The

HEARSTS

TO ORDER, CONTACT:
Telegraph Hill Press
562 B Lombard Street
San Francisco, CA 94133-2314
415-788-9112

The

HEARSTS

An American Dynasty

JUDITH ROBINSON

Telegraph Hill Press
San Francisco

To Betty Clapp Robinson and Ernest Kip Robinson, M.D.—
midwesterners who made their own places in history
—for their support and example.

Telegraph Hill Press
562 B Lombard Street
San Francisco, CA 94133-2314

Copyright © 1991 by Mary Judith Robinson
Third Printing, 2006
Front cover photographs courtesy of the California Historical Society, San Francisco
Library of Congress Catalog Card Number: 89-40768
ISBN: #0-9643382-1-1

Library of Congress Cataloging in Publication Data:

Robinson, Judith, 1939–
    The Hearsts : an American dynasty / Judith Robinson.
        p.   cm.
    Includes bibliographical references and index.
    1. Hearst, William Randolph, 1863–1951—Family.   2. Publishers and publishing—United
States—Bibliography.   3. Newspaper publishing—United States—History.   4. Hearst family.
I. Title.
Z473.H4R62   1991
070.5′092—dc20
[B]

                                                                                          89-40768
Printed in the U.S.A.   CIP

Contents

Preface

I am often asked how I chose Mrs. Hearst as a subject. I had determined to write a historical book based on letters and documents and for several years had explored subjects. One day, while visiting a friend's mother—a wise and gentle lady in her eighties who presided over her family's antebellum mansion and the remnants of a plantation in Fredericksburg, Virginia—I mentioned my interest. The woman, Mrs. Butler Franklin, an early feminist, gave me some ideas and then said, "You really should write about Phoebe Apperson Hearst." And I, as many people later said to me, asked, "Who is Phoebe Hearst?" Pointing to the primitive portrait of her grandfather, Captain Murray Forbes Taylor, which was usually askew in the mansion's front hall, she told me the following story.

Her grandfather, who had served with General Robert E. Lee at Appomatox, had abandoned the plantation during the Civil War and had moved south to raise cotton on his wife's family's plantation. A bollworm infestation had destroyed the cotton crop and there was nothing for Taylor to do but go West to seek his fortune. Knowing best how to run land and raise horses, Murray Taylor ended up near Bakersfield, California, raising racehorses for one of George Hearst's partners, James Ben Ali Haggin. Hearst hired Taylor to raise his own racehorses and cattle on the San Simeon ranch in the 1880s. Taylor became the Hearst's ranch manager, not only of San Simeon but of other vast Hearst holdings in Mexico and elsewhere, raising his family on the ranches and serving the Hearsts well until he decided to retire in 1905. Mrs. Hearst, who had relied on him for fifteen years since the death of her husband in 1891, asked, "Murray, what are you going to do?" He replied that he wanted to return to Virginia and try to buy back his family estate. Mrs. Hearst asked him how much he thought it would cost. He told her that he thought he could get it for $25,000, whereupon Mrs. Hearst sat down at a desk and wrote him two checks—one for $17,000 and the other on a different account of $8,000—his retirement fund from a grateful employer and friend. Taylor returned to Virginia, negotiated the purchase of his family lands, and deposited the checks in the Fredericksburg National Bank. But the check for $17,000 bounced. By that time Mrs. Hearst had gone to Paris for an extended stay in her lavish apartment facing the Eiffel Tower. The bank, somewhat apologetically, wired her the news. She promptly wired back, "Try another bank." She apparently had written the check on the grocery account.

There are many stories like that about Phoebe Hearst. People kept suggesting her as a logical subject for a biography that had not been adequately done. As I began to look into her life, I found that there was much that was not told or known of Phoebe Hearst: of her brightness, her domineering but capable managerial qualities, her thoughtfulness for people in the minutest of details, her constant giving to others in return for love, her frustrations with her husband and son—who were as stubborn and determined as she—and her inability to produce a daughter. It became obvious that she could not be dismissed simply as a rich Victorian woman who gave a lot of money to worthy causes. She was a strong, passionate, and influential woman who gave the world a son in much the same way that Pandora's box gave forth uncontrollable effects.

I have tried to reconstruct the lives of the Hearsts largely from correspondence and papers to give a sense of what life and America were like when they lived and of their participation in important historical events of the day.

The Hearst family extended many courtesies to me without endeavoring to influence the content of the biography, which they were anxious to see written about the family matriarch, of whom they are understandably proud. They shared personal family papers with me, allowed me to see many of Mrs. Hearst's treasures—silver and other precious artifacts, china, books, rare editions—and they invited me to visit the ranch house at San Simeon, which was built by George Hearst in 1875 and is probably the only building that remains much as when Phoebe Hearst occupied it. It was faithfully restored under the guidance of Mrs. Phoebe Hearst Cooke, a great-granddaughter of Phoebe Apperson Hearst, and contains many of the latter's furnishings and paintings, portraits of her and George, her "picnic" willow-pattern blue-and-white china. There I was allowed to sleep in Mrs. Hearst's bed in her bedroom, where I could hear the waves of the Pacific Ocean rolling onto the shore in the near distance and raccoons climbing on the wisteria-covered veranda outside the tall windows of the Victorian, white clapboard house (a reminder that the Hearsts loved animals). It was not difficult to evoke Phoebe Hearst's presence and to imagine the thoughts and sensations that she had experienced in those rooms and along the oak-lined creek running at the foot of the "Enchanted Hill." There her only child and beloved son later would build his own retreat on the top of the hill where he had picnicked as a child with Mama and Papa.

The story evolved into one about the family, George, Phoebe, and

Will, and their relationships. Although they were public figures, their private papers and personal correspondence reveal much about their motivations and the influences that shaped their personalities. They were products of the opening of the American West; they liked its expanses, opportunities, and the freedoms and liberalities that it afforded; and they believed that its development would be good for America and the world. They had visions of the future, no better expressed than in a postcard written by William Randolph Hearst to his mother from a train sometime in the first two decades of the twentieth century, that pours forth his deep-rooted love for California:

Dear Mother,
   We have just arrived in God Blessed California. The light is real sunlight, not artificial light, the heat is real sun heat, not steam heat, the Colorado river is real mud, the Yuma desert is real dirt, and the Indians are mostly real dirt, too.
   Some people may object to the horned toads, the cacti and the tarantulas but I like 'em. I like 'em not for what they are but for what they may become. The horned toad will soon be replaced by the Eastern tourist, the cactus by the orange grove, and the tarantula by the real estate agent. Most old Californians prefer the horned toads, the cacti and the tarantulas, but I am for progress and reform. I think California was the best country in the world and always will be no matter who comes into it or what is done to it. Nobody or no thing can shut out the beautiful sun or alter the glorious climate. The horned toad and the eastern tourist alike bask in the light and warmth, the cactus and the orange alike grow in the generous soil, the tarantula and the real estate agent alike live off the tenderfoot.
   Hurrah for dear old California.[1]

Acknowledgments

I am grateful to many people for personal and professional support throughout preparation of this work.

My special appreciation goes to William Randolph Hearst, Jr., who enthusiastically endorsed the project and made contacts with other members of the family so that I was afforded access to private family papers and artifacts, as well as the opportunity to visit the "Ranch" at San Simeon. His enthusiasm for a work about his grandmother was infectious. He did not in any way influence or control the manuscript, however, other than to provide valuable insights about his grandmother, whom he knew until her death when he was eleven, and about his "Pop."

Phoebe Hearst (Mrs. Jack) Cooke, great-granddaughter of her namesake and one of twin children of George Hearst, Jr., was extremely helpful and cordial in sharing with me private papers, Mrs. Hearst's china, silver, other treasures, and rare books, and in giving me a tangible sense of the woman and her tastes. The opportunity for me to stay in Mrs. Hearst's ranch house, sleep in her room, and savour her environment, which Mrs. Cooke recreated lovingly and carefully in restoring the family ranch house, was unique and memorable. Ann Miller, former curator of the Hearst San Simeon State Historical Monument, provided valuable help and information at the "castle" built by William Randolph Hearst, now a California State Park, which contains many treasures acquired by his mother, Phoebe Apperson Hearst.

I am grateful to Ann Hatch of San Francisco for the extended loan of *The Life and Personality of Phoebe Apperson Hearst*, volume 2, by Winifred Black Bonfils, of which one thousand gold-embossed, white leather, printed editions by J. H. Nash of San Francisco were commissioned and distributed by W. R. Hearst to family, friends, and libraries to commemorate his mother in 1928. Ann's copy had been given to her mother, the first wife of William Randolph Hearst, Jr.

I am indebted to W. A. Swanberg, author of *Citizen Hearst* (Charles Scribner's Sons, 1961), who kindly shared with me valuable notes from his interviews with Phoebe Hearst's niece, Anne Apperson Flint, who he said "came near reproaching me for writing about Hearst rather than his mother."

Dr. James Hart, the late director of The Bancroft Library, University of California, Berkeley, which houses the Hearst family papers, provided personal assistance, as did his professional staff, to whom I am grateful for their always willing, patient, and courteous help.

The California Historical Society staff in San Francisco provided the same kind of professional help and guidance.

The devoted members of the Phoebe Apperson Hearst Historical Society in St. Clair, Missouri, especially Mrs. Mabel Reed and Ralph Gregory, shared important information about the Hearst and Apperson families who settled in southeast Missouri in the early 1800s.

I am obliged to Henry S. Dakin for his generous support and expertise in preparation of the manuscript, and to Mary Goodell for her help.

To my immediate family and friends, who gave me continuing encouragement and support, I am especially grateful: my parents, Dr. and Mrs. Ernest Kip Robinson of Kansas City, Missouri; my brother John Kip and sister-in-law, Judy Robinson; and my brother Marc.

To Joanne Omang and David Burnham, thanks for generous hospitality in times of need. To other friends the following thanks: Helen Nelson for her friendship; Sylvia Siegel for allowing me to ply two trades; Arlene and Ken Brown of Mijas, Spain, for hospitality; Lynne Burwell and John Robiola for many kindnesses; Gregory E. Jones for his counsel; Lowell Groves for his access to old *Harper's Weeklies*.

Thanks to the many people who knew Phoebe Apperson Hearst or had information or knowledge that helped me piece the story together.

The Hearst Papers and photographs at The Bancroft Library, University of California, Berkeley, are used with the kind permission of Mr. William Randolph Hearst, Jr. Hearst, Peck, and Severance Papers are quoted with permission of The Huntington Library, San Marino, California. Hearst, Peck, and other papers and photographs cited from the California Historical Society are used with permission of the society. Hearst Papers at the Hearst San Simeon State Historical Monument are quoted with permission of the California Department of Parks and Recreation. Hearst Papers at the Phoebe Apperson Hearst Historical Society, Inc., St. Clair, Missouri, are quoted with permission of the Society.

Introduction

William Randolph Hearst, the famous American publisher, had equally famous parents, Phoebe Apperson Hearst and George Hearst, as well known in their lifetimes as Hearst came to be in his. The real Hearst, unlike the "Citizen Kane" depicted in a film about a strong-willed, rich, and eccentric publisher, was not sent away from his parents as a child to be raised and educated by a guardian. To the contrary, young Hearst was born almost literally with a golden spoon in his mouth and was doted upon by his mother and father. Not unlike the film, though, their lives had fairy-tale qualities. Phoebe and George Hearst were born and grew up in the American midwest in a rural Missouri community twenty miles east of the future town of Rosebud—the name of the metaphorical and mythical childhood sled that Kane, in the film, was forced to leave behind and that he sought to regain all of his life.

Phoebe Apperson Hearst was an American Cinderella, rising from modest beginnings to become one of the richest and most influential women in the world, but not because of a fairy godmother. Her life was filled with real gold that her husband, George, mined from the vast reaches of the American West. The Hearsts built real castles and lived lives that to many seemed like fairy-tale existences.

Their story, in many ways, could have happened only in nineteenth-century America, in a nation and a time that were rapidly changing, where the humble could suddenly become rich and powerful; in a nation that was growing geographically and industrially as new resources and fortunes were found and lost in an uncontrolled lusting of people after wealth and the good life; in a nation that still had a frontier, physically and psychologically.

Phoebe Apperson Hearst, influenced by her humble beginnings in frontier backwoods, became one of the greatest benefactors of her time to people less fortunate than herself. Like her husband, twenty-two years her senior and a miner who knew the undulations of Lady Luck, Phoebe appreciated the fact that luck had played a big part in her good fortune and that others were not so blessed.

Her story is also one of a family, of her relationships with a much older husband who followed different drummers, and a brilliant son who broke out of the mold that she designed for him. The three were strong individuals and their relationships were passionate, stormy, loving, respectful, and sometimes very strained.

Phoebe Hearst tenaciously carved out for herself a place in American history as an independent woman and unique philanthropist, willing to take chances on people and controversial causes. Briefly a school teacher with a rudimentary education, she was largely self-taught. Although she had little in common intellectually with her uncultured and uneducated husband, she was governed by the mores of the day and by her own recognition of the partnership's uniqueness. "If I married for money, I got it," she once was quoted as saying, partly in jest, to one of her attendant "court" lady friends who had posed the question.[1] Whatever prompted the marriage, it was marked by love, mutual respect, and honesty and was tested by the independence of their lives and many physical separations caused by George's mining ventures and Phoebe's wanderlust.

And it was tried by their only child, William Randolph Hearst. His respect for the origins of money was capricious, at best, because he always had lots of it. His, too, is a peculiarly American story—of the building of an unprecedented newspaper empire sometimes characterized by a more fervent desire to excite than to accurately inform, and not a little by a spirit of populist muckraking inspired by a concern for the underdog that he acquired from his parents.

His relationship to his Gold Rush father of simple airs and straightforward business decisions and to his culturally curious mother—who longed for a sister for Willie—was complex and tight, full of love and anger on both sides, frustration and willfulness, parental indulgence, and the child's desire to assert himself by shocking the world to prove that he could match, or surpass, his parents' achievements.

Each of these strong-minded individuals became influential in different ways. George's story is one of plodding determination to take advantage of the West's largesse in land and minerals; of simple devotion and obligations to Phoebe and "the Boy"—and perhaps some less-demanding affairs with other women; and of loyalty to the Democratic Party, which repaid him by placing him in high public office. Willie developed from spoiled child to visionary newsman and ambitious, liberal politician. Phoebe evolved from a farm girl into a sophisticated, intellectual, and powerful woman who, having had the barest essentials in her formative years, learned that she could hire the finest experts to accomplish what she wanted. She was particularly fond of transporting herself and others into fanciful settings, far from the real world that beset her with importunings and mundane demands.

Phoebe was a small woman, slightly more than five feet tall. Many photographs show her with tightly set lips and direct gray eyes. Her son inherited his mother's facial features and piercing eyes but he had his father's height of more than six feet and an unusually high-pitched voice. The few pictures of George give meager clues about his person-ality, showing only a somber, bearded man. Still, there is a twinkle in his eye. One can almost smell the cigar smoke and see the three of them in plush Victorian parlors, sharing a joke, quarreling, cajoling, encour-aging one another, Phoebe in lavender dresses and tight corsets and George enjoying a whiskey served by his faithful black butler, Robert Turner.

Phoebe had a rare quality of presence, an "aura" about her that people did not forget. It is evident in moving pictures made about 1916 and 1917 (the latter in color), possibly made by Hearst's chief cameraman, C. J. "Joe" Hubbell, at Phoebe's beloved Hacienda del Pozo de Verona in Pleasanton, California (overlooking the valley where her great-grand-daughter Patricia later would be imprisoned). A young woman guide at Hearst San Simeon State Historical Monument remarked that Mrs. Hearst seemed "elevated off the ground" in the home movie. "She had an aura around her that I have never seen. It was wonderful." Making entrances holding a parasol and much attended to by her family, Phoebe is clearly the "little commander," holding forth over her grand-children, who show off their riding prowess on ponies, along with their towering father on horseback. It must of have been the Fourth of July on one occasion since W. R. sets off a long string of firecrackers, to the delight of his three oldest sons. Pretty Millicent Hearst flutters about her mother-in-law, in whose arms rest the twin babies (born in 1915). Phoebe is the happy, proud, doting—and doted upon—grandmother and matriarch. The footage shows her candidly, unlike most of her photographs and portraits, in which she is staid, posed, and well ordered. She was not a spontaneous or impetuous person.

She was much admired and her detractors were few, usually those who had been cut off of her generous rolls or were jealous. It is hard to find a chink in her armor, as most of the surviving letters to her are effusive in praise and adulation, any others having been burned after her death, when most of her papers were carefully culled.

Phoebe was a pack rat; twelve trunks of papers were found in a storage warehouse and in her personal rooms at the Hacienda when she died in 1919. A secretary, Adele S. Brooks, undertook deciding what to save and what to destroy. The contents were reduced to fill three trunks, most of which was given by William Randolph Hearst, Jr., in 1972 to The Bancroft Library at the University of California—one of Mrs. Hearst's principal beneficiaries. After sorting through the papers, Mrs. Brooks wrote:

Hurried transfers made, at the Hacienda, from old and broken trunks, and from better ones required, after Mrs. Hearst's death, for other uses, resulted in the breaking up of all original order and continuity among the letters, which confusion was increased by the presence of quantities of telegrams, newspaper clippings, photographs, cards of occasion and greeting, paid bills, cancelled cheques, shopping tags, sale lists of collections and commodities of all kinds, notices of meetings and much other matter either valueless in itself or made so by the lapse of years.

Innumerable social invitations to every kind of function or celebration give evidence that both at home and abroad, society of the best quality and highest standing was open to Mrs. Hearst. These were set aside, but not destroyed.

The remaining mass of documents and letters, beginning with the marriage contract between "George Hearst and Phoebe E. Epperson," signed June 14, 1862, cover a period of nearly fifty-seven years, though very little was preserved during the first eight years of that time.

. . . Everything manifestly worthless was discarded [and] . . . burned. . . .

The confidential nature of the work made it impossible to make use of any clerical help. Destruction by fire could not be managed in private in a hotel. Matter of this kind was kept in locked suitcases until it could be taken to the Hacienda and burned there under supervision.

Numbers of begging letters (only a fraction of the quantity received during Mrs. Hearst's lifetime) were torn up, a few being kept as curiosities; but neither these nor any others among the many unclassified and now wholly insignificant papers preserved, were destroyed unread or unconsidered.[2]

She was perceived by the public and her admirers as angelic when in fact she was a tough little lady of no small brains who had personal dreams, fears, highs and lows, and problems like any other woman, wife, and mother. A saint to some, a determined and opinionated woman to others, she was a human being with strengths and frailties who happened to become a public figure, against her wishes on one hand and by her own doing on the other. Phoebe was a person of contradictions. She loved company but deplored a lack of privacy when her ever-present entourage of "court ladies," relatives, and friends became too much for her. She complained about the continuous flow of begging letters and demands on her time and money, but she derived great pleasure from giving. Chronically in poor health, she still had enormous reserves of energy, gaining sustenance from the pressures on her and the knowledge that many people needed and depended on her. She spent money lavishly and acquired obsessively but prided herself on her frugality, quick to rationalize her expenditures. She considered herself a progressive democrat who believed in human equality, yet she appreciated the advantages that wealth provided her and was happy not to have to mingle too often with the "hoi polloi." She deplored snobbery but basked in the company of royalty. She would listen thoughtfully and attentively to all kinds of people, but she had an aloof, slightly aristocratic air, a defense in large part for her shyness. She hated politics but publicly supported her husband's and son's political exploits. She adored and admired but frequently opposed and even sometimes despaired of her strong-willed and only son for his actions and refusal to knuckle under her thumb.

She was a powerful woman who was ahead of her time. In future years she might have been a senator or member of congress, chair of the board, or president of a company. She understood how to use power and came to know her own power. She also recognized that she could not have done what she did or achieved her stature without wealth. Thus she deferred to her husband and to the mores of her time. She was smart enough to know that she had no other option, and she played by the rules of the day. She made the most of the possibilities within the perimeters given her. She could not run for public office or vote during most of her lifetime, but she tightly governed her pet projects: the development and design of the University of California, important archaeological explorations, kindergarten teacher training, the founding of the Parent-Teacher Association, construction of the National Cathedral School for girls in Washington, D.C. She quietly lent her name to causes such as the Young Women's Christian Association, but because it was a name that carried great weight, it caught the attention of others, who joined in support. She was beseiged by requests to announce her support of women's suffrage, which she would not do for many years, believing public agitation undignified, but she privately donated money to the movement. She learned to gain the maximum benefit from her money toward the ends that she desired. And she expected a great deal from her beneficiaries.

The men with whom she dealt—a friend wrote that she had a "masculine grasp of financial affairs"—may have been frustrated at times by her strong will, admitting before making decisions, as the Board of Regents at the University of California often did, that they had to "consult Mrs. Hearst first."[3] But knowing she was smart and had good ideas, they listened to her and did not simply indulge her as a rich old woman. They paid her the ultimate respect of following her leads or advice.

She saw twenty-three presidents of the United States in her lifetime (1842–1919), the development of the automobile, airplane, electricity, telephone, and numerous appliances that made life easier. She loved new gadgets and inventions—she was a friend of Thomas Edison's and other innovators—and she poured over catalogues advertising the latest objects.

Phoebe would deplore the lack of social graces today (thank-you letters were written promptly for the slightest favor in her time), but she would delight in the equality between men and women—if not, perhaps, the equality of garb, the faded blue jeans and sloppy shirts common to both sexes.

She also would not be so pleased with the appearance and design of the University of California campus, whose plan she worked so hard to ensure would be grand, but which grew into a hodge-podge of many undistinguished and unattractive buildings, her high-minded hopes for a beautiful and cohesive campus not having been fully realized. But she would like to see herself in bronze, pertly perched on a pedestal in the Hearst Memorial Mining Building that she built to honor her husband, one of the loveliest buildings on the campus and a throwback to a time when good taste was affordable. George would have liked it, too, because it was what Phoebe wanted, and he gave her most of the material objects that she wanted, pleased when she was happy.

George quietly watched while Phoebe and Willie plunged into worlds that George cared little for. He wrote the checks and dug the fortune out of the ground with his hands and his instinct. He preferred racetracks to concerts, told jokes with Mark Twain, and handed out twenty-dollar gold pieces to mining cronies down on their luck while he determinedly amassed giant real estate and mining interests. He was fondly known in San Francisco as "Uncle George."

Willie was the smart-aleck but adoring son who felt guilty for displeasing his mother, with whom he shared a great devotion. Willie was glib and sharp and undeterred. He knew where his bread was buttered, but it piqued him that his mother controlled the family fortune. Old George, who confided in his diminutive wife his numerous, often risky business ventures, knew that his millions would be safe in Phoebe's careful hands, not in those of his impetuous, extravagant son. And so she, after George's death in 1891, inherited all of his $20 million fortune and doled it out when Will asked for it. She gave it sometimes grudgingly but nevertheless indulgently. Her dear son, who was "a great comfort" to her as a child, grew to be an individual with muses and thoughts of his own, and, like many an adoring parent, she was displeased when he would not do what she wanted.

Until she died, when he was fifty-six, Will had to ask his mother for money, even as he built his own newspaper empire. She wanted to "do right" by her boy, as George had exorted her in his simple will, but it was often at the point of exasperation. When Will asked for more money to acquire a newspaper in Chicago in 1899—she had "loaned" him some $10 million by that time—she wrote a confidant, artist Orrin Peck, whom she supported along with his family:

> I have been feeling greatly depressed and did not feel like writing. Will is <u>insisting</u> upon buying a paper in <u>Chicago.</u> Says he will come over to see me if

I do not go home very soon. It is impossible for me to throw away more money in any way, for the simple reason that he has already absorbed almost all. . . . It is madness. I never know when or how Wm. will break out into some additional expensive scheme. I cannot tell you how distressed I feel about the heavy monthly loss on the Journal. And then to contemplate starting another nightmare is a hopeless situation. I have written and telegraphed that no argument can induce me to commit such a folly as that of starting another newspaper.[4]

Nevertheless, she could not resist his implorings and persuasive arguments. Despite their conflicts, they maintained great loyalty to each other. When Will was publicly maligned, his mother was unfailingly supportive. Although vexed over his newspaper enterprises, she came to appreciate his muckraking mission and exposés of corporate exploitation. She canceled subscriptions to magazines that published offensive articles about him and felt that his political ambitions nullified his newspapers' worthiness because he was wrongly perceived as "buying" public office for his own ends. She wrote a politician in 1916:

> . . . I am sorry that there is any thought, on the part of any one, of suggesting my son's name as a candidate for the Presidency four years hence, for I think he can do more good in his fearless efforts to stand by and champion the cause of right through his newspapers than would be possible in any public office, even that of Chief Executive of the Nation. . . .
> I sincerely hope he will never accept the nomination for any office again, for the moment his name is mentioned as a candidate for office, his papers lose their influence for good and are accused of being used solely to further his own personal desires.[5]

While she privately winced at Will's newspaper ventures, she was quoted as telling a family friend who was alarmed at the papers' losses of a million dollars a year, "At that rate, William will last thirty years."[6]

Will's favorite editorial writer, Arthur Brisbane, wrote Phoebe in 1915,

> Many mothers get glory and public approval from the works of their sons—your son is helped in public esteem by his mother's work—and you are honored by the splendid public fights that he has made—a rare combination.[7]

Phoebe had big dreams for her only child and was torn by pride and disappointment as he became independent in his public and private affairs, choosing mistresses and a wife of whom his mother disapproved. Whether intentionally or not, she followed the advice and believed the predictions of a phrenologist whom she hired to read Will's character as a boy:

He is too tame and good, better if he were more wolfish. He is all candor and sincerity, hence easily victimized by the confidence men. . . . Has a brain rather small, but it is very smart and of the finest-grained quality. . . . is very strongly attached to his mother, provided she treats him lovingly . . . Will always be under petticoat government. Is gallant to the girls. Very fond of pets; friendly, cozy, fondling, doting. Has a woman's affectionate nature which he derives from his mother, though he derives his love of the opposite sex from his father—a very favorable combination. . . . Especially guard against disappointments in love—they will about use him up. Fortunately has considerable love of money—this will prove his great salvation because it will inspire combativeness in him, to fight for his dollars, and in general furnish a strong motive for effort. . . . Should be allowed to have his own will. Every time he is subdued he is made the more limp, like a rag. Is as conscientious a boy as ever was and can easily be governed by appeals to his sense of right. . . . His chief error is that he is too good and too smart. By all means let him go barefoot so as to force the blood from head to surface. Govern him by letting him govern himself.[8]

His mother gave in to Will while trying to control him, and the result was a brilliant, driven, controversial man whom people either worshiped or hated, whose admirers called a genius, and whose detractors called ruthless. He inherited from his mother a certain disdain for frivolous and superficial people and society and an independence from the pack, and so both were considered aloof by those whom they seemed to scorn. Will would come to be on the fringe of "old-guard" society, although Phoebe had impeccable credentials as matriarch of a "first family" of the West. She and Will, though, were intolerant of those who were supercilious or less bright than they, thus setting themselves apart.

Will's wise and down-to-earth father once told his son, when he was starting his newspaper career and complained of the number of fools in the world,

I would not be too hard on the fools if I were you, Willie. If everybody were very clever, you and I might have a pretty hard time getting along.[9]

They were a powerful and exceptional trio who knew they were making a mark in history. They lived in extraordinary pre-income-tax luxury, moving through rooms filled with treasures brought from faraway places, treasures that would be in museums one day. This, then, is their story.

1
Missouri Years and Apperson Family Roots

The carriage rolling and bumping up the road on an autumn day in Missouri in 1862 carried an uncommon couple: a great, gangling, bearded, soft-eyed man of forty-two years and his recent bride, about half his size and age. Her diminutive size and youth, nineteen years, could not disguise a strong and determined character. Cool, serious, gray eyes betrayed an intelligence and maturity beyond her age. The pair were en route to a train that would take them to St. Louis and New York, out of the lush Meramec River Valley, away from the Civil War that was being fought in their neighborhood and town squares.

Phoebe Apperson Hearst knew very little of what lay ahead, but she was not afraid. She was leaving the backwoods, a "miserable country," she later described it, where she had spent her life until that day.[1] She would not return to the poor farm life that she had known, although she was prepared for hard times ahead. Still, she knew there was an easier way to live and cultured people outside of the valley with its small farms and lead mines and God-fearing neighbors. The older man beside her, George Hearst, offered the promise of a better life.

He had struck it rich with a little-known silver mine at a place they called Comstock in the Sierra Nevadas far to the west of St. Clair, Missouri, where Phoebe and George had grown up on their family farms. He had made money after ten years in the gold fields. In her small purse Phoebe had a lengthy document, a contract with her husband that they had signed the day before they married. It gave Phebe Elizabeth Epperson, as her name was spelled, fifty shares of George's mining stock if he should die before she did.[2] She would be well cared for, but she did not know that one day she would be among the richest women in the world.

She had dreamed of richly furnished houses, servants, paintings by European masters, of stimulating conversation about books and philosophy, of concerts and plays, of Paris, London, and Rome. The man beside her could make those all possible. He was kind and gentle if a bit rough-hewn around the social edges. Perhaps she could refine him. Her plans included more than herself, for she was three months' pregnant and hoped for several other children as well.

She was pretty in a solemn sort of way, but she could not be called a beauty. Her brown hair was pulled simply and sternly back, parted in the middle. Her lips were full, her eyes clear and direct, her demeanor serious. Phoebe had the education of a rural farm girl with a few extra benefits: she had studied at a school in a neighboring county and had been tutored in French. She had taught school briefly, in the same one-room schoolhouse that she had attended as a child, and at the Meramec Iron Works school. She also had tutored the children of a family wealthy by local standards, in nearby St. James.

The man beside her had been a neighbor before leaving with a party for California in 1850. Phoebe had been seven years old at the time. George was the last man alive in his family, his father having died and left an estate of rich farmland and small lead-mining interests. Early in his life George had gained a reputation for finding minerals in the ground, an instinct learned while poking around the hills of south-eastern Missouri.

Phoebe and George were not totally dissimilar: they both came of Anglo-Scotch-Irish stock, although Phoebe had a strong German strain in her ancestry. The Hearsts and Phoebe's maternal grandparents, the Whitmires, had come to Missouri through the Cumberland Gap from South Carolina in the early 1800s. Phoebe's father's family, the Appersons, had come from Virginia. The Hearsts, though, were one of the few families in the area to have slaves and substantial land holdings. Most of the people in the valley eked a living out of the land and lead-filled mines in the neighborhood. It was a hard life for meager material rewards; it was the western frontier of young America. Everything eaten, worn, or used as tools was raised or made on the land.

Phoebe had been taught how to live and survive off the land. Her fingers had sewn, carded, cooked, planted, hoed, and milked. They had written lessons and sums and even poems. She had few books to read but she devoured all that she could lay her hands on, even those in French, which she studied avidly and longed to speak on the avenues and in the shops of Paris. The image of Paris was fixed in her mind from drawings in *Harper's Weekly Magazine*, where she read such stories as Charles Dickens's serialized "Great Expectations" and gazed at the elegant gowns of worldly women.

George and Phoebe had a strong bond of affection and respect for one another. He called her Puss, a pet name that her family and close friends had given her. Although in leaving Missouri her moreno dress was plain and her luggage meager, it one day would expand manyfold to trunks of shoes, dresses, gloves, and handsome jewelry.

The place she was leaving in Franklin County was not much given to change. Church was the center of social life, but Jesse James later would find its caves a hospitable hideout. St. Louis, forty-five miles north, was a growing metropolis with opera, theater, and cultural enticements that Phoebe had sampled only briefly. The rolling hills along the Meramec River were snow-covered in winter, verdant in summer. In spring the woods blossomed with dogwood and the river ran high. It would be many years before Phoebe again would see the seasons change so dramatically as in that country. If the land was rocky, the mines were rich. Towns to the southeast were aptly named Mines, Old Mines, Mineral Point, Leadwood, Anaconda, Steelville. A few miles to the west of St. Clair would grow the town of Rosebud.

A small band of frontier people had settled comfortably into the landscape in the early 1800s and Phoebe's and George's family roots had grown deep into the soil on the edge of the Ozarks. Tombstones and mailboxes would carry the names of early settlers' families for many years to come: Whitmire, Phoebe's mother's family who had given the place its first name, Whitmire Settlement; Clark, cousins to both the Appersons and Hearsts; Reed, Rowland, Isbell, Hill. Children bore familiar ancestors' names: Drusilla, Phoebe's mother; Randolph, Jacob.

Phoebe's and George's parents had been the first generation of eastern migrants to settle Missouri Territory before it became a state in 1821. Hearsts and Whitmires had been in a party from the Newberry and Abbeyville districts of South Carolina that trekked west for more than a year; several children were born en route as much as a year apart.[3]

As a child Phoebe had heard stories that Daniel Boone, already a legendary relative of several in the party, met the travelers in Potosi, where French miners had settled in the previous century. Boone had told them that a three-day drive by ox cart would bring them to the prettiest place they had ever seen. The party—including Phoebe's mother, Drusilla, who was about two years old (she had been born 24 September 1816 in Newberry District, South Carolina)—settled in 1818 or 1819 at a bend where Brush Creek enters the Meramec River near Meramec Caverns. The new frontier people claimed the land for themselves and began to build on, till, and clear it. Their migration had ended.[4]

The Cumberland party had been led by Colonel Moses Whitmire (1789–1836), whose father, Georg Fried Wiedmayer (George Fredrick Whitmire, 1742–1829), had immigrated from Stuttgart, Germany, to Philadelphia in 1767 and anglicized the name to Whitmire. He and a brother moved to Newberry District, South Carolina, an area known as the Ninety-Six District, where they had operated a tavern and trading post on a north-south highway. George Fredrick had served in the Revolutionary War. He and his wife, Sarah Phebe Hapgood (1752–1817), had eight children, the youngest of whom was Moses. Moses' brother Henry Whitmire (1776–1836), a member of the Cumberland party, and his wife Ruth Hill (1785–1843) were Phoebe's maternal grandparents. Phoebe's mother Drusilla was one of nine children.[5]

On 28 January 1841 Drusilla Whitmire had married Randolph Walker Apperson, the son of a Revolutionary War physician and veteran, Dr. John Apperson of Virginia. Phoebe's father was proud of his heritage despite his own modest state on the outer edge of the colonies. Apperson records, he had told his daughter, were among the earliest in St. Peter's Parish, New Kent County, Virginia, which had been established in 1654 and had a vestry book dating from 1682. Appersons, sometimes spelled with an "E," had a long Virginia history. Phoebe's paternal grandfather, Dr. John Apperson, born in 1763 in Spottsylvania County, Virginia, had married (in 1787) a Virginia woman named Alcey Favor, whose paternal grandmother was Isabella Randolph—the only connection found to the Randolph family. John Apperson had served in the Virginia Revolutionary Troops in 1780 and 1781, and in 1829 had migrated from Virginia to Missouri Territory, where he had practiced medicine and farmed. Randolph Apperson, Phoebe's father, was the youngest of twelve children, born 10 April 1809 in Washington County, Virginia.[6] The Appersons proudly claimed a coat of arms of English derivation, with symbols for nobility, military fortitude, and repentance.[7]

Phoebe Apperson and George Hearst actually were distantly related. Phoebe's aunt Phoebe Whitmire had married the Reverend Jacob Clark, whose mother was Mary Hearst, daughter of Martha Carson and Major John Hearst, son of John and Elizabeth Knox Hearst of South Carolina. There also were marriages between cousins within both the Hearst and Whitmire families.

It was of this frontier stock that Phoebe Elizabeth Apperson had been born at her maternal grandparents' farmhouse on 3 December 1842, nearly two years after her parents had married. It had been a cold winter day shortly before Christmas, which was to become her favorite holiday. She was named for her Aunt Phoebe and for George Hearst's mother, Elizabeth Collins Hearst, a neighbor and friend.

Phoebe's parents owned small parcels of land on which they farmed and raised livestock. They had little schooling but were practical and respected in the community. Her father was an elder in the Cumberland Presbyterian Church. Before his marriage, in the 1830s, he had clerked in a neighborhood general store where one of his regular customers had been William Hearst, George's father. Randolph Apperson also had worked on his father's and George Hearst's farms. After his marriage, when Phoebe had been quite small, the family had lived with the Whitmires or Appersons for periods of time. The Whitmires owned land along the Meramec River, including ninety-five acres that they had obtained with a federal patent in 1825.

In 1846 Randolph Apperson had purchased seventy-three acres of government homestead land along the river between farms owned by the Hearsts and the local schoolteacher, Hugh C. Berry. Phoebe had walked three and a half miles through the woods and crossed the river twice to attend the Salem District Public School.[8] She owed a great deal to that public school, whose lessons had opened new perspectives to her. Her sympathy for a good public education would reappear with force some years later.

Her father was hard-pressed to provide for his little family and had sold his land to Moses Whitmire, who subsequently sold it to George Hearst. The Appersons had moved around. Between 1848 and 1850, they had moved to the next county (then Crawford, later Dent), where Phoebe's father had operated a general store for several years and made some money.[9] There, her brother, Elbert Clark, had been born on 10 January 1851. Phoebe had just turned eight years old. At last there was a playmate for her. There had been disappointments when other pregnancies had failed to produce the expected brother or sister. But Phoebe and her brother were to have very different personalities.[10]

The general store business improved the family fortune enough to allow the Appersons to move back to Franklin County in 1853 and to acquire thirty acres. Although the Appersons were not rich, they were no poorer than most of their neighbors, with the exception of the affluent Hearsts. Phoebe's family was proud and lived comfortably enough off the land.

As a girl she had hauled buttermilk in the family wagon to sell it, for five cents a glass, to the sweaty railroad workers building the Southwestern Branch line, the first through the area. Phoebe performed her task dutifully, for she had been taught the value of managing money and of managing on little of it. Her frugality and fear of poverty, as well as her respect for money, would serve her well.

She also had had good training from her father. Despite his own lack of business sense, he had given Phoebe useful instruction in sums and accounting, another attribute for which she would be grateful. He had treated her much like a son in what he had taught and shared with her. They had spent long hours together, drafting poems or riding through the woods and farmland, Phoebe bareback on her pony. She was an excellent rider and could handle a team with competence. In fact, there was little that a man could do that she could not handle, feminine and diminutive as she was.[11]

If she recognized weaknessess in her kind and simple parents, she nevertheless respected them. But passivity and the somber strictness of their Protestant faith were antipathetic to Phoebe. She vowed that the heavy hand of religion would not dominate her life. Sundays would be days of pleasure, not penance, for herself, her children and her grandchildren. Sundays would not be dreaded.[12]

Little did she know just how much her life would change, that one day she would return in a private railroad car, pulled onto a siding at St. Clair while she drove through the community, dispensing gifts of shoes and clothing that she no longer needed. She would be a far more striking figure than when she left Franklin County in her homemade dress. She would dazzle the folk with her Paris gowns and jewels, a veritable Lady Bountiful.

Her neighbors remembered her as a "buxom country girl" who "wore farm-made linsey dresses . . . always kind-hearted, a general favorite in the community."[13] If her upbringing had been spartan, her charisma even then was catching. One acquaintance later wrote:

> Colonel A. W. Maupin of Union [Missouri] often recalls his visit to the Apperson home in 1855. Colonel Maupin was then deputy sheriff and a widower. His chief had assigned to him the duty of serving a paper upon her father. He had ridden a mile in the midst of a forest when he came upon a one-story log cabin eighteen by sixteen feet, with a little "lean-to" for a kitchen. . . . The deputy sheriff rode to the door and shouted, "Hello!" In response to his call, a girl of exceedingly beautiful features and who was clad in homespun, came to the door. The papers were duly served. The acquaintance of the young people progressed so rapidly that young Maupin found courage to invite the fair maiden to attend a ball which the county officials were to give in the court house at Union, 30 miles distant, two days later. She replied that she knew of no way of going to Union. The ardent young gallant was not to be baffled thus. He told her he was one of the committee on arrangements, so could not leave himself, but would send his own carriage for her. His persistence was rewarded. Phoebe Apperson was the belle of the ball, which lasted continuously for one day and two nights. The young people took turns at sleeping and dancing, so that the merriment continued without interruption for thirty-six hours. This was the greatest social event of Phoebe Apperson's girlhood.[14]

Phoebe had not been without beaux. But her life had been one of plain and honest habits, a spare existence deprived of the finer comforts. Books played an important role. From a one-room schoolhouse she had gone to a seminary in the next county—Steelville Academy, operated by the Cumberland Presbyterian Church, which she had attended for at least one year.[15]

With that rudimentary education she had become a teacher, first of farm children, and then (in 1859 or 1860), at the Meramec Iron Works in Phelps County, about thirty miles southeast of her home. Classes for the factory workers' children were held on the third floor of the Iron Works' boardinghouse, a wooden building that had seen better days. She was one of the most popular teachers at the Iron Works.[16]

Phoebe's reputation gained her a position in 1861 as a tutor and governess in the home of William James, a mining man who ran a smelter and was a friend of George Hearst's. There she had been part of the family, both as governess and student of a French tutor.[17]

She was an intelligent young woman who read and studied, expecting to advance herself. Poems written to her best friend, Ellen Patton, expressed a wistful yearning and hinted at forbidden love.

> Oh! heaven is where no secret dread
> May haunt love's meeting hour

she wrote, and in another,

> Few and by still conflicting powers
> > Forbidden here to meet,
> Such ties would make this life of ours
> > To fair for aught as fleet.[18]

The secret meetings may have been with George Hearst, who her parents thought too old for her. But Phoebe had become conscious of her womanly attractions. She had suitors from all over the countryside. "She was considered the 'belle,' being brunette, of medium height, thick build, with round face, dark hair. She was the leader of all parties and balls in the country—and the young man so lucky as to be favored with her company was looked upon with envy," her admirers remembered.[19]

The family physician, Dr. Gibson of Steelville, knew Phoebe well; he had watched her grow into an attractive, modest woman. It was no wonder that she had suitors. Even a member of the state legislature, Harrison H. Webb, was seen driving her from the Iron Works to Steelville in winter on a wagon loaded with meal and flour. But none of the suitors had turned her head like the tall man from California who had turned up in the late summer of 1860.

George Hearst had begun to call on Phoebe while she was teaching at the Iron Works, and soon the trips were made three times a week. He would stop en route to visit with Dr. Gibson. Rumors went around Steelviille, where people were suspicious of any clandestine activity in the war climate, that George Hearst and Dr. Gibson were organizing a "chapter" or "lodge" of the "Golden Circle," proslavery sympathizers plotting against the federal government.[20] George had war on his mind, but he also was thinking of Phoebe. He had persisted in a quiet, firm way in his suit. And Phoebe had responded.

Thus it was that in the autumn of 1862 George Hearst and his young, pregnant bride were leaving war-torn Missouri for the safety and riches of California.

2

George Hearst and Marriage

The man whom Phoebe chose to marry was not sure of his birthdate. It was 3 or 9 September 1820 or 1821, he thought. His parents were William G. and Elizabeth Collins Hearst. His family was one of the wealthiest in the Meramec valley and his roots were as deep in young America as Phoebe's.

The first Hearsts to arrive in America had come from Scotland in the seventeenth century. They were militant Presbyterian Covenanters, fiercely anti-Catholic, pledged to their religion as the only legitimate one in Scotland and the British Isles. The name was spelled Hyrst, a Saxon word meaning a thicket or cluster of trees, then Hurst and later Hearse in eighteenth-century South Carolina records. George's mother brought Irish to the lineage; her family was from Galway via Georgia.[1]

Descendants of the Scottish Hearsts made their way to Abbeville, South Carolina, in 1766. The neighborhood where they settled was known as the Hard Labor Section and Long Cane country. It was rich Cherokee Indian hunting ground, and Indian attacks on migrating white settlers were common only a few years earlier.

The Hearst family boasted several Revolutionary War soldiers, a state legislator, and two doctors. They were large plantation owners, had slaves, owned at least one mine, and were active in the local militia, Methodist, and Presbyterian churches. John and Joseph Hearst served in the revolutionary militia in 1782–83. John Hearst owned 116 acres in 1790 and two other tracts. Other Hearsts owned "large plantations and many stores" and had families of up to a dozen children. By 1790 there were four Hearsts (the name was often spelled Hearse) in the South Carolina census.[2]

George's father, William, had joined the migration west with the Whitmires and others from the Hard Labor Section who were seeking greater riches in the wilds of Indian territory. The Hearsts had rightly suspected that there were minerals to be mined in the unexploited western lands.

William G. Hearst, with his parents and his brother Joseph, had settled in the mining area along the "Merrimack," across from the mouth of Indian Creek near the remnants of an old Indian trail, not far from the town of Sullivan. In 1817 William married Elizabeth Collins, the daughter of a neighboring farmer. Soon after the marriage the couple had moved with their parents and others to Texas Territory, but the harshness of life and sickness (cholera had killed their livestock) had driven the Missouri families back to the lush banks of the Meramec, where the Hearsts purchased land from the government. A year later, their son George was born and named for his paternal grandfather. In 1830 William Hearst bought his brother Joseph's share in the homestead and became its sole owner. The property, consisting of some three hundred acres, lay in a big bend of the Meramec River.[3]

In memoirs that he composed in 1890, the year before he died, George later would recall his early life with a certain detachment. He was not given to sentiment or self-importance, but he was proud of his heritage. He related that his great-grandfather from Scotland, who had landed in America in 1680, "owned ten acres and nine niggers." His own father, who spoke with a Scottish accent, "was a very muscular man, not very large, but strong. He probably weighed about 175 pounds. He was a farmer, but I don't think there was his equal in the country for lifting weights and such like." He also liked to fight. "I can recollect that if anyone did anything outrageous towards him, he would try to clean him out; those were rough days, remember," George recalled. Still, his father had been "rather a progressive kind of man in his way," and "somewhat of a religious turn." He also "was a man of some considerable influence, and had the best farm, and indeed the best of everything in his neighborhood. At that time, they were a very poor lot of people in that section, and he certainly was the most prominent among them."

> He was a man of pretty good judgement and accumulated something. He always seemed to have plenty and was very kind to his neighbors, giving away a great deal. I remember that he was not very strict in the family; in fact I never got a licking from my mother or father at any time. I think it was his idea merely to set a good example. I was young when he died, but he seemed to have always taken to me kindly, and talked to me sensibly, telling me what was the best thing to do. Occasionally he would get mad, but as a rule he would not. I remember my mother once coming towards me with a little switch, but I do not think she meant to use it. My father took a great interest in public affairs, and he belonged to the militia, was first lieutenant, went on all parades, and in everything public evinced a public spirit.[4]

A stock raiser and landowner, William had been wealthy enough to put up "security" for a sheriff and the "Mineral" school district. When George was born the Hearsts were the wealthiest family in Meramec Township, owning nineteen of the forty-one slaves in the area and having mining interests.[5]

George was one of three children, with a sister, Martha, called Patsey (born in 1823), "a large, fleshy and rosy-cheeked girl," and a brother Jacob, called Jake (named for his maternal grandfather), a cripple.[6] George's mother and father were not always a happy couple. His father was quick to anger when provoked and he had shown an interest in another woman at one point; his mother refused to speak to him except as necessary.[7]

George remembered his mother as "quite a managing woman" who ran the farm until George was fifteen and took it over. At sixteen he had "laboring men" working under him. His mother was a woman of few words "but what she said was to the point, and I never recollect her to have been in the wrong":

> My mother lived until I was forty years old. She was a blond and weighed probably a hundred and sixty pounds when a girl. She was quite a good woman, and very conservative under all circumstances. I never saw her mad in all my life. She was very hard to excite on any subject, always cool and always gave good advice. I think I get most of my success from my mother, although my father was a very industrious man; yes, I believe I owe most of my success to her rather than to him.
>
> She was a woman of some education. She evidently came from a very good family because she had things you would not see nowadays, such as cashmere shawls, leghorn bonnets and things of that description, which were above the common.[8]

George was a dutiful son whose mother relied heavily on him and who accepted his responsibilities. His youth was a mixture of frontier adventure and hard work. Even though they had slaves, "Everybody had to be busy, as we had to make everything; in fact I never remember a time when there was not something to do," George recalled in his autobiography.

> My early childhood was spent in a wild sort of a way. Of course, we lived in a wilderness, and our surroundings were of the roughest kind. The Indians were around in every direction, and every summer visited us. The wolves would come time and again and make away with our chickens, geese and sheep. When I was old enough to work they used to set me at penning up the ducks and chickens at night, and later on to put the sheep in the fold to keep them away from the wolves. The geese we used to raise principally for the feathers to make feather beds, and of course we had to utilize the wool from the sheep for our clothes. A little fellow like me always had lots to do.

He had little schooling—"a part of three months when I was eight years old"—at the home of a neighbor or in an empty log cabin; when he was a teenager he went to school for fifteen months and again when he was twenty for about three months. "Two and a half years was all the time I ever spent in a school house," he said, but he "liked the school first-rate, and was very ambitious to learn everything, and it would worry me terribly if I could not succeed," he remembered. His teacher was impressed that George would hang about the school after hours to clear up what he had not understood in class. Berry, the teacher, "also said that there was another thing that was somewhat queer about me"— George's penchant for doing things his own way. "After he had put me into arithmetic, I never did a sum in the way the rule stated. I would always figure it out in my own way, I always had to have it my own way or not at all, and this has been my disposition all through life. I never could make a speech and let anybody else write it out for me. If a man wrote me a splendid speech, I would only make a botch of it, but if I thought it out I would do it well and everybody would know that it was me." From an early age he was independent, and, having little formal training, learned to "do it in my own way."

His religious upbringing was nearly as sparse, and his mother, if "a very conservative woman," made sure the children were not deprived of fun. In his autobiography he remembered,

> If she found any of us young people playing or fishing on Sunday she would say to us that that was not very nice, but she would never make much fuss over it. Indeed I recollect when people would say anything, unless we were doing something bad, she would say that children must have their fun, and would come out all right in the long run. She was always on the side of the young folks. She always took the bright side of things, and seemed to be always in a good humor.

She also "was the best spinner in that section and she could make cloth and cut it out with the best of them all."

Despite his lack of education, George had a sense that he might be special. In a persistent way he learned to teach himself what he had not been taught in school and developed a capacity to listen and observe:

> I never thought that I was a man until I was over 30 years old, and until that age never could make up my mind that I knew as much as anybody else. I was rather of a retiring disposition, and thought other people could do much better because they were older. I was always ready to give over and shirk everything of prominence, when I was able to.

He believed that he was part of a larger scheme and that his life was influenced by a destiny over which he had little or no control. It led him to mining, he figured, and protected him from the Indians, with whom he had an unspoken rapport:

> We never found the Indians to disturb us in the least. In fact, it is a strange thing that I have travelled all over the country and never had an Indian

molest me in my life. I hardly know how to account for this except in the way of destiny. Perhaps because I was a boy amongst them I had a better chance to study their nature and habits; anyway the Indians seemed to take to me and it may be because they felt that I understood them. I was never stagerobbed in my life, although I have travelled from the head of the Fraser river all over Montana and Idaho. I never met with any loss from anybody in my life in that way, although I often had from 20 to 30 thousand dollars about me. As I said before, the only way I can account for it is destiny.

When he had been in his early twenties George reportedly had taken a liking to Drusilla Whitmire (Phoebe's mother), a woman four years older than he. He had proposed to her, but she had rejected him. It was to be many years before he married.[9] Whether Phoebe ever knew of his attentions to her mother is lost to history. Perhaps he sought in the daughter his earlier unrequited love.

George had grown into a strong, handsome man more than six feet tall. He had gotten a reputation for having such an accurate nose for minerals that the local Indians called him "Boy-That-Earth-Talked-To."[10] In 1838 he had passed a grade school course at the Franklin County Mining School. He never was happier than when prospecting or trading and buying lands and mineral rights. He often tramped barefoot through the back hills, his pantaloons rolled up to his knees, a stick or wand in his hand, chasing hogs from their muddy baths on hot summer days, and cooling his blistered feet in the depths of the hog wallows.[11] He had hoped to stumble upon a rich vein, much as a local farmer once had done in discovering the Virginia lead mine, the biggest in the state. But George did not have such luck in the Missouri hills.[12]

George also had dabbled in politics and had been a delegate to a Democratic state convention at the age of twenty-six.[13] His friend W. V. N. Bay had urged him to study law. Bay thought that George "would unquestionably have made a good lawyer for he had a combination of traits which have always been deemed essential in a good lawyer . . . diligence, industry, perseverance, a love of truth, a detestation of falsehood, and a keen perception of what is just and proper between man and man upon a given state of facts . . . a searching and probing mind." But George rejected the idea because he felt it would take him away too long from his obligations to his family and his father, whom he helped on the farm. His absence and the cost of a college education "might possibly deprive others [in the family] of many of the comforts of life which they enjoyed," Bay recounted.[14]

George also had an exuberant spirit and liked lively company in which he could tell and enjoy stories and jokes. He was a convivial fellow. A mining friend once said that George took his conviviality "straight" and could stand a great deal of it. He would have made a poor parson, Bay thought.[15]

Although he had minimal formal education, George had a genuine thirst for knowledge and an ability to grasp and understand the importance of things. He borrowed numerous books from Bay's library. And he quickly learned to read business contracts.

His lack of decent schooling prompted George and his father to raise money for a much-needed seminary. They wanted to have the school endowed with rent from government property that Congress had donated to the township for educational purposes. According to Bay, a fund was raised that "reached $20,000 and would have soon reached $50,000 when both George and his father learned that the money had been loaned out by the County Court to irresponsible parties upon insufficient security, and was entirely lost." George was greatly disappointed at the plan's failure, but it presaged an interest throughout his life in providing educational opportunities for young people.[16]

In November 1844 George's father suddenly died, leaving him (then twenty-three or twenty-four) to care for his mother, sister, and crippled brother. Some of the family estate and slaves had to be sold to settle debts that William had incurred, in part by offering his property as security for community projects. At a sale of his father's property in 1845 George bought enough livestock and tools to continue working the farm. The sale brought them $954.75, including $500 for their twenty-eight-year-old black slave, Allen, and $200 for Tempey, the cook. Phoebe's father had been one of the appraisers.[17]

After the sale the estate still included six hundred acres of land, livestock, and a copper mine. Mrs. Hearst was allowed to keep Allen for the year 1846 "without charge as a remuneration for the care and attention of Jacob," who died a few years later when in his twenties. The farmland was much sought after and George rented part of it to others. Allen, who subsequently hired himself out, rented the Hearst homeplace, and when he died in 1854 owned considerable property in his own right. Phoebe's uncle, Moses Whitmire, then rented the property along the fertile Meramec River bottoms, which was worth between $12.50 and $20.00 an acre. Over the years George also had bought rich Meramec River bottom land from the Appersons and Whitmires. Early in life he appreciated the value of land.[18]

But his mother no longer lived on the property nor needed it. She had remarried four years after his father's death and moved into town. In 1848 she married Joseph Funk, a county judge and postmaster at Traveler's Repose. George bought the rights of his mother and stepfather to his father's estate a few days after the marriage, making him and his sister the only heirs to the estate. George lived and worked for a while with a well-to-do friend, James N. Inge, owner of a general store and postmaster at nearby Virginia Mines. Early in 1850 George bought his own general store at Judith Springs, which he managed with Emile Generally, a mine- and large landowner in the area. It was a busy commercial operation with a public house, blacksmith shop, garden, and other activities on forty acres at a trading crossroads. It was there that he first heard from travelers stopping at the trading post about the discovery of gold in California.[19]

George had become somewhat of an expert at mining, and credited French miners with teaching him all he knew.

> There was a big lead mine discovered near us. I got a little bit familiar with mining then, and when I was 22 years old I went to mining and made a little money out of it, and finally got interested in copper and iron, and made some money out of them, too. My father died in the meantime. I probably made about four or five thousand dollars out of mining copper and lead. This I made from 1842 to 1849, more or less after I was 21 years of age. Then the Gold fever broke out.
>
> As to the early mining in Missouri, where I was raised it was only a little bit to the lead mines and only about 15 miles to where there were smelting works owned by Frenchmen. My father knew these people very well and we used to make considerable money by driving pork to the miners and selling it to them. The Frenchmen used to mine in little shallow diggings and as soon as they got out a few hundred pounds of ore they would sell it, and I of course saw that there was money in it. I would always go with father when he drove the hogs there, or if he had to go for anything else. There were big merchants there that had every sort of nice French things. My people lived in log houses, and these French things were very extraordinary to us. We had tables and beds and chairs and that was about all, but these people had things which they brought from France which were very beautiful I thought. They were very fond of me and would give me lots of things to try and make me talk French. I used to stay about there a good deal. They were smelters, and bought from anybody, and I naturally saw that they had a good deal of money. I think that that was what induced me to go into mining. Farming was such a slow way to make money. You could make a living at it and that was about all. I used to hear father say that if he saved a couple of hundred dollars a year he was doing well.
>
> The men there were not very scientific, and I soon saw how things were done. My ideas seemed naturally to lead into mining. I can think of the places I saw when I was 15 years old, and can see them just as vividly today in my mind as then. When I was 15 years of age they found a big mine only a mile from our house. It was called the Virginia mine, and was right off from St. Clair. When I was a little fellow we would go down to see it. For a long time the miners would not wash anything out but would let us little fellows pick away into the big banks of dirt and we would often thus make from four to six bits a day. We would dig down and get little bits of lead. The ore was galena and limestone and a sort of clay. There were a great deal of little nuggets and these would pan out about 70 to 80 per cent galena; in fact there was not a better mine in the world.[20]

There was little to keep George in Missouri, scratching out a living in the valley. His mother was comfortably settled, his sister will cared for.

He was unobligated and unfettered, having no family of his own, and he had reached thirty years of age with little prospect for more of a life than that of a storekeeper and farmer.

Although he perceived himself to be a successful young man, the temptations of El Dorado overcame him and George reluctantly decided that he should try his hand in California:

> I mined along and farmed, that is, run a farm, and also a little store out on the public road that was called the old Springfield, until this fever broke out in California. I came very near going in 1849. I often then used to go to Mannie's Iron Works and would call on the old folks there; in fact I was quite sweet on his girl. I told him I had an intention of going to California, but he said, 'No, don't go. There is nothing new there. This gold was discovered some seventy-five years ago, by the Jesuits.' He went and pulled down some books and read it out to me. It was of course the Coast Range, as I now know, but I thought he might be right about it, and that this would blow out, too. Next year, however, I made up my mind sure to go. I had already a pretty fair success in life.
>
> I recollect talking over California with my mother. She did not like it at all, but when I told her they were making $40 and $50 dollars a day there and that it seemed to me it was by far the best thing to do, as it was pretty hard pulling here, she said that if they were doing that, she had no doubts I would make something, too, and she agreed for me to go.[21]

But there had been a good deal to arrange before he left. He convinced a respected country doctor, the family physician and good friend, William N. Patton (the father of Phoebe Apperson's dear friend Ellen) to handle his affairs and administer his father's estate in his absence. He gave Patton a deed to nearly all of the Hearst land and slaves and power of attorney to act as George's agent while he was gone. He expected to be away for a year or two. Of the arrangement, George later said,

> I made Mr. Patton my agent; I had all confidence in him; I was raised with him; he was my family physician; he had set by me many a night; I think he saved my life; and when he was in my neighborhood he always made my home his home; and I did his when I was in the neighborhood. I believed he was an honest, sterling man.[22]

To help finance his trip George sold his father's copper mines and seven other mineral tracts for $1,900. He left notes owing him with Dr. Patton, to be collected as they came due and paid against $900 in debts. At the time of his departure he had about a thousand dollars' worth of livestock and farming equipment that he left on the homeplace with Allen; one slave girl; and about $2,500 worth of notes and accounts receivable.

In early May 1850 George joined a party of fifteen, made up of several cousins and including women, that was heading for California. Phoebe

Apperson, then seven years old, may have watched the wagons head out for the mysterious territory beyond the sunset, wondering, as the party disappeared, what existed beyond the world of her farm chores.

George's mother and sister accompanied him for several days on horseback and then they parted, expecting to meet again in two years:

> Mother and sister came with me a couple of days and if it had not been for pride when my mother and sister left me I would not have thought of going; in fact, nothing would have induced me to leave them the way I did, if it had not been for pride. I felt it in my bones.[23]

George Hearst was not to return to Missouri for ten years. And he was never to see his sister again; she died in 1854.

George played down the hardships of the overland trek, which included death of fellow travelers, loss of his oxen in the Carson sink, sickness, and bad weather. "We did not have any incidents of much interest," he would later write, although he himself caught fever and cholera, the plague of the plains, at Fort Kearny, Wyoming. With the help of brandy, he recovered:

> I had a little bit of brandy which I gave $16 a gallon for in St. Louis, and took a drink of that and some pills which a man in St. Louis gave me; I took these according to his instructions and then felt like I wanted to lay down. My bowels just ran off like water. I did not suffer much and did not get the cramps. I recollect that the grass was about six feet high and I thought that if they would only let me lie there I would give anything, but after I took the brandy I felt better, and the next day was pretty well. It seemed that the cholera was worse when it was raining, but we had it all along the way. I don't suppose we saw more than half the graves, and yet we approached graves every mile. . . .
> I always had plenty to eat and never had any sickness except that touch of the cholera until we came to the desert about Humboldt, when I was nearly broken up with an attack of fever. Of course there were lots of incidents along the route but nothing of any particular consequence.[24]

He arrived the winter of 1850 in Eldorado County, California, weak from fever and broke but determined. He joined the crowd of miners at Hangtown, a makeshift boomtown in the Sierra foothills:

> When we got into California I had just a five-franc piece left. The last money of any account that I had, I paid for a sack of flour, $100 for a hundred pounds. The first place I stopped at was the other side of the mountains near Hangtown, now called Placerville.[25]

For nine long years after that, George's ability to find precious metals was not as keen as the Indians had led him to believe it was. Like thousands of other men—and a few women—George dug and scraped and panned with pick, shovel, and sluice through the Sierra Nevada with little success.

Money was so scarce at one point that he could not even afford a new pair of pants or fresh meat. The *Nevada City Herald* recounted how

> Hearst . . . a plain, very plain, sort of man . . . had been prospecting a long time with poor success and was getting hard up for money. His clothing was seedy and his stomach was empty. He went to one of the butcher shops that flourished here then and, addressing the butcher, said:
>
> "I'm all-fired hungry and I want some meat. I need a pair of overalls, too, the worst way, as these are ready to drop off. I've got six bits in my pocket. I can't get trusted for the overalls. Now what shall I do—go without the meat or the overalls?"
>
> The butcher told him to get the pants and he would trust him for the meat. Hearst did so and left the shop, feeling in much better spirits than when he entered.[26]

George thought he had struck it rich in December 1851, when he and some associates discovered a mine close to where others had built and abandoned a mill. They found it rich in gold-bearing quartz, traded some claims for it, and erected one of the earliest quartz mills in California. But after a year the gold gave out and they abandoned the claim. Then came a hard winter:

> 1852 was a very hard winter with us and we had a very hard time of it. The merchants ran out of everything and nothing could be purchased at less than a dollar a pound except beef which was 60 cents a pound. We could not do much that winter as there was so much snow on the ground.[27]

George took his proceeds from the quartz mine to Sacramento and entered the general merchandising business. He later had a similar business in Nevada City. But storekeeping was not to George's liking and he returned to placer mining until 1856, when, dead broke and disgusted, he decided to abandon its uncertainties and devote his energies to vein mining. With forty dollars, his entire available capital, he opened and developed some good mines in Nevada County, including the Lecompton mine, which would prove a good property. "I never succeeded much in placer mining," George said in his memoirs.[28]

Nor had his success at storekeeping been much better. One of his mercantile partners, Almarin Paul, who also alternated between mining and merchandising, wrote in his autobiography,

> In May [1852], I formed a co-partnership with George Hearst under the title of Hearst & Co. and we started business in Sacramento [at 92 K Street] but the times had so changed that we soon found there was no success in merchandising and we discontinued.[29]

George's adventures in gold country were varied. He invested in and managed a Nevada City theater and lecture hall above a store (it was to be the only time that he associated with show business). And on one occasion, while walking down the main street of Nevada City, George and a friend came upon a fire that threatened the local newspaper, the *Nevada Democrat*. One of its owners, Tallman H. Rolfe, wrote his brother Sam in San Bernardino May 28, 1858:

We have again been visited with a disastrous fire which originated in a Chinese wash house on Broad Street. . . . Our office narrowly escaped and we are under obligations to E. G. Waite and George Hearst for timely assistance in putting wet blankets on the gable on the Broad Street side and keeping them wet.[30]

It was George's first encounter with the fortunes of a newspaper, but it was not to be his last.

George was proud of his Missouri mining background and of the expertise that his colleagues had brought to California. He credited them with establishing the rules and techniques for mining in the West.

They carried on mining better than I have seen it done anywhere since except west of the Rockies. Of course we beat the world now, in fact nobody mines as well as we do. But I can say that I saw better mining done there [in Missouri] than I ever saw in any country. It was a pretty good school to graduate from.

The people in California got their education from Missourians or from southerners, but the southerners were not nearly as good as Missourians. Our whole mining arrangements originated with Missouri people, that is, the size of claims, the way to hold them, and the laws respecting them. For instance, in that section of Missouri, about 30 mile square, where there were mines found all over, if a man had a hundred acres, or five hundred acres, and another man went there and found mineral on it, the rule was that he had a right to a certain claim there and to work it, and that the price was regulated by certain conditions. In this way everybody was perfectly safe. It was an unwritten law, but men would not be allowed to stay in the country if they did not obey this law. It was an old French habit which they carried out there. If a digging were shallow and rich, they would cut you down to 14 feet square.

There was probably some five or six thousand people in that section [of Missouri] and out of them a great many went to California, and there scattered here and there and everywhere, so there were enough of them to make their mark and improve the regulations in California where there were no laws. They therefore made regulations there according to the old Missouri system. When a claim was dug you must do so much work every year, and make a statement to that effect. This was precisely the same rule as they had in Missouri.

When I went to California, if I found a rich gulch, as soon as the others would get on to it they would come over maybe 40 men or more and in fact would swallow it up, but they would not take my claim away. They would only make rules so that each man had so much. In the country I am telling you of, in a discovery of this kind, I was entitled to double what everyone else was entitled to, and so it was in California. The fellow who made the discovery had twice as big a claim as anyone else. These four or five thousand people of Missouri contributed more experienced miners to California than any other country, that is, more people who understood mining and its laws. Most of them came very early and went back early.[31]

That had been George's initial intent, but fate had stepped in. And in his absence, his affairs in Missouri had not gone much better than his mining ventures. About 1853, he later learned, he had been reported dead and for many months his Missouri relatives and friends had believed that to be the case. After his sister, Martha, had died, his uncle, Austin Clark, and George's lawyer, Elisha Betts Jeffress of Union, Missouri (who died in 1855), had been among the few who knew the particulars of George's arrangement with Dr. Patton. Word had gotten around that Hearst's land deeds could be attached for payment of some five hundred dollars to creditors, who began to bring suits against the real estate that Patton held as Hearst's. But payments had not been made by Patton and the lands were allowed to be sold by a county sheriff in 1855. The entire property (some eight hundred acres), including the homeplace and other Meramec River bottom lands, were sold for $228—a paltry sum for such valuable lands. Patton had tried to prevent the sales, claiming that the land belonged to him. But in 1856 he had become ill with a "head cancer" and died in 1858.[32]

George's stepfather, Joseph Funk, had sent him the bad news, but George was not anxious to return to Missouri. He saw that his fortunes lay in California.

Nevada City, March 19th, 1858

Dear Father:

. . . You say you would like for me to come home; now, I would like to see you and mother and some of the people, and particularly that little old dried up Uncle Austin and Aunt Ann, much better than you suppose, but to come home without money is out of the question; but if I have any kind of luck I will come home soon and stop awhile, though I do not expect to make this state [Missouri] my home; I am satisfied that I could not stand that climate. You need not be surprised to see me at any time after three months. This leaves me in fine health. You say I must not get out of heart; that is the greatest trouble in this country, but I have got the nerve and can stand anything until death calls for me, and then I must weaken, and not until then. The only thing that gives me much trouble is my old mother. I would like to see her have all that life could desire, and be with me a part of the time, but if God has fixed and ordained otherwise, so it must be.

I will also send you a power of attorney with all the power I could have if I were there myself, which you can use to the best of your judgement. . . .

As regards anything you may do about those lands, it will be all right, but if you have to pay anything like what they are worth, let them go, for I am not stuck after any kind of lands in that part of the world, and I am tired of sending good money after bad. If I had let all [go at] the start and went at something that would have paid me a good living, I think it would have been [better] for me today; but if you should see a chance to save something, do, for it is more than I have been able to do, and furthermore, I do not think that God intended for me to have one cent of that property. I will likely send you some more money soon. . . .

Yours,
George Hearst[33]

Still looking for the big bonanza, George heard in 1859 about a gold strike in neighboring Nevada Territory, across the Sierras in what was known as Washoe country, an inhospitable land of Indians, snowdrifts, and blizzards. Rumors were flying that a prospector had found a blue-black ore that contained gold. Miners were throwing the black stuff away, thinking it worthless. George and his friends, Melville Atwood and A. E. Head, suspected differently.

George resolved to see for himself, but he almost did not make it. Virtually broke, he set out on a horse for the Washoe area. At Nevada City he was stopped by a constable for payment of a forty-dollar debt to a storekeeper. When George turned out his pockets to show that he was penniless, the constable confiscated the horse and accused George of trying to leave California to avoid his creditors. Fortuitously his two mining friends, Atwood and Head, showed up and chipped in to pay the debt. Restored to his horse, George and his companions went on to Washoe, where they managed to raise enough money to buy a half-interest in a mining claim.[34]

They found only fifteen to twenty other men in the area when they arrived, as they had been only the second party to come over from California. George and his pals wasted no time in taking advantage of their jump on the claim. George borrowed one thousand dollars from a Nevada City hotelkeeper, sold his interest in the Lecompton mine, and paid an Irish prospector twenty-five hundred dollars for his interest in a claim called Ophir (a region mentioned in the Old Testament as a source of gold).[35]

George kept careful notes on all his Washoe dealings, scribbling them down with a blunt pencil in one of the leather notebooks that he carried.[36]

Fri., May 18, 1860

Puntes
Cash $500

| Hearst | $100 |
| Sam Custis | $40 |

His original investments in Washoe were picayune for the return they would bring. The mines, George quickly realized, were loaded with silver.[37] After all those years of quiet persistence, hard work, cold beef jerky and cheap whiskey in dirty mining towns, he had struck pay dirt. George tells the story in his understated way, remembering a moment of hesitation in the mountains before going down into the Washoe Valley:

> We ran the Lecompton mine until 1859, when the Washoe excitement came, and I went over there and spent a couple of months, then I came back and sold out what I had in the mine, borrowed some money and went back and took an interest in the Ophir mine, staying there until spring. We got hold of this on the first of June and got out lots of ore. Meantime I heard of a mine that they were digging down when they found it was black sulphurit of silver and that the gold was in that, and that they were breaking this up and throwing the rich silver away. I got a piece of this which had been melted and sent it to an assayer who told me it was worth about $3,000 a ton. The fellow who was digging this out said there was a lot of this stuff, and I said "All right, I am going over there." We talked around a couple of days, and finally one man put in $40 and another $40, I had about the same, and some other coming in, so we went over there.
>
> A strange thing I recollect, that while I was driving along I stopped, got down from my horse, sat on a log and played in the dust for 20 minutes, considering whether I should go on or return. I thought it was about 100 miles to the mountains and this looks like a wild-goose chase amongst the Indians; however, I soon had my mind made up and went on at a gallop. This same fellow that brought the ore over was coming back and they were about 12 miles from where the mine was. Finally we got on a great big mountain and saw below a tent where there were some people working; that was the Comstock.
>
> I did not know it was silver then, but stayed around for two or three days and with a fellow named Jim Southwell, went off prospecting a half mile away. We came back, took a drink together and walked up to where they were taking this ore out in large chunks. Then, after taking two or three drinks more this fellow said to me, "Do you know what this is?" I said, "I don't know except that it is metal." He took me off to one side and said "That is silver." It appears he was in the secret. I said, "How do you know?" and he said, "We are all sure of it." Well, I felt pretty good so I knocked round there and made a trade with a fellow for an interest in it after I had sold my interest in the little mine. The hotel man in Nevada City let me have a thousand dollars. We put a lot of this ore in our saddle bags, got on our horses, and started over the mountains, going along a slope by the side of the Truckee River. . . .
>
> I may say here that my interest in the mine was one sixth. We divided it into 12 parts and the size of a claim was 1500 feet. The good part of it was about 400 feet. In the meantime we got out enough to pay expenses, $2,000 a ton. We worked away till we got out about 45 tons. Some people said it was no good, and nobody believed that it was silver. Anyhow we knew the stuff was in it, but we did not know how to get it out, but we hired mules to get

some of the stuff to San Francisco. Nobody would pay any attention to it there. There was an Englishman by the name of Davis who said "We will ship it for you to England, paying you so much." We thought we could do better, and finally struck a German who said he could smelt it. He said he would build a furnace and smelt it for $450 a ton. We said all right. He then built a furnace and smelted the stuff, and we hauled it around to the Mint. People would not believe it was silver, it looked so much like lead; in fact, it had not been refined, and there was a great deal of lead in it. Everybody said it was lead and of no account, and that these fellows had got the stuff up from Mexico and were trying to work some kind of swindle. Finally the man in charge of the Mint said "Boys, come up tonight and I will give you some money." We went there and got our pockets filled, and then went downtown to see if it would pass for whiskey, and they took it. Then there was great excitement. That was the actual beginning of the Washoe excitement. After paying 25 cents a pound to get it over and $450 a ton for smelting, we cleared out of that $76,000, and besides that we sold slags for several thousand more, so we may say we cleared $80,000 for that lot.

Then the excitement commenced. This was along in March, 1860. The people began to flock there in crowds. It was about the first of April. . . . We started off and finally pulled through, although there was snow all over the country. Wheat was then 50 cents a pound, and I had then a fine mule for which I gave $400 and nothing to feed him on except this expensive stuff, so I let him browse around in the sage-brush. When the Indian war broke out I sold the mules, stayed there until June and then started home, the snow was not off even then. I went to San Francisco, left my traps there, and sold my mules to Ken Holliday. By the way, the Indians killed 65 out of a hundred at the two fights at Pyramid Lake and another place. This Indian war was playing the very Dickens with us. It cost us a good deal and I had to sell some of my ground, but when I got back we started the mill again, and so I went on there mostly up to 1866.[38]

The war with the Pyramid Lake Paiute Indians in the summer of 1860 was an "unnecessary and melancholy affair for the white people of central Nevada, and entailed great loss upon many, and among them was George Hearst," historians were to write in 1893. "He was forced thereby to dispose of a part of his interest in the Ophir."[39] When the uprising broke out, George and his colleagues frantically sent word to California calling for help to fight the Indians, whose last-stand effort to keep their lands was no match for the white men's greed and desire to exploit it.[40]

The Indians were subdued in a few months and the blasting of the mountains resumed at a feverish pace. A bustling city called Virginia had crawled up the valley sides in no time. New techniques for extracting the silver were being invented. George himself had invested in one developed by his old shopkeeping partner, Almarin Paul. It was called the "Electric Dry Amalgamating Process. A Revolution in Mining," according to Paul's advertising flyer. It had been a risk, but Paul had persuaded enough backers, including George, that his new system would work. On 11 August 1860, a steam whistle in Washoe's Gold Canyon signaled the first rise and fall of the twenty-four huge stamps in Paul's mill, the Washoe Gold and Silver Mining Company No. 1. The reverberation and the din were music to George's ears. His luck had turned for good. The lean years were over—forever, George thought. As Paul wrote in his newspaper column, under the pen name Cosmos, "Washoe was now the promised land for fortune hunters and all was life, vigor and prosperity."[41]

George and his cousin Joe Clark moved to Virginia City, whose population reached ten thousand in only a few months by the winter of 1860. It numbered more saloons than any other business, plenty of hotels that rented girls as well as rooms, and the *Territorial Enterprise*, a newspaper for miners, whose most popular writer was Mark Twain, a drinking pal of George's.

Twain would later describe the populace in *Roughing It* (1872) much as George remembered it.

> It was an assemblage of two-hundred thousand young men—not simpering, dainty, kid-gloved weaklings, but stalwart, muscular dauntless young braves, brimful of push and energy, and royally endowed with every attribute that goes to make up a peerless and magnificent manhood—the very pick and choice of the world's glorious ones.

Fortunes were made and lost at gambling tables, claims were jumped at gunpoint, and life was tough and lawless in Virginia City. While the Civil War was heating up two thousand miles to the east, millionaires were made overnight in Washoe. George himself had to hold on to his claims by force. A Texan named Dave Terry had decided to "take" Washoe for the Confederacy and to bring slaves to work the mountains for the cause of the South. He built forts in the area, one of which crossed the line onto George Hearst's Ophir holdings. Hearst hired a Kentuckian, Tom Andrews, a known gunfighter, to run Terry off his property—which he did, convincing Terry that Hearst meant business.[42]

But the mines were booming and George's investments expanded to include the Gould and Curry and other mines. Joe Clark wrote George on 16 March 1860:

> As Jack O'Brien goes over to Nevada today I send you this letter. I bought one hundred feet of ground from on the Sugar Loaf and Lady Bryan adjoining the Desert Co. for which I gave him an order on you for $2,300—I also Bot 100 feet of Arch McDonald in the same lead. He will not want his money for some time to come. Altogether I have bot 325 feet in this Co. I think it is the best Hill in the Flowery district. I have paid from $5 dollars to $25 per fot for [it]. I can sell now for $40—I am frozed to go out prospecting but can't go.

Can't leave here. Several parties are out now. I have got men at work on all our claims. Devil's Gate will be good. The Jumpers are getting good pay. In Hast,

Joe Clark[43]

But George had not been entirely preoccupied with mining. He had kept a sharp eye out for the ladies. With his new found riches and advancing age, he had begun to give serious thought to taking a bride. Every day on the way to the mines he passed a house on Main Street where a young girl from Missouri, Mary Dollarhide, would hang on the fence, prospecting for suitable young men. She lived with her older sister and her husband, who ran a store. George took a fancy to Mary and proposed marriage. He had not known it at the time, but the sister had scotched the deal, telling Mary, "You can't marry that worthless Hearst!"[44]

Just as things were going well, George learned from his stepfather that his mother was sick and would not get well. He wired George to come home immediately. George feared that he would not see his mother alive again. He sold his interest in the Ophir mine for a large profit, banked and invested part of his fortune, and left his mining affairs in the hands of partners Joe Clark, William M. Lent, Sam Custis, and others. George left Washoe in June 1860 and on the first of August sailed out of San Francisco Bay for Panama; after crossing the isthmus jungle, he took another steamer to New York and then a train to St. Louis. He arrived in St. Clair the first of September. The trip had taken only a month, far less than the overland trek of six months to California.

The journey home also had been made pleasanter by his traveling first class. He had taken first cabin on the steamer *John L. Stephens* from San Francisco, sharing cabin space with the Lord Bishop of Victoria, Hong Kong. But despite the urgency to see his mother, George had decided to stop in New York to visit friends and to take a short sight-seeing trip to Niagara Falls.[45]

He was met at the St. Clair depot by his old friend James Inge, who joined him on the train and, while the cars idled at the depot, told him of the sad state of his Missouri property affairs. When at last he arrived at his mother's in Crawford County, he found her failing badly from tuberculosis. She lived only until spring. George occupied himself with trying to straighten out his business affairs—and with calling on several women. His presence in Missouri caused quite a stir. He later would write:

Found my mother very low with consumption; staid with mother several days. Some time after I arrived, there was a little country fair at this town [Union]; I came down to St. Clair; took a horse and buggy and brought

Josephine Renfro over to the fair; remained two or three hours; saw James Halligan [a Union, Missouri, lawyer and later Missouri state senator] at the fair ground; spoke to him and he to me, very cordially; we went out to one side and sat on the grass. He asked me how long I calculated to stay in the country. I said that depended a good deal on the condition of my mother, who could not live perhaps more than two or three months, and I wanted to leave the country then. He said it was very important that I should stay here until these suits were determined. . . . I staid at Mr. Inge's a good portion of the time after the death of my mother, on 1st April, 1861. I staid in the country about 18 months after my mother died, for the purpose of bringing these suits to a close and settling up the matters every way; we finally got the suits to a trial in the district court here—two suits which is a matter of record—by the time the war broke out, which was in the spring of 1861, in April.[46]

The suits to recover his property were directed at Dr. Patton's heirs. George won his case in local courts, but a compromise in 1862 gave his friends Halligan and Inge title to the Hearst lands, and George had received a mere one thousand dollars. He expected to recover the title from his friends, but they had asked more than he had been prepared to pay, and so he lost his lands and the homestead where his grandfather had pioneered, where he had grown up and farmed, and where his father and brother were buried. He felt betrayed by men whom he had trusted as his friends.[47]

His fortunes were faring better out West, where his real interests lay. His partners were busy buying and selling shares in new Comstock Lode mines. "Money is d——d tight," Lent wrote George from San Francisco in October 1860, and income was assured "by telling the biggest stories yet heard of." George, as the richest among them, held financial leverage for his colleagues, so Lent asked,

If you can buy on the claims on Comstock, let us in for a share and we will try to get even with you. With many thanks for your many kindnesses. . . .

Truly yours, Wm. M. Lent.[48]

Lent was "looking after [George's] interests," and was encouraged about their fortunes: "When you return we will make more money, so you make haste to come back," he wrote to George on 8 June, 1861.[49]

George also had heard from his friend, J. B. Dickinson, with whom he had traveled from San Francisco and visited in New York. Dickinson was also looking after George's marital interests:

New York
October 17/60

My dear George,
    I duly received your letter a few days since and much regret to hear that

your mother's health is so bad, and trust it may yet prove that your fears have
made you look on the gloomy side.

My last date from San Francisco is Sept. 22 by pony. Lent was still at
Washoe. He says Central is greatly improving. They are taking out considerable quantity of the richest kind of ore—have the long tunnel in now, 900 ft.,
and expect [them] next to advise that it is in the lead. The crushing and
stamping mill is completed. They have made a contract to reduce 4 tons per
day by the Veitch process. The parties to be ready to commence in sixty days;
they are to pay $60 per hour.

He [Lent] says the Gould & Curry is a better mine than the Ophir and in less
than a year will sell for more. The mine is improving daily—the quantity of
metal is increasing. . . . In another letter they speak of the suit against the
Ophir as "Black Mail suits" that they [claim] amount to nothing—they do not
mention anything about the suit against the Gould & Curry—and I know
nothing about it except what I have seen in the papers. As you say, I never
heard of it before. I am inclined to think it is only to levy Black Mail—that it
will not amount to anything.

I am sorry to hear you have the Blues—that won't do—you must cheer up.
We shall send you papers, and hope you will be able to get this way and
spend a part of your time. I showed your letter to Mrs. Dickinson, she said tell
Mr. Hearst I will introduce him to a young lady that will suit him when he
comes here—she told me who—and I am inclined to think well of it. . . .

With my best wishes, I remain, my Dear George,

Yours most truly,
J. W. Dickinson.[50]

Even cousin Joe Clark had marriage on his mind. He had written from
Virginia City on 10 February 1861, "Girls—I don't know if I ever will
marry in that country. I am greatly in love with a pretty girl of Carson."
In the same letter, he said, "I am in favor of secession."[51] Like George,
his sympathies lay with the South.

The Civil War had begun to complicate George's life. In Missouri he
was caught in an act of regrettable indiscretion. Under the martial law
imposed in August 1861 by General Frémont he had been arrested for
uttering "alleged seditious language" in pro-Union St. Louis. He sent
word of his arrest back to the West, and the *Nevada City Morning
Transcript* printed an account of it on 12 September 1861:

We learn that a letter has been received in this city from Mr. George Hearst,
dated at St. Louis, Missouri, in which he says that he was placed under arrest
by the Federal authorities at that place, on account of alleged seditious
language. In former letters written by him, Mr. Hearst represented Missouri
as an intolerable place for a neutral man to live in. Indeed, such a thing as
neutrality was out of the question, neither Unionists or Secessionists allowing a man to occupy middle ground. He must be for them, else he is against
them. Mr. Hearst, it appears, expressed opinions in St. Louis deemed seditious by the authorities there, and hence his arrest. In giving vent to his
opinions, he did not probably realize the effects of martial law, as he never

before witnessed the workings of that institution. Mr. Hearst, as our citizens well know, is anything but a bad or dangerous man, and we hope he will be allowed to return to Washoe, where he can employ his time more profitably than with politics.[52]

Although he managed to get out of the matter, he could see that the fighting was spreading in Missouri. He had watched refugees pouring into St. Louis in December 1861, "destitute, half naked, benumbed with cold" and starving, as *Harper's Weekly* reported on 28 December.[53]

Some of George's relatives were fighting on the side of the Confederacy, and a cousin, William Hearst, would be taken prisoner the following spring. He wrote George from the military prison at Alton, Illinois, asking for help; George used what influence he had to try to get him released.[54]

Meanwhile, word traveled West, incorrectly, that George had become an officer in the Confederate army. William Lent wrote of his colleagues' surprise at the news.

> . . . you have caused so many moments of worryment—just previous to receiving your last letter. The report was that you was an officer in the Confederate Army. . . . Not having heard from you, I believed the story the day when at the G & C [Gould and Curry Mine] office there was a man inquiring about your stock who told [several?] that he had proof that you was in the rebel army. I came up to the office and immediately [sent?] to Joe [Clark] to come down. . . . I also sent for Judge Heydenfeldt [a lawyer and friend of Hearst's] and consulted him. During this time a number called and their conversation leading to enquiries what you were worth, saying, Lent, that friend of yours that went home has made a good thing. . . . My reply was that he had spent it. . . . This was on a Friday. On Friday night I thought the matter over and on Saturday I went into the market and sold 13 feet 3 feet at 1350$ and 10 feet at 1400$. . . . I felt the importance of the state of your affairs that I remained in town and Sunday when I received your letter I jumped for joy. The next morning when they inquired I told them that I had received letters and that you was <u>strong</u> [Union?]—I did not explain the kind of [Union?] I [meant?]. So much for neglecting to write.[55]

A few months later Lent wrote: "I am satisfied that at the time rumor placed you in Confederate employ, my letters were tampered with." At the same time, Lent expressed disillusionment with mining and encouraged George to sell all his mine stock and buy bonds:

> I am sick of mining and I am disposing of my stock as fast as possible. . . . it is hard to be poor, you are now rich and should take the advantage of it and place yourself in a position that you cannot be in danger of depending upon any man.[56]

But in no mood to stop a good thing, George decided to hold on to his mine shares. For the first time he had money in his pocket and a small fortune in the bank. Then forty years old, he decided that it was time to marry, so while in Missouri he began to look for a suitable wife. He cut quite a striking figure and was a good catch, even if his long blond beard and shirt front were stained with chewing tobacco, he liked to drink, and was prone to swearing. A *New York Times* writer described him as the "ideal young Western backwoodsman . . . straight as an arrow, long, swinging arms, big feet and hands, a somewhat awkward gait, a pleasant, ever-smiling face, a drawling but musical voice, and the pronounced accent of the Southerner of the slave days." He had the rough edge of the miner he had been for ten years, plain of manner and dress. Though "illiterate," the *Times* wrote, George was "of keen and observing mind and quick of perception . . . an experience once gained is never forgotten. He is a good judge of men and human nature and it takes a bright man to get the best of him." When in the company of his cronies, George was noted for delivering "himself of many wise, original and homely thoughts and phrases." But in dress the best that could be said was that he was "slouchy": "All the tailors on earth could not fix him up to make him look otherwise."[57]

There were not many unmarried women in Missouri, but Phoebe Apperson, the daughter of a woman he once had courted, was not spoken for. When he had left for California Phoebe was a child. Now she had grown into a pretty, charming young lady of eighteen. George Hearst was a mature man of the world who went about his business with a certain sureness. He was not boastful, but there was no doubt in Phoebe's mind that he had struck it rich in California. He certainly had made his mother's last months luxurious by local standards. But there were rivals for George's attention. Even Phoebe's best friend, Ellen Patton, was a serious contender; there were hints that George had proposed to her.

Phoebe's parents at first had been astonished that so old a man would call on their daughter. They hoped she would make a good match. She was their only daughter and they wanted the best for her. But a man twice her age, even if he did appear to have money, was worrisome; what would happen if he were to die, leaving her a young widow with children? They felt obliged to object to George's attentions to their Phoebe, but they did so less resolutely when it became clear, as spring and summer passed and another fall came, that the couple was courting. The attentions that George paid her led Phoebe to think that she might become his wife. They had an easy manner together. When they did not talk—George was given to long silences—she was content to feel his strong presence. She had written of her feelings in poems.

At last George proposed. He also agreed to a premarital contract, ensuring Phoebe financial security if he died before she did. She accepted his proposal. It was not clear whether George offered to make the contract or the Appersons requested it in return for Phoebe's hand.

They had reluctantly given their blessing to her marriage to this much older man only after it was apparent that their daughter knew what she wanted. She had been an obedient, thoughtful, and studious child. But she was determined. Her exposure to rich possibilities perhaps had planted ideas in her head and she had been convinced that she could go beyond the proscribed horizons of her simple life. She would leave behind an uncomplicated world for one that would tax her brain and stamina in ways that she could not imagine.

It was a sensible, unsentimental arrangement, George's taking a wife. The trust and fondness between them were not openly manifested, but they had a bond that was stronger than the objections that Phoebe's parents might have had to the marriage. That may have been why there was no church wedding and no family present at the ceremony.

On 14 June 1862 Phoebe and George went to the Steelville court-house, where the clerk had drawn up a contract in which George Hearst conveyed to "Phoebe E. Epperson" (misspelled) fifty shares of stock in the Gouldin (also misspelled) & Curry Gold & Silver Mining Company of Virginia City, Nevada Territory. The contract provided that Mrs. Hearst should hold the stock for life, and that it should revert to her husband if she should die first. The shares were to be free from any legal claim or judgment that might be obtained against George. "In consideration of said future marriage," it read, "it is further agreed that the said 50 shares of stock shall be her own separate estate and property, for her exclusive and separate use and benefit, and free from the interference and control of her said future husband during her natural life." Provisions also were made permitting the sale of the stock, with proceeds going to Phoebe. If she were to outlive her husband, the stock after her death would go to their heirs. "The said Phebe E. Epperson having no claim to the above described stock beyond her natural life has no power to convey or bequeath the same by any conveyance or will to any person for any purpose whatever at any time whether either before or after the death of the said George Hearst," it read.[58]

The next day, before noon, they were married by W. P. Renick, a Presbyterian minister, at A. J. Seay's home on Main Street in Steelville. Seay, although a Republican and a Union sympathizer, was a bachelor friend of George's and a lawyer who already had seen war service. No one from either the Hearst or Apperson families was present, and the event was not recorded in a photograph. Phoebe wore a simple dress that she had made. It was a hot summer day and a battle was in progress nearby, as it had been for several days. Union officers at the courthouse in Steelville had warned Phoebe and George to stay in hiding for several days since their lives might be in danger.[59]

They secluded themselves at the James home, where Phoebe had tutored, until they could safely return to St. Clair as a married couple. The deed had been done, signed, and sealed on paper.[60]

George's recollections of the event were prosaic, whatever passion that once existed in the relationship having been tempered by the time he set down his memoirs at the end of his life.

> When I went home I stayed about two years [and] got married. . . . The reason I came back was to see my mother more than anything else. My mother died six months after I arrived. She wrote me she was sick, and asked me to come home, and I started a little while after I got her letter. My wife was named after my mother [Elizabeth], but I had no idea how she looked like, I just knew there was such a person. Her name was Phoebe Elizabeth Apperson.

In only one other place in his autobiography would he refer to his wife, almost as if wives were commodities in Gold Rush California:

> I have been married since 1863 [actually 1862] and my wife has been with me ever since. As to the advantage of having a woman out west in those early days, of course, if she were a good woman, it was a good thing to have her; but outside of that there is not much that she could do. The first five years in California a woman was a curiosity, and they could coin money keeping little eating houses there; for we had to pay a dollar for any kind of meal. There was no kind of little place that could not take in a couple of hundred dollars a day.[61]

Phoebe did not expect to run a hotel or sling hash. George may have gotten more than he bargained for in Phoebe Apperson. But for better or worse, their bond was sealed for their lifetimes. And soon after the marriage Phoebe found herself pregnant.

It would be several months before George could conclude matters sufficiently to allow them to leave. George was anxious to return to California and to get away from the war. He had stayed far longer than he had intended and it was unsafe for his pregnant wife to stay in Missouri.[62]

By the time they were ready to leave, however, it was difficult to get through Union lines. George got his old mining friend and teacher, Dr. Silas Reed, who was working at a military hospital in St. Louis, to help arrange passage north, where Phoebe and George could take a train to New York. Because George was not in the Union army, he needed a passport before he could leave Missouri, which he was able to get.[63]

So it was that on a late September day Phoebe Hearst found herself in a buggy heading north with all that she owned or cared about in a trunk, a contract with the man beside her, and a child growing inside her.

3
Early San Francisco Years

The journey from Missouri to San Francisco was arduous, especially for one in the early stages of pregnancy. The Hearsts traveled by train to New York, where, on 11 October, they boarded a steamship, the *Ocean Queen*, for the Panama isthmus. They made their way across the steaming, mosquito-ridden jungle on a newly completed railroad from Aspinwall. From the west coast of Panama they sailed, first cabin, on the steamship *Sonora* for San Francisco, arriving at 10 P.M. 6 November 1862.

During the trip Phoebe became friends with Mr. and Mrs. James Peck, who were traveling from Kingston, New York, with their two-year-old son Orrin and other children. The 7 November 1862 *Daily Alta California*, reporting the *Sonora's* arrival, lists among the passengers "J. A. Peck . . . Mrs. Peck and 4 children . . . Mr. Hurst and wife and 170 others." Mrs. Peck looked after the pregnant young bride, for which Phoebe always would be grateful. They became lifelong friends and Phoebe a benefactress to the Peck family. She later paid for Orrin to study art in Europe and Janet music, and sent monthly checks to Mrs. Peck. Orrin would become a favorite both of Phoebe's and her son's and a familiar figure in the Hearst household.

To pass the time aboard ship, Phoebe sewed. Although she was a master worker with thread and needle, she later confessed an antipathy to that tedious work.[1] The story is told that during the journey up the West Coast, a dress on which she had been working disappeared; unknown to Phoebe, George had taken it. Not long after their arrival in San Francisco, seven made-to-order silk dresses, one for each day of the week, in different colors and in Phoebe's size, were delivered to her from Davidson's (later the White House) Department Store. George was said to have ordered the elegant gowns for his bride to replace her simple homemade dresses from Missouri.[2] The story may be apocryphal, but it was true that Phoebe developed a hearty taste for expensive fashions, which George happily provided.

When the ship carrying the Hearsts sailed through the Golden Gate, Phoebe gazed at the few lights twinkling from San Francisco's hills rising to the right and announced that she wanted to live on one where she could always see the Bay.[3] Ironically she would spend much of her later life on golden hills inland, far from the Bay and far from Missouri. As her fortunes rose, she found herself supporting numerous poor relations and friends, paying for their children to attend schools, "adopting" some in spirit if not legally, sending trunkloads of her hand-me-downs, jewelry, and shoes to Missouri, and on several occasions delivering the gifts herself.

But Missouri was far away on that night when Phoebe arrived in San Francisco. The Civil War was as remote in miles as in mind, Lincoln was President, Victoria was Queen of England, and San Francisco was a wide open town with a busy Barbary Coast of madams and gamblers along the waterfront and a growing number of "respectable" families in gingerbread houses rising on the hills above the Bay—Nob, Russian, Telegraph, Rincon. Social prominence rose proportionately to wealth, as did political power, in what was to become a San Francisco pattern. Hustle, fraud, speculation, and survival figured prominently, as did luck. Fortunes came and went with rapidity. Five major fires had virtually destroyed the city between 1850 and 1851, and the fire department held great political power in the city. It was, in fact, a town in which traditional rules of democratic government were waived in favor of raw gold- and silver-laden power grabs. It was a vulnerable city in which political control was directly related to the speed with which needs could be met—fighting fires, paving streets, constructing fire-proof buildings, controlling "undesirable" social and criminal elements. Vigilante groups governed the city.

San Francisco had been a Mexican village thirteen years before the Hearsts arrived. But by 1862 it boasted the largest building west of the Mississippi, the Montgomery Block, built in 1853. Montgomery Street had become a thriving "Wall Street West" with the newly formed (1862) Stock and Exchange Board. The city had pushed its waterfront one thousand feet into the Bay from the original water's edge. Gas lamps lit the stone, plank, or mud streets, pretentious buildings of granite from the Sierra Nevada rose in the commercial district, sand blew unmercifully from the dunes west of the hills during windy summers (Golden Gate Park had not yet been built to hold down the dunes), and rain turned the streets into mud wallows in winter. But the city had taken on a look of permanency. It had survived a bank panic and depression in 1855, and by 1862 silver speculation on the Comstock Lode was booming along Montgomery Street.

It was a city with a polyglot population: Americans, Spaniards, French, Italians, Germans, Austrians, Chinese, British, Irish, Australians, a few blacks and American Indians—all reflecting large waves of migration caused by economic depressions, revolutions, or famine in other parts of the world. California Indians recently had been murdered in cold blood not far from the city, and Chinese immigrants were soon to be a "problem" in the port town. The 1862 census reported that thirty thousand men and five thousand women lived in San Francisco, although the actual population was closer to one hundred thousand. There were twelve daily newspapers and a number of theaters in several languages, at least two literary magazines (*Golden Era*, 1852–98, and *Hesperian*, 1858–63—founded by women); hotels, cafés, saloons, boardinghouses, dance halls, whorehouses, and restaurants. More coffee, tea, champagne, and cigars were consumed in San Francisco in those days than in Boston, and the ladies' dresses were fashionable. There were at least forty bookstores, a thriving activity in trading of used books, and several libraries and book publishers. All of this was happening in a place of which Fitz Hugh Ludlow of New York (1836–70), who had come to town via Yosemite with landscape painter Albert Bierstadt, said, "To a traveler paying his first visit, it has the interest of a new planet." So it must have seemed to Phoebe. Another New Yorker, author Ada Clare (1836–74) wrote of Californians in *Golden Era*, "They seem to be people without any remembered Past save as it may sometimes come to them in a confused sense of having been born in some other place at some vaguely remote period."[4]

Richard Henry Dana, returning to San Francisco on 13 August 1859, twenty-three years after his first visit—which he chronicled in *Two Years before the Mast*—described the city much as Phoebe must have first seen it:

> We bore around the point towards the old anchoring-ground of the hide ships, and there, covering the sand hills and the valleys, stretching from the water's edge to the base of the great hills, and from the old Presidio to the mission, flickering all over with the lamps of its streets and houses, lay a city of one hundred thousand inhabitants.[5]

This was no backwater town, and its exotic hustle and bustle must have startled and exhilarated Phoebe Hearst as she stepped ashore and made her way down a long wharf, clutching her husband's arm.

San Francisco was a city seized by silver fever. Contemporary historian J. Ross Browne (1821–75) described the impact of the silver boom in the spring of 1860:

> [The news of silver was] borne on the wings of the wind from the Sierra Nevada, wafted through every street, lane, and alley . . . whirling around the drinking saloons, eddying over the counters of the banking offices, scattering up the dust among the Front Street merchants, arousing the slumbering

inmates of the Custom-House. . . . Nobody had any money, yet everybody was a millionaire in silver claims. Nobody had any credit, yet everybody bought thousands of feet of glittering ore. . . . All was silver underground, and deeds and mortgages on top, silver, silver everywhere, but scarce a dollar in coin.[6]

This was the city to which George Hearst brought his new bride. San Francisco was a month from New York by passenger ship and four to six months by cargo ship. It had begun to develop its own industries— banks, a mill to make cloth from California wool, sugar refineries, foundries, a silkworm farm, watch factory, carriage factory, rolling stock factory, and a furniture factory. The Hearst's arrival by ship in the winter of 1862 was on the eve of construction of a transcontinental railroad that four Sacramento storekeepers (Leland Stanford, Charles Crocker, Mark Hopkins, and Collis P. Huntington) and a visionary engineer (Theodore Judah) had pursued to reality despite opposition from steam-ship and stagecoach companies. Congress approved the Pacific Railroad Act in 1862, giving the "Big Four" large federal subsidies, huge land grants, and federal loans at 6 percent for thirty-year bonds. In January 1863 the roadbed started up the western slopes of the Sierra Nevada from Sacramento. Phoebe would travel that roadbed many times.[7]

The harbor on the nation's western edge was filled with clipper ships and other vessels, many of them abandoned by gold-seekers and used as foundations for wharves and buildings in the booming town.

What a moment of revelation it must have been for Phoebe, then several months' pregnant, as she walked along the busy bustling wharf into the noisy city—the biggest port and the only city west of St. Louis. She arrived in California in a plain brown dress with straight brown hair but it would not be long before she was adorned in lace, pearls, and curls. An observer of a photograph of her at that time later wrote that she was

. . . a beautiful nineteen-year-old girl with deep humid eyes, black hair, and the exquisite features of a Burnes-Jones painting. It was an interesting face, gentle, serene and lovely, but even then, at the age of nineteen, there was amazing strength and straight-eyed thinking in the picture.[8]

She did, indeed, have a determined look in her wide eyes.

The Hearsts stayed first at the ornate Lick House, built by James Lick, a piano-maker who had made a fortune in real estate. The Lick House had just opened in 1862 at the southwest corner of Sutter and Montgomery streets. It was the grandest hotel in town with 204 rooms, although it was only three stories high (there were no elevators). And it boasted a new attraction in San Francisco—a bridal suite—which

George no doubt secured for his wife's first nights in the city. Phoebe had seen nothing like it. Although the hotel was covered in *trompe l'oeil*—its exterior and interior walls were painted to simulate various kinds of marble or fancy wood—the three-room bridal suite was a Victorian sensation unmatched in San Francisco. Its parlor featured carved rosewood furniture, wall-to-wall carpeting to match the brocaded upholstery and curtains, a white marble mantel, gilt rococo mirrors, and two crystal chandeliers decorated with cupids. The big beds were covered with white linen and had soft and downy mattresses.[9] It was splendid beyond belief for a girl accustomed to the simple cabins of rural Missouri. Phoebe was surrounded by more opulence than she had ever seen—and she liked it. In a short time the Hearsts moved to the Stevenson House at California and Montgomery streets, an apartment-hotel where respectable people stayed in transient San Francisco. The following event apparently took place there; it surely was not in a hospital.

On 29 April 1863 she gave birth to a son. He was named for his paternal and maternal grandfathers, William Hearst and Randolph Apperson. Years afterward there was speculation that William Randolph was a twin and that the other died at birth. The fact has not been corroborated, and his birth records were destroyed in the 1906 San Francisco earthquake and fire. But a history of twins in Phoebe's family, the Appersons and Whitmires, preceded his birth, and there was a succession of twins from himself and his own progeny. Phoebe never admitted to having twins. In fact, she was quoted as saying, when William Randolph's twin sons were born in 1915, "I wonder where they came from. There's no history of twins in my family."[10] There was, of course, but we may never know whether she herself bore twins on the only occasion in her life when she gave birth.

Her niece Anne Drusilla Apperson Flint later speculated that the birth was difficult and that perhaps it was the cause of Phoebe's having no other children.[11] Subjects like that were not discussed in polite society, so the nature of William Randolph's coming into the world can only be speculated upon. He may have been a large baby since he grew to be a large man, like his father, rather than like his petite mother.

There also is some question about the date of William Randolph's arrival. Letters from William Lent to George Hearst in 1862 and 1863 discuss the boy as if he were born before 29 April 1863. In a letter dated 27 August 1862 that Lent sent from San Francisco to George in Missouri, telling of the rumors of George's being in the Confederate army, Lent also wrote:

> I would like to see you but [take?] your own pleasure. My regards to your wife and I would have written fully had you answered my letters or tele-

grams. When you come you can have a hearty welcome by myself and family. I have a fine boy and girl. I suppose I know the reason of your delay being an old married man. I can appreciate matters. Take no risks. I hope it will be as fine a boy as mine. Have you got a name for it? If not, call it Joe.[12]

Clearly Phoebe was pregnant then and even possibly had had the baby, although it is likely that Lent was speculating on the baby's being a boy.

In another letter addressed to George at Sullivan, Missouri, on 7 October 1862 (the same letter in which he urged George to get out of silver stock speculation), Lent wrote: "My best regards to your good lady and tell her to do me the favor and make you answer this immediately."[13] George already had developed a lifelong habit of not answering letters.

On 24 November 1862 Lent wrote from San Francisco to George at Virginia City, where he had hastened shortly after his arrival in California:

I was up to see Mr. Walters yesterday and found Mrs. Hearst very much improved. She told me to tell you that she walked to church and back without feeling fatigued. I told her I was agoing to write you not to return until you had accomplished everything so you would not have to go over this winter again. . . .

I sent up the carriage for Mrs. H. to go to her dressmakers, and will do all we can to make her happy. She looks like another person.[14]

Phoebe must have been recovering from her trip to California and possibly suffering discomfort from the pregnancy, as well as the shock of the transplant far from home to entirely new surroundings.

But on 20 January 1863—three months before the date given as William Randolph's birth—Lent, in San Francisco, again wrote George, still apparently in the mountains: "Your baby having the measels [sic] I was afraid to call [on Mrs. Hearst] as Mrs. Lent would worry about it as none but mothers can do. I will go up today some time."[15] Lent may have wrongly dated the year, it having just changed, and, in fact, it may have been 1864.

Whatever his date of birth, William Randolph was not baptized then, and when he was, several years later, it was without his parents' knowledge or blessing. Phoebe and George Hearst were not overly concerned about William Randolph's religious persuasion, instruction, or ticket to heaven.

The Hearsts hired an Irish Catholic governess, Eliza Pike, who also served as a wet-nurse for Willie until he was at least fourteen months old. The nurse worried about the infant's going to Hell unless he was baptized, and one day, while Phoebe was away, the nurse took Willie to a parish priest who baptized him in the Catholic church. When Phoebe returned to find the deed done, she protested, "But I am a Presbyterian."

"No matter, madam," the nurse replied, "the baby is a Christian."[16]

Shortly after Willie's arrival George Hearst bought a simple brick house on Rincon Hill, then the most fashionable part of town. On 13 October 1863 Lent wrote George from San Francisco:

> I was out to your house on Sunday. Mrs. H. was looking very well indeed. She has a very nice home and is much pleased with it. And no doubt you will be pleased also.[17]

Perhaps George had bought the house without seeing it. At any rate, he was off in the mountains. The father was to spend more time with his mines than with his young son and wife in San Francisco.

As a result, Phoebe turned most of her attention to her offspring and began a pattern of spoiling, indulging, and fussing over him. He early learned to take advantage of her permissiveness, as the rod was spared in the case of the former schoolteacher's own child. Willie's every act was the object of her rapt attention and she soon believed him to be a bright and superior child.[18] Phoebe desperately wanted a sister for him, but in the meantime, in her husband's absence Willie garnered all of her motherly affection and possessiveness.

Phoebe also had her parents for company. Early in 1863 the Appersons and Phoebe's brother, Elbert, accompanied by Ellen Patton, arrived in San Francisco. They would never return to live in Missouri and would be supported in large part by George, and later Phoebe, throughout their natural lives—which were made long and comfortable by their settling first on a pretty piece of ranch property near Santa Clara, some forty miles south of San Francisco. They preferred the country, and took up farming and ranching.

Lent wrote George from San Francisco on 15 January 1863, "I had a talk with Mr. Apperson and I do not think he likes the idea of going over the bay. He naturally wants to be as near you as possible and the communication easy."[19]

By 20 January (in the same letter dated in 1863, when Willie had the measles), Lent wrote George, "I saw Mr. Apperson and told him what you had told me. He's anxious to get at something to do. I told him not to be in a hurry and encouraged him as much as I could." He added, "I am giving my attention to the plans for the building of a race track. I found them so faulty that I rejected both and went to an architect to get plans made which will be done by the time this reaches you and when you come back I will give you my ideas."[20]

George may have had an ulterior motive in settling his parents-in-law in the country: he wanted to raise racehorses, which later became a passion with him. In 1864 he opened the Bayview racetrack at Hunter's Point, a few miles south of the heart of San Francisco.[21]

Meanwhile Phoebe began to take advantage of the cultural opportunities of the pretentious western city, with its opera, music, and other entertainments. She herself began to entertain, inviting to tea people who interested her—painters, musicians, and literary people. She preferred intellectual conversation about art, books, and music to society gossip and garnered a reputation as being somewhat aloof.[22] But she attracted many friends with her hospitality, discovering at the same time that she liked company and entertaining. Perhaps it was because she was lonely. George was gone most of the time.

Their great differences became more manifest: she was the self-learning, cultured lady; he the down-to-earth, uneducated man. He must have cut quite a swath on the occasions when he carried his great, gangling frame into Phoebe's social gatherings. He disliked fancy clothes and was far more at home playing poker with the boys for high stakes than he was in polite society. He walked and talked slowly, had a quiet sense of humor and a twinkle in his eye. He was well liked, but he and Phoebe were as different as they could be.

George preferred listening to talking and was taciturn in company, his mind often seeming far away. He would sit at a dining table crumbling bread with his long fingers, thinking of faraway places and fortunes. Robert Turner, the Hearsts' butler for thirty-five years, would brush away George's crumbs and bring him a fresh piece of bread, and George would continue crumbling, unconscious that his supply had been refurbished. He favored pork spareribs and hominy and string beans with two strips of bacon.[23]

His appearance has been described as

. . .tall, erect, rugged, with a broad brow, a well-formed high head, a striking aquiline nose and a long, graying pioneer's beard. He was slow-moving. He always wore a slouch hat down over his eyes, and on his feet were high-topped boots. He usually wore a cutaway coat, and occasionally, with great reluctance, he appeared in a frock coat.[24]

On one occasion George was reported to have arrived home in the midst of one of Phoebe's tea parties, entering "in his stocking feet, carefully carrying his boots in his right hand while his left supported the regulation crooked cane. He looked neither to the right nor to the left, but glided through the apartment like a ghost, to the intense amusement of the guests."[25]

A scene that must have been repeated many times was that described by a *New York Times* writer who professed to have known George for many years. One night he arrived home unexpectedly during a dinner party that Phoebe was holding. As his friend related, when George, the "inveterate tobacco chewer," became animated "in congenial company, he scatters the extract of the weed somewhat promiscuously over his shirt front." When he let himself into the bright and elegant gathering, he stood somewhat dazed as a hush fell on the party. Phoebe rushed over to hustle him out of sight and begged him to change into a fresh shirt. "Thrusting his hands in his breeches pockets—a habit of his—and drawing himself erect, he said in a voice loud enough for the company to hear: 'This is my ranch, and if these here folks don't like my shirt they can go home; it's time for folks to be in bed, anyhow, and I'm gwine thar,' and he steadied himself up the stairs to his apartment."[26]

It became apparent to Phoebe that he was not going to change, dress like a businessman instead of the miner that he was, or participate in her cultural improvement program. So they accommodated each other. He must have been delighted that his wife was adapting to California and taking her entertainment into her own hands, for he knew that he was neither capable nor desirous of joining her in the activities that she enjoyed. He indulged her desires and lavished material luxuries on her. She had running charge accounts at the best stores, servants, a comfortable home, a small child.

Phoebe realized that she would have to make her own social and intellectual life without George's participation. She was then in her early twenties; it was a time of great changes and decisions in her young life. It was not a time for tentative behavior. She boldly set out to make her own friends and amuse herself and her son.

4
Mother and Miner

Although George was away from home a good deal, he and Phoebe carried on a lively communication by letter between the city and the mountains, a distance that required traveling for a week or longer by horse, stagecoach, and the steamboats that linked San Francisco and Sacramento. In those early years of marriage and motherhood, the young bride complained of their separation and George of his missing her and "the Boy." It was a difficult time for both George and Phoebe.

A letter from George dated 14 September 1864 from Virginia City hints that they have had a disagreement, possibly over George's long absences. It tells much about his desire to please Phoebe, which conflicted with his devotion to business affairs and a yearning for a simpler life. His vision of the three of them living in the woods and surviving on beans is wistful, even comical, given the realities of their future, and surely must have amused his wife, luxuriating as she was in the comforts of her San Francisco home and riding about in a new carriage. Nevertheless, eloquent in its simplicity and directness, it is a poignant love letter.

Virginia, September 14, '64

My dear wife, this leaves me in good health. Hope you are [. . .] and [. . .] I am glad you are having a pleasant time but am sorry you are so low in spirits. I have been very homesick since I have been up here this time at best and [when] those bliss letters come I feel like giving up everything and let it all go. We can [go] into some valley and live on beans better. I am shure it will not take much to do me and if the Boy can be educated should he live, that will be sufficient. He can go in to the wood and make his own living. I hope he will have an easier time than I had before I succeeded.

I will come home as soon as this case is desided. It is going on first rate and I have no fears of them getting the best of it yet. If it was not well attended too we would loose shure and I have too much in it to loose unless I conclude that I have too much and then I had rather give it to some [Hearst?] people than to let a pack of thieves have it. As I am here I will do the best I can for this time, all though I feel very low spirited and feel just like I would just as soon be in some out of the way place where I could not see a person in a month as any other way. Just so I had enough of something to eat if it was only bacon and beans.

I suppose I will loose [the Watson matter?]. If so, so much the worse. I done what I thought was right. I thought he would pay it back of course and he and his wife have been so kind to you I culd not well deny him, so if it is gone I cant help it. I know I ought not to have done it now but could not see then. We might be just as well off if all we had had went at the same time.

You are unhappy because I have to be away looking after what we have and I am not happy here, for this is no company here for me and if we had nothing it might be different. If it was beans we could appreciate what we had had and been. If we were happier we would be glad of it. At all events, I am tired of this way and am agoing to change, for 200 dollars a year will do me and I had rather live on pork and beans than to receive such dispairing letters and if I am the cause of it, it must and shall be stopped, you can rely on that, that I am shure. I will stay until this suit is about over thin I go and when I leave again you will agree to it. If I [stopped], all would go into the sea.

You say in your letter you are sorry and that you are a fool for loving me as you do. I am sorry you think so. I did not know I had done anything so unworthy of your love. I know I would be sorry to have done anything rong and I am not sorry I love you and hope I never will be. I thought I would look after what I had here until I got it all right and out of trouble and then I would take it easy. But enough of this. I fear as you say I have wrote too much. But I have the Blues and feel very bad.

As to the carage, I am glad you got it. I told you to get it if you wanted. I meant just what I said. Of course I did not want it if you did not. All I have to say is if I live long you shall have those feet or its equivalent in what ever you say. You might have been better satisfied if I had done it sooner. But I know I can do it now and will. I thought it best to get in water stock or something shure. But we will have it fixed. I am going to try after this to please you.

Your husband, G. Hearst

A footnote scribbled on the front of the first page says, "Kiss the Boy for me I wish I could Kiss you for my self. GH."[1]

As in many subsequent letters to Phoebe, George complains of his loneliness without her while telling her that he will not be home for a while. Travel was tedious (there were no railroads yet running from San Francisco to the Sierras and East), and he stayed for months at a time in Nevada, Utah, Idaho, and later South Dakota, Montana, New Mexico, and Mexico. Political activities would keep him in Sacramento, the capital, for long periods.

This early letter is telling in many ways about the couple, so different in ages, education, and interests. Whatever their differences, though, George confided candidly in his wife throughout his life about his business ventures. In that regard it appears that they had few, if any, secrets. He was gentle and straightforward in his expressions to her in his letters. His writings, like his desires, were unpretentious—"200 dollars a year will do me." How little they then knew of his enormous fortune to come! In all of the letters, his handwriting is crude, the spelling phonetic, the punctuation nonexistent. His penmanship is erratic, growing sloppier and running off the page toward the ends of letters, possibly as candles burned down and whiskey bottles emptied in his tent or cabin somewhere in the mountains. His letterpaper was whatever happened to be at hand—plain, lined pad paper or stationery picked up from hotels or businesses.

Between visits to mines and saloons during long stays at Virginia City, George no doubt read the *Golden Era*, a gold rush literary journal that catered to miners, and the *Virginia City Territorial Enterprise*, which entertained the Comstock Lode crowd under the pseudonym bylines of Mark Twain and Dan DeQuille. Their aim was "to keep the universe thoroughly posted concerning murders and street fights, and balls and theaters, and packtrains, and churches, and lectures, and highway robberies, and Bible societies . . . and the thousand other things which it is in the province of local reporters to keep track of and magnify into undue importance for the readers of a daily newspaper."[2]

Exposure to those literary efforts did not improve George's ability to write legibly. Nevertheless he considered buying an interest in a newspaper at Virginia City, more for political than literary reasons. A letter to George dated 12 August 1863 from G. D. Roberts, a mining colleague, reads:

> In your conversation with me before you left here, you authorized me to draw on you for $500 for the Democratic paper here, if necessary.
>
> I can assure you that the life of the paper depends entirely on its friends, or the "Union League" have already arrayed their batteries against it. The paper is being conducted in an able, conservative, and loyal manner, but the name of Democracy is sufficient to bring upon it the Abolition cohorts. We therefore appeal to you for assistance in this hour of need.
>
> Please send your check for the $500, if agreeable to you, to order of Miss Linthicum and Hastings, proprietor of the paper. Your check payable twenty or thirty days after date will do.
>
> M. Linthicum and Hastings receives the money, when contributed in large amounts, as a loan.

On 21 September 1863, Roberts again wrote Hearst, "Please pay to the order of Miss Linthicum & Hastings, four hundred dollars, for the Democratic Standard, and much obliged."[3]

If Hearst obliged, it would have been his first foray into the newspaper business, motivated—as it would be later—by the need for a party organ.

Meanwhile Phoebe, whose own penmanship and grammar were almost impeccable, was teaching young Willie to read and write properly while George was developing a reputation as one of the savviest judges of mining potential in the West. He was in great demand to look at sites and was continuously exhorted to bring his knowledge and money to an investment. His fortunes were on the rise.

The Comstock Lode was booming. It ultimately would yield more than $400 million in ore. But the fortunes made from it were cornered by a few bankers and mining speculators such as George Hearst. Unlike gold, which anyone could dig out of the ground, silver was "bought" by those who had cash to invest in a mining operation, for which they were given paper representing "feet" of mines. Stock was traded on silver speculations, and those whose investments were honored and valid succeeded in making quick money; others, whose purchases were worth only the paper they were printed on, were either swindled or unlucky. The San Francisco Stock and Exchange Board, whose forty members were informally called "the Den of Forty Thieves," and the San Francisco and Pacific Boards of Brokers rang daily with names of the silver mines—Ophir, Yellow Jacket, Kentuck, Crown Point, Chollar-Potosi, Savage—and "feet" of Comstock claims were traded to the gambling populace. Silver stock was used as payment for bills; grocery clerks became millionaires overnight or lost their entire savings. William C. Ralston, a former steamboat clerk turned banker, who cornered the market on Comstock accounts and bankrolled some of San Francisco's early buildings, derisively referred to the Comstock Lode as "a hole in the ground with silver and gold in it."[4] George Hearst had opened the hole, and he and Phoebe were raking the profits in.

A letter to George from William Lent on 21 October 1863, Election Day, says, "I told [the local tax collector who is coming to look at your accounts] that you did not have any revenue for '62—but in this coming year you would have."[5]

Hearst avoided being swindled in the great stock manipulation craze that had resulted from the Comstock. He protected his interests and became a director of many mines, as did others whose names were to grace streets and hotels and leave legendary legacies in San Francisco: the "silver kings" James Graham Fair, John W. Mackay, James C. Flood, William S. O'Brien, and others.[6]

There is only one physical commemoration to George Hearst in San Francisco—a six-block street in a remote residential area was named George Hearst Avenue in 1895 (it parallels Flood Avenue). There is no other monument or other testimony to his wheelings and dealings and political influence in those boom times of California, perhaps because his interests were focused more on digging fortunes out of the ground than on currying favor and serving the public interest. His sights were on the rich mountains.

His mining buddies wrote him from Bullion City, Hot Creek, Eureka, Scott Bar, Granite Creek, Owyhee, Drytown, Humboldt, Grass Valley; and from Utah Territory (Skaggs Springs, Salt Lake City), Idaho Territory (Centerville), and Nevada Territory (Pioche, Treasure City, Mill City, Virginia City); even from Montana. They wrote him about mines called Savage, Sparrow Hawk, Black Cloud, Independent, Lawyer, White Pine, Argyle, Silver Glance, Lone Star, Eclipse, Buckeye, Rising Star, Shoshone. He scribbled notes and addresses, figures and dimensions and rough maps in his leather notecases, the names of people on the left and the numbers of feet of their shares on the right; he even wrote down bets ("Geoff Beach, 312 Front St., San Francisco, [Asbury] Harbending bets Roberts 100 that [he?] sells for 9, Shoshone County, Idaho Territory, July '64").[7] He listed his supplies:

1 canteen
1 hammer
4 lbs. tobacco
Meat
1 blanket, 13–20
Pick and shovel
1 gold pan
1 paper tax
Dry Beef

He made notes to himself ("Take affidavit from Joe Hall") and took orders for goods from the city:

Mrs. D. H. Hall, Eureka, Nevada.
1 small suit for winter for a girl, 6 years old
1 winter hat for same
1 ladies hat.[8]

George's willingness to bring supplies to others living in the mountains was characteristic of his generosity. Life in mining country was not comfortable—but it was profitable.

Sam Custis, one of George's original partners in Washoe, talked of their successes in letters from Virginia City. He wrote:

Virginia, 10 Aug/63

My Dear George,
    Home again, if this <u>delightful</u> place can be dignified with such a name. I arrived safe but at one time in the trip I supposed we were about to furnish an interesting item for the Newspapers. Going down the Backbone grade at night, our lead horses fell and brought the swing team down, all four were under the wheel. Horses in a [turmoil?], kicking right messily, the passengers

were out of the Stage quick and caught the horses, setting all right in a few minutes. No damage, a little scare and some benefit, as the little episode furnished a [stop?] to the fast driving the balance of the route.

I found everything progressing satisfactorily, the "Santiago No. 2" shaft is down 30 feet and in very good working rock. . . .

Andy Casamayou will start for Reese in a few days. His old mill at Steamboat has been burnt since he left. I will get the incorporation papers as fast as possible, for all the claims as yet are unincorporated.

Best respects to Mrs. Hearst and shake your son's hand for me. Regards to William Lent, Joe and all friends,

Ever very truly yours,
Sam Y. Custis

In another letter, Custis wrote:

Virginia, 17 Aug/63

My Dear George,

I will only write you a short letter tonight. I am considerably wearied with my days work, and besides am not at all well. I have been under the weather ever since I arrived back here. I cannot account for any illness unless it is caused by my stopping the imbibing of all Spiritous beverages, and going it alone on lemonade.

I write you this night principally about "Santiago No. 2 and Hearst Co." The Santiago shaft is down 35 feet, the rock getting softer and like the hanging wall of the Santiago mine. It is also thickly stained with colors incidental to that mine. Am very much pleased with it and think we will have a first rate mine. The Hearst is good beyond [prediction?]. I have cut the ledge in two places and find first rate ore on the surface. I will send a little of it down to you.

I think your good fortune must yet be in the ascendancy. I am preparing the incorporation papers and will send them down in a few days. We are hearing very big stories from Reese every day. Andy Casamayou starts next Thursday. The travel is so great now, seats home to be engaged 4 or 5 days ahead.

I will write you a long and full letter in a day or two. Compliments to Mrs. Hearst. Regards to Joe, and Wm. Lent,

Ever very truly yours,
Sam Y. Custis[9]

The "delightful" place, Virginia City, where George was spending most of his time, was an environmental disaster area. Wrote George Lyman in *The Saga of the Comstock Lode*,

Gold Cañon . . . was now one continuous line of sawmills, quartz-mills, tunnels, dumps, sluices, water-wheels, frame shanties, and adobes. . . . The main thoroughfare, cleaving to the old emigrant road, was flanked on both sides by brick stores with iron shutters, hotels, express offices, saloons, restaurants, and groggeries. The very walls of the Cañon were riddled and honeycombed with shafts, tunnels, and dumps. . . . Through this main artery rushed a strident current of sound—mingling of horse, mule, and ox, hissing of steam, clatter of machinery, and the whine of bullets. While above all soared the shouts of bull-whackers, mule-skinners, and the angry shriek of the Washoe zephyr—an uproar continuous in volume. . . . Over mountain and vale, cañon and ravine, mine and mill, night and day, hung dense clouds of swirling smoke and alkali—from which continually sifted powdered dust. . . . Everything you touched gritted with it.

By 1863, the business part of "C" Street presented the distinguishing features of a great metropolis—a bold, black, iron-faced city, doored and shuttered by great sheets of painted iron. Streets were lighted by gas jets on iron standards. The principal stores, saloons and hotels were ablaze with illumination. Large and substantial brick houses, four and six stories high, lined the main thoroughfares. Everyone of them disported a wide balcony, surrounded by black-painted iron balustrades, providing the walks beneath with a continuous, dark, irregular arcade, providing the second-stories with a gallery upon which French windows opened and iron stands filled with red geraniums stood.[10]

Such were the sights that greeted Phoebe when she traveled to Virginia City in 1864. There she would have met Mark Twain, who was a pal of George's and even borrowed his only clean white shirt once in Virginia City. As Twain later recalled the story at a dinner at the Hearst home in Washington, D.C., George—whose indifference to clean clothes was a constant source of annoyance and worry to Phoebe—had a new "biled" shirt sent to his room for some important occasion. Twain, lacking such a luxury, happened into George's room and deftly "borrowed" the shirt, leaving George to wear his ordinary one. When Twain described his own appearance in the fancy shirt, George replied, in characteristic wry humor, "That's so, Sam. And it's the only time you were ever well-dressed in your life."[11]

Phoebe made several trips to see the phenomenon with which George was preoccupied. One biographer claimed that

sometimes the little wife would pack a bag and go along on horseback, up the steepest trail, riding over the wildest mountains, happy all the way, interested, eager, never tired, never out of spirits. She loved the supper of bacon and pancakes, cooked on the prospector's fire in his lonely cabin, or, better still, smoking hot from a campfire in the deep woods on the edge of some terrifying gulch.[12]

Another biographer wrote:

Hearst was never so happy as when his wife went with him. The dainty, exquisite woman with a face like a dream of da Vinci had become a real miner's wife. Always on these trips of investigation and exploration the Hearsts were companioned by men with leathery, tanned cheeks and whose eyes held the far-seeing look that penetrates rocks and earth.[13]

Whether Phoebe became a "real miner's wife" is debatable, but she did travel to the mountains. Those early forays into the wilderness were a far cry from her later "camping" expeditions at San Simeon, south of San Francisco, for which she ordered a complete set of blue-and-white willow-pattern china from England, sufficient to serve a very large group. She called it her "picnic" china.

Phoebe was often exhorted by George's colleagues to join them in the mountains. In 1869, W. F. Walton invited her to accompany George to Hamilton, Montana (he also asked that Mrs. Hearst write if the recalcitrant George would not). On 4 March 1869 Walton wrote Phoebe:

> I cannot tell you, Mrs. Hearst, how happy I should be in your accompanying your husband to this place and I am now so situated in my new house that I could make you very comfortable and will promise you and your husband a room by yourselves and as good fare as the Lick House can give, Sunday dinner excepted. . . . I am anxious to have a talk with you about a certain [gent?] so you cannot misconstrue my assertions in my former letter. Never mind, we will yet have a talk on a subject and if everything makes a fair progression with your husband and myself, you may go with us to France next year. Am I not good in making promises to you, and consenting for you to go? . . .
>
> You are the same good kind "mind your own business," Mrs. Hearst, not an unkind word or charge against my own did I ever know or hear from your lips, but the like from lips of those that should have been my friends in adversity have caused me much trouble . . .
>
> I am glad you are not among the "Boux Monde," and obliged to keep Lent as I had rather hear you say no to such riligion [sic] as he professes.[14]

The latter double reference is to William Lent, whose business decisions affecting George did not please Phoebe. She refers to his owing them money in letters to another friend.

Although George may have talked about going to France when he struck it rich, he never actually made it. Going to France was more a symbol of success to him than a desire to be realized. Phoebe, on the other hand, dreamed of seeing Paris and was studying French avidly in San Francisco.

Walton did not give up his efforts to attract Phoebe to his humble abode, although it appears that she did not go. On 1 September 1869 he wrote George, "Have your wife come up with you. Weather is fine and I have a house of four rooms and kitchen. All good enough for a mountain."[15]

George Hearst's reputation preceded him in the mountains, where he was at home. He was paid as much as fifty thousand dollars for a single consultation.[16] As W. W. Allen and R. B. Avery wrote,

> There was no one who could so correctly estimate the character of a mine nor develop it to greater advantage than he. He had no equal in these

respects. All that was of practical value regarding minerals and mineral formations he knew. In this sense, his perception was so acute that it could be said of him, if it ever could be truthfully said of any one, that he was a natural mineralogist. Adding to his intuitions the lessons learned by observation and experience, he became a master miner, and was so recognized by all who were familiar with his achievements, or were capable of appreciating the combination of such instinct and acquirements in one man as made him the leader of practical mining in the United States. His maturity as a mining expert was probably reached during his connection with the Comstock; still, this was scarcely the beginning of his activity in enterprises that have formed an important part of the world's mining.[17]

Another colleague of George's, Asbury Harpending, recalled in his autobiography:

George Hearst was probably the greatest natural miner who ever had a chance to bring his talents into play on a large scale. He was not a geologist, had no special education to start with, was not overburdened with book learning, but he had a congenital instinct for mining, just as some other people have for mathematics, music or chess. He was not a man of showy parts, liked the company of a lot of cronies, to whom he was kind and serviceable—when he wasn't broke himself—was much inclined to take the world easy, but if anyone mentioned mines in his presence, it had the same effect as saying "Rats!" to a terrier. Hearst became alert and on dress parade in a moment.[18]

By 1865, concentrating on quartz mining, George Hearst was a millionaire. He came to be known as "Uncle George," particularly to this old mining cronies who were down on their luck. "The sight of him was worth a double eagle at any time to hundreds of old miners who had passed the time for handling the pick and shovel," Allen and Avery wrote.[19] It was said that George took one hundred dollars in twenty-dollar gold pieces when he left his office on Montgomery Street—where old miners made a point of loitering—and that by the time he reached Market Street and the Palace Hotel, where his regular poker game was held, the gold coins had disappeared into the hands of less lucky gold-seekers. One historian wrote,

A whole battalion of unsuccessful pioneers was pensioned by Uncle George and many a time he was seen to leave a party of important men in broadcloth and high hats to cross the street and shake hands with some ragged wreck of a pioneer whom he had known in the early days. . . .

Quite devoid of affectation, he was unimpressed by the shams and pretenses of society. He preferred the friendship of his mining camp acquaintances, regardless of their financial or social status, to that of snobs and pretenders in high places. Utterly independent, his long gray beard gave him the appearance of a patriarch; he talked slowly, walked slowly and never allowed himself to be hurried.[20]

One story is told of a traveling salesman who happened by the open door of the suite of rooms that Hearst and his pals rented at the Palace Hotel and inquired whether he could join the poker game going on. George Hearst invited him in but the stakes were too high for the salesman. The lowest chip was worth one hundred dollars.[21]

William Randolph remembered his father coming and going with valises full of quartz specimens.[22] Father was no skinflint with Willie, either. On his rare times at home he saw that his son had everything a child could want: a pony and cart, a Punch and Judy show, a large playhouse, two dogs—the first of many that he had throughout his life and for which he had a great fondness—pet rabbits, cats, mice, and fish. He had his first riding lesson while still a baby. And when he asked for ice cream money, Father lavished on him a twenty dollar gold piece.[23]

In 1864 George purchased a more elegant house, built by a Frenchman, at Chestnut and Leavenworth streets in San Francisco. It fulfilled Phoebe's dream of overlooking the Bay, perched as it was on the crest of Russian Hill. It was all that anyone could want for a suitable salon, nestled in a tropical garden above the street, along a toll road that led from the heart of the city through sand dunes to the Presidio. It was a favorite drive that Phoebe often took with Willie in the family carriage.

The following year, George—by then a big bankroller of the Democratic Party—was elected to the state legislature. And although politics required George to be away from home even more, Phoebe found that life in California was agreeing with her.

5
High Times, Low Times

Phoebe traveled a good deal when George was gone, driving her carriage to visit friends, her parents, scenic spots, and hot springs throughout California, often taking Willie with her. On one occasion, when visiting the Appersons at their Alviso ranch south of the city, Willie wandered away and became lost. The family was in a panic and the entire countryside was turned out until he was found. He had his mother's wanderlust at an early age.[1]

When she was away from Willie, Phoebe bemoaned the separation. In June 1864, Willie was sent to the baths at Santa Cruz with Eliza Pike, his nursemaid, with whom Phoebe regularly corresponded. His mother was arranging to move into the Chestnut Street house. Phoebe wrote daily and hoped that Willie would be weaned while away (he was one year old).

San Francisco, Calif.
16th June 1864

Dear Eliza and Willie,

It seems a month since you left. I am <u>terribly</u> lonely. I miss Baby every minute. I think and dream about him. We all feel low. . . .

I have had another letter from Mr. Hearst, brought by a gentleman from Reese River. He expects to be home soon, but don't say when he means by soon, a week or a month.

I hope you had a pleasant trip down and arrived safe and well. . . . Yesterday I was not well enough to go down to see about [your trunks]. I feel quite <u>miserable</u> this morning, have my "grandmother" yet and have taken cold. Also sore throat. I have sent Miles down to see about the trunks, will not finish this until he comes back. If they are not taken by the boat I must send them on the cars and stage.

Let me know how you are contented. If you don't feel satisfied, just back up and come back. Kiss Willie for me and write me how he is. I hope you will wean him. . . .

I am going to telegraph Mr. Hearst to know what to do about moving up on the hill. We have only two weeks more. I don't think I can come down to see you. I will be <u>very</u> busy. Write often, I feel anxious to hear from you. Oh, dear, what am I going to do, Mrs. Brady has just come in on the train this morning, is going to stay several days, perhaps a week, and just think, we're going to move, isn't it too bad? . . .

Yours,
P. E. Hearst

The letter is an early insight to Phoebe's domineering characteristics, her penchant for managing people and situations to her liking. No helpless female she, although complaints of illness appear in her letters throughout her lifetime—frequent references to unspecified malaises, the "blues," as George called them, monthly menstrual periods (the "grandmother" of this letter?). Letters functioned as the telephone of the time, and Phoebe's are full of daily trivia and gossip. She liked the daily doses of communication (in later life she would have secretaries handle her voluminous correspondence). Except for a consistent misspelling of "thier" and a fondness for the lower case, Phoebe's letters were neatly written in a fine hand. The early letters also evidence a wry sense of humor in places.

The following day she wrote:

San Francisco, Calif.
17th June, 1864

Dear Eliza,

I don't know that I can come down until I give up this house. I will have not a day to spare, though I don't know how I can wait so long to see Willie. We all miss him <u>terribly</u>. I have not been well for several days, think I would feel better if I could see Baby. . . . They were all glad that Willie sent them kisses, bless his little heart. I can see him now, tell him we take good care of Mike and Dicky [pet dogs].

Mrs. Magruder is still here, I told her what you said, she said she was quite anxious to go to Santa Cruz until you said the winds blew there, now she says she will take her baths in the bath tub, and play the Quadrills on the piano. . . .

I have not heard from Mr. Hearst since I wrote. . . . Write soon again, you know how fidgety I am about letters.

I am so glad you were not hurt when the wheel came off the Stage. You must have felt frightened.

Kiss Willie for me, tell him we had chicken for dinner yesterday and wished for him to have a leg. . . .

Write soon,
P. E. Hearst

P.S. I feel ashamed of this bad writing. Your's in haste.

After several weeks away from Baby and many more—possibly months—from her husband, Phoebe was anxious for both to return. The

welcome, or unwelcome, flow of houseguests and visitors was no con-
solation for the absence of the two people closest to her. In this letter
she worries about George's reaction to Willie's absence.

San Francisco, Calif.
25th June 1864

Dear Eliza,

I am so lonely, I don't know how to live. Pa and Ma moved last Thursday—
took Mike, Dicky and Rover, and everything that I thought I would not need. I
just think how I must have felt the first night. . . .

I had a telegram from Mr. Hearst. He left Austin Thursday and will be in
Virginia [City] today, if no misfortunes, and expects to be home next Monday
or Tuesday. You know I am glad he is coming, but I don't know what to do
about Willie. His Papa will think it <u>dreadful</u> not to find him here. But I think
you had better stay there until Mr. H. comes and then if he can we will come
down there and if not I will write you to come home. Ma and Pa are very
anxious to have you come there next week. They as well as myself are nearly
crazy to see Baby. Kiss him for me. . . .[2]

Accounts of Willie's growth and development filled many letters. He
was a fair-haired, handsome, blue-eyed boy who showed signs of growing into a large man. His every advance was cheered and remarked on
by his watchful and protective mother. He loved trips to his grandparents, where he could ride ponies until he was exhausted. As for
schooling, he was sent to a Presbyterian Sunday school and enrolled at
a private grammar school, his mother feeling the need to protect him
from the rough *hoi polloi* of public school. His fondness for animals of
all kinds was enhanced by frequent trips to Meiggs' Wharf, down the
hill from Chestnut Street, where a menagerie of strange birds and
animals collected by sailors from all over the world entranced him.[3]
They took the place of the brother or sister he did not have.

He was quiet and imaginative, not athletic, clearly intelligent, but
strong-willed and disobedient when he did not get his way. His closest
companions were adult women: besides his mother they were Eliza
Pike, for whom he developed a great fondness, and his Grandmother
Apperson, whom he also adored. His contemporary friends included
Orrin Peck, two years older, who lived near Mission Dolores and had
been on the same ship with the Hearsts when Willie (presumably) was
in the womb; Eugene Lent, the son of George's mining partner; Fred
Moody, a neighbor; and Katherine "Pussy" Soule, the girl next door and
his daily playmate. Willie once told his mother, in Pussy's presence,
that he was going to marry her when he grew up. Pussy later recalled
that Willie was a whiz at remembering rhymes and tunes, which he
often sang to her. "There was never a nicer, kinder, more sensitive boy
than Willie Hearst," she said.[4]

But Willie had a mischievous side that made him less popular with the victims of his pranks. Even his grandparents were stretched to limits in trying to discipline him. When he and Fred Moody were caught by a friend of Phoebe's, Miss Estrada, playing hooky from dancing school, Willie stuck out his tongue at and then sprayed Miss Estrada with a garden hose, ruining her dress. He hated dancing school so much that he threw a stone through the window of Monsieur Gallivotti's Académie de Danse, which accomplished just what he wanted: a ban from the dance class. He was known to frighten his mother's guests by setting off a mechanical mouse at receptions. He developed a flair for sensational surprises. When the Hearsts were redecorating and moved temporarily into a Nob Hill home of friends, the Addisons, Willie decided on April Fool's Day to liven things up and also show that he was not a sissy. So he set off some Bengal lights (flares that burned with a red glow), crying "Fire!" to the sleeping household after locking himself in his room with the flares, which glowed beneath the door. As his father and mother were battering down the door and firemen arriving, Willie opened the door and cheerily announced that it was all a joke. His mother was greatly relieved but his father appeared, at least, to be genuinely angry. By Willie's own account, George then asked him if he had been warm in the room while the fire was on. "No, Papa, I wasn't warm at all," Willie responded. Whereupon, George laid him across his knee, saying, "Well, you're going to be warmed now, son, where it will do you the most good."[5]

The spanking, Willie later recalled, was only a "pretense of severity," and it seems that Willie was a regular terror, subject to little serious discipline from his parents. Parental reprimands, however, may have taught him to apologize quickly so that he gained a reputation for being courteous.[6]

Often traveling with his mother, Willie lived a magical life full of new experiences and pets. Phoebe kept Eliza posted on their doings in letters that continued to the 1890s. About 1855 Eliza left her employ and moved elsewhere, ultimately back East (her husband disappeared, leaving her with her son, James).

San Jose, Calif.
2nd July, 1865

Dear Eliza,
      . . . I have been out of town four weeks. We are having our house made much larger, it will be yet a month before it is finished. You know me well enough to know that I will be glad to get home again, although I have been having a very nice time . . . went to Santa Cruz. . . . We drove on the beach, got a great quantity of beautiful seaweed. I brought the horses with me, so you know we had a nice time driving around. . . . I only stayed two days—the fare

at the hotel was so wretched that I could not stand it, baby ate little or nothing. If we had not taken some chicken and crackers with us, I don't know what the child would have done. I felt so uneasy about him, for they have cholera-morbus so badly in San Francisco and in fact everywhere that we hear of, I was so afraid he would take it. I thought it best for me to leave. . . .

I came back by Watsonville, the road was beautiful and the little town so pleasant. . . . Willie was as happy as a lark. He called my attention to every bird and flower, all the horses and little colts, cows and calves and everything else that could be seen. . . . am going to the warm springs, and as I go home overland will stop at Crystal Springs for three or four days. If my house is not finished by that time, I will go to Napa Springs for a little while. Don't you think we are traveling some?

You will wonder where Mr. Hearst is all this time. He has been on several little trips and the rest of the time in the City. He did not go to Santa Cruz but comes to see us once a week when he is in the City. I am very well this summer. Willie keeps well and fat though he grows tall. He is as brown as a berry and so active and mischievous, he is a very good boy. You have no idea how much he talks. You would be astonished. He seems to understand everything. He often talks of you. He likes his books so much. Can tell all about Cocky Locky and Henny Penny, knows more of Mother Goose than ever. His Prince is such a big dog he can't play with him, but Billy Williamson gave him a little rat terrier. He is a dear little puppy and will soon be very fond of Baby. Grandma has several little kittens. She has given us one. We will take it when we go to home. Willie kisses the dogs and cats all over. He says tell you to come and see the boy (he calls himself the boy). We rec'd the fishes. . . .

Before I came away we had been going out a great deal, there was a splendid operetta troupe at the Academy of Music. We went six or eight nights (not in succession), saw the best operas. I enjoyed it very much . . .

I tried very hard to get some good pictures of Willie, but did not succeed. He will not be still.

I think we will go to the Sandwich Islands sometime. It must be a delightful climate, but you know how foolish I am about leaving Mr. Hearst. . . .

When I write you again, will tell you all about how my house is arranged and how I am going to furnish it, etc. I have been doing splendidly in French, am sorry to lose all this time being away, but I read some every day so as to not forget. I have just finished a French novel which was very interesting. Willie knows several words in French. He is so cunning. We were just going to get in the rockaway that day when you passed on the ship. I showed it to Willie and told him you were going on that ship to the Sandwich Islands. He has never forgotten it. I did not see anyone wave a handkerchief. If I had been up at the house with a glass, I could have seen you plainly.

Accept my love and wishes for your success and happiness, and a great many kisses from Willie. If he could see you, he would have marvelous things to tell you. He is such a chatterbox. . . .

Yours,
P. E. Hearst

P.S. I had forgotten to tell you that I attended the school exhibitions at the Convent and College this summer. They were very fine. I have not time to go into particulars, but I would like to be in San Jose Convent if I was a young girl, it is splendid.[7]

It is no wonder that she wanted to write about the large Chestnut Street house, which boasted more than a dozen rooms, a garden, piazza, and servants' quarters. An inventory lists among its furnishings a billiard table, a Napoleon III easy chair, a rosewood library with glasses, gilt-trimmed porcelain dishes, crystal goblets, a dinner set including forty-five plates and four bottle stands, a piano and "12 boxes of music," a "playing table Louis XIV style (boule)," rosewood cabinets, chairs and tables with marble tops, Chinese and Japanese vases, trays, and lacquered chests. The meticulous inventory also includes a Rich sewing machine, a box with paint, brushes, and cartoons, a liquor tray and glasses, a leg-of-mutton holder, "gaz" fixtures and coal oil lamps, a French cooking range, oilcloth on the floors, a child's bathtub, a spring mattress covered with damask and an embroidered counterpane, a writing desk for a lady, many mirrors, a complete miniature theater, cast-iron garden furniture, an aquarium with gold fishes in a greenhouse—and a large wire aviary "with precious birds of which a Cardinal is worth 40$."[8] It was a far cry from the simple surroundings of southeast Missouri.

Notes from a diary kept by Phoebe between January and March 1866 tell much about her busy social life and trips to join George in Sacramento when the legislature was in session. Weak health is a continuing theme and there are references to financial troubles, George being nearly an "infidel," and Phoebe's desire to supplant the social whirl with more intellectual pursuits. A transcriber described Phoebe's activities in the third person; Phoebe's own words are in quotes.

Jan. 4—She, Miss Price and Miss Magruder went to a party and had a pleasant time. She did not dance but chatted with friends. Baby spilt castor oil on her handsome moire antique dress before she started for the party so she had to dress twice. She had a French lesson that afternoon.

Jan. 6—Mr. H. was going to the races that afternoon with Mr. Holmes. He had put off going to Sacramento until Monday and she and Baby were going with him, her trunk was all packed and ready.

Jan. 8—They went by boat to Sacramento, starting at 3 o'clock. Willie enjoyed the sea gulls. . . . Mrs. H conversed with a French lady, and read her French books.

Jan. 9—They were in Sacramento at the Brannan House. Willie was unhappy and homesick, as he missed his big playroom and many toys. They were on the 3rd floor in small but comfortable rooms. The only trouble was the stairs. "They almost kill me. Oh! how I wish I could be strong and well."

Jan. 10—Mrs. Gov. Stanford and her sister called, and they all took a long walk. . . . Willie was troublesome, did not rest well so she slept little. She was worn out and longed to be at home. Feared she was going to be ill again.

Jan. 11—. . . They saw all of Sacramento. The mud was terrible. Wives of several Members called—one a very nice little lady "but a Vermonter." Two Members who called were "good Democrats but that is all we know about them."

Jan. 12—. . . Mr. H. went to a dinner party at Mr. Hartley's—only Democrats invited—dinner "elegant." Baron Richtopher dined with Mrs. H. and party. "He is a Russian and very hard to entertain because it is so difficult to express ourselves so as to be understood. George came home at half past 11 and I was very tired and sleepy. I am more fully convinced that home is the best place for me."

Jan. 14—A quiet home Sunday. All too tired to go to church. Mr. H. felt unwell and weary and stayed in all day—very unusual. "How thankful we should feel for our many blessings," she wrote to Pa.

Jan. 16—Willie had his picture taken (an ivorytype). "Geo. sat for a photograph (colored), large size, also some cards which pleased me very much, for it was by long and frequent persuasions that I succeeded in having him take the trouble to sit for any kind of picture. He goes away to Sacramento today and I shall feel very lonely."

Jan. 18—. . . "I feel quite discouraged. Geo. has been so unfortunate in his business and has lost so much money lately I feel that we must live more quietly and be economical. I have sent the horses to Pa's. Poor Nig! I shall miss him. We have sold the Rockaway for $200. The coachman goes away tomorrow. By doing this we will save $100 every month. It is best to do this until we get our own stable."

Jan. 19—Not heard from Geo. but knows he is very busy, being member of Miner's Convention.

Jan. 20—Rained all day. Geo. came home at 10 p.m.—Sac. also dull and rainy and he felt lonely there.

Jan. 21 (Sunday)—Rained all day. Couldn't go to church—no carriage and the mud terrible. . . . Miss E. Patton came and stayed for dinner, also Judge Lindley. "He is a tiresome old widower who wants to marry and I believe is much pleased with Miss Cammie [Price]. It won't do him any good if he is. I was quite sick this evening from fatigue. I do wish my health would improve. It is very discouraging to be sick so much."

Jan. 24—They went to Maguire's Opera House to see *The Merchant of Venice* with actor: Baudmann [or Bandman?] in the role of Shylock and all enjoyed it very much, especially P.A.H. who had never seen it.

Jan. 26—". . . The weather is delightful, the view magnificient this morning with all the sails on the Bay and the sun shining so bright and warm . . ."

Jan. 27—. . . More calls. . . . "We even went away out to Larkin and California St. to see Mrs. Farish." . . . George came home, not at all well and couldn't go to the Amador Co. "I am sorry to have him sick but glad to have him home."

Jan. 28 (Sunday)—To church. Mr. H. stayed at home. Dr. Wadsworth delivered a fine sermon. "I like him and am sorry I cannot attend more regularly. No company. I am glad, do not approve of company on Sunday visiting either for myself or others."

Feb. 1—. . . "We waited nearly an hour for the carriage. Now I miss my own team very much, but I must not complain, for we must live according to our means. Oh, these parties are so foolish. I don't feel like going for my heart is very heavy, yet no one knows it is so."

Feb. 4—. . . "Dr. Wadsworth is going to deliver a course of lectures to the Y.M.C.A. on Moses. I want to hear them all if possible. . . . Oh, that we were not so worldly! Life is so short. We should be prepared to die at any time. My husband is not a member of any church, and comes so near to being an infidel it makes me shudder. It is hard for me to contend against this influence on my boy. He will soon be large enough to notice these things."

Feb. 7—"Instead of enjoying myself [at the Legislative Ball in Sacramento] I cried until I was almost sick. I felt uneasy about Baby and wanted to go home before Geo. was really ready. He was angry etc., etc." She was wretched all day. "I wish I never had to go to another party."

Feb. 9—They came back sleepy and tired at 4 a.m. Party delightful, "an immense number of persons there. I have never seen so many beautiful faces and elegant dresses at one assemblage. Many persons were masked. We were and had some fun." House large, handsome, entertainment handsome.

Feb. 11—All went to church . . . Willie left at home with little girl. "He is very full of mischief and I always feel anxious for fear he will act badly and disturb someone."

Feb. 13—They all had lunch with Mrs. Hunter. "They are from Lexington, Mo., have suffered terribly by the war. Their house was burned and everything taken from them by the Federals. They are quite poor now and it is hard, for they are getting old and have several children."

Feb. 15—They left [Sacramento] on the 1 o'clock boat. Trip pleasant but country around Sac. covered with water and looks forlorn. Willie troublesome and had to be taken away from the table. "But he was very sorry, cried and said he would be good."

Feb. 21—Lizzie went to the theatre with Mr. Dorherty, Mrs. H. studied her French. "I find there is no young lady of my acquaintance like Miss Price. These young girls are silly, shallow-brained creatures. Miss P. is so much company for me. I wish she was home." (She was in Sacramento.)

Feb. 23—Called on neighbors—mostly Yankees. "Do wish Geo. could stay home all the time. He is absent so much."

Feb. 27—"Now we are obliged to have dinner at 6 o'clock instead of 5. That is bad for Willie. It is too late, but I will have to manage the best I can."

Feb. 28—"I have sold my Imperial [mine stock] and lost some money on it."

Mar. 1—"Letter from Pa urging me to come down there and complaining about our having so much company. I will go down tomorrow with Willie."

Mar. 5—Mr. H. went to Sac., much troubled about his business.

Mar. 15—"Willie is as happy as a little King when he can have plenty of room to run and play with prince [the dog.][9]

Although ambivalent about company and parties, Phoebe surrounded herself with people, seeming not to want to be alone. In later years she enjoyed intellectual company of her own choosing, not the social butterflies of whom she complained in her 1866 diary.

The luxury in which she lived did not ameliorate a nagging desire. Phoebe desperately wanted a sister for Willie. In a letter describing a trip to the Northwest to meet George, who was exploring mines in Idaho, she speaks of it and of Willie's being "a great comfort" to her, talking like an "old man," and fearing her leaving him. She also speaks of putting up fruit, which, like many domestic chores, she still undertook herself.

San Francisco, Ca.
18th Sept. 1866

Dear Eliza,

I last wrote you from Portland, Oregon on my way to W. T. [Washington Territory] to see Geo. . . . I went on up the country, to Walla Walla and from there took the stage and went to a valley on the Lewiston road. There I waited three days until Geo. came. He was so glad to see me, it repaid me fully for the long trip. He had been sick, and looked worse than I ever saw him, he was not ready to come home, he was obliged to return to the mountains away out on the clear water above the Columbia River. So after staying there about 12 days I left for home. I could not go with him to the mines or be near him, but I was glad I went to see him. I enjoyed the trip very much, saw some of the finest scenery in the world. . . . enquired for your husband. Geo. also did but could hear nothing of him. I wish I could write you a full description of all I saw and heard, it would fill a [pile?] of paper and interest you.

I was gone just a month. . . . I was glad to get home again to see Willie, he was well and fat, he had grown tall, too. I stayed with Ma nearly two weeks, then came to my own home, and have been very busy putting up fruit. Mr. Bowles, (George's cousin from Grass Valley) came to see us. . . . We went to Santa Clara, San Jose and one Saturday went over to the new springs called Saratoga. . . . We all took a nice lunch and had a splendid picnic at the springs. The water is sulphur and magnesia. . . . They are really splendid. They are in the foothills towards Santa Cruz, about one mile from Pa's. When I came home, Mr. Bowles stayed several days with me. I think he has a strong notion of marrying, and fancies Miss Patton. Perhaps I will have the pleasure of writing to you of the marriage of one of the Miss P.s, but the other one, I am doubtful about. . . .

Willie talks a great deal about you. There is no danger of his ever forgetting you. He listened eagerly when I read your letter and kissed me a great many times for you, and gave me a big "queeze" for you. He grows more like a big boy every day. I do wish he had a little sister but no signs yet. I must have his picture taken soon, and send you one. He is very mischievous, but good and affectionate. . . .

In the first of my letter, I said I had been putting up fruit. You don't know how industrious I have been. I have made some of the nicest plum jelly. It is beautiful and a quantity of it, too. Have two dozen cans each of peaches and pears, also a few plums and am going to put up a quantity of tomatoes.

Alice [a new maid] is living with me now. . . . You know she is a splendid worker, but she has her failings. . . .

Old Madame was to see me yesterday. I will begin my French again the 1st of Oct., take one lesson per week until I can afford to take more. . . .

Geo. has not yet come home, I look for him the last of this month. . . . Willie is sound asleep. I wish you could see him—he is a great comfort to me. He talks to me sometimes when we are alone like an old man, he understands so much. He does not want to go to his Grandma's again, seems to be afraid all the time that I will go away and leave him again. He says he likes this home best, and loves me as big as the house and sky and everything. When I read your letter, I asked him how much he loved you, he said, he loved you that much, too. . . .

Accept our love and many kisses, with a big 'queeze from your boy,

> Your friend
> P.E. Hearst[10]

George's election to the state assembly in 1865 had added the new dimension of politics to her life. Phoebe and Willie joined George in Sacramento for much of the winter of 1865–66. They would take the Sacramento steamer sailing from San Francisco at four o'clock in the afternoon, have dinner on board in the company of legislators and lobbyists, spend the night on the river, and arrive the next morning in the Capitol. Phoebe's friend, Camilla Price, accompanied her on many of the trips, which involved packing and shipping large trunks to handle the gowns essential for Sacramento receptions.

George had not sought public office but accepted the call from the Democrats, who were on the side of the South. It was a divisive time in California because of the Civil War. A large body of secessionists had tried to turn California away from siding with the Union. In April 1865, when the Confederacy had surrendered and Lincoln had been assassinated, Democrats in California were suspected of being "rebels." The assembly in its sixteenth session (1865–66) was made up sixty-one Union men and nineteen Democrats (the state senate had thirty-one Unionists and nine Democrats). The convention at which Hearst was nominated was marked by fights between delegates wielding hickory canes, cuspidors, ink stands, and chair legs. Despite the fact that Democrats and Republicans in San Francisco were about even in number, Hearst won his seat.

He was a loyal Democrat with southern sympathies and could be relied on to protect his and his cronies' business interests. He seems not to have had a personal ambition to hold high political office, but he was ready to serve the party. He served on the assembly Committee of Mines and Mining Interests; voted against ratification of the Thirteenth Amendment to the Constitution, which abolished slavery (it passed 66–11); tried (unsuccessfully) to get the assembly to hear a lecture on public schools in the state (a continuing interest from his early unschooled days in Missouri); introduced a bill to encourage agriculture (which was not taken up); and otherwise kept his mouth shut.

He was reported to have "served with credit to himself and acceptably to the people whose interests he served." Mr. Hearst, a publication promoting "The Resources of California" stated in 1885, "is not an orator nor does he excel in debate, but he possesses those qualities of quick perception and ready adaptation to circumstances which enables him to do the right thing at the right time, qualities invaluable to a legislator."[11]

George also was characterized by independence in his politics and his aversion to joining groups. He said of himself, "I made up my mind that a good man was a good man anywhere, and that there was no occasion for joining any affiliation societies. I made up my mind to be independent, and decided not even to belong to a church."[12] Historians would later write,

> The course of [later] Senator Hearst was independent and pronounced. He never permitted himself to be compromised by interested parties who might desire to promote or hamper legislation for selfish ends, but remained free to exercise his judgement, exert his influence, and cast his vote purely in the interest of his constituents and the people of the whole United States, for whom he was a representative, not alone in name, but in fact. He was always a Democrat, but never a partisan. He was a Democrat solely because he regarded the policy of that party as best adapted to promote the welfare of the country. He was in no sense a politician, but in every sense a patriotic statesman.[13]

Mark Twain also referred to George's political independence, although Twain switched Hearst's party. George's political plans for his son may have been more prophetic than George wished. In 1906 Twain said in his autobiography:

> I had been accustomed to vote for Republicans more frequently than for Democrats, but I was never a Republican and never a Democrat. In the

community, I was regarded as a Republican, but I had never so regarded myself. As early as 1865 or '66 I had had this curious experience: that whereas up to that time I had considered myself a Republican, I was converted to a no-party independence by the wisdom of a rabid Republican. This was a man who was afterward a United States Senator, and upon whose character rests no blemish that I know of, except that he was the father of William R. Hearst of today, and therefore grandfather of Yellow Journalism—that calamity of calamities.

Hearst was a Missourian; I was a Missourian. He was a long, lean, practical, common-sense, uneducated man of fifty or thereabouts. I was shorter and better informed—at least I thought so. One day, in the Lick House in San Francisco, he said:

"I am a Republican; I expect to remain a Republican always. It is my purpose, and I am not a changeable person. But look at the condition of things. The Republican party goes right along, from year to year, scoring triumph after triumph, until it has come to think that the political power of the United States is its property and that it is a sort of insolence for any other party to aspire to any part of that power. Nothing can be worse for a country than this. To lodge all power in one party and keep it there is to insure bad government and the *sure and gradual deterioration of the public morals*. The parties ought to be so nearly equal in strength as to make it necessary for the leaders of both sides to choose the very best men they can find. Democratic fathers ought to divide up their sons between two parties if they can, and do their best in this way to equalize powers. I have only one son. He is a little boy, but I am already instructing him, persuading him, preparing him, to vote against me when he comes of age, and I want him to remain a good Democrat—until I become a Democrat myself. Then I shall shift him to the other party, if I can."

It seemed to me that this unlettered man was at least a wise one. And I have never voted a straight ticket from that day to this. I have never belonged to any church from that day to this. I have remained absolutely free in those matters. And in this independence I have found a spiritual comfort and peace of mind quite above price.[14]

George characteristically followed a noncontroversial path in politics, although in encouraging Willie to be contrary he may have gone too far!

Phoebe, then twenty-three, was not enthusiastic about these activities and grew to dislike the political arena, but she dutifully supported her husband throughout his public career. George tried to put her mind at ease about his legislative absences, writing Phoebe from Sacramento on one occasion, ". . . I am anxious to get home for I want to see you very much. You must not think I do not think of you for I do all the time. I can get along for one week but after that I am quite homesick."[15]

It was a one-term stay for George, who retired to private life. But he had learned how to apply his wealth to political interests, an asset he would find useful in the future.

About this time, George may have had affairs with one or more women. His wife's niece believed that the couple had become estranged by their great differences in style and interests.[16] When, and if, Phoebe learned of her husband's extramarital affairs, she must have been deeply affected, although we shall never know whether she was furious or devastated, or both. Her surviving letters do not speak of being betrayed by George.

There is no hard evidence that George had affairs with other women, although he certainly had plenty of opportunities since he traveled widely and most of the time without his wife. In his remaining papers are calling cards and memos written in his notebooks with women's names and addresses and occasional requests for clothes or help in paying for a house or making rent that reflect George's good-heartedness in helping down-and-out friends. On the back of one calling card is scribbled the name "Emily, Mrs. Smith, Tecumsah." And on the back of a torn menu offering "Bunker's Club House sausages, stewed kidneys, salt codfish, Shaker fashion, and frizzled beef," George has scrawled in his bold hand, "604, Mrs. Fionda, 6 sixth floor."[17]

Whatever the effect on young Phoebe of these developments, she continued to be the overly attentive mother, lavishing her love on her only child, who returned what she may not have been getting from her husband. George's long absences and extracurricular activities also may be why no "little sister" appeared.

At any rate, the bond between mother and son tightened. And Phoebe, not to be cowed, asserted herself. There is a story that when she and George quarreled, she would contact the White House department store and tell them to hold it open late so that she could go down and spend George's money on new clothes to ease her pain.[18] Such behavior was hardly characteristic of someone who manifested the control that Phoebe did, but she could make her unhappiness known when she wished.

George could afford her expensive tastes and habits. Not only were his mining interests paying off but he was acquiring large amounts of land. He had long realized the value of western land and had begun to acquire real estate in San Francisco and throughout California and the West. He anticipated the completion of a transcontinental railroad, then making its way up the slopes of the Sierra Nevada. Indeed, he later had passes, carried in a personalized green leather case and signed by the company presidents, to all the railroads running in California.

Besides the house on Chestnut Street, George purchased land in San Francisco between Pacific and Broadway, Dupont (now Grant Avenue) and Kearny streets. The latter deed, for which Hearst paid five hundred dollars as down payment, was for a house and lot owned by T. D. Bristol, on land "100 varas square, which was granted to one John Ramsford by the Mexican authorities in the year 1838." George also bought for $650 land in San Francisco bound by Dolores, eighteenth, and Fair Oaks streets, near the Mission Dolores.[19]

But his biggest coup in real estate in 1865 was the purchase for thirty thousand dollars of some forty thousand acres in the Santa Lucia Mountains along the Pacific Coast by San Simeon Bay, about 160 miles south of San Francisco. The ranch was called Piedra Blanca for the white rocks that jutted into the ocean along the little bay, one of the few safe harbors between Monterey and San Luis Obispo. Later (in 1868), George got the legislature to pass a special bill allowing him to build a wharf in the small "Sancimmion" port and charge a landing fee to coast steamers that docked there. It was called Port of Promise. In 1865 he fenced in orchards and began to raise beef and dairy cattle, poultry, and horses on the marine mountain range. He called his venture the Piedmont Land and Cattle Company.[20]

The land had been the property of early Spanish Californians, a few families of whom had received large grants (each one amounted to an area that one man with one horse could encircle in a day) from the Mexican government in exchange for living on and working the land after it was taken over from the church missions in 1834. Terrible droughts before 1865 set the stage for George Hearst to pick up large ranchos cheaply. Some said the deals were made in payment for bad debts.[21] Even so there was considerable dispute over the property lines of the ranchos and subsequent litigation over what Hearst actually got. The large tract initially had been granted in 1840 to Don Jose de Jesus Pico, called Topoi Pico, the first cousin of Pio Pico, Mexican governor of California, for service in the war against America.[22]

Besides the Piedra Blanca, George acquired neighboring ranchos: the three-thousand-acre Santa Rosa and the San Simeon ranch, both of which had belonged to the Mission of San Luis Obispo and had been granted to Estrada brothers of an early Spanish-California family. Estradas would later work on the ranches that had been their family property until George Hearst acquired 66,458 acres, ranging eleven miles inland and twenty-six miles along the coast. He also acquired the Evans range north of San Carpojo Creek and the Buckeye range in Monterey County. After George's death the Hearst land in the area totaled 240,000 acres, with ocean frontage of forty-five miles.

George's holdings in California ultimately included land in Tulare, Marin, Fresno, and Butte counties, and 4,500 acres in San Mateo County. He acquired timberland in Shasta (not the same land on which

Phoebe later would build a spectacular retreat) and in Siskiyou counties, and a large holding in Sacramento County. He picked up a small five-hundred-acre ranch on which to raise horses in Alameda County near Pleasanton (inland from the Bay) that would later be Phoebe's cherished Hacienda. In the Feather River Canyon, a railroad station was named Hearst because he was one of the early investors in the region.

George would also own a large piece of Texas; twenty-five-thousand acres near Phoenix, Arizona; and a quarter-million-acre cattle ranch called Victorio in New Mexico, with water sources that George and his partners controlled. He acquired vast holdings in Mexico as payment for surveying land for the Mexican government while mining in Durango. The payment from Mexican President Porfirio Diaz was six-hundred-thousand acres of timberland in southern Mexico that stretched through Vera Cruz, Campeche, and Yucatan. George picked up the giant Babicora Ranch in the state of Chihuahua, Mexico, for forty cents an acre in 1887, after Geronimo was captured and the Apaches subdued: the land had gone begging during the Apache "troubles." He rejected a bid by the Mormons to buy the Babicora for $1 million in 1890—they wanted to start a colony there—and the cattle ranch subsequently ranged over nine-hundred-thousand acres. At his death George Hearst owned more than one million acres throughout the West and Mexico.[23]

But it was the San Simeon property that interested him most in 1865. He set about consolidating a large contiguous block of land with coastal access and a port. Some of the landholders from whom he bought property felt that they were getting the short end of the deal, which left a bitter legacy that was passed down for generations over what some considered the heavy-handed, if not downright ruthless, way that George amassed the property. He was able to take advantage of hard times that had befallen many, but some observers speculated that he was garnering the property for his boy.

The Hearsts originally called the ranch Camp Hill. Phoebe, George, and Willie camped and picnicked in open areas overlooking the ocean or in shade along Oak Knoll creek, where they could hear the ocean breakers crashing. Phoebe liked the place and they often made the journey with friends from San Francisco, either by stagecoach to San Luis Obispo or directly to San Simeon by coastal steamer. There were horseback rides over mountains and valleys, hunting for the plentiful deer, quail, and other game, and fishing for trout in the streams.

An absentee buyer and landlord, George needed the aid of friends and agents in San Luis Obispo County in efforts to expand his holdings. He engaged as his attorney James Van Ness, previously a mayor of San

Francisco (1855–56) and later a judge. In an early letter regarding Hearst's transactions, Van Ness discussed prospects for land to buy (in this case, the Todos Santos Rancho):

. . . They [the owners] seem to prefer to sell outright and say that all the parties in interest are prepared to join in the conveyance. . . .

Now as to the price: They seem to have [picked?] up a remark made by you while you were conversing with them under the tree just before we left for [Sipona?], that "the land ought to be worth government price"—and this is their figure for the land. There are . . . in the Rancho . . . 22,220 acres, which at $1.25 per acre would be $27,775.00. In addition to this, they ask for the oil prospects the sum of $17,225, amounting in all to the respectable figure of $45,000. This is their offer. That they will fall some I have no doubt but how much it is impossible for me to conjecture.

The multiplicity of owners is the great difficulty in this as in other negotiations in these parts. . . . Now I believe there are in all interested in the Todos Santos property 13—perhaps 14—and this would give them, if they realized their price, about $3,000 apiece, which would do very well. If you reduce it much down, then they begin to wince—and the trade probably falls through. Thirty-thousand dollars would distribute $2,000 to each, and this might do. One thing is certain—they are all wretchedly poor, without one dollar, or the [conduit?] or industry to get it. It was deplorable to see them, and the conveyance with which they were travelling with the old lady and her daughter—once living, in the lifetime of Hartnell, in so much comfort at Monterey. . . .[24]

Getting the property that he wanted did not come easy for George. There were numerous suits disputing the property lines. He filed a suit against one claimant of the Santa Rosa property, a man named Pujol. In October 1865 Van Ness wrote:

Graves has filed his bill in the case of Hearst vs. Pujol, and when Pujol sees it, I think it will make him wince. . . . If the facts be as alleged in the complaint—and Graves says that they are susceptible of proof—I see not how he can hold the Santa Rosa Rancho.

Pujol, about two days ago, and the night before he left for San Francisco, had a long conversation with me, and expressed great anxiety to dispose of all his interests in this County, that his partners in San Francisco, Sanjingo & Bolado, were inclined to hold on for a stated price, but for his part he was willing to sell on very modest terms. He made no reference to the matter of this suit about the Santa Rosa, nor did I. He wished me to aid him to sell, and requested me to write him at San Francisco. I have done so, merely saying that I thought he held his lands in this County at too high a rate—and that if he would reduce his rates, I would endeavor to get men of means to come down and look at his lands.[25]

Land was not all that George wanted around San Simeon: copper had been found in the mountains and there were valuable mining prospects that Van Ness was keeping a secret from others in the neighborhood. George's land was rich, but there were continuing problems with the Spanish landowners. Van Ness wrote to George,

> San Luis Obispo
> November 28, 1865

Dear Sir:
    . . . In respect to the place where the red ore is found, it is on the Phoenix Claim. . . . There is no conflicting claim to the location, and there can be none. . . . It was abandoned, and the opinion was generally entertained that it would never again be touched by anyone.
    Last summer when I was up the Coast someone told me that the orchard and vineyard belonging to you on the Santa Rosa Rancho was in danger of being destroyed, that the fence was useless, and that the gate leading into the orchard was almost always open. I supposed that, much as Estrada's people had the privilege of using the fruit, they would see to this. If the stock running near, particularly horses, of which there were a good many, should get in, even a few horses, they might destroy it, and I sent word to a man living near to go over and repair the fence and fasten the gate, and at the same time to tell Estrada's people that there was no intention to prevent them from using the fruit. This expense will be but $4. or $5.
    . . . In respect to the matter of the exchange of the Pico part of the Rancho at San Simeon for the Clorio [Chorio?] belonging to the estate of John Young, I shall see Pico in a day or two, and learn from him what he wants, and what he is willing to do, and let you know without delay. I thought it would be the best opportunity that would occur in several years for you to get hold of the balance of that property—as these Spaniards, unless they are actually in the hands of the Sheriff without the power to extricate themselves, are the meanest and worst people to have any transactions with I ever fell in with.
    In respect to Mrs. Wilson's interest in the Port, you had better authorize me to close it at once for $2,000. It might possibly by waiting be got for a fraction under, but the chances are that it would cost more, or could not be got at all. She owns, as I told you, one fourth of the whole, and she is now very destitute, and must have money. Pacheco is not here, nor Pujol—as they might, and probably would, if they were here, put her up to asking more, or persuade her not to sell at all. Again, she might die, and then their interests would go into a dozen hands, and some of them minors, and you might have a terrible job, and one lasting for several years, to get the thing in shape. My advice to you is—close this matter at once, if you have any faith whatever in the future of San Simeon. With this interest secured you have three-fourths of the whole port—enough to enable you to arrange things pretty much as you like. I hope that you will not fail to let me hear from you by return mail about this matter. . . .
    I note all that you say about the Phoenix mine. I really believe that something very good will be found. I send up some more ore by this mail— explaining in note which accompanied it all about it.
    I have not yet told Boof, or any of the men at work, what the ore I sent up amounted to—and for several reasons I prefer not to do so. I simply said to them that you had written to me that the black rock contained some copper. I am afraid if I say anything to them, or others, of an encouraging character, or

that we have found anything promising, the whole mountain will be covered with people—putting on extensions or locating new claims—so therefore I keep my own counsel and the men at work can say nothing certain as to the value of the rock they find—without an assay of it. . . .

I do not know how you are to work it to get hold of more land in any reasonable time along the Coast. Everyday makes this land more valuable, and more tedious in securing, in view of the increase of population, and the success in finding mines. There is scarcely anywhere in California such land, and so admirably located, with so good a climate, as that laying along the whole Coast from here to San Simeon. Farmers who have recently come in say that the land on the Santa Rosa Rancho is the very best that they have ever seen in this state. I actually believe that the 1,400 acres you got from Estrada is worth today $30. per acre. You might not be able to sell it out all at once for this price, but the time is near at hand when it will command it. The finest wheat can be raised upon it, and its reproduction of barley, corn and potatoes is incredible. Gillespie has gathered off of about an acre of ground more than 100 sacks of as fine potatoes as you ever saw—planted in June, and having no irrigation. . . .

I have been asked recently if you would sell or rent the land which you bought of Estrada in small parcels. How about renting if anyone should want to use it for one, two or three years—and what would be your terms, if you are disposed to do anything of that kind? Please to let me know in season. There are many other things which I want to talk about, but this letter is as long probably as you like to read.

> Very truly,
> James Van Ness[26]

Van Ness also urged George to contribute to a road across his property between the port and ranches over the mountains. He pointed out that it would increase trade at the wharf, particularly in wool.

But George moved too slowly for Van Ness's taste and nearly lost an opportunity to control the port. In a letter to George's friend and lawyer, Judge Solomon Heydenfeldt, Van Ness complained:

You are of course not ignorant of the fact that I have from time to time, and as often as propriety permitted, called your attention to the interests of Mr. Hearst, of securing as much of the Port of San Simeon (he being now the owner of an undivided one half) as it was possible to do, and that a further interest of one-fourth could be had, and ought to be secured, as contributing to enhance greatly the interest held by Mr. Hearst.

I have been fearful for some months past and have so apprised you, that in consequence of the pressing necessities of Mrs. Wilson, the owner of one-fourth, she might be driven to make some disposition of her rights at the Port, and in so doing, embarrass the arrangements which it might be deemed advisable to inaugurate to make the property available and subservient to the wants of commerce.

My apprehensions have been [more than such?] as I find that on the 12th of this month a conveyance of this one-fourth interest in fact was executed by Mrs. Wilson to Moses Cerf [?]—a Jew merchant here—and who is among, in my opinion, the most disagreeable, impracticable, unscrupulous and offensive creatures I have ever seen of any tribe, sect or nation—and one who will never let go his grasp without the pound of flesh. How Mr. Hearst will relish the association it is not for me to say. I look upon Cerf's purchase of this interest as detracting materially from the value of the interest now held by Mr. Hearst, and as rendering the plans which Mr. H. might hereafter form for the development of the property much more difficult of execution if not altogether impracticable with an ownership so divided.[27]

Van Ness continued to push George to build a road so that commercial traffic would flow from the agricultural valleys inland through San Simeon harbor, paying George wharfage fees. In another letter, also possibly to Heydenfeldt, Van Ness expresses his unhappiness with Hearst's failure to act on the matter, noting that the local people believed Hearst was trying to avoid high real estate taxes by sitting on the land—holding it "for his boy"—rather than developing or selling it to exploit the land boom.

San Luis Obispo
February 17, 1869

. . . .If he has no intention of subdividing the land at San Simeon, and selling it, or of selling it in bulk, he will, I suppose, lease it—and I am told it is his intention to keep it—as one of the Supervisors remarked, when I was trying to reduce the assessment on it—"for his boy," which the Supervisor seemed to think was a reason for stiffening rather than ameliorating the tax. Where he learned the fact that Mr. Hearst was keeping it "for his boy"—or, if this were really so, how it affected the actual value of the property as a basis for taxation—were both mysteries to me. But assuming this to be so, and that it will be some years yet before his boy will be able to take charge of it, it may still be for rent.[28]

In other letters dated 1869, Van Ness refers to George's being blackmailed and apologizes for getting him into a "mess." Battles over the Hearst land went on for years. George was not popular with many in the area that he was buying up.[29]

McDowell R. Venable, a ranch manager, wrote George early in 1870:

Dear Sir,
Judge Van Ness returned on Saturday and after consultation with him I determined to go to Cambria and do whatever was necessary for the protection of your interest. Mr. Lull, who has been acting as your agent, informs me that Pujol has always claimed the possession of the land and that since it has been fenced he has used it as a pasture for his stock. . . . In order to prevent this and to bring to an issue the question of possession, I leased the place for one month to Morris Judd, a friend of Mr. Bowles and put him in possession, with instrucions to repair the fence and drive off all stock now on the Rancho and not to allow any other to come on, with the understanding that you will

defray the expense of any litigation which may arise as to the right of possession. I think it best to have someone on the place especially so as I think Mr. Lull has been, to say the least, very negligent in the matter. Grazing land is in demand and I think the place could be rented for a good price. . . . I have no doubt that Pujol will at once attempt to get possession; whether by force or law remains to be seen. . . .

Yours respectfully,
McD. R. Venable[30]

Pujol carried out his raid, and witnesses—whom Van Ness thought ungrateful and untrustworthy—had to be paid to show up to testify for George. In a letter dated 25 February 1870 Van Ness informed George of his concern for the Santa Rosa tract and of the true nature of Mr. Lull, who he thinks "means to throw you."[31]

George continued to acquire land around San Simeon and to develop a commercial wharf (in 1871 the wharf took in about $170 a month "wharfage"). It would prove to be one of the best investments he ever made "for his boy." But problems and litigation with unhappy local residents continued.

Venable wrote George on 7 June 1870:

Most of your tenants on the point refuse to pay rent. They say that Castro, Pujol and Mrs. Wilson have all told them that you had no right to collect the rents. As soon as Harris finishes his plats, we will bring a partition suit which is the simplest and quickest way to settle the matter. . . .

There is a 160-acre tract of land lying on the Morro Creek above and joining the Morro Rancho, upon which Goldtree has a mortgage of $1,800. The owner is anxious to sell and will take $2500 which is $15.62 per acre. . . .

Please send me a copy of the agreement between Grant, Lull and Co. and yourself with regard to the wharf. If the conditions are that you are to pay the original costs of the wharf if you take it before the expiration of the term, it would be better to go to work and construct an entirely new one, for the present wharf is made of pine logs which are already rotten and worthless. The only question is whether, under your present agreement with them, you can build a new wharf without buying them out. I also wish to see from the agreement whether the wages of the wharfinger are to be paid by Grant and Lull or to be paid out of the receipts of the wharf. . . .[32]

Although George's land dealings were expanding, other ventures were not faring well. In 1866 he had overextended himself in financial risks and found himself in debt. Phoebe must have feared that the Cinderella bubble had burst.

A business slump in the country at the end of the Civil War combined with the playing out of the Ophir mine to set George Hearst back. He had been buying and selling mining interests but suddenly found himself at the short end of a four-hundred-thousand-dollar deal. He lost an important lawsuit against the Raymond and Ely mine in Nevada and could not pay his creditors. Van Ness wrote, possibly to Heydenfeldt, "I am sorry of the embarrassments of Mr. Hearst, and regret exceedingly that in conveyances we're obliged to suspend operations here at a moment, too, when appearances are so favorable."[33]

A historian later said that "had his creditors pressed him, [Hearst] would have been insolvent in the amount of several hundred thousands of dollars. But the energy of the man was never more conspicuously displayed than when the tide of fortune was against him."[34]

He settled matters sufficiently to keep up social appearances and to begin to recoup his losses. "I quit the Comstock in 1867, and went into other things," George wrote in his autobiography, "went into real estate, for instance, in San Francisco, where I lost all the loose money I had. I had some real estate around San Francisco, and then I went and borrowed $30,000 and put it into a line down in Kern County and made money out of that."[35]

George was back in the mining business. In that deal he began a lifelong partnership that was to serve him well. He linked up with Kentuckians James Ben Ali Haggin (his maternal grandfather was from Turkey) and Haggin's brother-in-law, Lloyd Tevis. Thereafter George stayed clear of tying himself heavily to one mining property; he sat on boards or had controlling interests of many companies and increased his mining investments manyfold.[36]

Undaunted throughout his troubles, according to his friend Bay, George "felt an assurance that fortune in the end would smile upon him. To use an expression of his, 'He saw no necessity for going into mourning.' "[37] But during the time of reverses, sacrifices had to be made. The carriage was sold, although the family stayed in the Chestnut Street mansion.

In a letter to Phoebe, written from Idaho, George urged her to keep up her courage:

Lewiston
August 31, 1866

My dear wife,
    I have just received your very kind and good letter. Was much pleased to hear you got home all safe and found things all right about the house and that the Boy was all right. How much I would like to see him and be with you both. I have been waiting to see what course this R. thing would take but it is somewhat in a muddle as yet to me. . . . But I think the next letter or news I get will be that Mr. Robison has owned up that he has no mines. I do not think any man of sense could or would act as he does if he had a mine. At all events, I suppose we have the thing in such a shape that we will bring things to a close soon. We cannot be far from the last act unless R. gets away and that

I do not think he will do as one of the men that is along is one of the executive officers of the Vigilantes from Walla Walla and if R. don't look out he will get in a tight place if he don't find the mines.

You ask me what I think of Leland. I think he and Dyer understand each other but I do not think he is half as bad as Dyer nor do I think he thinks the thing has been done right.

I am sorry the carriage was sold. But keep your courage up. We can let the Bayview go and have enough left for us to live on and in any way we want to after a few months and then you can be assured that I will take off.[38]

Phoebe had not let the setbacks curtail her traveling. In the spring of 1866 she went to Hawaii—without Willie, who was sent to his grand-parents.

On 9 May 1866 she arrived in Honolulu aboard the barque *D. C. Murray,* accompanied by her brother Elbert, then sixteen. She stayed a month (Mark Twain was in the Islands at the same time, describing them in letters to the *Sacramento Union*). Ostensibly, the trip was for rest and recuperation from unknown ills, but for Phoebe, then twenty-four, it also was another adventure. The Sandwich Islands were exotic beyond belief for the girl from the backwoods of Missouri.

Phoebe had resigned herself to the family's precarious financial position and to George's long absences. She had Willie to amuse and occupy her, and she reveled in his growing dependence on her, as she wrote Eliza. Her brother "Eppy" was a problem, however.

San Francisco, Calif.
18th November, 1866

Dear Eliza,

. . . Willie has grown a great deal since you saw him, he has changed very little, though. Mr. Hearst arrived 1st Nov., he was absent from the City a long while, his trip was by no means profitable. He does not think of returning to that rough country. He looks fleshy and well now; in a few days he is going to Drytown. I don't think of going there this year with him. You know he can't stay at home long. I have made up my mind to not fret about it. I cannot help feeling lonely, but may as well take things quietly. I am so well and fleshy, you would be quite surprised. I was obliged to alter two or three of my closest fitting dresses, isn't that funny? But no signs of a little sister yet. . . .

Eppy is doing better than ever in his school, but he gives me a great deal of trouble in various ways. You know him as well as I can tell you. His disposition does not improve any. Willie is not so fond of him as he used to be. I scarcely ever leave Willie with anyone now. He can't bear to stay when I go downtown, and he is very good usually when he goes visiting with me. I don't think Alice is cross to him, but she is very careless and I dislike for him to learn any of her habits. His being with me so constantly has made him perfectly devoted to me. He is a real little calf about me. He never wants anyone else to do anything for him, and I think I love him better than ever before. Some days I do very little but amuse him. He knows several of his letters and will soon learn them all. He is very wise and sweet. I have wanted to have his picture taken, but he has had a small ringworm on his face, and I have been waiting for that to disappear entirely, which will soon be the case. I have taken him with us to church lately. He behaves quite well. . . .

Mrs. Montieth is coming here this week to do a little work for me. I am not going to have anything new, but old things made over. . . .

I don't remember if I wrote you about "Queen Emma", I called on her while she was here. . . .

Alice talks of going to New York in the Spring . . . She is not truthful but a good worker. If I am closely at home and tell her what I want done, she is splendid, but I can't trust her. I go out very little. Feeling as we do now, we shall live more quietly this winter than ever before. The carriage, horses and harness are sold. I don't like to see them on the street but then I have a great deal left to be thankful for. . . .

> Your ever true friend,
> P. E. Hearst[39]

There is little evidence that during these years Phoebe participated in much charity or community work; she was consumed by Willie, to whom she attributed greater abilities than a three-year-old deserved, and who even replaced George in bed, as the following letter shows.

> San Francisco, Calif.,'
> 9th December, 1866

Dear Eliza,

. . . I know you want to hear from Willie. He is very well and grows finely, has not been sick this winter at all. Lately he has talked much about you and when the last Steamer was due, he heard us talking about it, so the next day he found an old letter of mine, and began reading it. He said the Steamer would be in Saturday evening, and "Liza was comin" and we must have a good dinner for her. He knew she was coming because she wanted to see her Willie boy. He read a great string about what you would say, etc. He has improved very much. Knows several of his letters and is getting to be a very good boy sometimes. He was very much put out when Papa came home because he could not sleep with me. I talked to him and told him when his Papa went away again, he could sleep with me. He said, Well, he wished he would go. . . .

So far there has been no parties here. Next Thursday, Miss Clara Selby will be married and on that evening they will have a grand reception. We have red'd a card but will not go as we are not going to any parties this winter. . . .

Mr. Hearst sends love to you. Willie sends kisses and says tell you that "Saint Nicolas" is going to bring him some pretty things for Christmas. He is going to hang up his stockings. . . .

> Your friend,
> P. E. Hearst[40]

Willie was beginning to assert himself. His mother's adoration is never so evident as in the following letter. She wishes that "he could always be so pure and happy" and she hopes that "he will be a good man." "They are scarce," she says. But, she has begun to "feel more like married people" with George home more than before, his business affairs being slow.

San Francisco, Calif.
February 20, 1867

Dear Eliza,

. . . Willie was sick and I did not want to write until he was well. . . . He had fever and a severe cough, had taken violent cold in some way. For two weeks I did not leave him but once to go to market and attend to some things that I was obliged to do. He was very sick about three days, after that the fever was broken and he would be up but I had to watch him every minute to keep him in the room, not to let him get too warm or too cold. He had no appetite and got so tired of the house. I had to amuse him in every possible way. Willie and I both enjoyed it. When he was getting well, when he began to regain his appetite, he wanted to eat all the time, and said one day, "Oh, I am so hungry, I feel like I would eat up everything in the house." . . . Being with me so constantly, he became very babyish and wanted his Mama on all occasions. When he was sick, he would say so often day or night, "Mama, I want to tell you something." I would say, "What Willie?" and his answer would be, "I love you." His Papa laughed at me a great deal about it, saying Willie waked me up in the night to tell me he loved me, bless his little heart. I am delighted to have him well again. He looks thin, but is picking up rapidly. He has grown tall, but I think his features have changed very little, if any. . . .

Willie talks a great deal and in that manly way. He asks reasons for everything and when he tells anything he gives his reasons. He has improved very much, has fine ideas, thinks a great deal. I have taught him most of his letters. He loves books and play both. . . . He often sits down and writes a letter to you and then reads it to us. . . . I wish I could think of many little things he does, but it is not half so funny to hear of them as to see them. I have taken him with me when I go out so that he thinks I can't go without him and it is almost the case. I am unhappy if I trust him with Alice, for she is so very unreliable, her influence is bad. When he is rude, she laughs a big loud laugh and he, of course, thinks he has done something particularly smart. Then worse than that she encourages him to decieve [sic] me, but he is too honest. He will tell what happens, be it good or evil. Sometimes she tells me things in an exaggerated way and he will look with all his eyes and say, Why, Alice, no, and tell it his way. He is a great comfort to me and I hope he will be a good man. They are scarce. . . .

Mr. Hearst has been home all this winter, has been very well. We begin to feel more like married people than before, we have been very quiet, have not attended a single party, and only been to the theatre once, and to see the Japanese jugglers once. Took Willie both times. Those jugglers are splendid. . . . Willie tried to turn summersaults, climb poles, spin tops on a sword and all sorts of wonderful things that he saw them do. He has a great imagination. . . .

. . . The finest party ever given in California will be at the Lick House. . . . the dining room so surpasses anything I have ever seen. . . . We have an invitation but are not going. I would have to get a handsome dress, it would be both troublesome and expensive, and after all would not pay. I don't care about all the furbelows and vanity. Mr. Hearst wants to go to this party at the Lick—for a wonder . . .

I have scarcely visited any, therefore recieve [sic] very little company. That is dreadful for Miss P. [Price]. She is about the same, has changed some, looks older. As for her ever marrying, that surely will never take place. No one seems to fancy her. I think she misses the carriage, and dinner parties more than we do. We have a good home and enough to live on. That is much to be thankful for. If our little man is spared to us, we will try to give him a fine education if nothing more. . . .

Eppy is doing nicely in school—but he has not improved much in disposition. He is very trying. I try to be patient but don't always succeed . . .

I am still studying French, one lesson per week. Will soon be through. I can speak very well now. Madame is just as ugly as ever, and can eat as much cabbage and potatoes. . . .

A great many are going to the world's fair. I wish I could go, but I can't, and it does no good to think about it. My health is still very good, though I am hardly so fleshy. I have done considerable sewing this winter, have made Willie little full pants and socks, he looks very nice in them, have made him night drawers, and six new aprons of very nice brown linen trimmed with braid, worn long and full with a black morocco belt. They are so much nicer to play in than the old judies. These aprons look boyish and pretty. He has a very pretty felt hat, new style. . . .

> Your true friend,
> P. E. Hearst[41]

Willie was beginning to order his Papa about and to correct his speech, to Mama's delight. In a March 1867 letter she wrote, "I do wish you could hear him talk. You would laugh yourself almost sick. He takes particular pains to correct his Papa, and if he thinks I am teased about anything, he will say, 'Now you shant talk so to my Mama.' He is a great comfort to me. . . ."[42]

Between speculation on the marriage possibilities of various spinsters and widows in town and other gossip, Phoebe wrote of her daily life, of Willie's precociousness, and of George's comings and goings with no reference (in surviving letters) to his having affairs with other women. Her accounts are of a happy home and motherhood.

In the summer of 1867 George went to Idaho, where he was developing mining interests. Phoebe moved to her parents' farm and the Chestnut Street house was rented. She spent a good deal of time traveling about California with Willie. A June letter to Eliza describes these trips and refers to a chronic illness ("same old trouble") that plagued her. She concluded, "Everything is so uncertain. Bayview has been sold and paid off Lent's debts, mines that we have don't pay, all is a drawback. I don't see a bright future, but it is not that, but the way it has all happened. Lent has lately made some money. . . ."[43]

Lent's debts were a sore point for Phoebe, as she notes in a letter from Santa Clara in July: "It is said Lent has paid one-hundred-thousand dollars. I suppose it is true, but he has not paid his debts. . . ."

Of Willie she reported, "He observes closely and has a fine memory."[44]

George wrote Phoebe from the mountains, concerned over their long separations.

> Placerville
> August 27, 1867
>
> My Dear Wife,
>   I have been looking for a letter from you for a long time. I have got two letters from you in good time soon after my arrival but none since. I am sorry you do not write as it is a great pleasure to hear that you are getting along well and to hear all about the Boy and things generally and it is a great comfort to see a few lines from you. . . .
>   The mill will not start for 20 days yet and I will not go to San Francisco until it goes.
>   The time goes off hard when I think of you and I feel almost frightened when I think how much I am away from you when life is so short at best and in future, if God wills that I must go in the mountains, I must take you with me for if you were with me, all else that I might will or leave behind does not amount to anything save the Boy and I know he would do well at his great [?]. When I get to thinking of these things, I get very homesick. I must stop whining and cheer up and make the best out of it until I can see you. I am very anxious about the mill. I have some fear about the success of the concern, yet I hope it will be all right. But it is not certain. The mill is one of the best in the country.
>   Give my love to Ma and Pa and Kiss the Boy for me lots of times and accept the Love of your Husband,
>
> G. Hearst[45]

Phoebe's health continued to be poor, whether for physical or psychological reasons. After a serious illness that summer, during which she felt near death, she wrote Eliza on 15 September that life—and her boy—were more precious than ever.

> . . . I was scarcely able to read [your letter] when it was handed me, and am now not strong enough to write you a long letter. I have been very sick for five weeks, first had bilious fever, then enflammation between the stomach and bowels. For five days, I lived on ice. Nothing would stay on my stomach. By a great effort I kept down part of the medicine until the enflammation was checked. I had to be blistered and slightly salivated for three weeks. I did not eat enough to scarcely sustain life. I had a very good Dr. who was very attentive, but for a few days Pa and Ma were very uneasy. Mr. Hearst was and is still in Idaho (he went away in July, we expect him home soon). I have not been so sick since my marriage. My health was poor anyway and this severe sickness has changed me terribly.

A day or two ago, I was able to get downstairs. Pa had some scales to weigh his hay, so they weighed me. I was dressed thick and had on a shawl and only weighed 89 lbs., isn't that dreadful? I am recovering slowly, am so very weak, and have to be exceedingly careful in any diet; it will be many weeks before I am entirely well and strong.

I did not go to the Big Trees. . . . Instead of taking a trip to see the country and enjoy myself, I came very near taking a long journey across the dark river from whence no traveler returns, a change through which we must all pass sooner or later, but how little we realize it. We ought to think more of these things and less of the world with its gaudy trappings and emptiness. My precious boy would miss me more than all else. He needs me now, and I thank God that I am yet spared to him. If he lives to be a man, I do hope he will be a good one. . . .

You would be astounded to hear him speak and pronounce words of three letters, can count one hundred and knows what country, state and city he lives in, also who discovered America and about the world being round, and a great many little things that are well for him to know. He never studies or seems to think it is anything but play to say his lessons, but remembers what we tell him and brings it into conversation when we least expect it. He has a great idea of machinery—seeing the reaper, threshers etc., he asked innumerable questions, what this and that was for, and how and why. His Grandpa would have the machine stop and go slow so Willie would understand it, then he would come to the house and build machines. Some of his plans were very correct. Then he takes Prince to play baling hay with him. There is no baby here now, only a big boy. . . .

Instead of getting a Chinaman we have a girl about 16 years old. She was from Glasgow, Scotland, her mother died four years ago. . . . She has a very good, gentle disposition, is as steady as an old woman but innocent and childlike, has no pert independent ways . . . She is an exception. . . . Her name is "Alice Booth," she is quite pretty, fresh, good face. . . .

I think my family will be quite small this winter. Eppy will not be with me . . . and as for any young ladies staying with me, I am going to have it understood that I am in poor health, and am going to stay at home and entertain very little company. I will not wear myself out for people as I have done, have somethings of more importance to live for. . . .[46]

Her protestations to the contrary, Phoebe would entertain constantly all her life, housing friends and relatives under her roofs for long periods of time. She craved company and privacy at the same time and time to do what she wanted. In a letter dated 8 December 1867 she wrote Eliza that she "would like to be a thorough French scholar."[47] Her efforts paid off when she became fluent in French. Her eyes were on distant horizons.

Meanwhile George led a separate life of politics and business, but professed a longing to see more of Phoebe.

Sacramento City
December 11, 1867

My Dear Wife,
I am just now in receipt of your note and package, was very glad to hear

from you and sorry you did not come up as I do want to see you very much indeed and thought you would come shur or I would have gone home at all hazard. But as Willie is sick, it may be best for you not to come. I did not get your telegram yesterday in time to write you. . . .

I felt [very?] hard not to go [on another trip to Idaho] for several reasons. First, because I wanted to see you I think more than I ever did in my life, and I was shur you wanted to see me and would [wait?] for me, and I feared you would feel that I ought to have come home. I think I will get off tomorrow but may not, as I am in the fight and would not like to get badly beaten. I think this is my last trip in politics for I hait the nasty [?]. I am sorry you could not come. My love to all. Why did you not write me a [great?] long letter?

Your Loving Husband,
G. Hearst[48]

In 1867 George's business ventures turned upward and for the present the hard times were over. Phoebe decided to make a visit to her home state, where she would show off her wealth and her boy.

6
Travels and Tribulations

The opening of the transcontinental railroad in the late 1860s made it easier for Californians to travel to the "states" and also brought friends and relatives to California. One of those was Dr. Silas Reed's daughter, Clara, by then Mrs. Nathan Anthony of Boston. She and Phoebe went to Paso Robles Springs for their health. Like the Peck family, the Anthonys would be close friends of Phoebe's throughout her life and would benefit from their friendship in the form of monthly checks and expensive gifts from Phoebe, who provided a personal "family assistance" that allowed them to live comfortably and respectably. Another person enjoying the patronage of the Hearsts was cousin Joe Clark, who was a regular at the Hearst dinner table and supported by them off and on until he died in 1900. Phoebe found him fat and lazy.

She took quick advantage of the new link to the rest of the nation. In 1868, with six-year-old Willie, she made her first trip back to Missouri, using the passes that George's cronies had given him on the newly opened railroads. And Willie was "wild." On their trip East Willie tested his mother's patience to greater degrees than he had dared before. Phoebe left him with Eliza in Pennsylvania and traveled on to the East Coast with members of the James family from Missouri. She wrote Eliza from Baltimore, exhilarated by the sights of the "fine public buildings," parks and wide avenues, but missing Willie:

> . . . I am terribly lonely without Willie. I do hope he will not be troublesome. He has gotten so wild since we left home. Don't let him be rude for you know he will have to be punished to break him of it. Kiss him for me. Tell him to be truthful and good. I don't want people to think he has never been taught anything.[1]

She could not stand to be without her "old man" for very long, so she asked Eliza to bring Willie to Baltimore, advising her in detail how to take "the cars," tip the "darkey" for handling luggage, and wear a veil to avoid getting cinders in her eyes.[2] Phoebe liked having someone at her beck and call.

She made a quick trip to see Washington, D.C., and then took her son to Missouri. The places that had been battlegrounds when she left six years before were peaceful and verdant in the summer heat. She was besieged by relatives and friends—"I did not know I had so many"—and Willie was the center of attention. He was looking more and more like his mother.

> Everyone that has seen him thinks him splendid—they can't quit talking about how very large he is, and who he looks like. Some say he is handsome.[3]

They rode horseback, although Willie did not like riding behind his mother, "for he bumps his nose," which Phoebe thought "was the funniest objection I ever heard."[4]

Life in Missouri looked hard to Phoebe and she missed California:

> This is a poor country to enjoy oneself in except just to see friends and relatives. The country is so poor and rough, the people have to work so hard and many are so miserably poor, it makes me almost sick to see it, and worse than all, they think this is a good place to live. However, I suppose it is fortunate they are satisfied.[5]

By the end of July, after she and Willie had been sick with colds, dysentery, and the heat, she wrote, "I wish I was at home. This is a miserable country."[6]

Despite George's protestations of loneliness when Phoebe was gone, she continued to travel a good deal without him—to Salt Lake, Colorado Territory and Fort Laramie, Wyoming in the late 1860s. George, on the other hand, "as active and energetic as ever," was often at mines in Idaho and other western territories.[7] The two went their separate and independent ways.

The mining business was treating George well. He was an astute businessman who drove a hard bargain. Asbury Harpending wrote:

> Nothing could keep Hearst down in a mining region. Any capitalist was only too eager to back a man with such surpassing talents; but he had to pay an awful toll. For years, Hearst's projects were financed at 2½ per cent per month, compounded monthly, and any business that can stand that strain and come out ahead must have a solid foundation to build on. He was the real founder not only of his own, but of the vast Haggin and Tevis fortunes.[8]

Having survived a disastrous speculation, in which Lent involved George and Joe Clark (Lent owed George more than $200,000), George had recouped with his new mining comrades, J. B. Haggin and Lloyd Tevis.[9] Haggin, a card shark, had shifted his gambling winnings to mine speculations and relied heavily on George Hearst's geological wizardry.[10] To most people the western land looked barren on the surface, but George could see beneath the surface and find the angles of repose, the rich minerals unidentifiable except to a trained eye. Haggin backed George, cautiously at first, in mine purchases. He put up the money and gave George one-third of the profits.[11] Their first success was the Ontario mine in Utah. Others who had looked at it pronounced the area worthless, but George quietly watched for three weeks while a prospector dug away at a hole four feet deep and six feet long in the Salt Lake desert. George and Haggin then bought the hole for $33,000. It was to become one of the richest mines in the world, although the silver was recalcitrant and had to be "roasted" from the other ores before the mine became profitable.[12] But profitable it was. Hearst and Haggin, as their firm was called, made $14 million out of the Ontario, which put George back on his financial feet.

He next acquired the Sheep's Head gold mine in California, the Juacaschuta in Sonora, Mexico, and rapidly began to acquire others. His quiet doggedness became his trademark. In 1874, after the Sioux Indians had been subdued in the Black Hills, he and Haggin took a one-third interest in what looked to be a good gold mine in South Dakota. Some even said that Phoebe named it, calling it their "homestake."[13] Before long, Hearst and Haggin had bought out the syndicate that initially invested in it. The Homestake mine was to become the richest gold mine in the world. Hearst and Haggin also acquired water rights to the stamp mills and neighboring towns and built a railroad serving the area. In short, they built a company town in Lead, South Dakota, also owning the lumber mills, stores, and commissaries while providing the major source of employment.[14]

Their next major venture was at first not so successful. The Anaconda came to George's attention in 1881 through a foreman, Marcus Daly, who also had tipped him off about the Ontario. George urged Haggin to invest, but Haggin, in George's absence, failed to follow up and they nearly lost the deal. George managed to get in for a quarter interest without having seen the mine. They invested $4 to $5 million and dug a four hundred-foot pit, looking for silver, when a rich vein of copper ore was discovered. It was the biggest copper bonanza ever uncovered; it also contained gold and silver.[15] The Anaconda posed new engineering problems as the chasm grew wider and deeper, and just as it was starting to thrive, the plant and buildings were destroyed by fire. Hearst and company had a larger, fireproof plant constructed in the smoldering ruins.[16]

Hearst and Haggin were no-nonsense investors, and because of George's reputation for judging good risks and for fair dealing (he acted as broker between prospectors and investors), many miners brought property to their attention, frequently winding up as superintendents of

mines that Hearst and Haggin owned. If a mine paid off, the superintendent would be given one-tenth of the company's stock. Hearst and
Haggin stock was good value and sold quickly when offered on the New
York Stock Exchange.[17] They had two rules: Never buy an interest or
shares in a mine or property that was controlled by others; and never
pay more for a mine than the value of ore in sight. That way they kept
tight control of their ventures. They were not always successful, though.
They lost $900,000 in one speculation. But by that time they could
afford losses. The San Luis mine in Durango, Mexico, was another of
their notable successes.[18]

And their success was marvelous to behold. Hearst was not considered a ruthless robber baron who came by his riches by defrauding
others. His were hard-gotten gains, and he was respected for his hard
work, knowledge, and rapport with the earth. Those who were outwit-
ted—or outwaited—by him begrudged George his good fortune.

He also played by the rules of the West, which included "managing"
judges, witnesses, and juries in the numerous law suits that occurred
over title to claims and mines. George was no stranger to litigation, and
in "the management of some of these suits Hearst struck his strong
suit," a journalist remembered. Bribery was rampant. "Rich corporations absorbed the mines, and a poor man had as much show for his
rights as a clawless cat would have for his scalp in Hades," the journalist wrote. "Hearst distinguished himself in litigation of this sort, and
his tact and shrewdness in this, allied to his thorough knowledge of
mines and mining, made him an invaluable man to mining capitalists."[19]

His fortunes increased as he became a principal owner in the most
profitable mines in the United States, providing employment to three or
four thousand men.[20] He was highly sought after to examine prospective mine sites. A contemporary historian wrote:

> George Hearst has no superior as a miner on our slope. His opinion of a
> mine will command more confidence than that of any other man. It is well
> known that 4 or 5 of the richest mines on the continent were purchased by
> the present owners for relatively small sums under his advice. He is an expert
> whose trustworthiness has been accredited by experience. Lloyd Tevis and
> J. B. Haggin have been well rewarded for relying on him. Their best mines
> have been obtained with his help.[21]

Haggin and Tevis were an odd pair who complemented one another
as business partners. Haggin was cold and calculating but given to
speculation, while Tevis was outgoing but cautious in his business
ventures:

Haggin had nothing in common with good fellowship. He was always silent, sober and cold. But under it all he must have had a heart. . . . Every man, without exception, who rendered Haggin faithful, efficient service he made rich. And he was very loyal to his friends.[22]

Tevis, like George Hearst, had come overland to California in 1850, penniless. He talked his way into a job as scribe at the County Recorder's office in Sacramento, and managed to lay away $250 a month. With his savings, he and Haggin made a loan of one thousand dollars at 10 percent per month, from which they collected five thousand dollars in interest before the principal was paid. That launched Tevis as a capitalist and banker. He became president of the Wells Fargo & Company banking and express firm. He was quoted as saying,

When I came to California, young, poor, ambitious, I had to decide whether I would strike for political fame or for money. I concluded to go for money.[23]

Like Haggin, Tevis was a lawyer but there the resemblance ended—except for their common penchant for making money, and the fact that they were married to sisters, daughters of a Mississippi colonel.

These, then, were George Hearst's business partners. They were astute and calculating venture capitalists who grabbed opportunities, unflamboyantly but tenaciously, in the virgin West.

George's business affairs typically were fraught with disputes over money, property lines, and secret deals. Haggin's letters to George were full of references to "bargains," the need to keep their prospects secret, and problems with worthless employees. But by the mid–1870s George's fortune was assured. He had consolidated his land around San Simeon and was buying parcels of land in San Francisco and elsewhere in California. He was raising sheep, cattle, and horses. In 1869 he had purchased, for $1,750 in gold coin and three $1,500 promissory notes, the fifteen-hundred-acre Forbes Ranch in Alameda County.[24] By the time George was just over fifty years old, his bank account was fat, if occasionally overdrawn by several thousand dollars.

George's canniness at mine speculation prevented his being taken, as were others whose greed exceeded their judgment, in a "great diamond hoax." In November 1872 Haggin wrote George, "Write me all you know about diamonds. It is important for me to know everything."[25]

They found out enough not to invest in the diamond "mine" that two clever prospectors had salted in Utah and sold to San Francisco banker William C. Ralston and fellow speculators only after Charles Tiffany, the popular New York jeweler (who had little experience with rough gems), pronounced the diamonds genuine.[26] Ralston and many others

were well swindled before a government geologist, Clarence King, discovered the hoax. George had sent Dr. Silas Reed to scout the situation.
Reed wrote back on 2 December 1872:

> I am truly glad that you did not lend your name to the sale of an interest in
> it after you heard it was probably a fraud. You could not, as you say in your
> letters, afford to make money out of what you had reason to believe was not a
> genuine thing. . . . How could [they] have been so badly fooled? . . . The
> papers' exposure came here yesterday from San Francisco. It is terrible to
> contemplate.[27]

King became the toast of San Francisco, the "King of Diamonds" and
the darling of society, feted at all the mansions, including Phoebe's. He
was a popular wit and scholarly geologist, a well-educated dandy. But
he and George were incompatible rivals. George disliked King's style
and pretensions, and King disparaged old George Hearst as a wolf in
sheep's clothing, saying that "Hearst was bitten on the privates by a
scorpion; the latter fell dead."[28]

George's toughness already was legend. He himself wrote of his ups
and downs in the mining business more prosaically. He did not like
being accused of stealing, and occasionally, very grudgingly, he gave up
portions of claims when challenged on his rights. He became angry
when he was double-crossed, and he was not averse to rearranging the
environment to meet his needs. Mining was his life.

> I . . . wanted to go to mining again so I went into mining in Idaho, and lost
> $92,000. Jim Fair was with me in that and some of those Comstock fellows. I
> then started out to see if I could not get hold of some good mines, and I
> started to go to Pioche. I had been getting a lot of letters from Mineral Hill,
> and finally I went out, more as an expert than anything else. When I got over
> there and looked at the mines I wrote back to San Francisco to these fellows
> to get some money as I had made a trade for them. It was $400,000 to be paid
> down, and $600,000 afterwards. We, that is I and my partner, got $80,000 and
> a piece out of it. This was known as the "Eureka" mine. I got this mine from a
> lot of Irishmen, and bought it for myself, Bill Thompson, George Roberts, and
> some others. I borrowed $40,000 for my part from Haggin. Then those outside
> got to quarreling and said we were stealing and I got mad and sold out.
> I then went to Pioche but did not do much. Just knocked around a little.
> Got in with some men who had a set of Pioche mines, sunk a shaft down,
> struck a bed of ore, got into a big law suit over it, got out of that, making some
> $250,000. From there I went back to "Eureka" . . . and then to Salt Lake. I lay
> around there but did not see much that I could do; so I went back home and
> there found a telegram awaiting me about the biggest mine in the world.
> There was great excitement. I said I would go up to look at it. Several others
> looked at it, too, but said it was a failure.
> In the meantime I saw Marcus Daly who told me he had been out there and
> that the mine was of no account; but that there was a little mine a fellow was
> digging into, a little hole of about four feet, he said. . . . We went to look at it.

I found there was a hole about as deep as your shoulder and about six feet long. It was sunk round the side of a vein. I looked at it and dug away a little when a fellow who was standing on the bank said, "You can tear that down all you want to," so I dug down a while. He then said, "I had a chance to make a stake and go home three times since I came here and I must get some money out of this thing now. I am going to sell." . . .I asked him how much he wanted and he said $25,000. All that was there was just this hole about six feet long. . . . The boys were going to Pioche and came to wake me up next morning but I said, "I am going to stay right here and watch this little mine." I lay round there about three weeks until they sank another hole. They took out a lot of rock from this and I then took some and had it sampled. Finally without waiting further I decided to give $30,000 to them for the mine and $3,000 to another fellow to get him out of the way. The was the "Ontario" Mine. . . .

[It] yielded us net about $14 million. . . . Haggin was with me in this mine and I carried a little interest for Chambers which made him rich. . . .

From the $30,000 everything else came. We went to the Black Hills about a sheep ranch and now have got 600 stamps running there. From there we went to Montana and got hold of the copper mine "Anaconda" and have not done much since. . . .

As to the [Homestake] mine, the way we got on to that was as follows: There was a wild fellow that when broke always used to come to me to get money to go somewhere or other. I believe he wanted to go to Chicago this time but before he went he sent me word of this mine. The first I saw of it was a sample at Salt Lake in which I could see gold. I took it and had it assayed. I think that was in August 1875. . . . (T)he next year I made arrangements for Chambers to go [to the Black Hills] in September but the Indians got so bad that it was as much as a man's life was worth to go there. Next summer, however, this man Sevenoaks dropped in there and got hold of a little lead mine. I was very sick at the time but he kept telegraphing me and when I got well I suppose there was about $400 worth of telegrams lying on the table. . . . At that time there was a man whom I knew used to hang around the mill and I telegraphed to Chambers to send him to the Black Hills. . . . He . . . went pretty slow but finally he said he thought it was a good thing. I telegraphed him at once to get a bond, which he did.

Then some other fellows came along and there was quite a stir about it. I finally promised to let these fellows have a little. Then I went to Haggin and told him about it. He said, "It is too far off, I don't want it." I then . . . told them they could have all but one quarter which I would take myself and they agreed to do this. This was all right but when it came to paying the money it was not forthcoming. . . . There was a regular row about it as I found they wanted to get everything and this made me mad. . . .

Along in March things began to look pretty bad, things seemed to be going to pot. . . . I . . . telegraphed Haggin we must either sell all or buy the control. . . . He telegraphed me back he would buy control of it. He went ahead and bought control and then we bought up the side claims and spent a lot of money building a couple of hundred stamps that season. . . .

Besides that we . . . got a water right. I made an arrangement for a little ditch and paid a pretty good price for it. I bought some water rights and some springs and we got the water in at a cost of $170,000 and it has brought us in $8,000 a month ever since. I went off nine or ten miles and got a spring here and a spring there and running them round to a point finally got them all into one creek and it has been the best thing in the whole outfit for it does not cost more than $2,000 a month to run it. We get a couple of thousand from the towns and have the use of the water for our mills.

Then we have a railroad. Haggin and myself own that. That pays too. . . . By these two schemes we supply water to these two towns, to other people around and to our mills, and the railroad brings in wood. So as long as the mills run it is a good scheme for us to keep them going.

The next big venture was the "Anaconda." We got this through Marcus Daly, the fellow that told me about the "Ontario." . . . We started a railroad there too which delivers freight . . . and there is also a fine hotel there. . . .

I have been in a great many mining enterprises outside of these and lost a good deal of money by them. . . . I have confined myself to mining since I was 21 years old. Everything else was incidental. . . .

The general character of my mining has been to get the ore out, reduce it to bullion and sell it . . . in other words, we were engaged in what is called legitimate mining. I never sold any stock in any mine that was not in operation. We would always sell a little . . . but very often, we would not even do that. . . .

On the whole, I think that mining is about the best business of all. Of course, there may be chances in some railroad scheme that are better; but for a regular business, I think I would prefer mining. . . . if I were going to start out to make $10 million, I would most assuredly go to mining. As to farming, that is hardly a business at all. The farmer, of course, is sure of making a living, and that is about all.[29]

Mining was George's destiny. "Without being the possessor of brilliant talents," wrote one of his contemporaries, "yet he has those qualities of quick and ready adaptation to circumstances, and a personal magnetism which brings success in his particular enterprises to a greater degree than many who boast of a university education and great intellectual endowments." George's ability to recoup after business losses, the same historian wrote, "arises from the fact that from his mental organization he allows nothing to worry, alarm, or make him nervous, and therefore, in times of disaster, he is ready to take advantage of business opportunities, and while others are nervous, sick and alarmed, he is employing his expert experience and knowledge of men and mines to his advantage."[30]

Some speculators, to their misfortunes, did not take George's advice. In one instance, involving the Little Emma mine in Salt Lake, he tried to warn some English mining "experts" against developing the mine as a big stock speculation. George thought the mine "was like a turnip turned upside down," with only a pocket or large lump of ore that would not last. The "experts" refused to believe him, thinking they had a mountain full of ore. "The result turned out just as Hearst predicted," his lawyer, Clarence Greathouse, later reported; "they were working on the top of a turnip," and thousands of investors were ruined.[31]

George wrote Phoebe in detail about his mining enterprises, how construction of the mills were coming along, how much things cost, what the expected return was, who was involved. Whatever their relationship at that time, their letters continued to be affectionate. George told her on one occasion that he would like to carry her around in his pocket, as he was happier in the mountains than in San Francisco.

> Hamilton, [Montana]
> January 30, 1869

My dear wife,

I arrived here all well and have been in good health ever since cam, eat first rate and am well pleased with the place. But miss you very much. If I could carry you around in my pocket I had just about as soon be here as any place. But you do not know how much I think of you. It is a horable life for me to live without you. I have a good place to sleep in . . . and have as good a time as I could have without you. But this place will not do for you as the cold wind and light atmosphere would be hard for your throat. It might do in the summer time. I wish it was a good climate so you could live here. We would make plenty money. But I do not know that I can stand it to stay here without you.

I saw Mrs. Sheaster. She told me she knew you first rate and is a good friend of all the McDonalds. . . . She is a very smart lady and is a lady. . . . She is the only lady I have seen since my arrival. There are some women here, but Oh, what hard looking ones. . . .

This is a great place for small folks to make money. . . . The whiskey bars and restaurants are crowded, as full as they can . . . as there is all the places that we can get to [live in?] and they are taking in piles of gold. Many persons cannot get a bed and have to set up all night or sleep in a chair or on a stool and some have no money to get a bed. But no one need go without money as all can get work that will. But there is more broken down businesses here than any place I ever saw. But if they will leave off whiskey and will try, they will make money. . . .

If I don't come out with plenty, you can blame me for it. . . .

> Your
> George[32]

In November of the same year, George wrote from Wyoming Territory, ". . . I had the Blues badly as you felt so bad when I left, I felt bad all day and thought of you and the Boy often and felt terable, hope you have got over your Blues."[33]

Many letters explain that he would not be home. And when he was in the mountains, he stayed through holidays. From Montezuma [Colorado?] on 18 December 1871, he wrote,

> . . . and should I go, I will not be home at Christmas. I never was so anxious to see you in all my life. I am homesick and sometimes I think I will start and go at once. But that would not be manly and as long as I pretend to do

anything to make money, I must attend to business before my own happiness or wants.

I have traveled on the outside of this camp some 2 or 3 days, found nothing that will do for an opperation and hate to go home without something to put on the mantle. It would be so nice to start something the first of the year. If I had you along with me, I would not think of San Francisco once a month. I never missed you so much on a trip ever before. . . .

Kiss the Boy for me. If I should not be home for Christmas dinner, think of me and wish I was there.

Your
George[34]

For her part, Phoebe also expressed loneliness in George's absence during these years. She signed her name Puss, the affectionate name that George and her close family called her but that was never used after George died. When she herself was traveling, she continually berated George for not writing and urged him to visit her parents in Santa Clara. George was reluctant to do both. Writing was a chore for him and he was often far from Santa Clara on business. Phoebe, on the other hand, wrote long and detailed letters, which George looked forward to getting.

From Sullivan, Missouri, she wrote:

I do hope you will have respect enough for yourself and me to keep yourself <u>well</u> dressed and <u>clean</u>—nothing can make me feel worse than to think you are going about shabby and dirty. I suppose you are at the Hotel. You did not say. Please write me if you have any new clothes and if you have your washing done, and be sure not to forget to pay for it. I know how careless and forgetful you are, though you don't intend to be so.[35]

In the same letter she exhorts George to get rid of Lent—"he is a <u>very</u> dangerous man"—and offers advice about George's mining ventures. All her relatives and friends in Missouri looked old and overworked, and many would "not last long," she predicted. Nearly all were poor, some were "ruined by the war," and others had lost their wheat crops to "the bugs." Phoebe more and more appreciated her advantages. She gave a poor cousin "a calico dress and some other little things." A friend's daughter, Eliza Jane, had "gone <u>to bad</u> and <u>very bad</u>," having left her children and run off to St. Louis and Rolla, Missouri. And a relative of Cousin Joe Clark was imposing on Uncle Austin; the man "needs his neck broken . . . he is no account, rough and low, everyone knows it," Phoebe said. But everyone "fell in love with Willie—some say he looks like you and your family, others say he is like me. . . . Everyone thinks he is so large and smart. You need not fear that I will be the least careless about him; if anything happened to him, I should be almost

heartbroken," she wrote. Willie was getting lots of attention and domi-
nating his playmates wherever possible. One of them, Phoebe wrote,
"says Willie has to be Conductor, Brakeman, Engine and all."[36]

The absences tested their love for one another. Phoebe did not want
hers doubted. She also hoped that she was pregnant, having had irregular menstrual periods. In a subsequent letter from Missouri, she wrote
George:

> From the tone of your letter, you seem to doubt my writing at all. You say
> "Even if I wrote it would be a long time, etc." As for my neglecting to write
> you or being careless about you, it hurts me very much for you to think that
> for a moment. I cannot think you doubt my love. You know me too well for
> that. I did wrong not to write you even though I was sick, but it was through
> love and not neglect or thoughtlessness. I did not wish to distress you and
> hoped everyday to be better. . . .
>
> If you and I live to be very old, you will not find that I do not love you, or
> am careless about you. . . .
>
> I wrote you about having my courses before getting to Panama. It was 18th
> May. From that time until yesterday, I did not come unwell, near two and a
> half months. I had come to the conclusion I must be pregnant. The Dr. said
> some persons were unwell once after being in that condition. I did not know
> what to do about it, and was afraid to take any medicine to bring me right,
> fearing to produce miscarriage. I suppose the cold I had was the cause of the
> trouble. I think my health will be much better as I now have my menses,
> don't be uneasy. . . .
>
> I will be anxious to see you and be with you, but as I am here and may
> never come again, I would like to go to some places that it will be impossible
> to do if I start [home] a month sooner, but just as you say. It seems almost a
> year since I saw you. No wonder you feel out of patience and lonely if the
> time seems so long to you. . . . Take care of your clothes and keep neat and
> clean . . .
>
> Give my love to friends that you know I like. Willie sends kisses.
>
>   Your wife,
>   Puss[37]

Her protestations to the contrary, it was hard to keep Phoebe from her
travels. She had an insatiable curiosity and desire to see the world. In
August she went to New York and then to Niagara Falls. She was
dazzled by New York and the elegantly dressed and sophisticated
women. Her health improved immediately on arriving in New York.
The sights and diversions invigorated her and whetted her appetite for
more. She felt a bit plain, and a tinge of jealousy permeates her letter to
George from the Fifth Avenue Hotel:

> . . . Mrs. Forbes talks of going to the different watering places. She has
> many acquaintances here, seemed to be enjoying herself, was surrounded by

gentlemen, and was elegantly dressed, enough so to attend a party. She said she was going out this evening to some place of amusement. . . .

This week I feel quite well. Think Missouri does not agree with me. There is no doubt about it, the people live magnificently here, and certainly cannot be surpassed in dress. I thought I had a few handsome dresses—but mine are very small potatoes, after all. I often think what a farce it is, how fortunate it is, that the dress does not make the person.[38]

Niagara, too, dazzled her. In a September letter to George she said they had "enjoyed everything so very much, I cannot tell you how I love this grand scenery." The trip was a great success, despite having been detoured "into wagons, and driven around two miles to another train" because "beyond Schenectady a bridge was washed away the day before," and she and Willie were forced to spend the night "in the cars." It did not dampen her enjoyment, nor Willie's, who was entranced by the wonders of travel to exotic places. But Phoebe complained of being exploited as tourists: ". . . I never saw such places as this or the White Mountains. They exact a dollar from you to turn around."[39]

Willie, however, got food poisoning while staying with Eliza in Reading. He was "bilious and troubled with worms the day before he was sick," had "spasms" and "was insensible for more than two hours. . . . He had eaten something he ought not, which completely upset him." By the time his mama arrived, he could not "bear for me to get out of his sight," and he wanted to go home. Phoebe was beside herself with fear of losing him; their "little man" was "everything" to them, she wrote George.

> . . . last night (he) let me sleep some and Eliza watched him, but if he felt a little badly, it was "Oh, Mama, I want you." He said yesterday he wished Papa was here, and this morning he said, "let us just get on the steamer and go home, for I don't want to go back to Missouri again."
> . . . I will do everything for him, bless his life. He is everything to us. He is such a little man. . . .[40]

Phoebe shared his desire to start for California: "It is bad enough to be separated so long without making each other miserable by writing disagreeable things," she wrote George again from Reading on 4 October 1868. "If you have read my letters, you will see by them that I have been having a good time. The only thing lacking was to have you with me, but that could not be." She hoped that George would join them in Missouri and take them back to California. That, too, was not to be. She was reluctant to return overland "by the cars" without George or "some gentleman acquaintance . . . as much as I would like to see the country." She returned to Missouri to await George's reply. And she got in another lick at Lent: ". . . I am very sorry indeed that Lent always manages to have things his own way. Am afraid the <u>big</u> Idaho mine will never benefit <u>us.</u> I was thinking matters would be different. However, it is no use to worry about it."[41]

She took Willie to an opera and fair in St. Louis. "It is amusing to see the fruits and vegetables on exhibition," she wrote, comparing them to the better quality in California. Willie, she found, was remarkably "fond of music," but indiscriminating. He particularly liked the brass bands in a "grand democratic" parade that they viewed from their hotel window: "he enjoyed that very much."[42]

George did not come to fetch them, so she booked passage to California on steamers from New York and Panama. She had two country cousins in tow—Jake and Joe Whitmire—who were moving to California. "They could not do worse than stay where they were," Phoebe wrote George from New York, 29 November 1868. Nevertheless, she was disgusted with the "mean" exorbitant fare for steamer passage. "The fare has risen still more. They [the cousins] will have to go second cabin," she told George, complaining that her and Willie's fares were outrageous: "$300 for myself, $150 for Willie, but we can't help it, we are very anxious to see our dear papa." She was always conscious of being frugal but quick to justify going first class. The cousins were "utterly ignorant . . . they were more care than two babies," she wrote Eliza, complaining that she had to handle all the travel arrangements, a skill for which she developed a worldly capacity.[43]

Phoebe was anxious to be home after six months away and to ascertain whether a 21 October earthquake had damaged their Chestnut Street house. To George she wrote:

> I hope we will get home in time to eat Christmas dinner at Pa's. I suppose you will be home before we get there. We will look for you as soon as the steamer gets up near the wharf. . . . I will be with you . . . soon . . . that is, if we reach there in safety. . . . Goodbye until we meet.[44]

They sailed at noon on December first for California: "I believe I prefer that place to any other, after all," she wrote Eliza.[45]

Despite good sailing weather, the trip was made miserable by the fact that Willie contracted typhoid fever about the time they reached Acapulco. Phoebe feared "he would not live to reach home." She and the ship's doctor nursed Willie on a little port wine and teaspoonfuls of beef tea, "just to keep life in him," she later wrote Eliza. "Poor little fellow was lower than I ever saw him. You can imagine what he and I both suffered. He would let no one touch him but me." Nine days after leaving Acapulco they sailed into San Francisco Bay on Christmas Eve day. George and Cousin Joe Clark met them, but "papa felt terribly to find his little 'Billy Buster' so sick." They stayed at the Lick House, and George, in atypical behavior, hung about day and night while they nursed Willie back to health. He "scarcely went to the office at all, it was like being married over again. You would have laughed to see how foolish he was about us. He says we shall never go away again without him and I am sure we do not want to undertake another trip alone," she wrote Eliza.[46] Phoebe was pleased to "hear good accounts of how many clean clothes" George had worn in her absence, but, she confided to Eliza, "I came back and found him almost destitute of shirts and underclothes; he loses them."[47]

Christmas festivities were postponed, although Willie was given "some very pretty toys—a gun, some books, a farm with animals, a regiment of soldiers with full brass band and some other things." They went to the Appersons where Willie's appetite—always hearty in good health—returned. He loved his grandmother's fried chicken and years later longed for it. The family prepared to move back into the Chestnut Street house in hopes of avoiding exposure to a smallpox epidemic that was rampant in California. Anyone who lived in a hotel and came down with it was sent to a crowded "pest house" on the outskirts of town, where care was poor; Phoebe wanted no part of that. Although she had been vaccinated thirteen times and had had several more given herself and Willie on the steamer and after returning home, she feared hers had not taken.

Nevertheless, life was not all sickness and epidemics. In a long letter to Eliza Phoebe added a gossipy footnote about a woman who was to be a colorful legend in her own time in San Francisco: Lillie Hitchock Coit, who followed fire brigades and left money in her will to honor firemen and beautify the city. Coit Tower on Telegraph Hill was constructed with her legacy. Cousin Joe Clark apparently had fancied Lillie.

> Oh, I had forgotten to tell you the all-important gossip of the day. Lillie Hitchcock is married to a young man named Coit. Her parents are so angry they have gone east overland and gone south, have disinherited her. I have not time to write you particulars, but will reserve that for my next. Cousin Joe bears it all well.[48]

Life for the Hearsts returned to normal, with George pursuing mining riches and Phoebe redecorating their house in lilac and gilt-striped wallpaper (lilac was her favorite color). San Francisco, she wrote Eliza on 20 June 1869, "is growing fast and improving wonderfully, you would be astonished." George was home more than usual—"Isn't he improving?"—but had "many annoyances and anxieties" trying to make money. Phoebe wanted success for him as much as he did. He was then hoping for a strike in the White Pine district of Nevada: "The mines are principally silver and <u>wonderfully</u> rich, no humbug about it. . . . They far surpass Virginia City in its best days," Phoebe had written Eliza back in February. But Lent, who continued to owe George money, was a curse on their fortunes, Phoebe felt.

> Mr. Hearst writes that he is very much pleased with the place and thinks <u>he</u> can make some money there. His mine in Idaho has not proven such a rich one as they had expected. The mill is running and some bullion has been sent down, but they fear the ore will not pay as much as it ought to. It seems that he has a hard time. He tries so hard to make money, and has lost so much. The way Lent offers to pay up what he owes them is in old notes and "wild cat" mining stock and I don't believe they will succeed in getting anything else. Lent ought to be sent to the Penitentiary for life.[49]

Phoebe's brother Eppy also continued to be a problem. In the same letter, she wrote, "He has been extra kind this time, at least, to me, but he is very disrespectful to Pa and Ma, don't know what is to be done with him," she confided to Eliza.

Those were happy years except for the fact that no "little sister" appeared. She was "fleshy," weighing 120 pounds, and content. "Home is the most comfortable place," she found.[50] George bought the adjacent lot to the Chestnut Street house and put it in Phoebe's name. They built a large stable on it and kept a cow, chickens, a pony for Willie, two dogs, two cats, carriage horses and two carriages, and a gentle horse and buggy that Phoebe drove. She entertained with large luncheon and dinner parties. She began a pattern of filling the house with rare and exotic flowers when she entertained, to transform the place into one of fantasy. She had several servants—a cook, a chauffeur who doubled as gardener, and a "neat and smart" Chinese house boy from whom Willie was learning Chinese. They often had company, who would stay for weeks or months at a time. She felt obligated to put up guests but did not always enjoy having them. At times the company became too much for her. She described it all to Eliza:

> . . . During that time, Caleb Bowles, wife and baby came, so we had them all, it was awful. I just told Mr. Hearst I could not stand it, they should leave or I would. So he went out and hunted them up a small house, rented and furnished it and sent them groceries enough to last six months, then gave them some money and got them away from here. They live on Union Street. The day they moved from here I was sick in bed with fainting spells. I was completely exhausted. The next day George Bowles and his wife came. They have all sold out their mines and moved down here. So we then had all the Bowles. In fact, George B. and his wife are here yet and I suppose they will stay all winter.
> Caleb has bought a nice farm down at San Luis Obispo. They have moved down there. Ellen has a very pretty little girl, but she is spoiled. Ellen is not at

all neat. It was very hard to have her here for I was busy cleaning after her and trying to keep the diapers out of sight of other company.

. . . It took all my money to buy something to eat. Our market bills were enormous. . . . I had a letter from Pa scolding about my not going down to see them for such a long time. He said just leave and let the "Hotel" take care of itself. . . . Ma has new teeth and likes them very much. I am anxious to see her with them. Pa wrote that she looked much improved.[51]

She complained of "hangers on" draining their coffers. And, with an ironic insight to the future, she worried that money might corrupt Willie. She hoped he would be a "talented man."

Times are duller here than I can remember their being. Money is tight. Many think greenbacks will have to be used yet. Our finances are about the same. We would have all we want, were it not always our fate to be weighed down with so many hangers on. Well, I suppose it is best. We might want too much of this world's goods and forget our father who cares for us all.

I am not ambitious to leave my boy rich, for it might injure him more than benefit, but we want to educate him well, take him travelling. He has a good memory, and, we hope, will make a talented man.[52]

Phoebe was frugal but had expensive tastes. She mended and remade dresses but loved new gowns, which George gave her at Christmas. In 1869 he gave her a large sable fur cape that cost three hundred dollars. He had gotten a deal on it by knowing a friend of the furrier, thereby saving fifty dollars. That same Christmas, Phoebe gave her mother her used Singer sewing machine and bought the new, improved model for herself. "She would as soon have it as a new style Singer," Phoebe wrote Eliza.[53]

It was during those years that Phoebe took in the first of many young women whom she protected, educated, and launched into society. Alice Booth was an orphaned girl sent from her native Scotland to relatives in California. The relatives were about to take the homesick girl to British Columbia when the Hearsts agreed to take her in. She did light domestic work in return for room and board, education, and the privilege of being introduced to polite society by Phoebe. Alice was the first of many surrogate daughters whom Phoebe would mother. She saw to it that Alice learned proper social manners and had suitable suitors. Nothing pleased Phoebe more than to see her protégés happily—or at least successfully—married. Alice was the first; five years after Phoebe took her under her wing, the girl was married in the Hearsts' parlor to an old friend of George's, H. Jasper McDonald, a man of some means.[54]

Alice, while living with the Hearsts, took over many of the domestic, menial tasks that Phoebe had been accustomed to doing, such as sewing and putting up fruit—the latter a job that Phoebe was "not sorry to lose," she told Eliza.[55]

As for George and Willie, George was often sick or away, so Phoebe moved Willie into a bedroom adjoining hers. "It is such a universal occurrence for (George) to be sick, it makes me uneasy and anxious," Phoebe wrote Eliza in January 1870.[56] She did not want to lose George, and was genuinely concerned with his health. When he was not overly indulging Willie, he was at mining sites. "You know how fond he is of rocks," Phoebe wrote Eliza. "It is very difficult to persuade him to go anywhere for pleasure. If there is any prospect of finding a mine, he is ready."[57]

So she began to take Willie on more trips. He "is now old enough to appreciate sight-seeing and is a very good little escort."[58] Willie was learning French and attending a private school a few blocks away on Vallejo Street, to which he walked. Phoebe was determined to "keep him out of bad boys' company." The servants helped. "They are all good to Willie and if they see him doing wrong, let me know."[59] Phoebe thought him an "innocent child," but he had a penchant for attracting attention by doing clever mimics to the amusement of his classmates. In 1870 Phoebe wrote Eliza:

He is learning fast. . . . He talks incessantly, asking for things in French. It is very amusing to hear him. He has been going to school just about one month, is in a class with some children who have been going to school for two years. We feel very proud of our boy. The teacher is fond of him. She has only 12 little scholars and says Willie is the favorite with them all. He is such a mimic—sings, dances and plays so as to much amuse all of them. he is growing very fast and is in good health.

I have made him a good supply of nice warm clothing. He wears boots! And to see him trudging off to school with books and lunch—he looks so "big." I begin to feel old.[60]

When she took him traveling with her, she kept up his lessons. "He learns easily and retains all," she said.[61] There was no doubt that he was Mama's boy.

It is no trouble for him to get a lesson. He is fond of reading interesting books. I take great pleasure in amusing and interesting him at home so that he may be kept as much as possible from bad children. Of course, I must allow him to have company often but I manage to watch them closely. So far he is a very innocent child and I mean to keep him so just as long as I can. Whenever he hears anything from other children, he comes straight to me with it.

He is a great comfort to us. Mr. Hearst is so proud of him and too indulgent to try to keep from spoiling him. Am decided with him. He is all the more devoted to me for it.

Mr. Hearst often says he would not like to have Willie on a jury if his Mama was concerned for whether it was justice or not, he would decide in my favor.[62]

Her greatest sadness was her failure to conceive another child. She kept herself healthy, took iron tablets, and hoped. But it was not to be.

> I am so sorry we have no other children. We love babies so dearly. Why we are not blessed I cannot understand. I have tried to be careful of myself this spring, hoping for <u>something</u> but no change yet. I suppose we must be patient.

Always anxious to please Phoebe—or perhaps to avoid her displeasure—George in 1872 talked of taking the family to Europe the following year to attend the World's Fair at Vienna. Phoebe studied her French even more diligently and took up German in order to be prepared.

Although George was never to see Europe, Phoebe and Willie would.

7
Europe and Beyond

It was the realization of Phoebe's dreams—the Grand Tour of Europe—and she joined a parade of newly rich Californians crossing the Atlantic to take in Old-World culture. The Lent, Tevis, and Head families were among acquaintances traveling abroad in 1873, when Phoebe and Willie, then ten years old, embarked for eighteen months of European sightseeing and Continental education. George, who Phoebe kept hoping would join them, never did. "Mr. Hearst will never cross the ocean with us. Even if he should, he would disapprove of all that we might enjoy," she later had to admit in a letter to Mrs. James Peck, a close friend since their voyage to San Francisco in 1862.[1] But for Phoebe, Europe fulfilled her highest expectations and she was reluctant to come home, even after the prolonged absence from George. Her wanderlust and insatiable curiosity were stronger than her nesting instincts.

The Chestnut Street house was rented for $125 a month "to nice people who have no children." The couple, Phoebe hoped, would "keep the place in order, which is equal to fifty dollars more a month. They will perhaps buy our horses and carriage. The buggy horse we will send to Pa's, also the buggy. Will sell the rockaway horses, cow, dogs, etc. I really feel sad to break up my nice home," Phoebe wrote Eliza, "but now is such a good time to travel I had best take advantage of it.[2]

George gave Willie a watch and he and Phoebe set out on their adventure. George was expected to join them in New York but the farther away Phoebe got, the more remote became the possibility of his joining her. He was involved in several legal suits and had other worries. The cultural grand tour was of little interest to him—he would much rather go to the mines and make money than spend it in Europe. Business was tentative at that time, although Phoebe's grand tour was a surface show of their wealth. In fact, George had debts and was waiting for mines to produce a "proffit," as he spelled it. George wrote Phoebe from Pioche shortly after she left and while she was visiting relatives in Missouri.

I am in much better health than usual in the mountains. I feel first rate. And feel I will make some money this year for the Babies. And it is quite possible I may be in London this summer or fall. I will want to see the Babies very much. In fact, I feel you have been gone a great while now. For outside of you and the Boy, all is [vanity?] . . .

I do not see how I am to get my letters to you in Europe. But you will post me as best you can as soon as possible. As to the money you will need in or on your trip, dont give yourself any trouble about [that]. I will see that you have it at any cost. . . .

Have a good time and think of me. Kiss the Boy for me often and dont let him forget me.

> Your loving husband,
> George Hearst[3]

George, Phoebe later noted, was "away from San Francisco nearly all the time since we left; when he is there, he seems much more lonely than when in the mines."[4]

Nevertheless, she worried that George was at a disadvantage with his partners, Haggin and Tevis:

> We miss you very much and do wish you were here, but from the tone of your letters, I can see things are _very_ bad and I feel extremely anxious as to the result. If there should be no new trial granted to the R. and E. Co., it will in a measure relieve you, but I fear the worst, then "Monitor" dragging so heavily, and that dead weight in "Cariboo" is enough to carry one down forever.
>
> I am afraid Haggin and Tevis may not wait the turn of events. You are undoubtedly completely in their power. I know you feel it, and I do. I am sure you are doing the very best you can _now_ for it is impossible to remedy evils when you cannot realize [a] sale for anything. I am dreadfully sorry that Dr. Stallard did not sell "Ontario," that would have been some help.[5]

Their precarious financial situation did not deter Phoebe from spending, however, and George even encouraged it.

During her absence, Phoebe wrote copious and effusive letters to her husband, expressing her love for him on elaborately monogrammed paper, which changed as she moved from country to country. He responded simply and shortly—to her frustration—expressing his affection and fear for the safety of her and "the Boy." However much he was away, he found that the disruption of his small home left him lonely and empty. Phoebe's absence this time was the cementing of a pattern of separations. Her level of sophistication rose daily. She learned tricks about traveling, quickly perceiving the advantage of tipping porters, museum guards, and hoteliers to gain favors and avoid crowds. While constantly justifying expenditures and defending her frugality, she was submitting to temptations to buy things. She loved the opportunities to meet educated and cosmopolitan people of breeding and money. And she and Willie dreamed of one day having rooms as grand as those they walked through in the palaces of England, Germany, Italy, and France.

The trip across the American continent was not an easy beginning. It rained, snowed, and sleeted wherever they went. They stopped in Missouri to visit relatives, where Willie encountered snow for the first time. She wrote George,

> He is so delighted over the snow, wants to play in it all the time. I dare not allow him to do so, but where it drifted against the window we gathered some and ate it, also made a few snow balls. Willie tried some experiments with it. He did not seem to realize it would melt so easily.[6]

She worried about Willie's getting smallpox or "something like the spotted fever—it is called 'spinal meningitis.' " And she regretted going to Missouri. In the dreadful weather, two wheels came off a wagon and they were thrown out: "I would have been killed if the horses had run but they stood perfectly quiet." She found her relatives "frail" and "pitiful."[7]

Willie already wanted to go home. They made a nostalgic 24-hour visit to Eliza in Bloomington, Illinois, leaving the train at three o'clock in the morning in a rainstorm. Eliza prophetically told Phoebe she thought Willie would "make a great man." For the moment, though, he had lost his rubber sling in Chicago, which upset him. They were delayed by floods en route to Boston, where they stayed with the Anthonys and Phoebe basked in the social life.

She needed to obtain a letter of credit, which required a visit to the hated Tevis, who sent her to the more-despised Haggin:

> . . . you positively told me the amount would be ten thousand dollars and assured me it would be right and Tevis would attend to it. When I went to see him, I could not find him. He left word for me to go to Haggin. I would just as soon have taken an ice bath at once. Haggin was polite and agreeable enough, but gave me the amount he thought necessary. Now you know that I should spend no more, if my letter of credit called for twenty thousand, than I shall, as it is, and I consider that I might have the benefit of any attention it might secure me. . . .
>
> I am not the least afraid but I will have enough. You will supply me with all needed funds, but what wounded me was to be set aside in that way, as though it was of no consequence. I was at first very angry and would not trust myself to write to you, fearing I might say something to regret and you would feel annoyed. This matter should have been all arranged before our departure. I know you are dreadfully busy.[8]

Phoebe did not like to be crossed or put on "hold," particularly by men whom she did not respect nor trust. Her anger brought a reaction.

George gave "J. B. . . . a blowing up about it, and I think Mr. Tevis did [also] for he [Haggin] appeared to feel very badly. . . . He saw I was much hurt about it for I talked to him as he has not been for some time," George wrote Phoebe. He was ready to send her all the money she needed to buy whatever she wished to bring home. He even suggested that she get "a nice piece of cloth . . . to have me some nice close made here."[9] "Spend as much money as is necessary for your pleasure and not think of it, for if you are to feel that you are doing rong you loose all your pleasure and all is lost," he wrote Phoebe in another letter.

> So do not write me that you are feeling bad about what it costs. You will get all you want for your pleasure and comfort and it only makes me hapy for you to have the money to use in that way.
> . . . we will come out all right in time and no fear. So give yourself no trouble. I know you are sensable and know what is about right.
>
> Your loving husband,
> George[10]

In one of his musings about their future, he wrote wistfully, "I long for the time when we will be settled down in our own little nest and enjoy ourselves the ballance of our lives with our dear Boy."[11]

Phoebe gave scant attention to his wishful dreams, feeling the burdens of practical life more than she considered her due. She exhorted George to give money to some poor relations in her absence, saying that "you will not attend to them unless there is someone to remind you. . . . somehow this way of shouldering others' burdens will cling to me."[12]

On 19 April, armed with letters of introduction, Phoebe and Willie sailed for Europe on the White Star Line steamer *Adriatic*. Life would never be the same for the two of them.

In Ireland, their first stop, they saw another side of life: Old-World wealth contrasted with extreme industrial-age poverty. Riding through Dublin in an elegant carriage provided by a gentleman to whom they had been referred, they saw poverty such as they had never imagined. Phoebe described it graphically to George in her first letter from abroad:

> Belfast, Ireland
> 11th May, 1873
>
> . . . The people are much more formal than with us. Many of them highly educated, warm hearted and hospitable, but the poor classes are terribly poor. Willie wanted to give away all his money and clothes, too, and really, I felt the same way. If we could have relieved half of them. The Irish are a strange people, a combination of deceit and kindness.
> . . . Willie says he does not like this country very much because the men are so bad to the women and horses. He saw the women working out

barefooted and thinly clad. The horses in the south of Ireland are so poor and overworked. The whole country is beautifully cultivated.[13]

Willie was "greatly amused" however, by the judges and lawyers in the Queen's Court, wearing "funny curled grey wigs and strange black gowns." They were invited to the home of a doctor when Willie got a bad cold and the doctor's mother "took a fancy to Willie and seemed very anxious to have us stay longer," Phoebe also wrote. Willie was on his best behavior—but not nearly so interesting, his mother thought.

> You know Willie is always interesting when not well and full of pranks. He talked so quietly and was very good, but I would have felt happier to have him well and a little bad.

Phoebe confessed in the same letter to George that she had many "unpleasant dreams—cannot help fearing something is wrong." She felt "a little homesick" and she missed him but said that she and her little escort managed to get along well. She assured George that she was trying to save money and deplored the fact that "Americans are fast spoiling everyone [on the Continent], many of them are such fools and so extravagant." She continued to offer advice on George's business affairs, which George heard but rarely followed. He wrote from San Francisco that "Times are very dull and all most impossible to sell a thing. I note all you say about [settling?] up all my matters and will give it my attention, of this you can rest assured."[14]

Dinner at "Allice's" was "all that appears like home," he wrote, but it did not ameliorate his feeling at loose ends without Phoebe. He wrote her plaintively on 30 May that "a man without a home is just about no man at all":

> I hope you are having a good time for I have missed you very much since I have been back. We have been together so long I have become weaned from nearly everyone and scarsley know anyone and find the Hotel a very stupid place and nothing to interest me. A man without a home is just about no man at all. Be shure to write me all about your travels. I am very anxious for you and the Boy for fear you will never get back safe. I will think the time long until you return. I hope I may get off and meet you yet.
>
> Your husband,
> George[15]

The meeting was not to take place, as George was embroiled in battles over mining stakes. His ventures were "paying a good proffit."[16]

Phoebe and Willie were spending the profits in Glasgow and Edinburgh, where Willie was fascinated by Rob Roy's dirk and wanted a kilt.

His eyes were wide open to new experiences and his sense of drama was fed by visits to old castles, which he loved. His mother was titillated by the linens and glassware. It was the beginning of a buying spree that, despite her protestations of frugality, would become an obsession and one that Willie later emulated. At a large linen manufacturer she was "tempted to indulge my taste to a greater extent, but my better judgement said <u>wait</u> and see how matters go at home before spending much for even such useful articles," she wrote George.[17]

Although she and Willie occasionally traveled with friends, they preferred being on their own. "Willie often says we can see more alone, for we, as you know, have energy and perseverance," she told George.[18] Willie, though, was sometimes homesick, uprooted as he was, and he had caught whooping cough. Phoebe, determined not to miss anything, did not allow it to slow them down, although she assured George that she was being "exceedingly careful."

> You need not be uneasy . . . for you know I will not leave anything undone to cure him and keep him safe and well. You would feel life a blank without him.[19]

Still, she felt "it would never do for me to have such a good time without something to mar the pleasure." They both craved "some good home vegetables and fruits—Willie looks in disgust at the poor supply we have here."[20]

She thought, quite wrongly as it turned out, that she would "probably never have another opportunity to come abroad" and had to make the most of the time she had.[21] That was her rationale for spending. She paid the extravagant sum of twenty dollars for a ticket to a command performance of the London opera for the Shah of Persia ("he was a blaze of diamonds") and explained to George:

> I shall try to get the <u>worth</u> of my journey. It will be one of the grandest affairs that has ever been in London. If there had been another seat, I would have taken Willie, but that could not be done. I don't know what you will think of this, hope you will tell me. I must say that I feel worried about spending so much, but must stay at home if I do not. My seat at opera is only a plain stall. The boxes and most elegant departments brought one and two hundred dollars. There is a <u>pang</u> with the pleasure when I keep thinking of our debts and difficulties and of you working and anxious. I cannot help it. We have certainly seen everything as thoroughly and in as little time as any one could under the circumstances. . . .
>
> I have done my best to be moderate and it <u>will</u> cost me $50.00 per week for our living. Then add cab hire, railways, trips or excursions, theatres, operas, concerts, etc. and the amount runs up to nearly $100.00 per week. Then I want you to know that I <u>never</u> take the very expensive seats at places of amusements, only if they are nice and respectable. I certainly am no display of lavish expenditure.[22]

The temptations were too great to resist, however. She commissioned a portrait of herself—"for you and Willie," she rationalized to George— at a cost of three hundred dollars, which she feared he would "consider a great piece of extravagance." She had gotten a good deal, though, she explained. The artist, Pope, was a friend of a friend, and had charged a more reasonable fee than those commanded by "the swell noted artists who paint only the very rich people [and who] would not paint my portrait for less than four or five thousand dollars. . . . If I had it done abroad, I would have to rely entirely upon my own judgment and perhaps be cheated. . . . I hope you will be pleased," she wrote her husband.[23]

While spending his money she worried about his business alliances: "I hope you will write me how business is with you and what you are doing. I feel very nervous and uneasy about your position with Haggin and Tevis. If there is not a favorable change in some direction, I can't see the way clear."[24]

Phoebe enjoyed the luxuries of London and the proximity to royalty. She and Willie never missed an opportunity to watch the gentry on parade. Outside of St. Paul's Cathedral, where a special service for members of the royal family was held, they "sat in a cab and had a splendid view: Prince and Princess of Wales, Duke of Edinburgh and several of their suite passed almost touching us."[25] Willie delighted in seeing "the magnificient turnouts, elegantly dressed ladies, and swell Englishmen" riding through Hyde Park. "It is a sight never to be forgotten," she wrote. "The English know how to live," and she and Willie were getting ideas:

> In the old and poor parts, many streets are very narrow, gloomy and crowded. In the better portions, there are thousands of handsome and comfortable homes. In the stylish and elegant parts are thousands of magnificient residences, hundreds are perfect palaces, and how they do spend money—a dozen or more servants to each family, coachman, footmen, butlers, etc., horses, carriages, and every luxury. Talk of dress, it is marvelous to see some of these grand people at the Opera. The formality and distinctions of class seem a little strange to an American at first, but we must admit, the English know how to live. They seem to get so much more for their money than we.[26]

Willie said he "would have liked to live at Windsor Castle."[27] He, too, was displaying the first signs of a passion for conspicuous consumption. "He has a mania for antiquities, poor old boy," Phoebe told his father. "If you could see him studying and prying into everything." He also had a mania for animals and loved zoological gardens, aviaries, and aquariums, even fancying having his own zoo one day. He took up drawing with a modicum of talent. But most of all Willie liked talking about the things they were going to take home. He was impressed by the palaces and was fond of very tall towers—the taller they were, the better he liked them, climbing to their tops wherever possible. The Baden Baden astronomical clock, with its "full powers displayed at noon . . . made a lasting impression on Willie." He also loved noisy spectaculars with fireworks.[28]

For her part, Phoebe protested that she was practicing "self-denial" on purchases of Belgian lace and other treasures, but she "wickedly" coveted a German Landau carriage, she confessed to George, and Willie wanted four of the German white horses that were specially bred to pull the English royal carriages.[29]

Willie was often obstinate and difficult for his mother. The two were headstrong and frequently clashed. But he redeemed himself with his genuine curiosity and capacity to charm himself back into his mother's good graces. It was a skill that he learned early and well and that would serve him well in future. Phoebe wrote,

> Willie sometimes almost kills me. He wants all sorts of things and fre-
> quently at just the most important places he does not want to go, or if he
> does, gets tired and insists upon going to the hotel, thereby destroying my
> pleasure as well as fatiguing me greatly, though I try to be patient, and he is
> sometimes so pleased and interested and good. Altogether he is a great
> protection to me.[30]

"Sightseeing is very hard work," she concluded, although a "work" that she avidly enjoyed. Her constitution, she found, was strong enough for rigorous travel. Her health often improved when she was traveling and indulging her thirst for new knowledge and experiences. With a sharp eye and keen perception she noted every detail. It was "desirable to go twice to museums . . . to charge one's memory with all," she thought. Still, it could be overwhelming. There were too many statues at Westminster Abbey, and the Tower of London was full of "instruments of torture and death . . . everything to destroy life, but nothing to prolong and preserve it . . . think of all the headless bodies interred there." Willie shared it all with her. When he missed the opera in London because of his whooping cough, Phoebe described the performance to him and they had "a little laugh" imagining what would have happened "had he whooped just as Nilsson came on stage."[31]

In a small moment of nostalgia, she wondered if George remembered their eleventh wedding anniversary: "I wondered where you were and if you thought of us."[32]

George missed them, or at least he said so in his letters from the mines.

I feel very badly that I am not with you on your trip, as it is about all the trip I was anxious to make. But if I do not meet you before you return, I never will see the Old World and will be satisfied with your description.[33]

In the same letter he told of giving money to a little boy who had lost a foot when run over by a wagon. George had a soft heart for the underdog.

Tell Willie I want to see him very much and I am very lonely with no Boy. And that I met a nice little Boy who had his foot mashed off with a waggon running over it and he was about Willie's size and was going on one foot and crutch. I gave him money enough to send to Philadelphia and have a cork foot made for him. If he had been let grow up that way he would have been all out of shape. But if he gets good attention from this on, he will hardly miss his foot, as it is only off from the instep.

He also promised to send Phoebe his measurements "for I do not know as nice a thing to do as to bring some nice cloase in the way of cloth and linen."

He continued to worry that he might never see his "Babies" again because "some boat might blow up or some accident [happen] on a railroad," but he reported that his business affairs were improving—"have plenty of money in the bank"—and that he was making more than six thousand dollars a month from some mines, and expected to reap thirty thousand dollars from another, despite the fact that "times are very dull . . . stocks are flatter than they have been since '66." He added: "I am getting quite fleshy—I am sorry as you know I have a horror of fat."[34]

Although Phoebe dreamed that George was angry with her for her expensive travels while he was in debt, she comforted herself "with the remembrance that you love me even if you never say you miss me—we cannot all be demonstrative."[35] She and Willie were drinking up the European culture like the wine they drank instead of water, for fear of cholera. They also tried to avoid "common" Americans, revealing a certain snobbishness. "No wonder Europeans laugh at our people when our country is represented by this class of common people," she wrote George. "Many of them [in one group] were public school teachers, principally Yankees. You can imagine what they are like."[36] She was proud to be an American, though, and resented hearing derogations of her homeland. Encountering in London a "pompous and disgusting" American colonel who was moving to the Continent and who "remarked that in six months, I would be ashamed of America, I gave him an answer the he may remember sometime. Europe is certainly superior in many respects, but I see no reason why American women cannot come abroad and return clear-headed," she wrote George.[37]

The subjugation and inequality of European women astonished Phoebe. She considered herself an equal to men, at least intellectually. The sight of Prussian women working in the fields angered her: "Such dreadful looking creatures. . . . Females are degraded among the lower classes." Revealing a growing boldness, she noted that she was at first "timid" to go about alone, but quickly overcame that, and, when attending the Shah of Persia's command performance in London, turned her opera glass on the royal box and "stared as long as others did. Why should I care, modesty is never appreciated." Meeting the William Tevis family on the ship over and in London, she was annoyed at Mr. Tevis' indifference to her as an equal.

> I think at first Mr. Tevis was very indifferent or thought I did not amount to much. I made it a point to show him, in a very quiet way, I had a head of my own. He finally became quite agreeable. . . . I don't mean to have you think that I feel myself of importance, but do feel that I have a right to respect even from Tevises. . . . Mr. T. and I talked business, etc. At first they all asked me questions about travelling alone, but at last concluded that I could take care of myself.[38]

Willie displayed several similarities to his father that Phoebe deplored. He was "lazy about writing—but promises many things." George's failure to write her often was an indifference for which he was not sorry, she felt. She was forever forgiving them both for ignoring her, it seemed: "Sometimes when Willie has grieved me very much he says, 'Oh, Mama, don't say anything. I am sorry.' So I won't say anything. Don't think you are sorry, though."[39]

Willie wrote his papa that he liked speaking German much better than French, and that he was "reading a great many books but don't like to write. Mama says she will have me write every week now so that I may improve." Mama, in a postscript, said,

> I have allowed Willie to write this without any assistance from me. Although the writing is bad, he can express himself moderately well. He reminds me of you in his aversion to writing, but if practice and perseverance can change him, I will try it.[40]

It was an aversion that Willie overcame; as an adult he developed an ability to express himself that influenced or enraged millions of people.

Phoebe wanted to put him in a Protestant German school instead of a Roman Catholic school in France, and she asked George's blessing to stay longer in Europe. At the same time she fussed over George's appearance in her absence. She had enough trouble keeping him tidy when she was at home:

> Tonie wrote me she saw you and your clothes looked like "Pioche." You had no necktie, etc. and looked 'don't care.' I felt very badly and wish you would be more careful in your appearance for my sake.[41]

She asked him to dress up, "look your best!" for a photographer, and to send her a picture; "everyone with whom I become acquainted wants to see your picture."[42] At one point, Alice wrote that she thought George did not know where his clothes were.[43] Phoebe told him,

> I hope when you go home with Mr. Clarence Greathouse, you have clean clothes. However, I shall not fret about things I cannot change. I know you are good, but careless.[44]

Phoebe was conflicted by her desire to stay longer in Europe and by guilt at her long absence from George, whose approval she continually sought. From Germany in August 1873, five months after their departure, she wrote:

> I am very anxious now to have you write me how long you are willing to have us remain abroad. If you are fully decided you cannot come, I shall not feel contented to remain away many months longer, though as we are here, and never likely to come again, we ought to see all that it is possible to see and try not to be homesick. I want you to write me what you think. I am sure you are lonely and need us to cheer you. I feel conscience stricken about having so much enjoyment with you at home worrying and working. Does my love and my society when with you compensate for all? I hope we will yet have many happy years together. Willie certainly will have great benefit by this trip. It is in many respects better than school.[45]

They liked Germany, spoke German at meals, and Willie played with German boys. Phoebe was impressed by the art collections and free concerts in the parks, but did not like the Germans' intransigence nor their discrimination by social class. "One could never convince a German to act differently from orders or his routine of duties," she observed.[46] The aristocrats were "unapproachable" while the working classes received "very small wages" and had "few privileges." In Dresden she wrote:

> We see many poor here, and I think I have never seen so many deformed and afflicted people on the streets of a city. I have been through many of the poor streets, just to see, and have remarked this. There are numerous charitable institutions. They seem to be well managed, but there are always sufferers.[47]

She was derisive of the way "Many Americans rush through Europe and lose all the <u>best</u> that is to be seen, then they talk of where they have been, but can give no clear idea of important objects. I would as soon not go at all."[48] And she was disappointed in the display from the United States at the Vienna International exhibition: "Every country was better represented than our own, for which I felt very sorry. . . . The greatest display they made was of <u>sewing machines, soda water</u> and <u>dentistry.</u>[49]

In Munich Willie tried to bribe a guard when he was prevented from seeing an exhibit of statuary and frescoes because the King of Prussia had ruled that no one under seventeen was to be allowed in:

> Willie felt very badly, and said he meant to come here again when he was 17 to show that Keeper that he <u>would</u> go in. There is not the slightest objection to the collection in any way, but I believe the King made that rule so that children would be excluded. Everything is so rare and fine. [If] they should indeed not be touched by children, they must then exclude all. . . . Willie tried to bribe him, but no go. He was very good natured and let him <u>look</u> into three rooms.[50]

After the magnificent museums of Europe, Woodward's Gardens in San Francisco paled. Still, she asked for more money and more time to absorb the culture of Europe: "In my last letter, I did what is very unpleasant to me, that is, asking for more money. I did not mention any amount for you will send me what you think best."[51]

In Switzerland Willie could indulge his love of heights. He was "in love with Switzerland," his mother wrote. They rode a small train to the top of Rigi Peak, tugged by "a puffing, blowing little engine that looked, as Willie expressed it, like a big bottle." There they watched the sunrise the next morning. "Willie dressed in about five minutes and made a rush for the highest point, fearing he might miss something." He was intrigued by William Tell's monument, where Tell was supposed to have shot the apple off his son's head, and wanted to have "all the carvings in wood that we see." He went fishing on Lake Lucerne, where one day he caught twenty-one fish, seventeen of them "good to eat—<u>it was good fun,</u>" he wrote his papa.[52]

By that time Willie had read at least a dozen books and was growing rapidly. His mother worried that he read too much and exercised too little, and that he would be far behind when he returned to school. She again urged George to let her enroll Willie in a European school. In another observation about her son that would be close to the mark in the future, she told George, "He is a great reader, and has a good memory, but no tact for relating to others what he has seen or read."[53]

Willie also took an intense interest in how things were made and was petulant when interrupted. He was "so engrossed in all he saw" at a Swiss watch manufactory that when his mother "called his attention to something different from the object he was then examining, he so nervously said, 'Oh! I can't look.' that everyone laughed."[54]

George, meanwhile, had been sick, requiring a trip to hot springs. "If anything should happen to you during my absence," Phoebe wrote him, "I should never forgive myself for not being with you. I hope we will have the happiness to be again together, without any sad regrets." She was pleased to learn from friends in San Francisco that he "looked as neat as anybody's husband."[55] Things looked bright for his mining ventures, George wrote Phoebe, despite a recent financial panic in America and the litigation over his Missouri lands.[56] He urged Phoebe to stay in Europe until she was satisfied that they had seen everything.

> . . . Get through as soon as you can and brake for home. I do not mean for you to hurry for as you are their I want you to see all the important places or at least so much that you will not regret you did not stay longer. I hate what you say about money. I will attend to it. I am glad you did not leave Willie at school as he would not learn as he will with you and he is company to you, all though he may give you some trouble. At all events I would not like for you to leave him alone in a strange country.
>
> And do not go yourself or take him where their is the least danger in any way for I fear something will happen to you [even] with the greatest precaution. Take always the safest route and go nowhere their is the slightest danger.[57]

In one of her few allusions to the unorthodoxness of their marriage, Phoebe wrote George from Milan:

> I will be weary with traveling and not enjoy visiting when I come home. I dread the visitors. If we could only be quiet for a time. I will have so much to tell you and be so glad to see you, that it will be a great annoyance to have people calling, half of them insincere and curious only to see if I am back without having eloped, and to discover if you are glad to see me or not. What a queer world this is. . . . We may not wish to keep house for awhile when I return. Willie must go in school and I shall follow you. I have not much hope of having you settle down at home and now I should be terribly lonely when you were away, not having Alice. If I could only have a little girl of my own, how delighted I should be. I know you like boys best, but as I am not likely to be soon blessed with either, I will say no more on the subject.[58]

She had her thirty-first birthday in Florence, and wrote George nostalgically, "Today is my birthday, did you remember it? We are both growing old, but I hope we may enjoy many happy years together."[59]

She and Willie loved Italy, but she was "suspicious of Italians, they are not trustworthy." In Milan, Willie pulled out a tooth himself and Mama gave him the money that he saved by not having to go to a dentist.[60] Together they read Shakespeare's *Romeo and Juliet* and *Two Gentlemen of Verona* before going to Venice and Verona, where they saw an old well head *(pozzo)* that they coveted.[61]

In Florence Willie's interest in pictures and drawing was aroused:

> He is begging me to allow him to take drawing lessons, but I am afraid it would not be best to undertake so many things. He would do none well. However, I will see about it. He is picture crazy. I do not mean to say he has any special talent, and would not wish him to be an artist (unless a great one) but he frequently surprises me in his expressions concerning the best pictures. If he only learns to sketch enough to amuse and interest himself, I should be glad. I am very proud of his advancement in German. He likes it, and learns quickly. . . . He . . . was rather backward in [arithmetic].[62]

In Venice, the full force of their exotic experiences and distance from home hit Phoebe when she stepped into a gondola on the Grand Canal.

> At first it seemed so unreal, so like a dream that I should be there, so far from my native land amid the scenes of which we have often read. . . .
> I was disappointed in the gondolas. I knew they were no longer gay and elegant as in the palmy days that have passed away forever, but I certainly was not prepared to see them look like hearses, all black, and felt glad of the approaching darkness that their defects might be hid. I felt afraid of being upset, too, for we shot around corners at an alarming rate and the dexterous gondoliers wound their way through innumerable barges, etc. Willie and I held our breath and sat close together. At last, we arrived at our hotel on the Grand Canal, where we obtained a nice room fronting on the Canal. The view from the windows was so fascinating, I never could satisfactorily settle myself even to study the guide book in the evenings.[63]

There, too, the temptation to shop was irresistible. At a Venetian glass factory, Phoebe had difficulty convincing Willie that "there were other places to see and we could not buy all we saw. He gets so fascinated, his reason and judgement foresake him. I, too, acknowledge the temptation."[64]

She wrote Eliza that she was not buying clothes because she "would rather spend the money to fill my mind with what will give me pleasure all my life than to put it on my back."[65] She urged George to sell the San Francisco house to save money, which she thought could be better spent on statuary and pictures.

> I feel uneasy about home. Am afraid Harris will kill our horses and wear out the carriage and leave the house before I come. That would be a chapter of misfortunes. As for hoping to have a new house, that will be out of all reason, and I may be glad to have the old one, though I sincerely wish you could sell it, and then I will try to follow you, and leave Willie at school. We could live much cheaper. The money required to keep up that place is too much. I wish I had the amounts spent in repairs to purchase some statuary and pictures to

give pleasure to ourselves and friends all our lifetime. It is a mistake to wait until we are about ready to die before we treat ourselves to such things.[66]

Phoebe spent many hours at the Uffizi Gallery in Florence, gazing at the paintings, which in the same letter to George she described in detail:

> It is necessary to study them and know what I am looking at, to what era they belong, and the peculiarities of each master . . .
>
> I suppose you would not care to hear so much of pictures. I am more enthusiastic about them than I ever supposed I should be. The inspiration of the old masters was a sacred flame and with it, they painted love and prayer, praise and sorrow, with inevitable power, however strange and hard their lines and shapes, but finally grace and beauty of form were added more and more, till Raphael's time.

Surrounded by monuments to the dead, she wondered about posterity and why great men were rarely honored in their lifetimes. She added,

> The Florentines would feel ashamed of so long neglecting such a great man [Dante]. It seems as if nations made a point of putting their greatest men to despair, completely desolating the earth for them, and, then, when fame can be nothing to them, when they can no longer suffer or feel joy or favor, wrong or neglect, at the safe distance of a century or two, how thickly fall the honors. Churches contain their monuments, cities quarrel for their bones, geniuses cut out their glory in marble, or emblazon it upon canvas. How costly then is earthly renown.

The Italians had known better times, she thought, not producing much "modern work" of importance, which she blamed on "the corruptions of the Roman church, which have defiled the land." The priests, she thought, were guilty of unspeakable acts. She continued to George,

> [Italy] has suffered under an incubus that is now gradually being lifted. The appearance of the priests here is almost invariably repulsive and gross. It is said they are particularly depraved. They are fat with flabby, coarse cheeks, chins and throats of very earthly aspect. I can compare them only to hogs. It is shocking that such men are in a holy garb, set apart for the constant worship of God, and under the cover of superior sanctity, becoming the most corrupt of human beings. Recently the suppression of monasteries and convents have brought to light some fearful facts, too terrible to write, unless I knew no eyes but yours would read.
>
> About 10 days ago a mob attacked one of the churches to kill the priests, and were only prevented by the military. The cause was the conduct of the priest towards the mothers, wives and sisters of the men.

When not with his mother at museums, Willie played in the Pitti Palace gardens and nearly "bankrupt" them by taking chances and "patronizing the grab bag" at a fair to benefit Protestant orphans. "I really could not refuse him the pleasure." He won a "very pretty little cushion" that he gallantly presented to his arithmetic teacher.[67] They spent Christmas at the American consul's palace in Florence, then went to Rome, where curiously they had an audience with the pope, despite Phoebe's antipapist fervor. It was the thing to do, a privileged point on the Grand Tour.

> He was so kind, gentle and lovely, spoke altogether in French, asked where we were from, etc. When he came to Willie he placed his hand on his head and blessed him. He also blessed several articles that I wish to give to Catholic friends.[68]

George spent a less cheery Christmas. He was sick with a severe cold that settled in his "bronkel tubes." He longed for sun and warm weather; the damp of San Francisco "seems to chill me through." He blamed his chronic tendency to colds on the city, which hemmed him in. It had been a "terable" winter, and he worried that he might die soon and have lost precious time with his Babies. In January 1874 he wrote Phoebe,

> You do not know how much I miss you when I am confined in town and more particularly when I have to spend most of my time indoors. I think of you and the Boy and think I may not live long or at least might not, and if so, what a frightful loss of time.
> But of course when I am away I am hapy knowing that you are having a good time and of course could not improve my condition by being in this city. I would leave the city at once were it not so cold and wet in all directions. . . . I am anxious to get out of this place. . . .
> Of course, when I get away and am fully employed, I do not feel so blue as when I am here and not well.[69]

As to Phoebe's returning, he told her to be "governed by your pleasure," but to avoid dangerous places—"There is plenty to be seen where there is no risk."[70] With this correspondence he sent her a letter of credit for another three thousand dollars and would send more if she needed it. He wrote wistfully of attending the Calico Ball—a fundraising event to benefit the poor of San Francisco—where none of the ladies were as pretty as his Phoebe:

> I was there and I gave my mite for the poor. Did not dance and soon got tired and left.
> I did not see so good a looking woman at the party as yourself and that is saying a good deal. I hope the Boy will surpass either of us in all things.

George also wrote Willie news of his pets and farm animals. On that subject they shared a common interest:

I am glad to hear from my Boy and see with my eyes his own letters. I think you do very well. Hope you will try to improve. I saw Mrs. Peck's Boy, he is a very nice, smart boy and behaves like a little man, he asks about you often.

I was down to Gran Pa's and had a good time. Saw all of the dogs. Franky and Pennie and Eppy's dog. The little dog sleeps in a box by the stove and is the nicest little fellow you ever did see.

"Dock" is as fat as he can be and all of the horses are fat. But old "Jim", he has never got over the epazutic and as he is so old, I suppose he never will.

Gran Pa has about a dozen of the nicest pigs in the county, and as fat as they can be. They are so fat or something else that their tails all drop off. Gran Ma sais she wants to see you very much and wants you to come home. She sais she will take good care of the little dog and "Dock" for you and Ma until you come home.

Your Father,
G. Hearst[71]

Robert Craig Chambers, superintendent of the Ontario mine, worried that George was overdoing it.

I fear you are still taking too many chances by making those long and tiresome trips, especially in bad weather. And I hope Mrs. H. will soon return to take care of you and put the brake upon you when necessary.[72]

George prepared to go to Missouri to deal with the litigation over his property, fearing, rightly, "that Missouri things will cost more than they are worth."[73] He disliked having to go back.

. . . it will be cold and disagreeable and I have but few relations in that part of the world that has much atraction for me. I have been away so long that I have become weaned from all my former associations, both landmarks or persons, and all of my recollections of that place are not very pleasant, but rather sad than otherwise.[74]

George was appalled at the state of the country and his kin in Missouri. He longed for a "little nest" with Phoebe where the rest of the world would leave them alone.

They all look care worn and poor and miserable. . . . Find the country not improved but if possible in a worse condition than when we left the state and in no way as good a country as Cal. I am glad I left it though I have lost all I was worth. If I should lose this case, I will wash my hands of this part of the country and never will I trouble these people again, and hope we will live longer and better than those we have left behind, with all their ill-gotten gains. I think we live more in one year than these people do in 12 years. . . .

I do not wonder at your not wishing to see this part of the country again. I would not give an hour in Cal. for all that our friends have.

How would you like to come and live among them in Franklin again? The more I see, the more I want you back and let us settle down in a little nest and be as happy as possible and let the ballance of the world wag along as it pleases.

Love to the Boy and your good little self,

Yours ever,
George[75]

George resolved not to be such an easy touch for poor relatives and friends in the future. When he urged his cousin Joe Clark to send money to his aging and poor parents—which Phoebe had encouraged George to do—he said that Joe "burst into tears." He had not sent any money because he kept expecting to make some and had failed, and "knowing I was hard up and that I had done so much for his family, I supposed he could not ask me to do it." But again George helped out.

> I have been in dreadful bad luck for a year and a half. I told him I would raise the money some way and send it Monday if I had to leave off all comforts for myself. So you see that will be attended to and I shall trust to the gods to help me along. I do not fear if we have our health . . . we will have all we need, for the worst of my load is over. I must do for Aunt Clark as long as she lives. The Hearst boys must look out for themselves and all the rest of my poor kin and I assure you I am done helping persons as friends. 1874 shut down on that sort of thing.[76]

The suit to regain his property looked "doubtful." If he had returned sooner, when his former friend Inge was being examined in court, George believed he "could have made him give testimony more in my interest . . . he has sworn to things very contrary to my recollections of the facts and of course very detrimental to me in many particulars. But we may get them yet," he wrote Phoebe.[77] As it turned out, he did not.

By then Phoebe and Willie were in Paris, the culmination of their trip. She had made the tour in reverse of what most Americans did. She told Eliza,

> I am so glad we have taken the route we did. I have saved time and seen more. Nearly all Americans rush to Paris, and get bewildered with dress and gayety. I do not assume to be superior to the rest, but determined to not buy a single article for myself that I could do without. It only adds weight to the baggage and is more care. I want all new things when going home.[78]

In Paris Willie was put in school with the Lent boys—"He gets very lonely having nothing to do," said his mother. They lived at a *pension* and spoke only French at table. Mrs. Lent's unassuming American demeanor was a refreshing change on the Continent: "Mrs. Lent is just the same good woman. Paris and all the world could not change her. It does me good to see her."[79]

But George's mining affairs again were tenuous and his obligations substantial, particularly to his partners, Haggin and Tevis. Phoebe was preparing for belt-tightening. In the same letter she wrote George,

> . . . I fear everything is very dark for us, unless "Ontario" or "Cariboo" should prove very rich. I see no way to keep on any longer, for it will take about everything we have to pay Haggin and Tevis. It seems as if everything had gone wrong. I hope you will succeed in selling our place, horses and carriage and all, that will lighten the load some. Now is a good time to sell. We can board in Oakland and live much cheaper. I think you will find I am right about it. Let the money for the place be invested or put at interest for Willie and I, it may be all we will have to educate him.

But it was April in Paris and she wished to stay abroad until fall. Somewhat plaintively she asked George: "If we stay and anything should turn out good in your business, can I get some nice things to bring home? I mean if you can spare the money."

She stayed until October. It had been a year and a half since she and Willie had left San Francisco. In her April letter to George she wrote that she wanted to avoid grasping Missouri cousins en route back across the United States.

> There would be no pleasure in it and [it] would be very expensive, every 42nd cousin would expect a present because I had come from Europe. They imagine we have plenty of money. . . .

She filled one trunk with objects ordered by friends, had a flurry of dressmaking in Paris, bought more china and glass, and got the name of a customs officer in New York who might be sympathetic. She was becoming adept at clearing customs with quantities of purchases, which in time would arrive by the crateload. On the tenth of October she and Willie sailed from Liverpool on the Cunard Liner *Cuba*. It was a stormy voyage, with waves washing over the deck, but neither was prone to sea-sickness, an advantage for the many Atlantic crossings that would follow that first trip. On 23 October 1874 Phoebe wired George of their safe arrival.[80] They were going home, but they had opened Pandora's box.

George Hearst, possibly about the time he married Phoebe Apperson, when he was forty-two years old. *Courtesy of The Bancroft Library, University of California, Berkeley.*

The earliest known photo of Phoebe Apperson Hearst, ca. 1862, possibly in her wedding dress. *Courtesy of The Bancroft Library, University of California, Berkeley.*

Phoebe Hearst, ca. 1863, shortly after arriving in San Francisco as a pregnant bride. *Courtesy of the California Historical Society, San Francisco.*

Phoebe Hearst with infant son, William Randolph, born 1863 in San Francisco. *Courtesy of the* San Francisco Examiner.

William Randolph Hearst as a small boy. *Courtesy of The Bancroft Library, University of California, Berkeley.*

Phoebe Hearst, ca. 1874, San Francisco social leader. Note her increasingly elaborate hair styles and gowns as George Hearst's mining fortunes rose. *Courtesy of the California Historical Society, San Francisco.* Photo by Morse's Palace of Art, San Francisco.

Phoebe Hearst's parents, Drusilla Whitmire, who died at age 87 in 1904, and Randolph Walker Apperson, who died in 1900 at age 91; painting by Orrin Peck. *Courtesy, Phoebe Apperson Hearst Historical Society, St. Clair, Mo.*

Phoebe Hearst as a young woman in new finery. *Courtesy, Phoebe Apperson Hearst Historical Society, St. Clair, Mo.*

William Randolph Hearst, c. 1879, when he was about 16. *Courtesy of the California Historical Society, San Francisco;* photo, Morse's Palace of Art, San Francisco.

William Randolph Hearst as a youth. *Courtesy of the California Historical Society, San Francisco.* Photo, Thors, San Francisco.

Will Hearst at Harvard, ca. 1884. He was a natty dresser and *bon vivant.*
Courtesy of the California Historical Society, San Francisco. Photo, Pach
Brothers, Cambridge, Mass.

Phoebe Hearst tent-camping at San Simeon ranch, ca. 1884. Note photo of
Will, when at Harvard, on desk. *Courtesy of the Hearst San Simeon State
Historical Monument Archives.* Photo, Ron Chinitz.

George Hearst, ca. 1888, when a U.S. Senator. He died in office in 1891. *Courtesy of the California Historical Society, San Francisco.*

George Hearst, ca. 1888. *Courtesy of the California Historical Society, San Francisco.* Photo, George Prince, Washington, D.C.

Anne Apperson, Mrs. Hearst's niece, whom she raised. *Courtesy of the California Historical Society, San Francisco.*

Washington, D.C., house near Dupont Circle, ca. 1889, which Phoebe had remodeled when George became Senator. The house no longer stands. *Courtesy of the California Historical Society, San Francisco.* Photo, Frances Benjamin Johnston.

Washington, D.C., house; music room hung with Aubusson and Gobelin tapestries. *Courtesy of the California Historical Society, San Francisco;* photo, Frances Benjamin Johnston.

Mrs. Hearst's Hacienda Music Room, Pleasanton, California, filled with artifacts that she collected, including American Indian rugs and baskets (displayed in the rafters) which became part of the permanent collection at the University of California's Robert H. Lowie Museum of Anthropology, renamed in 1992 for Phoebe Apperson Hearst. *Courtesy of the California Historical Society, San Francisco.*

Will Hearst about the time when he was the young proprietor of the *San Francisco Examiner,* in his late twenties. *Courtesy of the California Historical Society, San Francisco.*

Phoebe Hearst showing off her jewelry, elegant gown, and fur. *Courtesy of the California Historical Society, San Francisco.* Photo, George Prince.

Entrance of the Hacienda del Pozo de Verona, showing wellhead ("pozzo") and distinctive mission-style architecture. The Hacienda became a country club after Phoebe's death and burned in 1969. *Courtesy, Bill Jamieson, Castlewood Country Club, Pleasanton, Calif.*

Dining room of the Hacienda, with table set for guests of Mrs. Hearst. *Courtesy, Bill Jamieson, Castlewood Country Club, Pleasanton, Calif.*

William Randolph Hearst portrait by Orrin Peck, his lifelong friend, painted in 1894 when Hearst was 31 and owner of the *San Francisco Examiner.* *Courtesy of the Hearst San Simeon State Historical Monument.*

Phoebe Hearst in lavish finery, jewels, and ermine cape. Note brooch and ring on left hand. *Courtesy of the California Historical Society, San Francisco.*

Phoebe Hearst in her Washington, D.C., house, ca. February 1897, when the National Congress of Mothers, forerunner of the Parent-Teacher Association, was founded. *Courtesy of the Phoebe Apperson Hearst Historical Society, St. Clair, Mo.*

8
Prosperity and Politics

They returned to a bleak financial front in San Francisco and a need for economy. The Ontario mine had not yet proven its worth and the Chestnut Street house and all its trappings, horses, and carriages had to be sold. It was a bitter experience for Phoebe, who suddenly discovered the difference between real friends and those "whose well-feigned previous regard for her . . . went no deeper than a time-serving interest," as historian H. H. Bancroft wrote in her lifetime.[1]

Willie went to four different grammar schools between 1874 and 1878, either because his mother kept moving him or because her precocious boy was asked to leave certain schools for being disruptive, demanding attention, and showing off. After a year and a half in the almost exclusive company of his adoring and tolerant mother, he must have had difficulty adjusting to the regimen of school and the society of his peers. He attended both private and public schools, including Lincoln Grammar School, which had a distinguished alumni in San Francisco. His father won a brief round, over his mother's mild protests, in favor of taking Willie out of private school. George thought that his son was not learning anything practical and should be exposed to the realities of life in public schools. Writing many years later of that crisis in his family, Willie related that his father did not "see anything particularly delicate" about his son, but rather that he had "more than the usual amount of misdirected youthful energy. . . . 'If the public schools are rough-and-tumble,' George thought, 'they will do him good. So is the world rough-and-tumble. Willie might as well learn to face it.' . . . Willie was distressed to see that his mother did not put up much of a fight in his behalf and in behalf of private tuition, but seemed readily to agree with Willie's father."[2]

So Willie went to public school. Mother, however, generally prevailed where Willie was concerned, and his tenure at public school was not long.

In 1875 the Ontario came in, bringing George the "proffit" that he had suspected lay in its shafts. The family again "went to housekeeping," renting a furnished house at Sutter and Jones, hoping that by the end of the year a new avenue would be completed to the North Beach section of town, where they had some property and thought of building a house. George was not adversely affected by the failure of the Bank of California (its owner, William Ralston, had walked into the Bay and drowned when it collapsed) but it had been a year of "disaster to California," as Phoebe wrote Eliza.

> . . . so many misfortunes, failures of banks, deaths of useful citizens, floods, fires and loss of life by sea. We did not lose by the failure of Bank of California but business was so much depressed that Mr. Hearst was a sufferer to a certain extent. . . . It was very sad about Mr. Ralston's death. He is greatly missed.[3]

To add to their misfortunes, the Virginia mine burned, Willie got a high fever and had to have his head shaved, and Phoebe was becoming resigned to having no more children.

> There seems to be no hope for any more babies in this family. The other day a friend remarked that it was better to have one splendid boy than several ordinary ones, though that does not reconcile me.[4]

In 1876 Phoebe and Willie went to the Centennial Exposition in Philadelphia, which she found "quite as fine as the Vienna Exhibition, all except the picture gallery" and the 257,000 other people who attended: "it was dreadful."[5]

They went to Boston and New York, where they called on Samuel J. Tilden, then running for President on the Democratic ticket. The call may have been prompted by George's offer to help the candidate financially or by a desire to obtain support for George's own political activities. Whatever the reason, Tilden was reported to have put his hand on Willie's head and told him to be a good Democrat like his father. That was certainly the boy's intention at the time.[6]

While in the East, Phoebe received word that Eppy planned to be married at the end of December. He had been courting a young English girl and working for George for one hundred dollars a month on the San Simeon ranch. Despite her plans to be home by Christmas in time for her brother's wedding, it took place without her. Missing the ceremony indicated her strained relations with her brother, with whom she had little in common. George gave the newlyweds one hundred dollars in gold and Phoebe brought the bride a necklace, locket, and earrings—"not elaborate but fine and good." At the time she and her parents were pleased with the match, but it was not to be a happy one.[7]

The Hearsts again gave up housekeeping and in 1877 boarded with friends on California Street near Powell ("they keep a nice table and are most excellent southern people") who were down on their luck. Phoebe dreamed of building her own house, though, which was not to happen in San Francisco. The Ontario was beginning to spew forth its riches. "It is considered a great success," she wrote Eliza, adding that Willie had learned a new song-and-dance routine.[8]

He also was up to his usual tricks. He got his pet rabbit drunk on champagne and wrote his father about it.

March 29, 1878

My dear Papa,
. . . I spent most of the vacation with Andrew at the springs and enjoyed myself very much. We killed a few rabbits and squirrels though game was very scarce. . . .
I wish I could spend a few days in the Black Hills, I would like to have a shot at some of those deer, elk and maybe grizzly bears I heard you talk about.
Bunny took some champagne last night and it made him tight; Mama was very much provoked with me but mad as she was she could not help laughing at him. He has learned to open his cage and now we can scarcely keep it fastened. . . .

With much love,
Your affectionate son,
W. R. Hearst[9]

It was time to think about putting Willie into a school that would prepare him for Harvard, for Phoebe had her sights set on her son's attending at that time the finest university in America. But first they indulged in a second trip to Europe, in 1879. This time they took a tutor, Thomas Barry, a recent graduate of the University of California. It was an opportunity for Barry to see Europe free of charge, but it was a trying trip because of Willie's rambunctiousness and penchant for pranks. He had a companion in crime on this trip—Eugene Lent—who came with his mother. Phoebe's energy and health were not at the level they had been on the previous trip. She had to take a rest cure at Carterets in the High Pyrenees.

Willie's letters to his papa conspicuously omitted his hijinks. He reported seeing the Coliseum by moonlight and reading Roman history while in Rome. "Whenever I read of anything especially interesting, I can see the exact spot where it happened," he told his father. He made more progress in six weeks of fencing lessons than most boys made in months, his mother proudly wrote George, and, "as usual, wanted all the relics I could carry away" at the site of Etruscan tombs near Orvieto.[10] To work off his energy, Willie went daily to local gymnasiums for exercise. But by the time they reached Paris, Willie was not inclined to wander through museums with his mother. He and Genie Lent devised their own entertainment, which defied his mother's imagination.

On their first day in Paris, where they stayed at a pension opposite the Tuileries Gardens, ("That was the nuts for Willie and Genie," Will later wrote), a gendarme brought them home by the ears for catching goldfish with bent pins in the fountains. Their mothers ordered them to stay in, which was a mistake. They got hold of the pension owner's Persian cat, and, while Willie held it, Genie tied a string around its tail. The cat was then the wildest animal Paris had seen for many a day:

> It went around Mme. Pincee's prim salon like a streak of blue lightning, only touching the side walls and the ceiling and going right through the Louis Quinze bric-a-brac cabinets. . . .
> It took Mme. Pincee's whole staff to catch that accelerated feline.[11]

The madame was somewhat mollified by the knowledge that the boys would be punished. They were locked into their room upstairs, yet another mistake. Willie had a little brass cannon and some powder, so they started shooting out the windows at pigeons. But Willie burned his hand while pouring powder down the muzzle of the cannon. Genie recommended that the best remedy was to put Willie's hand in a bowl of alcohol to remove the powderburn pain. That was almost a fatal mistake. Willie got the idea of having a fire at "sea" using a model ship that was on the mantle. They floated the ship in the alcohol, which they ignited, causing the bowl to crack and sending flaming alcohol all over the floor. Genie broke open one of the shutters, which fell through the glass roof of the pension kitchen, sending the chef to the hospital for three weeks. The Parisian pompiers arrived to put out the fire, dousing the guests on the floor below. And the Lents and the Hearsts were asked to leave.

The group moved to the Hotel d'Albe on the Champs Elysées, which was more elegant and ripe for the mischievous ruffians from the Wild West. Willie and Genie managed to buy a chasspot, an old gun that had a blank cartridge and a ramrod. Back at the hotel, they succeeded in firing the gun and driving the ramrod through the cherubs dancing on the plaster ceiling of the suite's drawing room. The concierge was summoned, and succeeded in pulling the whole ceiling down when he tried to dislodge the ramrod. It was an unexpected expense that cut short the trip to Europe.[12] Many years later, when expelled from France in 1930 for having published secret Anglo-French treaties, Willie considered that he had gotten off easily in 1879.[13]

Willie's youthful pranks presaged his later behavior and had their roots in early fears. He was afraid of being a sissy; he wanted to be a pirate. He later admitted that he knew he was a brat and a "mother's boy," but was "mighty glad of it." Beginning in his early teens to realize his own strength of personality and powers of persuasion, Willie developed a habit of humorous self-deprecation. It reflected in part guilt about his overbearing demeanor and his actions, of which he knew many disapproved. He did not curb his spirit or his determination, however, nor did he apologize once he had made up his mind to do or to get something. He realized that some people—such as his pal, Eugene Lent—secretly admired his abilities and imagination. But he later wrote of himself, "I really should have turned out better with such fine forebears. . . . If Willie had been more fertile soil, the harvest would have been more gratifying."[14]

In Europe in 1879, Willie was a terror for his tutor as well as his mother. Barry was charged with taking the boys sightseeing and to gymnasiums for exercise. He gave Willie lessons in the mornings and evenings, wrote letters for Phoebe, and accompanied her to museums and artists' studios in the afternoon. He wrote in his diary on 5 June 1879 that he would be glad to be relieved of his charges when the trip was cut short.

> It is decided that we must return in August. Deeply as I regret giving up my European tour as I had favored it, I heartily rejoice that I soon shall be relieved of my charges. In a few brief months, I will be myself once more.[15]

Barry told his diary that Willie was "convulsed" when the tutor responded in French as a joke to a "simpering Englishwoman" who asked directions to the Invalides, in front of which she was standing; that Willie preferred the Vatican Venus, the "one with bronze sheath or drapery" to all others in the Louvre; and that he was made to study extra half-hours for "morning transgressions." Willie was "rude to the [gymnasium] master with idiotic attempts at fun which highly amused Eugene." A high point for all of them was a Grand Prix horse race in the Bois de Boulogne, where they drank champagne and watched the impressionistic scene, which Barry described in his diary.[16]

Phoebe stayed at the Carterets and Barry took Willie and Eugene back to America. Willie had one of his colds, which he treated from a homeopathic medicine chest that his mother had given him and taught him how to use. He was still a shy boy in the presence of others. Barry wrote Phoebe that Willie "did not have 'gumshun' enough to kiss the lovely [French] madame [who packed his trunk] although I could see that she rather expected it of him. Why are the good things of this world thrown before those who cannot appreciate them?"[17]

The voyage home aboard the *Bothinia* was rough but it did not curb Willie's prodigious appetite and taste for champagne at a jolly table that included a clergyman who "convulsed us for half an hour with anecdotes relating to the cloth" and "five sober-looking Englishmen [who showed] themselves to be thoroughly pleasant and good-natured. . . . Our table was very gay . . . all sorts of practical jokes were played. . . . We were so uproarious as to attract the attention of the room," Barry told Phoebe.[18] On the Sunday before they reached New York, Willie put on a mimic performance that Barry described with amusement:

> He felt the spiritual influences of the day so strongly that he buttoned his coat up to his throat, donned my broad-brimmed straw hat, placed his spectacles solemnly upon his nose, dragged a seedy pair of gloves upon his hands, carefully bearing the finger ends, stuck his Latin Dictionary under his arm and walked about the saloon in a slow and solemn fashion to the huge delight of Eugene.
>   I don't know whether he went on deck, but I told him not to be irreverent nor to wound the feelings of religiously-minded persons.[19]

Otherwise, Barry wrote, Willie was "amiable," "docile" and "tractable," faithfully doing his lessons. He did not want to leave the ship when the journey ended. No wonder. It was to be his last taste of freedom for some time and the beginning of his first extended separation from his mother, who was by then manifesting the chronic illnesses for which she would continually seek cures. Whether the separation from her only child triggered the illnesses can only be speculated.

That fall Willie was sent to St. Paul's School near Concord, New Hampshire. He was sixteen years old and it was a devastating experience for him. Although he roomed with Will Tevis, son of his father's partner, he was dreadfully homesick and lonesome for his mother and father. His mother was still in Europe when his papa wrote Willie, sympathetically:

> November 4th, 1879
> My Dear Son,
>   . . . I am hapy to know you are well, and much pleased to learn you are doing so well in your class. But sorry you are so lonly and dont feel so hapy as you might. I know the managers are always a lot of persons that are not much company to boys and some times are not very careful of their wants. But I hope you will stand in like a man and take it as it comes, good and bad, until I see you and we will talk it over and we may be able to sift out some of the objectionable parts. . . .
>
> Your affectionat Father,
> G. Hearst[20]

Will, as he was by then called, stoically stuck it out but longed to be allowed to leave. Although he belonged to a cricket club, he was bored with the sport, preferring baseball. He was put off by the three High

Episcopal services that the boys were required to attend each day, and thought the religious persuasion hypocritical. His letters home were brave but plaintive. In his first month at St. Paul's, he wrote his mama,

> This is the best place to get homesick that I ever saw. Everything is so dull, I am just homesick all the time.
> I want to see you so bad. If I could only talk, how much more I could say than I can write in a letter.
> You only put a 15c stamp on your letter and it ought to be 25. I was very sorry to hear you had been sick. I suppose it was the effect of the waters and of Dr. Sarrand's big bill.[21]

Later, he complained of the food, his lack of spending money and the boring repetition of the regimen:

> We fast nearly all the time but we have a special fish and potato fast on Friday.
> We can only go into town once a month, and only have four dollars a month to spend and out of that have to come bats and balls and all such things.
> The Dr. [headmaster] spoke to me tonight about my studying so much, he says he will excuse me in some lesser study so that I will have more time for the more important, but I think I will try and take all. . . .
> I have settled into a state of perpetual homesickness, which although not quite so bad as when I first came is pretty bad and I think it will continue until I see you again. I never knew how much time there was in two months before and how long it could be strung out. . . .
> There is never anything new to write about in this place. Every day is like another except now and then there is only a substitution of Church for playtime and Sacred History for Latin, Greek, etc.
> I have received quite a number of letters from you, one with a paper cutting of proverbs, etc. I have read them and hope that I am the cork. Although the string that holds me down has not yet been broken, I hope it will before the end of the term.
> As I study so hard I knew you would not care if I took boxing for exercise so I have begun with a Professor of Gymnastics which is at school.
> On Saturdays I generally play baseball. . . .

> Your affectionate son,
> W. R. Hearst[22]

He became captain of a baseball team (it was the fourth best in the school), got no bad reports for sniggering in church or other infractions, and ranked in the middle of his class's scholastic ratings. He moved out of the room with "little Tevis," who went to bed at nine o'clock while Will had to stay up and study, which he did most of the time (nine hours a day) except when in church or on the baseball field. He also had a tutor. In another letter to his mother, he deplored the heavy religious hand on the place.

> I have really nothing to write about, but I feel that I would like to say something to you so bad that I must write. . . .
>
> We have a new minister almost every Sunday. Last Sunday we had a German, he talked "shus" like Gus Williams. Nearly half the boys in school got a report for laughing. Speaking of reports, I have not had one report yet. . . .
>
> The Sunday before we had a minister who kept forgetting his place and every time he did so he would repeat his text until he found it. . . .
>
> I believe that every old minister in this country comes here to practice on us, and shove off old sermons that no one else will listen to, and I would not either if I did not have to. The Dr. preaches pretty well but hollers too much. . . .
>
> It is almost like a catholic church. We have to bow whenever we come to Jesus Christ in the creed, and Dr. spoke the other day of the holy virgin.
>
> I think he is an old hypocrite and I know you will think so when you see him.[23]

He hoped his mother might spend the winter near him in Concord, but realized that she probably could not tolerate the twenty-five-degree-below-zero weather. At one point, he wrote her,

> I feel very despondent and lonely all the time and wish for you to come awful bad.
>
> It has been over a week since I received a letter, and I feel very anxious for fear you are sick.
>
> If you are I would rather know. It is the next thing to speaking with you to write and receive a letter.
>
> It is all I can do to keep from crying sometimes when how much alone I am and how far away you are. . . . the only thing that comforts me is that the time is getting shorter every day till you will be here. . . .
>
> Your loving son,
W. R. Hearst[24]

His concern for his mother's health prompted an outpouring of promises and confessions.

> If you get well, you shall never have anything to make you sick again, if I can help it. . . . I often think how bad I have been and how many unkind words I have said, and I am sure that when you come back I will . . . never be so bad again. . . .[25]

His grades were not outstanding, partly because he was "not quite up to the work," according to his tutor. A friend of the family wrote to encourage Will but also to admonish him to look to his future and to his

mother's health and hopes for her "dear boy." The threat of disappoint-
ing his family is heavy in the letter, which Will kept all his life.

> San Francisco
> Sept. 20, 1879

Dearest Willie:

. . . . I am sure, my dear boy, that your pride will prompt an effort commensurate with the task of not only making up the necessary deficiency but of
taking an honorable rank in your studies. . . . There is no reason, if your
health continues good, why you should not graduate at the head of your
class. . . .

Stoop to nothing that may ever mantle your cheek with a blush of shame—
to nothing that can compromise your own self-respect or your standing with
those who are laboring for your advancement—in a word, Willie, do nothing
that has not the unqualified sanction of both your own sense of right and
Mamma's approbation.

A single indiscretion has only too often blighted a whole after-life. . . .

Have the manliness to decline any proposition not entirely consistent with
what you know to be right. . . .

Your last promise to me was that you would do all in your power to make
Mamma's life as sunny and as happy as possible.

I am satisfied that but few years yet remain to her and you in a great
measure hold her weal or woe in your own hands and I conjure you, dearest
Willie, to lay up for yourself no bitter recollections of thoughtlessness,
neglect or cruel selfishness.

Let no unguarded words or act add to the heavy burden that her heart
already bears. . . .

Think for a moment what life would be to you without her and then
consider how much more thoughtful she has always been for your happiness
and welfare than you possibly could be for hers. . . .

You and I know better than any one else what her struggle, aim and
ambition have been since you first had your being, and I cherish the fond
hope that she will yet realize in her only boy all for which she has so yearned
and for which she has so often wept and prayed. . . .

> William A. Robertson
> 2701 Bush St.[26]

Will himself later wrote that St. Paul's was "a very nice school—much
nicer than Willie. So Willie was thoroughly unhappy there." He was
shown Harvard "where he might wind up if he did not mend his ways—
and he did not mend his ways."[27]

For his mother, Will's letters from St. Paul's were painful. She also
deplored the separation. Will was growing tall and she knew he would
no longer be her little boy. She had written Eliza that he grew "so
rapidly he will soon be a man, then how I shall miss his childhood."[28]
She realized that she would no longer have her favorite escort with her,
and that she would have to find other companions and diversions. But

the bond between them was fixed so strongly that neither would ever really sever it.

Phoebe returned from her European cures in November, for the first time accompanied by a maid. She was weak and frail.[29] She went immediately to visit Will and took him to Cambridge to see Harvard. She resisted his implorings to take him home, although she arranged to have him with her in New York during the holidays. He liked visiting New York. He developed (so he said) another one of his sore throats and was allowed to stay out of school until March.

Phoebe did not return to California until the spring of 1880. Will was left to finish his term and return to St. Paul's the next year. The cold, bleak New England winter was broken only by a few trips to New York, which he spent with Orrin Peck's uncle, a Mr. Hughes. On one occasion, his demanding qualities manifested themselves. After politely asking if he could spend the holidays with Hughes and getting no answer, he fired off a telegram, making his request more of a demand: "For God's sake, please ask me to New York."[30] He got his way.

His mother found her diversions in two ways: a busy social life and charitable activities. In September 1880 the Hearsts moved from the Baldwin Hotel to a leased house at 1315 Van Ness Avenue, on millionaires' row.[31] Shortly after that they bought an imposing mansion at 1501 Van Ness Avenue. They built a new wing for an art gallery, but somehow the house was never quite to Phoebe's liking, although it was the first of several large mansions that she would own.[32]

Phoebe had a continuous string of houseguests and gave large parties, introducing several new kinds of entertainments, such as dancing parties for unmarrieds and a New York-style luncheon party. A society writer said:

> Mrs. Hearst introduced the New York-type of monster luncheon party, with 20 to 25 tepoys disposed around the room, the place looking like a restaurant of the most unexceptional tone such as Beaconfield would write up.
> She inaugurated a gay dancing party for unmarrieds only, which was a new idea and a whopping success. She began a series of regular Saturday night dinners and gave a smart reception and dance for Lord and Lady Waterlow.[33]

Phoebe knew that her invitations were coveted and she liked that. She issued them to people who amused and interested her, not to the insipid social set whose fair-weather friendship and insincerity had hurt her in hard times. She showed a fondness for startling her guests with pleasure and transforming the environment for entertainments, filling the house with walls of flowers hung on fishnets and three-foot-deep banks of violets. She presided over a French-style intellectual *salon* in what had become a bustling city of contrasts, where wealthy citizens attended operas while sailors were still "Shanghaied" on the waterfront and the Chinese population, which supplied most of the city's domestic servants, was becoming a "problem." It was a time of political and intellectual energy in San Francisco. Isadora Duncan danced on the beach, and a local politician, Dennis Kearny, led a campaign to rid the place of the "oriental problem." A lawlessness reminiscent of the Gold Rush still existed.

One night, in front of the Hearst's house, which was guarded by two stone lions, a sullen mob gathered and was urged by its leader to climb up and tear down George Hearst's lions, considered symbols of predatory wealth. Calmer voices prevailed and the lions stayed. But Phoebe was angry, hurt, and astonished. At that moment, she considered leaving the city and never returning.[34]

But Phoebe stayed, next to George and all he provided her. And, at the age of forty, with her only child away in school, she began to devote a large amount of time and energy to charitable activities. Her wealth now certain, she began to give it away. At her parties and through friends, she discreetly learned about young men and women who showed promise of talents but who lacked sufficient money to advance them. She began a pattern of quietly making the necessary funds available, more often than not anonymously. The happy recipients, however, often children of acquaintances who were widows with limited means, generally learned the identity of their benefactress and were grateful that Phoebe knew they would be embarrassed to accept charity publicly.

Those years saw the genesis of what would become a far-reaching personal kind of philanthropy. It began modestly but had a theme that was to become constant: support of education to enable people to help themselves. Phoebe lent support to one of the first settlement houses in San Francisco—in the South Park section—and to orphan asylums and free kindergartens. She became president of the board of directors of the San Francisco Homeopathic Hospital, a training school for women physicians that was staffed by women. A lifelong devotee of homeopathic treatment, she presided over a merger with the Hahnemann Medical College in 1883.

Phoebe was not alone in her charitable efforts since most wealthy women and widows of the West were substantial givers to needy causes, competing for the prestige that accompanied their generosity. No one understood the dynamics of charitable competition better than Mrs. Sarah B. Cooper, the driving, devoted founder of the Golden Gate Kindergarten Association. She counted among her board members the wealthiest women in San Francisco—Mrs. George Hearst, Mrs. Leland Stanford, Mrs. Charles Lux, Mrs. William Crocker, and many others.

The concept of free kindergartens for poor children who otherwise would be running unsupervised in the streets while their parents worked to make ends meet was new in America in 1879 when Sarah Cooper's First Congregational Church Bible Class organized the Golden Gate Kindergarten Association and opened a school in the heart of San Francisco's "Barbary Coast." It was the second kindergarten west of the Rockies.

Cooper's "liberal" concept of helping children through "preventive" charity was considered unorthodox and viewed with suspicion by the Presbyterian leaders of the church where she initially began her kindergarten as a bible class. The church deacons demanded that the class be disassociated from the church and dismissed Cooper from the congregation. A full-scale heresy trial ensued, which Cooper used to her advantage. She moved her class to the First Congregational Church and circulated a pamphlet portraying her opponents as narrow-minded bigots and herself as a true Christian trying "to do good among the neglected little children of the city." Public opinion favored Cooper and a year after the trial, contributions to her kindergarten doubled.[35]

But the very notion of kindergarten was controversial. It took children away from their mothers and homes at an early age. And it justified play as an educational and training tool. Mrs. Cooper's contention was that "children too young to learn to read and write can greatly benefit by schooling adapted to their age level needs." The proponents were following the teachings of Frederick Froebel, who had founded the first kindergarten in 1837 in Germany.

Kate Douglas Wiggin had opened the first one in San Francisco in 1878 with $130 raised by Felix Adler of New York (leader of the Free Religious society and the Society for Ethical Culture) on a visit to the city that year. She had been trained by German educator Emma Marwedal of "The Froebel Union" of New England, who in 1876 had opened a kindergarten teacher-training school in Los Angeles. (Phoebe became her principal patron, providing Miss Marwedal with a pension in her later years.)

The demand for Mrs. Cooper's kindergarten exceeded all expectations and two more were opened in 1880. The following year, in 1881, Sarah Cooper happened to be on a "chance errand" to Phoebe (it may not have been so inadvertent as she later described it). She wrote of the meeting:

> The mission had been accomplished and the leave-taking was going on. "I wish to ask you about the Kindergarten work, in which I feel a deep interest," was the genial and earnest suggestion [of Mrs. Hearst]. A brief, very brief recital of the work, and the pressing need for increased facilities for many children who were turned away for want of room, elicited the prompt and

tender response: "Oh! they must be cared for! I will gladly sustain a Kindergarten for these little ones."

It was only a few words; only a moment's interchange, but the results of
that brief interview will last through endless ages. For, from that time . . . the
Hearst Kindergarten has been fairly thronged with little children, and they
have been nurtured and trained into ways of goodness.[36]

Phoebe's love for children had found an outlet. She would soon have
several hundred to care for. She believed in the purposes of kindergarten—to rescue what Sarah Cooper called "these little, neglected,
sad-faced, prematurely old, weary-eyed little ones in the purlieus of
vice and crime"—and to set them on paths toward being productive
citizens by giving them gentle care and guidance in pleasant surroundings. Froebel had said, "The plays of childhood are the buds of the
whole future life." It was a philosophy dear to Phoebe's heart and
experience with her own son. "It teaches how to work, what to do, and
not to be ashamed of work. . . . Mrs. Hearst lays great emphasis upon
these facts," Mrs. Cooper wrote in her 1890 annual report.[37]

Newspapers took up the cause and editorially championed it, noting
that the movement "continues to spread and bloom and bear fruit
through all the harrowing and raking it gets from the uncomprehend-
ing, who try to limit it to the region of modern fads." Kindergartens
would "effectually make hoodlumism a thing of the past" and provide
the solution to "the great problem that has puzzled social philosophers
and philanthropists for generations—how to get at and control the
source of the streams of crime, disease, misery, and degradation that
rise in a thousand places. . . . The Kindergarten idea is to begin earlier
and to teach the endangered little ones how to walk in the paths of
pleasantness and peace, so that they will never slip at all."[38]

After the "chance" encounter with Sarah Cooper, Phoebe offered in
1881 to finance an entire kindergarten. She was the first of the Golden
Gate Association's patrons to do so, and began a trend of patronage of
kindergartens that were named for their benefactors. The first Hearst
Free Kindergarten was on Union Street in San Francisco's North Beach
district, or "Latin Quarter," as it was called for its population of Italians
and other immigrants. Jane Stanford followed suit on the death of her
only son, Leland, Jr., in 1884, as did others. In time there would be
seven Hearst Kindergartens and five Stanford kindergartens in San
Francisco. Mrs. Stanford established an endowment of one hundred
thousand dollars to perpetuate the kindergartens after she was gone.
Phoebe and others also provided endowments that allowed the Golden
Gate Kindergarten Association to survive to the present day with the
same basic objectives that Sarah Cooper set forth and that Phoebe and
others initially endorsed with their dollars. The free kindergartens were

so successful that merchants at the Produce Exchange claimed the street gamins no longer were stealing their fruit and vegetables, and they made a voluntary contribution that underwrote another kindergarten in the produce district. Four other commercial organizations followed that example—merchants, lawyers, insurance and real estate brokers—each sustaining a kindergarten bearing the name of their organization. Sarah Cooper was quick to appreciate the value of public relations to generate support for her cause and sent out annual reports by the thousands, worldwide, which were widely published. She credited the press as second only to "wise and liberal-hearted men and women" for the "rapid growth of the kindergarten work in San Francisco."[39]

The movement did not stop there. By 1896 it was estimated that 287 free kindergartens had been organized throughout the United States and in other countries as a direct result of the Golden Gate example. In addition, a free Normal Training School for Kindergarten Teachers was established from which more than two hundred teachers had graduated by 1896. They were in great demand, and Phoebe was a major supporter of the training effort, believing that carefully trained teachers were the key to the success of the movement. Small minds should not be guinea pigs nor kindergarten places for experiments by untrained young women, she strongly felt. She also led a movement to have the kindergartens integrated into public school systems[40] and to provide kindergartens for Afro-Americans. She advocated and supported a training course for black women and she underwrote a kindergarten for black children in Washington, where she also supported several kindergartens for white children. The free kindergartens were used as demonstration classes for the training school. A newspaper in 1901 stated:

> Among the philanthropic work of the day ought to be mentioned the kindergartens established through Mrs. Hearst's generosity for the little negro children in the poorer parts of Washington. They have struggled against a great race prejudice but they are doing a wonderfully good work. . . .
> Mrs. Hearst is also associated in an Eastern movement, which promises much in the way of practical results. . . .
> After all, sometimes you can trust women to get at a practical solution of a difficult problem. It seems very sensible of them to suggest that the only practical solution of the race problem will be found in the homes of the people.[41]

For while the kindergartens were designed to prepare children for training in trades, their influence was also intended to spill over into the homes and lives of the poor and downtrodden. To that end the mothers were asked to attend Mothers' Meetings, where they were taught various home economics skills, health care, and training of children. Getting to the roots of the problem of poverty was the larger objective, with which Phoebe had great sympathy. Said *The Evangelist* magazine in 1896:

> What wonder that the children love the bright, beautiful, sunny kindergarten, full of light and joy? What wonder that they take something of the spirit of the kindergarten back to their shadowed homes in their bright faces, cheery smiles, and their loving, tender hearts? These little hands are the tendrils by which many an erring, sin-fettered parent will climb heavenward.[42]

The mothers in Phoebe's Latin Quarter school were of such disparate nationalities that English was not the common language, and they at first came to the meetings reluctantly. Later they were enthusiastic participants, although they were not given the same "lessons" that other mothers received from the kindergarten teachers. The international mothers (some thirty-five nationalities were represented) participated in entertainments and such activities as paper-folding and cutting, raffia work, and clay modeling. Still, it was an aspect of the movement that Phoebe believed was one of the most valuable, a forerunner of another movement with which she would be associated, the founding of the Parent-Teacher Association.

The kindergartens so interested Phoebe that she had continued to offer support for more classes. In 1889 she wrote Mrs. Cooper from Washington:

> . . . I am very anxious to take in the twenty-five little applicants. I will gladly supply the funds, if you can arrange for the room. No doubt the number will be increased twenty-five more before the end of the year. I shall be glad and thankful if I can help them. I do not know the cost of the sittings, or the preparation of a suitable room, but if you will let me know, I will send the amount. . . .
>
> I agree with you that this is a blessed work, and the love of human hearts is a priceless boon to anyone. There is nothing sweeter than the love of little children.
>
> In regard to the disposal of the large doll—in the fall, when entertainments are being given, no doubt it can be disposed of to advantage, and the sum appropriated to the little necessities of the sick and suffering among the children.
>
> With fervent well-wishes for great success in the good work,
>
> > I am ever most sincerely yours,
> > Phoebe A Hearst[43]

The doll referred to was a creation dressed by a European princess for a charity fête in Washington. Phoebe had purchased it and sent it to the Kindergarten Association to be sold as a fundraiser. She took a great interest in the subject of education and during a trip to Europe in 1889, visited Froebel's widow and niece.

Hearst Free Kindergarten No. 2 opened in August 1889 and a third opened the following year, after Phoebe wrote Mrs. Cooper:

> I feel that I would like to support another Kindergarten. If you will kindly select a suitable locality and rooms I shall be very glad to have another group of little ones. I am most anxious to do this. I am satisfied that money expended in this way, for little children, accomplishes more good than in almost any other way. . . . I have thought a great deal, during the last few weeks, about this matter, and am quite decided to have No. 3. I find great happiness in caring for these little children. . . . Let me know when you find the desired locality. I hope it may be very soon.
>
> Yours affectionately,
> Phoebe A. Hearst[44]

The kindergartens served about sixty children each, ages two-and-a-half to six, and operated at a cost of some six hundred dollars a year. The "graduates" proved to be better-than-average students once they entered public school. The teachers prided themselves on the fact that often the most unruly ruffians became serious and obedient students, and at least one went on to become an attorney of much promise.[45]

In 1902 Phoebe built, at a cost of forty thousand dollars, a kindergarten school at 560 Union Street in San Francisco's North Beach, where the seven Hearst classes were housed. The building was considered a model of its kind, the finest kindergarten school in the world. Phoebe had made a careful study of kindergarten needs and her ideas were incorporated in the design and construction. It included small steps for toddlers, child-size plumbing fixtures, tables and chairs designed at Pratt Institute in Brooklyn, New York, flowers and plants at the windows, sliding partitions, a steam heat system that allowed the atmosphere to be entirely changed in a few minutes without opening doors or windows, and a sandbox filled with white beach sand from Monterey. The stone and red-tiled building stood out in a neighborhood that the association's 1903 annual report noted was "occupied chiefly by crowded tenements."[46]

Phoebe also supplied Thanksgiving and Christmas feasts for the children and on at least two occasions enticed George to attend the festivities. At a Thanksgiving dinner in 1888, his "face fairly glowed with pleasure as he watched with eager interest the movements of the little children," one press report said. His great, gangling frame moved among the three hundred youngsters, and he took special delight in refilling cups with milk and loading up plates with second helpings of cranberry sauce, saying: "I haven't forgotten how it was when I was a boy. I want to see these children filled full. . . . That little fellow is not full yet. This will never do—This is Thanksgiving [and] Thanksgiving comes but once a year."[47]

George became intrigued with the possibilities of helping needy youngsters improve their lot through care and training for useful work, which he and Phoebe concluded was a productive way to spend their money. In 1890, Phoebe surprised the Golden Gate Kindergarten by announcing that she would endow a Manual Training School where children over six years old, after graduating from the Free Kindergartens, could learn the arts and industries. She intended to pattern it after the North Bennet Street Industrial School of Boston (established in 1880) and others that she saw in Europe. Like the free kindergartens, she hoped that the vocational school would be integrated into the public school system and regarded with respect, which such schools had not been in the past. Despite her long-contemplated and best intentions, the manual school did not come to fruition. But Phoebe's dedication to the kindergarten cause was lifelong and genuinely inspired by a love for children and the belief that they could be set on happy and productive paths if channeled at an early age.

But Sarah Cooper's involvement in kindergarten work was to end in 1896 with her tragic death, which, like many actions of her sixty-two years, caused shock in the community. Her disturbed, pock-marked daughter for some years had shown signs of mental illness, which Sarah feared was congenital from her husband, who had killed himself. The daughter, Harriet, suffered from insomnia and nervousness and in her late thirties bgan to express resentment and hostility toward her protective mother. In 1895 Harriet and Sarah helped arrange a lecture tour in California for suffrage leader Anna Howard Shaw. Harriet became emotionally and passionately attached to Shaw, with whom she exchanged love letters. Shaw withdrew from the relationship. In depression and anger, Harriet threw her energies into a trial of the Coopers' minister, who was accused of sexual indiscretions with his female assistant. Harriet and Sarah testified against the minister as a "sexual monster," for which they were publicly hissed at the trial and socially ostracized. Harriet, then forty, grew increasingly agitated, complained of great pain in her head, and begged for opiates. Sarah sent her to a sanitarium for a "rest," but soon brought her home against the advice of doctors. Harriet began to attack her mother physically and to talk of suicide. On 11 December 1896, eleven years to the month after the suicide of her husband, Sarah Cooper was found dead with her daughter in a room full of gas. Newspapers speculated that Harriet had either waited for her mother to sleep or had subdued her by force, then turned on the gas.

Sarah had a premonition of the death, writing in her will, "If my daughter should take my life, I want the world to know that she was not to blame." Phoebe sent a tribute to the *Examiner*, saying, "Children have lost a wise and loving friend in Mrs. Cooper, and the needy and heartbroken a helpful and sympathetic spirit. All classes have been touched and benefited by her influence."[48]

George's interests, meanwhile, lay more along political lines. By the 1880s the Democratic Party in California needed a mouthpiece and George offered to buy it one. He thought of it—the southern-leaning, conservative San Francisco *Examiner*, which had been struggling along for some years under different names—as another "property." As the *Democratic Press* it had advocated secession for the South, and when President Lincoln had been assassinated, the paper's offices had been wrecked by a mob. It had been forced to change its name to the *Daily Examiner* in order to resume publication.[49]

On 30 October 1880 the evening *Examiner* was sold to "W. T. Baggett and Company"—a front for George Hearst, who thought that his political pals would help foot the bill for it. Some said that George got it in partial payment for a debt owed him by its principal owner. At any rate, George found himself the sole owner of a daily newspaper. Knowing nothing about the newspaper business, he put his lawyer and friend, Clarence R. Greathouse, in charge as manager, and the *Examiner* was changed to a morning paper.[50]

George himself later described the purchase this way:

> As to my connection with the *Examiner* newspaper, I may say that I always took a great interest in politics, and when some of my friends came to me and stated that the party needed a paper and offered to subscribe something toward starting one, I said, "There is no use in doing that. Why not buy up the old *Examiner*?" There was never any disgrace attached to it. However, when it came to paying for it, I found that I had to put in all the money myself. I knew no more about a newspaper than the man in the moon, and when I looked over the property, I said this looks very like a quartz mill to me, and it will take a great deal of money to manage it. The boys said they would attend to that, and turn it into a morning paper and it would not cost more than 10 or 12 thousand dollars. It ran on for some two or three years, and I kept sinking money in it all the time, until I found that it was worth 65 thousand dollars less than nothing. I believe that I lost some three or four thousand dollars a month by it.[51]

Phoebe was skeptical about the acquisition as a business venture, but George sought to reassure her that it would "be good property" in time. She also observed an unusual interest in the paper on the part of Will, who expressed a desire to work on it—after he graduated from college, of course. George, looking to Will's future and understanding the power of the press, wrote Phoebe from Arizona, where he was exploring mining properties in December 1882:

> I think the *Examiner* will be good property after this [and we?] will get all of the patranige, so you see we have some good luck. Some people are very jelous and some talk of starting another democratic paper. I say go ahead, they will soon go [under?]. It can't be done by talk, as we know, and but few will put up the coin.
>
> I hope the Boy will be able, as I think he will, to take charge of the paper soon after he leaves college, as it will give him more [power?] than anything else.[52]

Phoebe could not have foreseen at that moment the long-range involvement that she would have in the publishing business. If she had she would have rued the day that her husband brought a newspaper into the family. But, although she had doubts about the wisdom of the enterprise, she agreed to help in the undertaking. When the Hearsts undertook anything, it often became a family project, and, while they might disagree on how to proceed, they nevertheless offered one another advice. Writing Phoebe in December 1884, when she was in the East, George asked her to find out about "the newspaper men":

> . . . I have been quite lonsam at all times. Home is no home, it is only a stoping place. . . . What is a home without a wife and baby? . . . I want to see the Boy very much, so anxious for him to get through . . . I think I am almost a tramp. No place to go and no place to stay. . . .
>
> Can you find out about the newspaper men? What we want is a man that understands the press business from the bottom up and all the way through, so as to be able to take full charge of the paper and direct the business in every department, also the business part, or rather the financial part also.
>
> We know such a man is hard to get. But he must understand and know just what is wanted to get out the paper at the least possible expence. The financial or business can be more easly filed [filled] and can be got here, no doubt.
>
> Or course, this man [may] be of use if he is first class editorial writer. . . . But if the paper is not run at the least possible expence, you can see it must be a failure, no matter how good a paper may be brought out.
>
> First is good circulation, 2nd a good paper and 3rd to know how and get the paper out for the least possible cost. And to do that the man must know just how many men he wants. . . . In other words, does this man know all about the business from the tipe room to the press until the money is paid in? Or is he only a strong writer?
>
> And will he come out here and if so, for how much a month, and will he want an interest in the paper? Circulation 16,000 dayleys + 18,000 weekleys. . . .
>
> . . . Perhaps Will can attend to it.[53]

Will in 1881 had talked his parents into bringing him home from St. Paul's. He was a tall, attractive eighteen-year-old, and he had discovered girls. He wrote letters to an Anna Hamilton, who read one "aloud in a tremulous voice which was extremely touching in one so young," her mother wrote Phoebe. He was still shy about kissing women: "I enjoyed the kiss he gave me at Oakland, even if in his hurry he did plant it on my nose with a fury which threatened <u>dislocating</u> that valuable member," Mrs. Hamilton added.[54]

He was experiencing the first flutterings of the heart for the opposite sex. About that time, he was taken with Sybil Sanderson, the daughter of a California Supreme Court Justice; her mother and Phoebe were friends and encouraged the match. Sybil was acceptable socially and very beautiful, but selfish, cold, and determined to lead her own life. An engagement may have been announced, although Will's cousin, Anne Apperson, believed that the two were not actually engaged.[55] For whatever reasons, Sybil was whisked off to Europe to study voice. Will was devastated. In an undated letter to his mother, he exhibited that capacity for humorous self-deprecation and honesty—as well as a way with words—that was becoming characteristic of his relationship with his mother.

> On the train yesterday I saw the prettiest girl I have ever yet seen. Every love from Sybil to Miss Henderson sank unheeded into the dim mists of obscurity when the fair unknown beamed upon me. She smiled and when she smiled my poor intoxicated little heart butted up against my ribs in a way that, I fear, has permanently injured it—flattened it out probably till it looks like a Dutch pancake.
>
> Why can't a fellow go through life without being continually led like a lamb to the slaughter, a sacrifice to beauty? Why can't he see the prettiest girl <u>first</u> so that all others forever after will seem tame and homely and he may rest in peace without being at the necessity of repeatedly repairing an organ which is as often mutilated again? I feel, however, that I have at last seen the prettiest of girls and from this time on will probably never be troubled again. Whether my battered heart will ever resume its wonted shape is a different matter, but after mature deliberation, I have concluded that I should not be surprised if it did. It's rather elastic as a rule. And in that respect also it is <u>very</u> much like a Dutch pancake.[56]

Also in 1881 George bought a ranch in a valley forty miles east of San Francisco, near Pleasanton, where he wanted to raise race horses. The property would be the site of Phoebe's estate in future years. But their immediate concern was Will's higher education. He entered Harvard in the fall of 1881. In honor of his departure, his mother gave an elegant dinner party, "the house looking pretty as ever, the veiled lady in marble flanked by Mrs. Hearst and her son, looking superb and somewhat crowded in the alcove," a society writer reported.[57] Phoebe took Will to Cambridge and installed him in a suite of three rooms at Matthews Hall, spending four thousand dollars on furniture to set him up in style.[58]

En route to Europe in 1882, she visited Will, who was the life of the party and the source of "much amusement" at the sailing on 18 January 1882. But it was a sad day for her. She wrote in her diary, "What a hard day this has been, leaving my dear boy, going so far away. We sailed at 3 p.m. Dear Will was brave and kept trying to make us laugh."[59]

She felt "weary and dull" and wanted to sleep all the way across. She confessed, "How I miss my dear Will. He is indeed a part of my life."[60]

In her party was a pretty, ambitious young girl who aspired to be an actress and who would soon become more a part of Phoebe's and Will's lives than Phoebe would like. Her name was Eleanor Calhoun and her ancestors included South Carolina politician and two-time Vice-President, John C. Calhoun of Phoebe's ancestral hometown, Abbeville.[61]

Will's life at Harvard offered new diversions and amusements. Quick to learn, he mistakenly thought that he could get by easily in his studies. He devoted a good deal of attention to extracurricular activities and was not inclined to adhere to the discipline and rules that were de rigueur at Harvard. He had developed a certain scorn and intolerance, instilled by his parents in their different ways, to stuffiness and class snobbishness, considering them insincere and unnecessary for social success. He was, after all, a child of the frontier and the West, and he was proud of it and of his parents. He had nothing to be ashamed of. He also was as rich or richer than many of his classmates, which he flaunted as a way of getting attention and justifying equality with his peers. His mother made sure that he had plenty of spending money to insure him a place in the right clubs and circles. She would come to regret her open-handedness with Will's allowance.

He wrote his "Mummer" and father often, in letters full of humor. George offered recommendations for his son's curriculum—Spanish and engineering, so that Will could take over his father's expanding mining and ranching businesses in Mexico and the Southwest. George could see no earthly use for Latin and Greek, a point on which Will agreed. Discussing his Harvard courses, Will wrote his father on 30 December 1882, after spending Christmas in New York with his mother:

> I was pleasantly surprised by a letter from you, and I suppose it was for me although you signed yourself "Your loving husband."
> You spoke about my studying Spanish and Engineering, so I will give you a sketch of what I am doing this year as the work for Freshmen is prescribed. . . .
> Latin—   three hours per week

Greek—   "   "   "   "
German—   "   "   "   "
Conic sections—two hours per week
Physics—   "   "   "   "
Algebra—one hour per week

And then we have, every Monday afternoon, a lecture on Greek and Roman writers and their works. . . .

To prepare these you spend as much time as you consider necessary. . . . So you see, a fellow can study or loaf just as he pleases and if he manages to skim through his examinations all right, nothing is said. It is hard to get very high marks at Harvard without regularly "grinding" for the examinations are three hours long. . . . I think a fellow ought to get an average of 70% and that is what I shall try for. . . .

I shall drop Latin and Greek next year and take something else in their place. I don't believe they do you any good. . . .

Next year I can choose whatever studies I please and will take Spanish and whatever else you wish. . . .

You are a daisy to promise [to come to visit]. Don't you remember that you said you were coming to New York to spend Xmas with your Billy Buster? Well, I didn't much believe it then, but I wish you would come on and see the College. I saw Will Crocker the other day. It's lucky that he went to Yale. He will do as a Yale man, but you could not find him at all at Harvard. . . .

> Your affectionate son,
> W. R. Hearst[62]

Will and his mother shared a fond resignation to George's unpretentious styles and manner. After one trip with George, Will aptly described his father's no-nonsense ways:

Dear Mummer,

If variety is the spice of life, I am at present enjoying the most highly flavored existence imaginable. There are a brace of twins on board, sweet blue-eyed, red-headed Irish twins. There is no mistaking the nationality of the darlings for "they're up all night till broad daylight a skipping the tra-la-la-loo" and then one is named Mike and the other Dan. Micky and Dan, think o' that will yez and moind the trouble I'm having.

I left Papa last night at Sacramento without having talked very much for we sat most of the way wrapped in gloom and staring woefully at each other. The silence was once disturbed by a real estate broker who wanted to sell some land, but Papa excused himself in rather a novel manner. He took the man gently by the arm and assisted him out of the section, remarking in a very audible undertone that if there was anything he did despise it was a blanked impertinent real estate broker. The broker retired in confusion and Papa relapsed into silence and gloom.

. . . I hope Miss Crockett will forgive me for having sacrificed one or two of the candies to silencing those awful twins. By the way, doesn't it strike you that there is a curious antithesis between twins and preserved pears, for, mark you, while the pears are preserved let us hope that the twins will be everlastingly jammed! Ha, ha! . . . Well, hoping they'll grow up and subscribe to the Examiner, I drink their health and close my letter. . . .[63]

Will had two California friends with him at Harvard, Eugene Lent and Jack Follansbee. The three cut a merry swath through the beer halls of Cambridge and Boston, once hiring a cab to bring them back to campus from the city and throwing oranges at policemen en route.[64] Will's expertise at pranks did not fail him at Harvard. He once threw custard pies at performers in a Boston theater. He wore flashy clothes and plaid suits and kept a pet alligator that he delighted in getting drunk on champagne.[65] His behavior would not have pleased his mama but he was not out of the ordinary for a rich college kid.

Phoebe's influence prevailed in another way, however. Will was not a big drinker. His father's fondness for a good bottle of whiskey perhaps had a negative effect on Will since he saw how it affected his mother.

Will also had a high-pitched voice that startled people unfamiliar with it (much like another six-footer, Charlemagne). Although his voice box may have been damaged by frequent colds and sore throats as a child, it is more likely that his voice was congenital. His voice never changed to a lower register, and as a grown man and later powerful editor-in-chief of a vast publishing empire, he once was mistaken by one of his own editors, who thought the Chief was a crank woman caller ordering the front page remade.[66]

Will's best friend, Jack Follansbee, was forced by financial reasons to leave Harvard in 1883, and Will made an impassioned plea to his father to give his pal a job. He did not want to lose track of Jack and in fact made him a part of his family, much like the brother that he did not have. In April 1883 he implored George not to "throw . . . aside" his letters and to help Jack out. He also speculated on what lay ahead on "the road of life." It presaged his power of editorial persuasion.

46 Matthews
Cambridge, Massachusetts
April 19, 1883

Dear Father,
    The letter I am about to write is full of importance to me and I hope you will read it carefully and consider well what I have to say. . . .
    . . . as I can't talk with you, I want you to pay strict attention to this letter and to do what I ask just as if I were there to keep reminding you of it; and don't throw this aside, and never think of it again and don't neglect it for a few days even, for I shall anxiously await a reply.
    Jack Follansbee, whose father you must have known in early days and whose mother Mama is well acquainted with, is obliged to leave college and go into business. I do not know the reason why he is compelled to leave, but I think it is through the financial embarrassment of his uncle Jim Keene who is supporting Jack here at college. . . .
    Jack's college course has been very successful and his habits and deport-

ment have been such as to make him a favorite not only with the fellows but with the professors as well, so that there is general regret at his departure.

He is in the class above me but has been very kind—giving me good advice and the benefit of his experience. In fact, he has been the best friend I have had in College so far, and I shall be sadder to see him go than I would have been at the departure of any number of fellow freshmen.

But he must go, he says, and make some money, and this is where I want you to help him. He is a splendid fellow, Papa, and in aiding him you will be aiding yourself, for I don't know where you can find a young man with the brightness, the sound sense and the pluck that Jack Follansbee has.

He is a tall, strong fellow with an honest, attractive countenance and he is highly honorable and proud, for when a wealthy classmate proposed to let him have enough money to complete his college year, he refused, saying that he had enough education to give him a good start and he must now make some money. And it takes a good deal of courage to leave college in the middle of a successful course, and to refuse the money with which he might stay and complete it.

Now, what I want you to do is to get him a good position and one where he will have a chance to rise—as he surely will if the opportunity offers. He has the determination and "where there's a will there's a way" sure enough. But the way may be long and steep and rugged and hard and the weary traveler may drop by the wayside.

The road of life may be a path of flowers through pleasant woods where glimpses of his destination through clefts between the trees urge the traveler on and encourage him; or it may be a toilsome march through a trackless desert where deluding mirages mock the wanderer with vain hopes of rest only to melt into empty air as he draws near.

But this is a digression, considerable of a digression, but let us return to Jack. Do please get him a fine position with a fine salary. Could you not send him down to "Victoria" where Mr. Head is or get him a place in the city? He is fully capable of filling a high position in any business you may see fit to put him. . . .

Do please pay attention to this matter and write soon and favorably and gratify

Your loving son,
W. R. Hearst[67]

He also asked his mother to intervene on Jack's behalf. She had concerns about Jack's influence on Will—Jack liked to make merry with a drink or two—but she could not deny her only son a good friend. For the rest of his life, Jack was one of Will's favorite companions, joining him at a moment's notice in travels and other amusements, including a trip in their college days to "scout" the Southwest, from which Will, Gene Lent, and Jack had to be rescued.[68]

Phoebe was sympathetic to Jack's plight and recognized that her husband often needed prodding. "You know that your father is slow to act and has to be managed. Though he is fond of Jack, he does not arrange matters quickly. He needs you to talk to him."[69]

Will seemed to enjoy writing long letters, particularly to his mother, and he evidenced a fondness for words and description that must have delighted her, after all her years of tutoring. Every letter was a treasure to her, she longed for more than she got and complained when he failed to write that he was just like his father. His college letters are full of purple prose. He wrote about the weather until his mother wished he would stop and about running short of money, despite an allowance of one hundred dollars a month.

Dear Mother,

I haven't written sooner because I couldn't have said "all well" without prevaricating, and you know how tender my conscience is and how averse I am to telling an untruth. . . .

I had a slight sore throat . . . so I went to the doctor and had it touched with essence of asafoetida, or some other beastly preparation and now I am able to sign myself yours in health Lydia Pink-bah! . . .

. . . the sore throat has gone . . . either fumigated out by that awful essence of asafoetida or thawed out by a few warm days that we have had and the sun baths that I enjoyed. I rather think that the latter remedy was the most effective, although I believe that the asafoetida was capable, fully capable, of ousting any sensible sore throat—at least I know that if I were a sore throat I wouldn't stay about a man who smelled like a veterinary hospital.

It has been raining all day long and the sun has kept his face hidden from view, but just now, as his royal highness is sinking to rest among the Western hills, he parts the curtains of his bed and bids us a gracious goodnight. The splendor of his countenance lights up the grim old college buildings and they seem like venerable students linking up for a moment to admire the beauty of the scene. . . .

The birds that flit from tree to tree are golden birds and drops that fall from the rustling leaves are jewels, bright and rare. And one might almost fancy himself in the enchanted gardens of Aladdin were it not for the prosaic surrounding and the cigar sign, "Havana Cigars, two for five cents." Alas! Alas! What use of a magic lamp when we can get pure Havana's at two for five cents? . . . how these "Yankees" can lie.[70]

He did not imagine that fifteen years later he would be in Cuba, fomenting a war. Spring had come at last to Harvard.

Oh spring, beautiful spring; gentle, balmy, enervating spring. How pleasant it is to be able to open the window and let in a breath of fresh air without letting in diptheria along with it; how pleasant to take long walks over the sunny fields, to lay down and go to sleep under the cool shade of some spreading tree, and to wake up and find that some tramp has made off with your watch and pocketbook.

It is now, when the gentle zephyrs, laden with the scent of budding flowers, toss the auburn tresses of the dude, that he recklessly invests in patent leather pumps and silk stockings and catches pneumonia. It is now that the Cambridge matron, while wending her peaceful way homeward, is surprised by the flying baseball and knocked silly. It is now, when the fences are heavy with spring advertisements, that the William Goat abandons the luscious hoop skirt and the succulent kerosene can and regales himself on the gaudy circus poster. It is now that the tatooed man arrays himself in a fresh coat of blue paint preparatory to a tour in the country.

It is now that the susceptible Freshmen warbles plaintively upon the midnight air a ballad to his lady love and is arrested for disturbing the peace, &c, &c, &c.

For further particulars consult "Puck."[71]

His mother sent him money when he ran short but required that he account for his expenses, which included such items as "carriage hire for the month, $85; silk underwear, $4; servants, $9; gave Janitor's wife, $20; loan to one of the boys, $75."[72] In one letter he wrote:

It is very kind of you to send me more money and I am much pleased for I know by that that you understand my position and do not believe that I am recklessly extravagant or squandering my money in a wrong way; and this is as much a comfort to my feelings as the money is to my empty pocket.[73]

And in another:

I need a lot of money and will specify what for in full.

Lense, blow pipe, magnet, knife, streaker, forceps, platinum wire, &c, chemical outfit, about	$50.00
Tutors	44.00
Changing Z Y rooms, assessment	35.00
Entrance fee into a certain society	100.00
Term bill	135.00
Board and lodging in New York during coming vacation, bet $50 and $100	75.00
Brass bull frog omitted	15.00
Grand total	$454.00

Please remit and oblige,

Your affectionate son,
W. R. Hearst

P.S. Tell Papa I get the papers. Many thanks.[74]

Will admitted an impatience with routine when he was dropped from a play because he failed to turn up at rehearsals.

When we returned to Cambridge we found that the fellows had started on a new play and that I had not had the honor of being cast in it because, they said, they had discovered in the last play a certain tendency of mine to cut rehearsals and make myself generally scarce at a time when I was most needed. Well, I didn't express any regret at being left out and so in a few days

> I was waited upon by a delegation and now have permission to cut as much as I please, just so I know my part on the evening of the performance. I wish the faculty would adopt the same measures as regards recitations.[75]

He was good at performing and once was asked to do three encores, including an imitation of Henry Irving, which was a great hit with his fellow students.[76]

Jack Follansbee left Harvard in a tearful parting, with Will's blessing and $130 that Will had borrowed from Orrin Peck to see Jack safely to San Francisco. His exhortations to his mother on Jack's behalf anticipated Will's stepping into his father's shoes.

> . . . I should think it would be to Papa's interest to obtain the services of young, vigorous, honest and enterprising men to put in responsible positions. Men who will be to me what Chambers and McMasters have been to Papa. Men who have grown up in the business and who have a knowledge and an interest in it as well as a friendship for me; for I know I have few better friends than Jack and there is no one that I am fonder of.[77]

He asked his mother to deposit $50 in the Nevada Bank for Jack until he got on his feet.

> Jack will pay us back as soon as he gets a position. And if "Billy Buster" ever gets knocked out, you would like to have somebody help him. . . .
> All mothers are pretty much alike—at least all good ones are.[78]

Jack went West and worked for George, overseeing Mexican and other ranching interests. He did not realize that the job involved Indian attacks by Apaches, to which he was subjected late in 1883, when A. E. Head sent him on a scouting mission in the Southwest, which Will thought reckless on Head's part. Will accused Head of being "invincible in peace and invisible in war" in a letter to his father, accompanied by cartoonlike stick drawings that he occasionally used to illustrate his points.[79]

Will settled back into Harvard life, got pinkeye, and stopped smoking, a habit that he gave up for life. But he longed for the West and a ranch that he could run with Jack. He wrote his mother:

> I have had the "molly grubs" for the last week or so. I am beginning to get awfully tired of this place, and I long to get out West somewhere where I can stretch myself without coming in contact with the narrow walls with which the prejudice of the beaneaters has surrounded us.
> I long to get out in the woods and breathe the fresh mountain air and listen to the moaning of the pines. It makes me almost crazy with homesickness when I think of it and I hate their weak, pretty New England scenery with its gently rolling hills, its pea green foilage, its vistas, tame enough to begin with

but totally disfigured by houses and barns which could not be told apart save for the respective inhabitants.

I hate it as I do a weak pretty face without force or character. I long to see our own woods, the jagged rocks and towering mountains, the majestic pines, the grand impressive scenery of the "far West."

I shall never live anywhere but in California. I like to be away for a while only to appreciate it the more when I return.[80]

He realized that he was not good at managing money—he was always lending it out and running out—and he began to speculate about a political career. He told his mother:

I think I shall take a Political Economy course in hopes that it will teach me to regulate my money affairs better. . . .

Oh, my, Harvard is no place for a poor boy. . . .

Now I hope Papa will understand that I know that I may have to work my way in the world and that I do not feel terrified at the prospect, although of course, I should prefer to have enough money to be able to turn my time to politics or science or something where I could make a name.[81]

He frequently entertained in his handsomely furnished rooms that his landlady delighted in showing off. And he was not averse to an increase in allowance:

I didn't talk to Papa about my allowance, but if he sees fit to increase it, he shall have all the thanks of a thoroughly worthy and appreciative son.[82]

Although he would much have preferred "exams in baseball, tennis and physical development," his grades were above the 75 percent mark. But, despite his busy social life, on his twenty-first birthday he was lonely and homesick.

I have the dumps today and I feel rather homesick and I wish I could enjoy my birthday at home and with you and father instead of with a lot of fellows who don't care whether I am 21 or 30 so long as the dinner is good and the wine plenty.

Talk of college friendships lasting for life. There are very few that I should care to have last longer than the four years here; and doubtless fewer still that will last. . . .

I shan't bring anybody home with me this summer. . . .

I for my part don't see why anyone should rejoice on entering upon the duties and responsibilities which are supposed to attend the age of manhood. I should prefer to be 19 again and be 21 only when it is necessary to leave College and begin the work of my life in earnest.[83]

He had gotten into some sort of trouble, and referred to himself as "your reformed child": "The faculty has very kindly left me alone lately but there is no telling when they will break out again although I am doing all I can to pacify them."[84]

Phoebe, who was suffering from "muscular rheumatism" and was in great pain, had sent him one hundred dollars for his birthday—he said he "used it for a splendid time, without getting loaded."[85] She also ordered a present for him from London, and wrote him, "May you have many happy years and never know what it is to be neglected by those you love."[86]

Her rheumatism may have been triggered by a feeling of neglect from her husband and by the realization that she was losing her boy. The fact of the matter was that she felt sorry for herself. She had gotten very thin and "lost interest in everything but my boy," she wrote Will; "It does seem as if I had more than my share of aches and pains." She asked Will to give her a miniature portrait that he had had made that showed him with hair parted in the middle and intense eyes: "When we hear and know so little of you, it would be gratifying to have something to look at, to remind us we have a boy."[87]

She also was annoyed when he ignored or failed to honor her wishes. It was hard for her to accept that she could no longer control her son's life and actions, even his packing:

> It grieves me deeply that you never regard any promise made to your mother. If you ever realize how I feel about it, I cannot understand how it is possible for you to be so utterly indifferent to my wishes. I am mortified and grieved beyond your comprehension.
> I wish you to let me know when you will start home. I insist that Rachel is to do your packing, for she knows my wishes about things you are to bring. . . . When will you start and what route do you intend coming? Answer.
> . . . I hope you will remember about not needing thin summer clothing here. You know last year you could not wear your very light suits. Did you find your overcoat? Of course, I know you will never answer this question, but it may remind you that you need it and must find it. I shall be happy when we hear from you.[88]

George had sent his son two hundred dollars for his twenty-first birthday but an admonishing mother wrote, "You might probably have had more if you had only taken the trouble to write a good letter to your father."[89]

Still, they celebrated their absent son's matriculation to manhood with a gay party in San Francisco. Phoebe stayed up all evening, there were merry toasts to Will, dancing—"a most hilarious quadrille, yes, right on my fine inlaid floor"—and the flowers on the table were arranged to form the figures 21. When George was asked to make a toast, he demurred, saying that "it would be taken for granted that the father and mother would 'boil over' about him," Phoebe wrote Will.[90]

A new worry was confronting her and she implored Will to "write to your father about politics in most emphatic terms."[91] George had begun a campaign for high public office and the newspapers were giving him a hard time. Phoebe did not like the public scrutiny and merciless derogation.

> I sent you the San Franciscan, a new paper here. In one copy you will find an extremely severe article about your father. As usual, Greathouse was more to blame for it than your father. It troubles me very much for Papa to be in politics.
> When you come home, I hope you can induce him to give it up.[92]

Phoebe was not fooled by the glorification of political life. She saw the duplicity of it, recognizing that elections were not necessarily a show of popular support for candidates, but a carefully contrived and purchased event. There was not much honor in politics, she believed. And she did not like the nasty things the newspapers said about her husband, who she knew to be a good man.

But in 1882 George sought the Democratic nomination for governor of California with the blessing of the Democratic machine boss, blind Christopher Buckley of San Francisco. The Oakland Daily Tribune reported that George's friends warned him against running.

> "George, you don't want to run. They'll dig up every glass of gin you ever drank in your life, and make it a burden to you."
> "If any of them fellows lie about me," said Hearst, "I'll make 'em take it back if I have to stand in front of 'em behind a rifle. I ain't scared to defend my life and my record."[93]

Protestations aside, he was clearly the candidate of the party bosses. Before the convention one paper said that a clear majority

> "was done up and labeled Hearst," who made his immense fortune by luckily gambling on the winning mining stocks. He possesses no qualification of statesmanship, of experience in public affairs, of character, or of anything essential for fitness for the Gubernatorial office, except the one solitary and questionable qualification of a plethoric purse. This, it is understood, he will use with a lavish hand to buy his way to the place of honor and trust to which he aspires.[94]

Another paper said he "has no better qualifications for Governor than a squealing pig," although the writer thought him "a good fellow" whom he had known "when [Hearst] hadn't money enough to pay a chinaman for washing his shirt."[95] There was considerable derision in the papers about George's "buying" the nomination: "Hearst owns the San Francisco delegation, because he has bought and paid for it," said the *Sacramento Bee*.[96] The cruel criticism of her husband appalled Phoebe. One commentator wrote:

> Outside of a rather limited circle of capitalists and speculators, George Hearst has been an unknown man, until he bought a newspaper and commenced to fix things to suit himself to secure for himself the Democratic nomination for Governor. What his opinions have been upon matters of public concern, says the Oakland *Times*, is a matter entirely of conjecture. Whether he is a man who has any opinions, is still a query, for his letter announcing his candidacy gives no clue to any.
>
> In that, he proposes to endorse anything the Democratic convention may favor. He will be railroad or anti-railroad, slickens or anti-slickens, Sunday Law or anti-Sunday Law or anything else that may be decided by the assemblage of politicians which will convene at San Jose. Outwardly, there is no more reason why he should be nominated for such an office. . . .
>
> But he is a formidable candidate; he has an income of a thousand dollars a day, it is said, and the substratum of Democracy sees in prospective an enormous corruption fund. They like to secure the nomination of wealthy and vain men, as they can generally play upon their ambition and their nervousness, and secure heavy gifts of money. A man who is foolish enough to pay for the maintenance of such a paper as the *Examiner* would naturally be weak enough to squander his money upon the manipulators, political bummers and sharks who generally handle the Democratic machine in San Francisco.[97]

The convention was a horse trader's delight, a veritable "cock fight at the race track." George's patrons, however, failed to garner enough votes for their candidate, despite a "formidable army of Hearst workers," who included Haggin, Tevis, and Wells Fargo & Company agents. Friends who he thought would support him betrayed him, including the railroad magnates, who feared his independence. George was "mad as a hornet when he found the railroad opposing him, and he took part in an anti-railroad fight the following four years that made Fourth and Townsend Street sick," one political observer later wrote.[98]

George was hooted down when one of his supporters called for three cheers on his behalf. After fourteen ballots, he lost the nomination to a former Union cavalry leader, General George Stoneman. Phoebe was not there to see it. It was men's work.[99]

But George and his sponsors were not defeated in spirit. Their sights were set on the U.S. Senate, into which they thought the governorship automatically would have sprung George. Money was no object; cold cash was the ticket to the Senate, even for the "people's party." And George had plenty of it. It was pouring into his bank account from the Homestake, Anaconda, and Ontario mines.

His wife and son did their best to dissuade him from a political path but to no avail. George and the Democratic party were formidable adversaries in that round, although George had lost money by bankrolling the Democrats in California in the 1884 presidential election, "for he would insist that it must go democratic, which it didn't," Phoebe wrote Will in November. She hoped that "the republican majority in California has settled the vexed question of your father's senatorial aspirations. It will be a cheap arrangement for us. If this state had gone democratic, no one could have induced your father to abandon his wish. Now he must do so at any rate."[100] But it was wishful thinking on her part. Politics were to become an inextricable part of their lives. Ironically, given his own later political aspirations, Will wrote his mother in 1884 discussing, among other things, his constant need for money:

> Expensive to be sure, but not half as costly nor yet as exasperating as Senatorial aspirations. A terrible disease this, and I'm told it runs in the family.
>
> Every man, in this world, has his specialty, and when a man is fortunate enough to have found it, he is foolish beyond measure to leave it for something else.
>
> Number the successful men you know. You can almost do it on your fingers. These are the men who have found and pursued the path in which their talents lay. And the myriads of unfortunates are those who insist upon attempting what they are not naturally fitted for. Why my father should abandon the nag which has carried him faithfully for so many years to mount the fickle animal that has thrown him once is more than I can understand. It is more than folly. It is tempting providence.
>
> If Thackeray had attempted politics his name would have been buried beneath his ashes. If Jay Gould had fostered a mania for literature, the acme of his success would probably have been a serial story in the Boys and Girls Weekly.

He then wrote her a long parable, suggesting that George was out of his element.

> And this is to show that those who stray from the path that nature has marked out for them are prone to run against snags, long and sharp and multitudinous.
>
> And this tale is to be found in the fourth chapter of the ninth book of Herodotus and the name of the man is U.S. Grant.[101]

George was not to be equated with political "reform." He was a team player, and in 1886, thanks to going along with boss Buckley, he was appointed to the U.S. Senate by Governor Stoneman to fill out the unexpired term at the death of John F. Miller. The New York Times reported "from inside political circles" that "members of the Legislature who were elected by the use of Mr. Hearst's money have made up their minds that if they are going to be covered with infamy for sending Mr. Hearst to the Senate, they ought to be paid accordingly."[102] The following year, on 19 January, the California legislature elected George Hearst to a six-year term in the club of millionaires. When his Republican colleague, Leland Stanford, escorted George down the middle aisle of the Senate to be sworn in, "it was remarked that those two individuals could buy out all the rest of the Senate if they wanted to."[103]

The *New York Times* fired another shot at George: "For six years California will be represented in the United States Senate by a man whose sole claim to preferment . . . is that he is rich. He can neither talk nor write well, and he is surrounded by a gang who flatter him in every way solely for the purpose of making all they can out of him." The latter was a view that Phoebe shared. The successful election had cost George half a million dollars.[104]

George's donations to the Democratic Party had paid off and his newspaper had done its part. It had campaigned for George while denying that the *Examiner* was "run in any way subservient to the personal ambition of George Hearst. . . . No man in the State has a better right to run for the Senate than George Hearst. He has proven himself a faithful and zealous Democrat, and such men are worthy to be and deserve to be rewarded."[105]

The night of George's triumphal return from Sacramento, Phoebe arranged a victory banquet for his cronies at the house they then were renting (the Head's) at 1105 Taylor Street on the top of Nob Hill. Eighty members of the Iroquois Club (Democratic boosters) marched in a heavy rain to the Hearst house to serenade the senator-elect. A band played and when George and his party came up in a carriage, the serenaders gave three lusty cheers. They then were invited into the brightly lit mansion where they were received in the billiard room. A true politician, George told the crowd,

> . . . that if he had the choosing of a U.S. Senator, he might not have chosen George Hearst, but as the people had chosen him, all he could say was that during his six years in office he hoped to do something for his fellow citizens of California that would make them as proud of him as he was of them. . . .
>
> At the conclusion of the speeches the guests were ushered into the dining room, where a sumptuous repast was served, with champagne *ad libitum*. Toasts were drunk and the enthusiasm of the serenaders rose with the popping of the cork of each wine bottle.[106]

For Phoebe it meant a new and public life as a senator's wife and hostess. And it meant moving to Washington. Contemporary historian H. H. Bancroft noted,

It will be cause for no slight gratification also, for California to realize that the wife of their honorable Senator, a lady of the rarest gifts and most liberal culture, will preside over his household in Washington, exemplifying in that center of refinement the very best forms of social life on the Pacific Coast.[107]

Phoebe disliked the public spotlight but she accepted her responsibilities and obligations to serve her husband. The contradictions with which she wrestled throughout her life were never so strong as when she took on the role of political wife. The prospect of having to be in the public eye actually terrified her, her niece recalled, although Phoebe enjoyed entertaining on a grand scale. Her graciousness disguised a shyness and an aversion to publicity, which she considered an invasion of her privacy. Nevertheless, she grit her teeth and made herself do what was expected of her. She did not know at the outset that she actually would grow to like the perquisites that accompanied the job—the special courtesies extended to her, the special doors that opened, the deference paid to her. So as not to appear arrogant, she developed a slightly deprecating manner, which was her way of seeming to remain humble. It was as if she were apologizing, ever so slightly, for being a rich senator's wife.[108]

Will also changed his view, some years later writing his mother:

I want to say that when I spoke against my father going into politics I was very young and very foolish.

There is nothing that I am prouder of today than my father's record as senator and of the high esteem in which he is held and still remembered by men high in place in the nation.

That record and that opportunity to show the whole people his fine character is the greatest thing of the many good things he bequeathed us.

George Hearst Senator is better known and wider known than George Hearst miner and we share the advantage of that and I am proud of it and glad today that he went into the service of the nation.

Sincerely and truthfully,
Will[109]

9
Challenges and Disappointments

The decade of the 1880s was a trying time for Phoebe. George was embroiled in politics, which she deplored. The *Examiner* continued to lose money. Will was in trouble at Harvard. Her health was poor. And the Homestake mine was draining their resources. Unable to foresee how richly the Homestake would serve her one day, Phoebe then wished that George "would close out that store," she wrote Will. "It is not doing much. If he would take the money out of it and invest it in a range for you and Jack, it would be better," she said, adding a warning to her son about his relations with his father: "He is so difficult to move and every year becomes more so. You make a great mistake in not writing an occasional nice letter to your father."[1]

Even San Francisco had become tiresome. The doorbell rang incessantly with callers, to whom Phoebe was always gracious but who privately often annoyed her. The Van Ness Avenue house was for sale, but few buyers were willing to pay the Hearst's price. "How I hate to live in S.F.!" she blurted out to Will in one of many letters excoriating him for failing to keep his promises to her, for not calling on her friends in the East, as she requested, for failing to write more often—in short, for going his own way, out from under his mother's apron strings.[2]

She was anxious that George get a ranch for Will and Jack Follansbee to operate when Will graduated from college—a prospect that began to appear in jeopardy:

> Write your father at once, and do take care to write him the best possible letter. This is no doubt a fine range and I am so anxious for you and Jack to have it. . . . Don't make a mistake, but write your father in the right way.[3]

Will's Harvard career was by that time a source of great anxiety to his mother. His grades were unimpressive, and by July 1884 he was deficient in several courses and had failed to pass Political Economy 4, which course examination he had skipped.[4] He was on probation and his mother was beside herself.

Harold Wheeler called here yesterday evening. He <u>kindly</u> remarked that you had what was called an <u>incentive</u> to study this year. Of course, I knew he meant that you <u>must</u> work or be suspended, and I am <u>very</u> much afraid it will be the latter. You cannot realize my extreme anxiety about you. It would almost kill me if you should not go through college in a creditable manner.[5]

He had taken a great interest in politics and the election of the man whom his father supported for President, Grover Cleveland, the first Democrat to be elected since the Civil War. Will footed the bill for a big celebration of the election that startled staid Cambridge with fireworks, roosters let loose in Harvard Yard, and noisy carousing. But he had lost bets on the election. Little did his mother know the truth when she wrote, shortly after the election,

I am afraid that all this excitement has caused you to neglect your studies . . .

I suppose you bet something on the election and lost and your father's sanguine hope that Cal. would go democratic was probably the cause of your loss. So I shall see that you have the amount of coin necessary, not only to pay up losses but subscriptions and dues.[6]

The Van Ness house at last was sold and Phoebe went East to be with "my dear boy" and to try to straighten him out. He was partying too much. Phoebe reported to George, after hosting Will and some of his chums in New York, that he "could not settle down to do much and he looked badly."

Late hours and dissipation affect him. Of course, I don't know how much he drank, but I do know he was not intoxicated at all, nor even <u>funny</u>, as they call it but even the amount he must have drunk did him <u>no good</u>. Theatres, horse shows, late suppers and <u>women</u> consumed the two hundred dollars quickly. . . .

You should write to him. As I said . . . he is all right the last two days. . . . He is very bright and capable and has many good traits, but has his weaknesses and faults. . . .

. . . he would not be likely to drink too much and have me see him. I <u>never</u> go to bed until he comes in and never shall as long as I can hold together. . . .

The day after the college fellows left, I was suffering dreadfully. [Mrs. Anthony] said she did not think I could possibly live through the year if that state of things went on, but I don't believe heartaches kill and I am plucky if not strong. I think my energy and strong will must pull me through until Spring. I shall do everything possible to have Will do right.[7]

A family friend told Will to take his father's advice and "stand in like a man and stick to [your] studies 'til the end." Will was asking permission to leave Harvard in the spring of 1885 so he could go to work on the *Examiner*.

Your father realizes, if you do not, the contemptuous estimate of a man (even in a money-making community like this) which is sure to stick to one who has failed in a contest that is distinctively a test of brains. . . .

A Harvard degree, if it means nothing else, does mean that a man has made the beginning of a liberally intelligent life. . . .

Whatever occupation you may choose as a business, I venture to say, unless I am greatly mistaken in you, you will never lose an interest in intellectual things, but will feel from year to year that they hold a place of growing importance in your life.[8]

But Will continued to put pleasure before his studies and to devise new pranks to amuse himself and his friends, to the growing disapproval of college deans. He joined Delta Kappa Epsilon fraternity, was elected to the elite Hasty Pudding club, and was fond of giving dinner parties with Gene Lent in his luxurious rooms. His college chums later reported that "Billy Hearst was one of the best fellows in college."

He was quiet and reserved, and the last man you'd think of in any . . . scrape. He was a wholesouled, generous fellow, and paid the expenses of two students throughout the college course. . . .

While he was here he was anything but a lady's man. He had the reputation of being the coolest and longest-headed man in college. He was not enthusiastic over anything, and least of all over girls. He was a calculating fellow, and I never knew him to do anything rash.[9]

From Harvard, Will reassured his mother,

I have signed the pledge—total abstinence, not because I needed it myself but to get Eugene to sign it with me. I think it will be the saving of Gene if he sticks it out and I think he will. Ginger ale is good enough for me nowadays, and I'm not too high for plain cold water.

Oh, I wanted to tell you that I had changed one of my electives. The one Papa didn't like from the first—Philosophy 6. It is too dry and learned and full of big words and generally incomprehensible for me. He got up one day and began to talk about the "as it wereness of the sometimes" and I lit out.[10]

He changed his course of study to English—"I think it will be more interesting and of more practical benefit than that Philosophy."[11] And he had joined the staff of the Harvard *Lampoon*, to help out his friend Lent, the hapless business manager of the humor magazine, which was chronically in debt. Will took on the challenge with enthusiasm, organized subscriptions among alumni, and sold advertisements to local businesses, of which he was a high-spending patron. He wrote his mother:

I am a man of business now, and spend all my spare time in "booming" the *Lampoon*. . . . Eugene and I are business managers, or managing editors; we drum up subscriptions and advertisements, keep the books, send the exchanges, and attend to all the business of the paper.

   . . . now we stand on a firm basis with a subscription list of 450 and $900 in advertising, making a grand total of $2,250 and leaving the $650 clear profit after the debt is paid.

   Show this to Papa and tell him just to wait till Gene and I get hold of the old *Examiner* and we'll boom her in the same way she needs it.[12]

The magazine's finances began to show a profit, and the project occupied Will's interest far more than his classes. He even enlisted his mother as a West Coast subscription agent.

   I am going to send out about fifty copies of the Harvard *Lampoon*—first number—out to San Francisco and I want you to get the addresses of all the Harvard Club and mail a circular and a *Lampoon* to all that you think may subscribe. . . . For Harvard is the only College which is able to furnish sufficient talent—literary and artistic—to run such a paper.

   The *Lampoon* is peculiarly Harvard, beginning with its red cover, and all the way through; and it ought to be supported by Harvard men with contributions and subscriptions. . . .

   Eugene and I expect a great deal from California and I hope we shall not be disappointed.[13]

Meanwhile, Will was looking to his future in anticipation of graduating in 1886. He wrote his father, wryly offering him advice on how to run his affairs, and, in particular, the *Examiner.* Will had no great love for Greathouse, whom he accused of procrastination. In January 1885 Will suggested that they hire as managing editor Ballard Smith, an editor at the *New York World*, and pay him the high price he commanded. (Smith never took the job and when Will himself later offered it, Smith astutely suggested that Will be his own editor.)[14]

   The most striking objection to Mr. Ballard Smith is that he is very high priced. But I am convinced and I think you are that the paper must be built up and that cheap labor has been entirely ineffectual. . . . The only thing that remains to be tried is first class talent and corresponding wages. You could not even sell the paper at present so I think this is the only thing to be done.

   I will give you the benefit of my large head and great experience on this subject—and not charge you a cent. . . .

   Under those conditions I am willing to bet that in one year the paper will be paying expenses at any rate. By that time I will be out of college and if I have succeeded in developing any talent for writing, I will take a minor position in the office and endeavor to learn the business. If by the time I graduate, I find that I am fit for nothing in God's world, I shall go into politics. But neither Steve Elkins or Greathouse shall manage my campaign, you bet your sweet life. . . .

   I shall expect an answer to all these questions for I feel that I ought to know a little of your business by the time I get out of college which is not now far off.[15]

He also continued to ask that his father "procure some kind of a ranch, mine, line of steamships or something that Jack and I can go into."[16] Like his father, he saw land as a sure value and source of income:

> The landlords are always a wealthy class. Every infant born in a country makes their land more valuable. Every mouth to be fed, every body to be clothed, increase the demand for the products of the soil and thus raises the value of land. . . . The Landlord sits calm and serene on his paternal acres peacefully surveying the situation and conscious of the fact that every atom of humanity added to the struggling mass means another figure to his bank account.[17]

"Will you kindly take some slight notice of your only son," he begged ironically of his father, "and let him know that you at least appreciate his kindness in allowing you to draw upon his large experience and gigantic intellect?"[18]

He went home to California in the summer of 1885 expecting to continue at Harvard, where his popularity, at least with his fellow students, was rewarding. He had been elected president of the Harvard Base Ball Association and was campaigning to be vice-president of the Intercollegiate Base Ball Association by throwing a dinner for the championship competitors. He had acquired a number of friends through his genuine brightness, humor, and strong personality, and, no doubt, through his generosity at the dinner table and tavern. His political savvy was improving—but his days at Harvard were numbered. His jollity and optimism to his mother were misleading.

> Well, only a few days now and I'll be on my way to San Francisco, and I hope with a carload of Eastern college boys so you may advertise for the benefit of the San Francisco belles as follows:
> New Invoice of College Boys.
> Large and varied Assortment Going at a Sacrifice.
> Genuine American, all wool dudes, every bit as good as the English article, will be sacrificed for 50c on the $1.
> Boston Blue Bloods—slightly damaged by water—selling below cost price.
> Pay your money and take your choice.[19]

The following fall, Harvard informed Will that he was not welcome back for his final term unless he made serious amends on several fronts, academic and social. A classmate wrote Will that he had heard a "horrible report . . . to the effect that the faculty have decided the air is too bracing for you in Cambridge. . . . It can't be that the college has failed to appreciate your ability to guide the youths in college to a higher standard—morally and otherwise. If any such action has been taken it is a damn shame and I should be most proud and happy to say as much to that august body of blockheads."[20] President Charles W. Eliot, who granted Will a personal audience at Eliot's home the afternoon of 4 October, was willing to consider a reprieve if Will made up his academic failings. He wired his parents 4 October 1885,

> Saw the Dean, requested not to return. Saw the President, said if I went to a good climate and studied with a competent instructor, I should probably be allowed to pass my examinations in June. Shall I engage instructor? What salary are you willing to pay?[21]

Phoebe was stunned and incredulous. Her niece, Anne Apperson, who had just come to live with the Hearsts, remembered going into her aunt's room while she was dressing in the morning after receiving the news, and finding Phoebe in tears—a devastating sight because her aunt was usually calm and reserved. Phoebe said to her, "I'm very unhappy about something. Will has been into mischief, and he's been punished for it by being expelled." It was one of the greatest disappointments of her life.[22] Orrin Peck tried to reassure her that it was not the end of the world. He defended Will's behavior as not entirely reprehensible, writing Phoebe from Munich, where he was studying art under her patronage. As he often did, he addressed her "My other Mother."

> You have no reason to cry over what dear Will does. He will never do anything to disgrace himself or his friends. In the first place, nastiness is not born in him and I would hate him if he didn't possess a mixture of boyishness and devilishness—neatly spiced with a college wittiness surging here and there on to wickedness. He will graduate, mind you, and well.
>
> In the first place, I don't think you and Mr. Hearst have had any one great trial with Will—but, my dear, have you not often worried over little things that in themselves were really nothing? And that is what the stupid faculty have been doing. There is a certain amount of red tape which at college must be stretched or broken, and Will didn't think about it but cut the string, was discovered and ousted—better that kind of a boy than a quiet hide-around-the-fence sort of fellow.[23]

Phoebe wired Will, asking whether the faculty had met and the decision was final. She was willing to pay any price for instruction to reinstate her son in good standing. And George sent a large donation (four hundred pounds) of mining specimens, possibly in hopes of changing the learned gentlemen's minds. But it was to no avail.[24]

Will had finally stepped over the bounds of Harvard's tolerance. Whether it was the apocryphal chamber pot prank or something else, he had gotten himself thrown out. Legend later held that he had ordered delivered to each of his instructors a large chamber pot with the name of the professor elaborately baked into the bottom of the pot.[25]

Phoebe went to Boston and Will was glad to have his mother at hand in his time of trial. She persisted in trying to get him to pursue tutored studies that would allow him to graduate. At President Eliot's suggestion, they secured a tutor in a place where the environment was conducive to study and far enough away from Will's college chums to prevent heinous activities of the kind that had gotten him into trouble. They chose Baltimore for its proximity to Johns Hopkins University. "Will feels badly about the state of affairs," Phoebe wrote George from New York in October 1885, "and says he wants to get his degree, especially as he thinks the Dean don't want him to have it. My faith in his perseverance is weak but if he can be away from last year's associations, he may redeem himself."[26]

His experience with the Dean had been impressive:

> When Will went to see the Dean, he was obliged to wait until that stern individual was ready to look up and speak to him. The Dean then said, "You here again! I thought the letter I sent to San Francisco would keep you there." He would not give Will any encouragement and evidently wanted to get rid of him.

In the same letter Phoebe implored George to help restrain Will's spendthrift habits. It was time his "vacation" ended, she thought.

> He insisted today upon drawing money as usual and I can do very little unless you help me. If he continues to spend too much money and neglect study, it will not be my fault, and you can take the blame upon yourself. I will not be held responsible when you go on giving him the means to do just as he pleases.
>
> I cannot give you a full account of my conversation with Will upon this subject. It was very hard for me. I, of course, want him to have a moderate amount of spending money, but if he is to have $250 per month, I can tell you that he will not study much. . . .
>
> It is only throwing temptation in his way, for he will come to New York and meet the fellows and have dinners and go on in a way that will surely bring us sorrow. . . .
>
> I remarked that he had been enjoying one long vacation all of his life. . . .[27]

Her quiet but determined insistence brought Will around, at least outwardly. She wrote George,

> I know you will be glad to learn that Will has appeared to change very much since I last wrote to you. He has selected a fine course of study and is very much in earnest. I talked to him a great deal, in a quiet way, and not too much at one time, telling how we were distressed on his account and then I thought it best he should not feel that we had lost faith in him, so I said we thought he would redeem himself.
>
> Gradually he seemed to realize everything and is now perfectly reasonable and willing to do genuine work. I hope this may continue.[28]

She had him on a regular regimen, including exercise with dumb-bells in the morning, and kept him away from his friends, who kept telegraphing with invitations to club dinners. Even so, Will invited three of his pals to New York for a long weekend to see a horse show.

> . . . Will did absolutely <u>nothing</u> while they were here, excepting spend money on them or with them. During that time he spent two hundred dollars, and the bills for their rooms and <u>restaurant</u> charges were sent to me and I had to pay one hundred and seventy dollars. So that was almost four hundred dollars thrown away. It was simply outrageous. I told him that I should never pay any more.[29]

On top of that, one friend bounced a check that Will had endorsed and Phoebe had to make it good. She was fed up but still the forgiving mother: "Will's friends are expensive and I am sure I could live without them."[30]

Will also was spending time at the theater and dinner parties with Eleanor Calhoun and her sister, who had accompanied Phoebe East. They were sailing for Europe. "Will and I have enjoyed having them with us," Phoebe told George. She did not tell him, nor may she have perceived at the time, the extent of Will's interest in the pretty, aspiring actress from Tulare County, California. She was several years older than he.[31]

Phoebe worried about George, who was spending time in the south-west: "If you go south telegraph me and be careful. You have often wished to <u>be</u> an Indian, but I don't believe you would be fond of the Apaches."[32] But most of all she worried about herself. She noted to George that she was giving up medical treatment for what had become a chronic illness in order to look after Will, who, she felt, was unfeeling about her own needs and ungrateful.[33]

Her poor health was all-absorbing. She referred to her "usual sick time," telling George in one letter that she had "gone two months and a half and have suffered terribly for two days." Her monthly menstrual cycles apparently were irregular. On another occasion she referred to "nothing unusual—only one of my days of suffering and utter inability to retain even a spoonful of food." And once she told George, "There is such danger of peritonitis the Dr. finds it necessary to be extremely careful."[34] While self-pitying, she also tried to reassure George that she was making an effort to get well, recognizing that her constant sickness made her a poor companion.

> I have been under very strict discipline and extremely trying treatment. Am now somewhat better, and try to hope that I may be well sometime. . . .
> A woman in ill health, with every nerve worn threadbare, is not very companionable or interesting, though you like me anyway, I know. Consider-

ing all this, it may be just as well that I have been alone. I hope to be much better when you come and shall be glad to see you.[35]

She and Will went to Baltimore but Will was more drawn to Washington and picked out a house for them in anticipation of George's becoming a senator. The political bug also had bitten Will. In a November 1885 letter to his father, with tongue partly in cheek, Will wrote about his political dreams, at the same time urging George to buy a particular house that could be had for $159,000.

We have decided to spend the winter in Washington not only because the climate there is delightful and very conducive to mental exertion, but because I will have there opportunities of hearing the debates in Congress, familiarizing myself with legislative methods of procedure, and thus at once assisting my present college studies and preparing the way for a brilliant entree into the political arena, some time in the future.

My three ambitions, as you know, are law, politics and journalism, and under favorable circumstances it might be possible to combine all three. And so while you are serving your country from the Senator's bench, the pride and support of your declining years will be expanding himself so as to be able to wear gracefully the mantle that will one day fall upon him, and not be completely hidden by its ample folds.

In fact, we may one day read in the papers that "The Honorable Geo. Hearst, having served twelve years as Senator of the United States is about to retire from public life. The loss of such an ardent advocate of their rights will be greatly deplored by the people throughout the Union, but they will be partially compensated by the knowledge that his son has just been elected to Congress and has devoted himself to the cause which the elder Hearst has so nobly upheld."

Now if this prophetic vision comes true, as seems extremely likely, our home will be Washington as our political pursuits will demand an almost constant residence in that city. . . .

The selection of an abode for the future leaders of the Democratic party and arbiters of this country's destiny is a difficult and complicated affair. . . . To that end it must be imposing but unassuming. Imposing, that it may seem to appreciate the importance of its position in sheltering two such immortals, and unassuming as if it were at the same time sensible of the views of the occupants towards the people.

. . . the interior must possess comfort and yet not display that arrogance of wealth that is so offensive to the people, and here again our house is marvelously complete. . . . It is surrounded on all sides by land belonging to us and this gives the impression that we might have built a larger house had we desired but that we had limited ourselves to the existing modest structure.

. . . there is no better place for the location of [a] home than Washington. The climate is delightful; and then the society there is composed neither of wealthy boors nor of aristocratic imbeciles but of men of science and letters and is therefore well worth cultivating.[36]

Will made a pretense at studying but he had perceived that his days at Harvard were over. In fact, he had told his mother earlier in the year that he thought it a waste of time to stay in college when he could be out helping his father in his many affairs. She had written George when she went East in January 1885,

Our boy is very much interested [in the *Examiner* and in finding a good managing editor for it], and anxious about it. He says it seems dreadful to stay another year in college when he might be at work doing something to help you along with all the business you have.[37]

In the same letter, written shortly after Christmas, she betrayed her acquisitive side and a desire to keep up with her rich friends. But her conscience was bothering her.

Mrs. Bryan wrote me that you had handed her a large diamond for her to send to me with your Christmas greeting. This was a very great surprise to me. . . . You know how it pleases me to be thought of, and I thank you very much, but I fear that with the present bad times, you could not afford to send me such a handsome present. My conscience troubles me now that I said a word about wanting Mrs. Barreda's beautiful diamonds. I only meant that I should like them very much if we had money and no debts. I am afraid that you thought I wanted this diamond. You mentioned one being for sale, but I don't remember saying much about it.

She still expected Will to graduate and in early 1886 she got a proper Bostonian friend to intercede on Will's behalf. The university laid out a series of requirements under which Will might be reinstated. After seeing President Eliot, the Hearst's supplicant wrote Phoebe, laying out Harvard's terms and blaming Will's associates for whatever the final deed of attrition had been, but pointing out that Will had to cooperate.

My dear Mrs. Hearst,

I have seen President Eliot and was much pleased to find him in a very amiable mood. After talking Will's case over with him I came to the following conclusion: If Will goes to work the right way, there is a good chance of his getting back and graduating with his class.

He must petition the faculty at once to allow him to return. He must let the faculty understand that he means to work and that he will work and that there will be no more "punches" or suppers in his rooms, that he will not leave Cambridge during the term.

With his petition he must send a letter from his tutor saying that he has studied well during the winter and that he (the tutor) thinks the faculty will have no cause to regret having taken him back.

I told Mr. Eliot that if he would take Will back I would occasionally go over to Cambridge to see that all was going on well and keep a strict watch over the young man.

Mr. Eliot agreed with me that it was Will's associates rather than Will himself who did wrong and I came away with the idea that the President was very favorably disposed towards [helping?] Will and would do his part if the young man would agree to do this.

There is a faculty meeting a week from next Tuesday (16 February) and I beg you will have Willie send the petition at once. Don't fail to have the tutor's letter accompany the petition.

As soon as Will comes in let him call upon me and I will tell him what I haven't time to write to you now. Make him promise that there shall be no more punches and suppers. Otherwise, the faculty will refuse the degree at the last minute.

Trusting you and Mr. Hearst are quite well, I am, sincerely yours,

J. P. Oliver[38]

The terms were stiff and Will would not accept them. Phoebe had to admit that the jig was up. Will telegraphed her on 6 May 1886,

The honor I proposed to confer upon the College declined with thanks alack aday. My presence aroused too many slumbering memories of the past and flagranisings. . . . The Dean nailed his colors a bit of alive plush to the Moil and went down without a murmur, his poor old slate colored head erect and his eyes flashing defiance in five or six directions at once. . . . What are you going to do about it?[39]

That was the end of Will's higher education, and he disdained formal education for the rest of his life, instilling his disdain in his children. Everything worth learning, he thought, could be learned outside the halls of academe. "It takes a good mind to resist education," he believed. No Hearst graduated from college until the middle of the twentieth century.[40]

In truth the *Examiner* kept tantalizing Will, drawing him to it. He pored over copies that he regularly received, advising his father and suggesting improvements. In an early 1886 letter to George that compared their West Coast sheet with the sophisticated New York dailies, he recommended cleaning up the *Examiner*'s typesetting, increasing the number of columns from six to seven, and using more illustrations, although he believed "It is a positive insult to our readers to set before them . . . pictures of repulsive deformity." He cautioned against inflammatory pieces such as a *New York Sunday World* "article that comes to a climax with a piece of imbecility so detestable that it would render the death of the writer justifiable homicide." He also offered "to look around and try to find some capable people for the dad gasted old paper," as he affectionately called it. His ideas on sensational copy would soon change, however.[41]

Will went to work for the *New York World*, for which he had great admiration, to learn the business. George begged him to come to Washington "to talk about the paper and other business that I think of much importance . . . as something must be done about things on the other side [out West] and I cannot do all."[42]

About that time, in 1886, Will wrote his father a long letter, outlining his ideas for "our miserable little sheet," and begging to be given full control of it.

Dear Father,

I have just finished and dispatched a letter to the editor of the *Examiner* in which I recommended Eugene Lent to his favorable notice, and commented on the illustrations, if you may call them such, which have lately disfigured the paper. I really believe that the *Examiner* has furnished what is thus far the crowning absurdity of illustrated Journalism, in illustrating an article on the chicken show by means of the identical democratic roosters used during the late campaign.

In my letter to the editor, however, I did not refer to this for fear of offending him, but I did tell him that in my opinion the cuts that have recently appeared in the paper bore an unquestionable resemblance to the Cuticura Soap advertisements, and I am really inclined to believe that our editor has illustrated many of his articles from his stock on hand of cuts representing gentlemen before and after using that efficacious remedy.

In case my remarks should have no effect and he should continue in his career of desolation, let me beg of you to remonstrate with him and thus prevent him from giving the finishing stroke to our miserable little sheet.

I have begun to have a strange fondness for our little paper—a tenderness like unto that which a mother feels for a puny or deformed offspring, and I should hate to see it die now after it had battled so long and so nobly for existence; in fact, to tell the truth, I am possessed of the weakness, which at some time or other of their lives, pervades most men. I am convinced that I could run a newspaper successfully.

Now, if you should make over to me the *Examiner*—with enough money to carry out my schemes—I'll tell you what I would do. In the first place, I would change the general appearance of the paper and make seven wide columns where we now have nine narrow ones. Then I would have the type spaced more, and these two changes would give the pages a much cleaner and neater appearance. Secondly, it would be well to make the paper as far as possible original, to clip only some such leading journal as the New York *World* which is undoubtedly the best paper of that class to which the *Examiner* belongs—that class which appeals to the people and which depends for its success upon enterprise, energy and a certain startling originality and not upon the wisdom of its political opinions or the lofty style of its editorials. And to accomplish this we must have—as the *World* has— active, intelligent and energetic young men; we must have men who come out west in the hopeful buoyancy of youth for the purpose of making their fortunes and not a worthless scum that has been carried there by the eddies of repeated failures. Thirdly, we must advertise the paper from Oregon to New Mexico and must also increase our number of advertisements if we have to lower our rates to do it. Thus we can put on the first page that our circulation is such and our advertisements so and so and constantly increasing. And now having spoken of the three great essential points, let us turn to details.

The illustrations are a detail, though a very important one. Illustrations embellish a page; illustrations attract the eye and stimulate the imagination of the lower classes and materially aid the comprehension of an unaccustomed reader and thus are of particular importance to that class of people which the *Examiner* claims to address. Such illustrations, however, as have heretofore appeared in the paper, nauseate rather than stimulate the imagination and certainly do anything but embellish a page.

Another detail of questionable importance is that we actually or apparently establish some connection between ourselves and the New York *World*, and obtain a certain prestige in bearing some relation to that paper. We might contract to have important private telegrams forwarded or something of that sort, but understand that the principal advantage we are to derive is from the attention such a connection would excite and from the advertisement we could make of it. Whether the *World* would consent to such an arrangement for any reasonable sum is very doubtful for its net profit is over one thousand dollars a day and no doubt it would consider the *Examiner* as beneath its notice. Just think, over one thousand dollars a day and four years ago it belonged to Jay Gould and was losing money rapidly.

And now to close with a suggestion of great consequence, namely, that all these changes be made not by degrees but at once so that the improvement will be very marked and noticeable and will attract universal attention and comment. . . .[43]

George continued to hope that his son would go into mining or other legitimate business. Will made several forays into the field to satisfy his father, but his heart was not in it. On one trip to the Anaconda he confessed that he knew nothing about the mining business and had not the slightest interest in learning. It was a miserable business and a miserable life.

His father at last agreed to let his son work on the paper, where he was headed when he stopped off at the Anaconda and wrote George, in a letter "Relating to We, Us and Company":

After having thoroughly been soaked with dust, choken up by the Narrow Gauge and prostrated by the heat, I am now, at last, safely arrived at the Anaconda Mine. . . . Why! Pa this is the damnedest hole I have ever struck.

As far as one can see—which isn't very far because of the dust and smoke—there is nothing but reddish yellow leprous looking hills with an occasional splotch of dead-grey sage brush that rather serves to heighten the dreariness of the scene.

In the town below . . . stands the bank, the church, the hotel, a few dwelling houses, saloons innumerable and the jail—and next to the saloons I have no doubt that the jail is the most frequented and best patronized place of the entire neighborhood.

. . . I would just as soon live in a jail as anywhere else in this country and I am sure that the four walls of a prison could not present any greater or more melancholy monotony than one obtains from the summit of the Anaconda mine.

A very few days will exhaust this place or rather in a very few days this place will exhaust me and then I shall sally for San Francisco and begin more agreeable work on the *Examiner*.

You see, the trouble with me is that I don't know anything about this mining business. I don't know a drift from a vein or a dump from a tunnel and as a consequence, it is difficult for me to display any extraordinary interest in the proceedings.

However, I will learn as much as I can—not very much I guess with you not here . . . and I shall then be able to return with a satisfying sense of having done my duty.[44]

Will had fallen in love with two things—the *Examiner* and Eleanor Calhoun.

If his mother thought she had had problems with her son before, she now had the biggest challenge of her life: weaning Will away from Eleanor, whom she had entertained and chaperoned as a friend of the family and whose acting studies she had helped underwrite. It had not occurred to her that Will might fall in love with the pretty and enticing actress, whom, though of a reasonably good family, Phoebe increasingly disliked and saw as a gold digger. The newspapers were rapturous in their praise of the young lady, but Phoebe grew to despise her for entangling Will. The enchanter had publicly announced her engagement to Will, although it was supposed to be a secret. The papers described Eleanor as "the beautiful debutante" whose "bright young dramatic career . . . promises so splendidly and seems unmarred by vanity, by affectation, or any other taint. . . . Miss Calhoun possesses beauty of the highest order" and a "fascinating personality." But the *Washington Post* reported a rumor that the Senator and Mrs. Hearst opposed the marriage, which they publicly denied. The *San Francisco Call* 7 February, 1887 said the Hearsts recognized that "Miss Calhoun has few equals among young women in intelligence and culture," which was why they had "taken so deep an interest in her, and expended large sums in advancing her dramatic education." But George was said to have sent word to a friend from a sick room, where he was confined by his doctor because of a "severe nervous attack," that he felt the marriage was "inopportune." "This rumored engagement is said by intimate friends of the Senator to be one of the causes which led to his present sickness and prostration," the newspaper reported. "He is extremely averse to the match, not because of any objection to the lady, but for the reason that he considers the conditions unfavorable. His son is but a youth scarce through his college course . . ."[45]

Phoebe was distraught. In a letter to her close friend Mrs. Peck, she said,

I am so distressed about Will that I don't really know how I can live if he marries Eleanor Calhoun. She is determined to marry him and it seems as if he must be in the toils of the Devil fish. . . .

We are trying to delay matters. . . . I am so heartbroken I have no pleasure or pride in anything.[46]

But Will was not the only problem confronting her. Her brother, Elbert, had taken to drink, his wife was a "beast," and the health of her parents was failing, as was her own. She had agreed to take in her nine-year-old niece, Anne Apperson, to remove her from family conflicts. George was fond of the little girl and wanted to adopt her, but Phoebe was opposed to it, saying that it would be unfair to Will. Anne went to live with them in Washington and George always made a point of asking where she was when he came home. He liked to have her sit at his feet on an ottoman in his study while he read the paper and smoked his endless cigars, unconsciously tousling her short hair as if he were petting a dog.[47]

Anne and her "Aunty" did not always agree, however, and were sometimes at odds with each other. Janet Peck thought the girl "petty" and "ungrateful" at times and prone to scheming to deceive her aunt. It could not have been an entirely happy arrangement for the girl, separated from her parents and raised by a kind but domineering aunt. One Christmas, Janet wrote her brother Orrin from the Hearst's Washington house after Annie's parents, Elbert and Lizzie, had come to see her.

Annie says they are unhappy and feel "Aunty" has changed. Little devil has to be making a quiet [mess?] somehow all the time. I think Mrs. Hearst extremely kind and thoughtful about them. . . .

I can see Miss Egan has a very detailed knowledge of all that passed between Mrs. Hearst and Annie. Mrs. Hearst when angry with Annie was pushed to the wall when Miss Egan tried to shield the child and to let her know considerable of what was [written?]. It was a grave mistake for Annie to use my name with her own for I naturally did not know she was playing double and gave her away every breath. She has learned a good lesson and gained by having it no older. The girl has not many friends, I fear, and she will need a good strong one the rest of her life whether she deserves one or not.

I was amused the other day when she was dressed up and looked very pretty. She said in a "verry" English accent—"How I wish my cousin were here. I miss him so much. I think he would like this gown, don't you?" And I am afraid he will and the girl in it. But I was amused at little Miss Calculation. . . .

Mrs. Hearst is much rested and is sweetness itself. I ought to keep a journal in this house. The friction among the servants would be enough to make some humorous chapters.[48]

For Phoebe the friction in her family was almost more than she could bear. Shortly before George had been elected to the Senate, Phoebe had written what she admitted was a "doleful" letter to Orrin, who had become as much a confidant of Phoebe's as a friend of Will's. She poured out her troubles to him. "Something I cannot write" was bothering her, but she kept up a brave front.

> . . . I must tell you about myself in my own way. . . . I have suffered enough to kill most women and yet I am alive, though not <u>very active</u>. First was the worry about Elbert, then Will, and later something that I cannot write. My nerves were in such a state that neuralgia tortured me, and it became almost impossible for me to digest any food. Finally I had rheumatic fever, and during the six weeks I have had three severe operations performed. Now I am getting on well and hope to be about in a few days, and then the weight of sorrow that is almost more than I can bear crushes me and I am down again for days.
>
> As I gain strength my courage increases, and I have determined to keep my mind and heart in a better condition, and rise above the trying influences that have so burdened me. During all this terrible strain, I have smiled and entertained and been bored, when able to be out of bed. Good clothes, an artistic "make up" and a brave spirit have deceived the world, but the hours alone at night when sleep <u>would not</u> come and the heart ache had its own way, cannot be easily forgotten. The weeks have seemed months and I have been afraid that I should get into a state of depression impossible to throw off. . . .
>
> I shall first tell you about Elbert. He was in a dreadful state when I came home. No one could do anything with him. He did nothing, would lie about in a stupor for days. You know what a temper Lizzie has, and when E. was sober, life was not worth anything as she never gave him a moment's peace. To make matters worse, father and mother were unreasonable with me when I insisted upon radical measures. Lizzie wanted to come to the city for awhile and I really considered it best. Elbert could then go to father's and be taken care of.
>
> They decided to let Annie stay with me for a year or more. I sent East for some medicine and Elbert at last consented to take it. . . . For ten weeks Lizzie remained away from home. She was here part of the time and then went to Fresno and visited some of her relatives. She grew fat while the rest of us fretted, grieved and grew thin. The truth is, she is a beast.
>
> Of course, I do not excuse poor Elbert for his course, but when he tries to do better she does not help him. The old people have failed and broken, mother especially. For a few weeks Elbert has not been drinking at all, they hope. I have not much faith in reform, but do all I can to help him. . . .
>
> I expect to take Annie East with me and try to make something of her. Don't know if it can be done; however, I shall try. She is bright but has some of Lizzie's hard nature.
>
> I shall now tell you of Will. You well know all that I have been to him, the devotion lavished upon him. You also know he is selfish, indifferent and undemonstrative as his father. Both have their good qualities, but the other sides of their natures are most trying. Will is a brilliant fellow, has improved wonderfully in many respects, has not bad habits, given up the foolishness and carelessness of a great part of his college life, and is immensely interested in business. You would be greatly surprised to see how he works and how very capable he is. Mr. Hearst is very much pleased with Will's business abilities.
>
> You will wonder how it is with all this I am so unhappy about my boy. You

will understand when I tell you that he is <u>desperately</u> in love with Miss Calhoun, the <u>actress</u>. He has simply gone mad about her, and she is quite willing for she wants to marry a man who has money. She is about two years older than Will and in worldly experience and craft she is twenty years his senior. She is in poor health, has not been doing much in her profession for more than a year, and—oh! dear! if I could tell you half of all I have gone through in connection with this affair, you would be astonished.

We oppose the marriage but may not be able to prevent it. I feel that it will ruin my boy's life to marry such a designing woman and he will have to be burdened with the whole family of <u>eight</u>. Miss Calhoun is wonderfully bright and even brilliant, but so erratic, visionary, indolent and utterly wanting in order and neatness with extravagant tastes and no appreciation of values. All she cares for is to spend money, enjoy luxury and receive admiration. Will would be disillusionized in a few years and when just in his prime be burdened with an old invalid wife.

Now you know a little of my anxiety. Miss C. knows that we oppose their plans and has made Will so <u>ugly</u> and cruel to me, I can never forgive her. Don't on any account let Will know that I have told you a word of this. He would only be more determined and disagreeable. . . .

Business affairs are not as cheerful as they might be, but might be worse. I hate politics so that it is difficult for me to mention the subject. Mr. Hearst expects to be elected to the Senate for six years but the matter cannot be decided until the Legislature meet and elect whoever may be <u>their</u> choice. There is a democratic majority and it is thought they must elect Mr. Hearst but I have <u>no</u> faith in politicians. One can never depend on them. . . .

I like Washington, but could enjoy more there if not in political life. A Senator's wife has her trials, I assure you, and I don't consider that there is much honor in politics.

You know I am always obliged to carry all social responsibilities. Will don't like society, and I need not tell you how I have to manage Mr. Hearst to keep him even near the right thing.

How I should love to go to Germany and have a long rest from worry, fatigue and pain. Weak as I am, I seem to be the anchor for awhile longer and must do my best. I am actually ashamed to send you such a doleful letter. . . .[49]

Will had to be sent away, his mother felt, in the hope that he would get over his infatuation. In the fall of 1886 he agreed to go to Mexico with Jack Follansbee to look over his father's huge Babicora ranch in Chihuahua, acquired because of geological favors to Mexican President Porfirio Diaz. The idea was that Will would take over the ranch and Jack would manage it, but Will turned down the offer. He asked that *Examiners* be sent to him regularly while he was away so that he could critique them. Not unlike his mother, he had become ill under the stress of quarreling with his parents and pining for Eleanor. His mother had argued, as she always did, that a trip would do him good and restore his health. He wrote her en route to Mexico,

Everything is blooming so far, and I have no doubt but I will have a very healthful trip. I am equally certain, however, that I shall get very tired of this business before three months are over but I guess I can stand it for the sake of the benefit it will do me. You know I will have to build up my constitution considerably in view of the threatening misfortunes. Send my letters when they—if indeed they ever do—come to Chihuahua and let me hear the latest news of yourself, herself, themselves and things in general.[50]

In other letters he referred to the tension between himself and his parents.

Dear Mummy,
   I am almost afraid to send you this letter lest you faint away with surprise on receipt of it. I wanted to talk to you and fix things all up but I couldn't do it. You were nervous and I was nervous and I thought the best thing I could do was wait and write—so here's the letter. . . .
   I hope you are feeling better now that you are away from the malign influence of your infant.[51]

When he had decided against taking the ranch he wrote, "I am sorry I was so decided about the ranch business if it distressed Papa but I am nervous and irritable, I expect, and it seemed outrageous that my father should think so poorly of me."[52]

Will also had asked for a boat, which he had been denied; he was peeved. He was accustomed to getting his way: "I am all broke up about the boat. I don't want to complain, but I think it would be a mighty good thing to get me."[53]

From Mexico he wrote his "Mama" that he still loved Eleanor and would not change his mind about marrying her. That news, which his mother did not want to hear, was contained in a postscript to a letter full of advice for his father about property interests in Mexico and the senatorial election. He was looking to his family's, and his own, future fortunes.

   We are pioneers in Mexico. We have all the opportunities open to us that ever pioneers in California had and we should improve them. . . . You also have great influence with the government here . . . connections and a reputation in the east. . . . Your election to the Senate, if you get it, will be worth a million dollars to you at the very least here in Mexico. It will give you so much power, it will so impress these fellows.
   . . . there is no reason why we should not soon be as rich as Crocker or anybody.

But it was the postscript that discussed what was on his mind.

   P.S. Young Georgie Gould and young Jimmy Blaine have both gone and done it. Who said next? I am sure of one thing, however, the son of Senator Hearst from California will lead them all as far as his selection is concerned. Yes, will lead them all, meaning everybody and not George and Jim and Willie Crocker alone—but all. And if, as you say, in a few years I could pick the girl of all the girls I wanted in the world, I would not change my mind. Nay, my Pop. There has been time to give my love a chance to cool were it so inclined but it obstinately refuses so to do. If I were serious before, I am desperately in earnest now and if she should ever reconsider her decision, why I would just go down on one of these southern plantations and raise rice and sugar cane and hell till our friend, the busy and grim visaged warrior, came along and doubled me up with a swoop of his scythe. You bet you, Pop.[54]

Eleanor's "decision" no doubt was strongly influenced by the Hearsts. She was over her head, and neither she nor Will was a match for Phoebe when she harnessed George to the cause. A financial incentive may have been offered Eleanor to leave their son alone. Whatever the inducement, Miss Calhoun went away. She dreamed of a glamorous stage career. Both were strong women, but Phoebe cleverly had worn her down after a painful series of meetings in which the older woman was overtly kind, protective, and understanding, but firm and unrelenting. "Cold, hard" Lloyd Tevis did the dirty work, acting as intermediary and negotiator, unknown to Will. Phoebe's tactics of patient but stubborn cajoling, delaying, and persuading had worked. Eleanor went off to pursue a successful theatrical career and did not enter the Hearst house again.

Phoebe wrote George of the arrangement and of Will's giving in and seeing reason at last. She asked George to have the letter destroyed, and, in a stunning aside, asked that George stop going around telling "people that your wife is crazy."

Their separate paths had become more divergent, yet they were tightly bound and in an inexplicable way continued to be fond of one another, or at least respectful. George, however, in his blunt style, was not averse to expressing his opinions about his wife's activities. Phoebe wrote him:

My dear Husband,

Since the first of the month, I have been in such a state of distress and extreme anxiety that it has been impossible to write letters. At present my mind is not relieved of the burdens, but things have assumed a somewhat different aspect and we are at least sure of delay, and Will is not insane nor is he so unreasonable. He says that he will not do anything rash and I believe he will keep his word.

Miss C. has been most foolish and announced the engagement and caused all the publicity. There is no doubt that she did this to make the thing secure. By this action she has placed herself in an unenviable position, but I have done nothing to compromise her. I have refused to see reporters here—would make no statement whatever.

Today Miss C. came to see me, and we had a long talk. We began at the same time when she and Will first told me, and she said she felt satisfied that I was delighted. I replied that I was by no means happy, but thought best to refrain from any expressions of disapproval to her, for I did not then, and never have believed that <u>she</u> was in love, that I earnestly hoped that in a few months they would both feel differently, and just here let me say that in a few days after Will had spoken to her on this subject, he reproached me with showing a change of manner, and said that <u>Eleanor felt</u> it. So you see, she could <u>not</u> have thought me jubilant.

I also said at the time that I felt sure you would not approve, and I thought best not to worry you with it <u>then</u>. I saw that Will had completely lost his reasoning faculties, and I stood in constant dread of a sudden marriage, which Will <u>now</u> tells me <u>he urged</u>. I now think that they <u>would</u> have been married last summer if we had strongly opposed it. I was very unhappy about the understanding between them, but truly considered the matter from every point, and decided that it was best for her to return to London and go on with her play. I hoped for delay.

After you came home, I wrote her a kind letter, but told her of your objections to the marriage, and urged delay. She then plainly took a stubborn stand, and has forced matters as much as <u>possible</u> up to the present.

There is so much more that I can tell you when you come here. I talked <u>very</u> plainly today, but told her that I would do anything reasonable to protect her and place her right before the world. Will and I had a talk tonight, and he has regained his reason, and wants to do all that is right and best.

He proposed going to S. F. So he starts tomorrow morning. He tells her that he goes there to see you, and he will then write her a blue letter, telling her that you will do nothing more and will not consent and that he would not be willing to marry her unless he could place her well. This would give her an opportunity to break the engagement, which I think she will do when she finds there is no <u>money</u> in it. She looks old and thin and told me today that she had fever most of the time.

Will feels right towards you. I told him that he must surely know how much you love him and that your only wish was for his happiness. We both feel most positive that this marriage could result in nothing but misery. He has behaved well and is manly and honorable.

We must be firm and kind and help him get out of this. He will talk freely with you but will feel sensitive about any comments from others. I know it was hard for you to take the stand you did but it was right and best. Nothing can convince me that E. loves Will. She is such a clever actress that she makes almost everyone believe that black is white, but I <u>know</u> and <u>feel</u> that she is <u>acting</u>.

I think her mother should come east. Then we can arrange matters more satisfactorily. If Mrs. Calhoun comes, that will obviate the necessity of E. going to Cal. which she will do unless her mother comes here. It is best to meet that expense and get rid of of this thing as well as possible. I think Mrs. Calhoun can influence E. and also her presence here will place E. properly. Will and I think this best. It would be bad for us and for Will to have E. go to Cal.

Will is so deeply interested in the paper that he will be all right. He worried a great deal for two or three days, but he eats and sleeps well, and has too much strength of character to be seriously affected by this. He has been as good and tender and confidential as I could wish, and I think he feels that it has been some comfort to have Mother here.

Mr. Tevis has had numerous interviews with Miss C. and myself. I cannot see that he has aided a great deal in adjusting matters, and I am <u>always</u>

suspicious of him. I do not believe in his friendship. He is a very cold, hard man, and no man's friend excepting L. Tevis. I did not tell Will that Mr. T. had anything to do with this, and it is best not to let him know.

I want our dear Mary to read this letter and then <u>burn</u> it.

I also especially request that you will not tell people that your wife is <u>crazy</u>. I resent that.

. . . I return to Washington tomorrow and shall be glad, as I have been under a great strain here and need rest. On Monday, I am going to a luncheon given by Mrs. Cleveland and shall try to enjoy it. Lent begins so soon there will be very little going on after that. . . .

> Your loving wife,
> Phebe[55]

Will asked that his parents treat Eleanor with consideration:

I had a letter from Mrs. Calhoun today and I shall go down to see her tomorrow. I am sorry I didn't have a talk with my father on this affair for while I have determined to comply with his and your wishes in this matter, I insist upon Eleanor being treated with all consideration possible. You know how terribly unfortunate this is for her.

I have heard only twice from her since I left and while she doesn't say much she appears to be in the most intense anxiety over the outcome of your opposition.[56]

Possibly as a "reward" for having acquiesced to his parents' wishes, or as a diversion, Will got the other object of his affection. George at last relented and, on 4 March 1887, the day that he was sworn in as senator, his son, at age twenty-four, officially took over the *Examiner*.[57]

He wrote his father enthusiastically:

I shall be through here on the 10th of February, and I shall go immediately to San Francisco if I can catch you before you come here. I am anxious to begin work on the *Examiner*. I have all my pipes laid, and it only remains to turn on the gas. One year from the day I take hold of the thing our circulation will have increased ten thousand.

It is necessary that the *Examiner* destroy every possibility of being considered an organ. I know it is not an organ devoted exclusively to your interests, but there are many people who do not know this, and so, the influence and accordingly the sale of the paper is thus largely affected. . . .

We must be alarmingly enterprising, and we must be startlingly original. We must be honest and fearless. We must have greater variety than we have ever had. We must print more matter than we have ever printed. We must increase our force, and enlarge our editorial building. . . .

There are some things that I intend to do new and striking which will constitute a revolution in the sleepy journalism of the Pacific slope and will focus the eyes of all that section on the *Examiner*. I am not going to write you what these are, for the letter might get lost, or you might leak. . . . In a year we will have increased at least ten thousand in circulation. In two years we will be paying. And in five years we will be the biggest paper on the Pacific slope.

We won't be paying for two years because up to that time I propose turning back into the improvement of the paper every cent that comes in.[58]

It was an ambitious set of goals, but Will had no doubt that they would be realized. His determination, and his reaction to the recent trauma of his personal life, made him plunge into work, day and night, at the paper. He hired several of his college chums to help him. Shortly after becoming editor-in-chief, he wrote his mother:

> I don't suppose I will live more than two or three weeks if this strain keeps up. I don't get to bed until about two o'clock and I wake up at about seven in the morning and can't get to sleep again, for I must see the paper and compare it with the Chronicle. If we are the best, I can turn over and go to sleep with quiet satisfaction but if the Chronicle happens to scoop us, that lets me out of all sleep for the day.
>
> The newspaper business is no fun and I had no idea quite how hard a job I was undertaking when I entered upon the editorial management of the Examiner. Thank heaven for one thing: Our efforts are appreciated.
>
> The great people, the great and good people of California, want the Examiner. They don't want it very bad; they don't want it much harder than at the rate of about thirty additional copies a day, but in time this will count and if we can manage to keep ahead we will have in a year from thirty to thirty-two thousand subscribers. That will put us away ahead of the Call and well up with the Chronicle.[59]

By the time Will took it over, the paper had lost George a quarter of a million dollars; and before it turned around, it cost George some seven hundred thousand dollars out of pocket.[60] But Will wrote his father positively, begging him to use his influence with friends to buy goods only from Examiner advertisers and to exert political pressure to have certain local officials, who boycotted and criticized the Examiner, removed from office. Will called them "dadgasted unpopular snobs" and "conceited, insolent popinjays." "We are doing mighty well," he wrote his father, "but we would do a great deal better and would get on much faster if we could only work all the forces and influences that ought to be at our command." In the beginning Will sought his father's approval for and made an effort to involve him in decisions affecting the paper and its content, but as time went on Will and his staff made the decisions without George's input. In a letter to his father not long after becoming editor, Will said:

> The Examiner is doing very well—very well indeed. We get out a very good paper, but we might get out a first class paper if we only had a few more advertisements. . . .
>
> What we are straining for now is circulation. The paper has become good enough to please most anybody—so good, in fact, that many republicans are subscribing for it, and it only remains now for us to bring it prominently

before the eyes of the people and to convince them that the present excel-
lence of the paper will endure. . . .

We might go ahead much quicker and with much less expenditure if some
of our violent opponents in federal office were removed and *Examiner*
democrats were appointed in their places. If you can get these . . . removed,
you will do away with . . . great obstacles, not only to the success of the
Examiner but to the success of the Democratic Party in California. . . .

Damn 'em, they make me mad. Have them bounced. Assert your rights. You
are not given half the consideration you deserve. . . .

I have got so that I won't buy anything of anyone that don't advertise in the
paper, and I want you and Mama to be the same way, and I want you to use
your political influence for it and I want you to come home as soon as
possible and help me for awhile. We are bound to succeed but whether we
succeed in one year or in five depends largely upon the work of all of us.

Mike De Young said to [Army General Irwin] McDowell the other day that
he had hoped the *Examiner* would drop out but he realized now that it had
come to stay . . .[61]

Indeed, it had come to stay. Will even valued the daily editorial
criticisms of the *Examiner* by other papers as good publicity. But
despite his best efforts, the paper continued to lose money. Several large
advertisers withdrew, including George's business partner, Tevis. Will
felt betrayed. He wrote his father:

. . . I positively will go simply crazy about this paper unless I get some
help.

. . . As these sons of bitches are principally indebted to you for whatever
they have, I think this is the goddamndest low down business I ever heard of.
I don't apologize for the swear words for I think the circumstances excuse
me.

Now if you will telegraph Stump a hot telegram to withdraw all your
business from these firms, if you have any there, and not to give them any
more until they advertise in the Examiner and not in the Chronicle, I think
we can accomplish something.

. . . Nobody takes any interest in the paper or helps us at all. It's dam
discouraging.

I am very much obliged for your kind offer of a thousand dollars for a Xmas
present but money is so tight and Stump borrowing so much that I guess I
won't take it—not till much later anyhow. It will be all the Xmas I want if you
will use your influence for the paper and help us in the way I have mentioned.[62]

Will figured out a way to get money from his father without his
knowledge to keep the paper going when George was ready to give it up
as a losing proposition. Will needed fifty thousand dollars in a hurry,
which his father refused to put up. So Will talked a Democratic commit-
teeman into giving the paper one-half of George's one-hundred-thousand-dollar pledge to the party.[63] It was several years before the
Examiner began to show a profit, but with Will's manic perseverance

and George's money, it became the paper to be reckoned with in San Francisco.

"Young Hearst's success with the *Examiner* has upset all our cherished ideas regarding the experience necessary for the successful management of a newspaper," a prominent journalist (and later librarian of Congress) John Russell Young said in 1888. The young upstart editor, "with a tremendous amount of nervous energy and a genius for hard work," had "set a hot pace from the start," a trade publication, *The Journalist*, stated in its 29 December 1888 issue. To attract readers, Will began printing cablegrams from Europe, telegraphic coverage of eastern sporting events, and daily illustrations; he hired special trains to distribute the paper outside the city and gave the local zoo a grizzly bear named "Monarch of the Dailies." His efforts, *The Journalist* noted, brought from "his alarmed contemporaries" the charge of "sensationalism," which Will did not deny. In fact, he defended it in an article in *Overland Monthly* magazine, saying that "intelligent sensationalism" was just what he was striving for. He sent an artist up in a balloon to draw the first aerial view of San Francisco, which was sent to the paper by homing pigeon. A reporter was sent to one of California's insane asylums to get the inside story on cruelty to inmates. Another was ordered to get himself locked up in the San Francisco Home for Inebriates, where he spent three unhappy weeks to prove that anyone could be indefinitely imprisoned there without cause. And one hapless reporter jumped from an Oakland ferry into icy San Francisco Bay to demonstrate the ferry company's incompetence in handling life boats. It was all good, lively muckraking—even his father's party politicians were not exempt—and it attracted attention to the *Examiner*. That was just what Will wanted. His genius for getting attention was paying off. He told *The Journalist*: "I hoped I made the *Examiner* a first-class newspaper entirely aside from its sensational features, but I had to get the people to look at the paper before they could see its general improvements, so I had to do many things out of the usual order."[64]

Still, Will had a hard time keeping his father interested. It took all of his most persuasive talents. He had grandiose schemes for getting the paper in the hands of readers—including free oyster roasts and boat rides on the Bay—and he encouraged George to use his position as a senator to win friends for the *Examiner*:

Dear Father,

We are having a hard fight with the *Examiner* against the other papers out there and against the prejudice and conservatism of the people of the coast. The *Examiner* is admitted to be the best paper now published in San Francisco and this admission is made even by the employees of the other papers, "but," they say, "you cannot keep ahead." If we do keep ahead, we will win for even the prejudice of people against the paper—that is, the belief that the *Examiner* will shortly relapse into its former flaccid state—even the prejudice and conservatism is giving way before our enterprise.

Our circulation is increasing more rapidly. Formerly it increased at the rate of about 40 or 50 a week and now it increases at about 50 a day. If we can keep this increase up we will be on a paying basis in a little over a year. Now we must bring every force and influence under our control to bear upon this object. You are the most powerful help we have and you must not hesitate to do all you possibly can for us.

Right now is a crisis in the history of our paper. If we hesitate a moment or fall back a step we are lost and we can never hope to make anything out of the *Examiner* while it remains in our hands. At present people are talking about the paper and looking at it, and some of the more adventurous ones are even subscribing to it. There is a boom that must be kept up and the interest of the public must be held on the paper and soon when the people see that our superiority over the other papers is an actual and lasting fact we will get all that vast majority of subscribers that take the best paper no matter what its politics.

Papa, you must do your best for us and you must do it immediately. Delay would be as fatal as neglect.

First, see Senator Stanford and try to get him interested in the progress of the paper. A man like Senator Stanford ought to feel some interest in a paper whose object is to do the right thing, the strong thing and the best thing by the people of the coast. He will know that our paper will be honest and pure and that it will never be guilty of any blackmailing schemes or filthy transactions of any kind such as have distinguished our papers here. He will know this and he will feel I am sure that it is the duty of honorable men to support such a paper if only to offset the opposition which scoundrels would naturally make against it. If we can get Senator Stanford to take an interest in the prosperity of our paper, the greatest stroke towards its success will have been made.

At present the news companies on the trains—especially the S.P.—discriminate against the *Examiner* for the benefit of the *Chronicle*. This may not be due to railroad opposition but it would be prevented by railroad favors. We receive letters constantly saying that they can't get *Examiners* on the train and coming home. I had a conversation with one of the news boys on the train and he said that the news company only gave him 15 *Examiners* but that he could sell 50.

Then when summer comes and the people leave the city and go to Monterey and Santa Cruz and Menlo, etc., along the line of that southern road, I want to run a special engine and deliver papers at every station along the route. This will procure us six or eight thousand subscribers and the prestige of the thing—for it has never been done in California—will bring advertising in far greater proportions. We can and will do this if the engine would not cost us too much and perhaps Senator Stanford might here interfere in our behalf and get us a rate that we could afford. Please try to get him to do this for us. . . .

One thing more. I have telegraphed you a letter of introduction to Mr. Cockrill of the *World* and also to Mr. Turner and Mr. Ballard Smith of the *World*. If you haven't seen these gentlemen already, please go to see them immediately now. The most important thing we can do for our paper is to make friends with these powerful eastern newspaper men. They would appreciate a visit from a U.S. Senator, they would feel flattered. Make yourself agreeable to them. Tell them how you admire the newspaper business and how you determined your son should be a newspaper man—if you found he possessed talent enough. That you were determined that he should not be simply a newspaper proprietor, but should be an editor, a newspaper man, etc., etc. Tickle them a little. Say that I told you what a great paper the World was and you wanted to see it, etc., etc.

Then the first thing you know they will do anything they can for us. . . .

See Mr. Nordhoff of the Herald in Washington. There is no need of any of the aforesaid funny business to him. He is a fine man and I am greatly indebted to him. Moreover, I am for the Herald with all my force. It is an honest and brave paper and one can respect it. It is the kind of paper I should like the Examiner to be, while the World is, because of the Jew that owns it, a nasty, unscrupulous, damned sheet that I despise but which is too powerful for us to insult. At present, especially, we must make friends with the World as some one has just gone east from the San Francisco Call to get the World Cable News and we want to keep the World from giving them this if we can possibly.

I work on the paper from ten o'clock in the morning till one o'clock at night and every one in the office from the reporters to the editors are working like beavers. There is a woeful lack of system about the Examiner but this we will soon correct.

Please, please attempt to do what I have written you. It is <u>very important indeed</u>.

> Your loving son.
> W. R. Hearst

Wednesday morning.

The Chronicle comes out this morning with the World Cables. However, we can get the World on our side yet if you will make yourself agreeable to the editors. De Young is not a U. S. Senator.

> W. R. H.[65]

Will's cajoling of his father was a sign of his growing sophistication in the world of politics and journalism, but it also betrayed his lack of knowledge about how George operated—quietly, in the back rooms with the boys—and of the realities of the "club" of power, on the fringe of which Will always would operate, never really belonging, as his father did.

Will was optimistic in thinking that Stanford, a Republican, would help out a Democratic party organ, even with a train engine. But Stanford would rue the day he turned Will down. The Examiner later would lead a fight, almost a personal vendetta, against Stanford and his railroad cronies' efforts to extend the time for repayment of federal loans.

From George's perspective, several years later, the *Examiner* had been a business failure that his son turned into a success. "I did not realize the boy's got grit," he told historian H. H. Bancroft.[66] In his biographical reminiscences in 1890, George said of Will and the *Examiner*:

> I tried all sorts of people to make it a success, because, of course, I had not time to attend to it, and could not pretend to run it. After I had lost about a quarter of a million by the paper, my boy Will came out of school, and said he wanted to try his hand at the paper. I thought it was the very worst thing he could do; and told him so, adding that I could not make it pay. He said, however, that the reason that the paper did not pay was because it was not the best paper in the country.
>
> He said that if he had it, he would make it the best paper in the country . . . and then it would pay. I then put him in it, and made him a deed of the whole property from top to bottom, and agreed to stand by him for two years. Now, I don't think there is a better paper in the country, and if I wanted to get all the news, I would rather have the *Examiner* than any of them. It has got just as good eastern news as any of the other papers and a great deal better western news.
>
> My son Will is one of the hardest workers I ever saw, and he thought at the time that he would tire of it as there was so much drudgery in it, but he did not. He is now 27 years of age, having been born in California in 1863, and before he went to Harvard spent six months in one of the New England common schools. He was four years in Harvard. I do not think, however, that he worked very hard there, because he was too fond of fun.
>
> Before the *Examiner* was put on a paying basis, it cost me from six to seven-hundred-thousand dollars; but I believe it is now worth upwards of a million. While I did not for a good while pay any personal attention to the conducting of the paper, still I took pains, now and then, to find out what the people needed, and inaugurated reforms which made it a valuable family paper in all respects.[67]

Phoebe took a less generous view of the *Examiner's* expenses and of her son's free hand to spend whatever George would give him. Will was spending more than she and George together—and they were not penurious, what with Phoebe's travels and maintaining a house in Washington and George's keeping a stable of expensive racehorses. She asked George to rein in their son, on the advice of Stump, their business manager, who, Phoebe wrote George,

> . . . said that Will had been spending an enormous amount of money, more than you and me together. Some time ago he talked to Will about it, and the last two months there was a decrease in expenditure. He said you have never limited the supply and he, of course, could not refuse payment. He thinks it a kindness to Will and the only means of aiding him to do right will be for you to make a reasonable allowance and not permit matters to go on as they have been.
>
> This can be done in a perfectly kind way but would be <u>best</u> for the boy. . . .
> I will talk more with Will . . . and get an idea of the needs and expenses of

the paper and a more thorough understanding of personal affairs. . . . Things have been going on in rather a bad way.[68]

In one year, she reported to George, from August 1887 to August 1888, Will personally had spent $47,939 and had drawn $184,513 for the Examiner. He had no idea of the amount of money he was spending. He simply drew it when he wanted it. "If you have any courage, it might be well to say a few words to Will," Phoebe suggested to George, who was largely deaf to her importunings.[69]

Much of Will's personal expenses went to keeping a mistress in his Sausalito home and to running a steam yacht, the Aquila, which he finally had acquired and in which he commuted to San Francisco, across the Bay. The mistress, Tessie Powers, had first been Jack Follansbee's girl and Will had inherited her when Jack left Harvard. Tessie had been a waitress in Cambridge who was down on her luck.[70] Will's soft spot for the underdog made him even more vulnerable to her attractions. And he may have been retaliating for his parents' breaking off his engagement with Eleanor Calhoun. Phoebe was appalled that he lived openly with Tessie, out of wedlock, flaunting social convention. A story is told that on one occasion he rented a San Francisco apartment and filled it with furniture ordered from the best department store in town, Sloan's, asking that the bill be sent to his mother. Phoebe paid it— and then ordered all the furniture sent back to the store.[71] But Will was further announcing his independence from his mother—and his similarities to his father. His relationship with Phoebe was developing into a tug-of-war between devotion and resistance, and it went one way or the other as she complained or caressed, and as his financial dependence on his parents grated on him. One moment he was the attentive, amusing, and adoring son, the next, hateful and inconsiderate, Phoebe thought. On her return to San Francisco in July 1888 she wrote George that Will

> . . . really seems glad to see me and has shown me more kind feeling and affection during the last four hours than he has shown during as many years. We have already had a quiet, reasonable and thorough discussion of the subject that has caused anxiety.[72]

Will was making up for his meanness to his mother. He did not want to bite the hand that fed him. And he could charm and delight his mother as no one else could. He knew how to win her over. He "was very sorry for having spent so much money" and agreed to adopt a new plan for the Examiner in which he would not draw more than five thousand dollars a month until the end of 1888, after which he hoped the paper would be self-sustaining. Phoebe wrote George from Yellowstone Park that

> . . . Will is very anxious to cut down but, of course, not to the extent of injuring the paper.
> I know you are glad to have me feel contented about Will, and I do. It has been such a comfort to be with him so much and to have him talk, not grunt and be ugly. He has been kind, thoughtful and considerate and has shown me so much affection that I scarcely know how to express my happiness. I feel ten years younger. Tenderness and love is more to a mother than all else.[73]

She was feeling affectionate toward George on that trip and, in another letter, closed by saying, "I send you much love, and hope you think often of your wife."[74]

Besides her husband and son, she had many things to occupy her—charities, travels, and the necessity of establishing a home in Washington. In 1889, her focus shifted to the nation's Capitol, where she would have the grandest salon in town.

10
Love, Death, and Independence

Phoebe found Washington and the people with whom she could surround herself stimulating. She wanted a mansion in which she could entertain and show off her treasures from Europe. George was content to live in a hotel and had no interest in social affairs, which he called his wife's "rackets." He had a daily routine that included discharging his senatorial duties with a minimum of effort and drinking with the boys at Chamberlain's bar, which had the kind of southern food that George liked—spareribs and hominy. But Phoebe had grander ideas about how a senator and his family should live, and George left that business to her. Although they rented a pleasant house (on Highland Terrace), she set about convincing George to purchase a large, handsome residence at 1400 New Hampshire Avenue, near fashionable Dupont Circle.

> Now about the house. I know it is not at all the kind of house that we would build, but you are not by any means willing to build. The Fairchild house is well located, healthy, stands on a corner, and has light and air. It will increase in value, that is sure. We have room there to make some changes that will suit you, and not be extravagant. We will have a home for four years, and then it will sell. I can make the house pretty and attractive and there will be people who appreciate that and will buy it.
>
> I have been anxious to feel somewhat settled, but I don't want to urge you against your better judgement and your wishes in the matter. I know you wish to please me, but I don't want to be unreasonable. If you buy this house, I shall hope that you will be happy and comfortable in it. If not, I shall feel that you knew best and we may find another desirable place.[1]

The house was purchased. And in June 1889 she set off on an extensive trip through Europe and Russia while the house was being remodeled. Much of the trip was devoted to research on innovative educational systems, in which she had taken a keen interest.

She sailed 26 June aboard the *City of New York*. The passenger list read like a *Who's Who* of New York society and newly rich Americans, with names like Rockefeller, Aldrich, Auchincloss, Bloomfield, Andrew Carnegie, John J. Deering, Jacob Livingston, James H. Kidder, Peter E. Studebaker, and Henry Saltonstall.

Phoebe went to the Bayreuth Wagner festival in Germany, and wrote George from Berlin that

> While over here I am anxious to obtain all the information possible about the Froebel system of kindergartens, and also the Sloyd system, which teaches manual labor. Although the social and political conditions are different in our country, we may profit somewhat by their experiences over here. I had a long talk today with a very intelligent and agreeable woman, who is doing admirable work here among the poor. She has been in America and fully understands our institutions and our people. She said, "Your country is the place for the fuller development of these methods of instruction."[2]

She visited several archaeological museums, which fascinated her, and found her friend Mary W. Kincaid, a teacher and fellow board member of the Golden Gate Kindergarten, a knowledgeable guide and traveling companion. Nevertheless, her heart ached when she thought of Will, who, she felt, "does not recognize the fact that I am in existence."[3]

Russia took her mind off her troubles. Her privileged party received red-carpet treatment, thanks to a letter of introduction from the American secretary of state. "The distances are great and everything is on such a colossal scale," she wrote, that it was hard to see all they wished. They were given special permits to the Hermitage, which was closed to the public, and visited the School of Mines—"said to be the finest in the world . . . Russia supplies the world with platinum," she wrote George.[4]

She again hoped that George would meet her in Europe, at the exposition in Paris, but he would not come. "You could have brought Robert to take care of you and I would have spoken French for you and gone about with you when you wished me," she wrote him. The prospect of George's visiting Paris was unrealistic. So Phoebe, resigned to the incompatibility of their interests, urged him not "to drink too much and sit up all night," and to free himself "from leeches and parasites, who cling, flatter and want all they can get. . . . I assure you, I am taking great comfort in being free from importunities and incessant interruptions and worries."[5]

Mary Kincaid wrote George from Russia:

> Your wife has worked every day the whole day at looking into the most valuable means of improvement and into the history and development of the people of this northern world. Not a single hour has she given to social life or show.
>
> I can't help thinking what a difference between her and Mrs. Mackay, for the latter came here in as much grand state as a queen, spent her time in foolish ostentation, in dancing around the Court here and displaying her rare

clothes and jewels, traveling about in private car, and all such unreality as a superficial woman would delight in . . . leaving here without a single idea of how this country grew and struggled out of the Tartar grasp into the autocratic magnificence that she was. . . .[6]

Phoebe now had ample justification for her travels and the expenses she incurred. This was to be an instructive trip, from which she would take back new information to apply to good works in the States. George's racehorses could hardly be so justified, and she remonstrated him about such wastefulness.

> I cannot feel reconciled that you and Joe [Clark] did not come over. You surely have not had any pleasure with your horses, nor have they been, or ever will be, any benefit to you. The money is thrown away so far as a racing stable is concerned.
>
> I have been travelling and spending some money, too, but have had a great deal of genuine pleasure, have gained information and seen much that will remain with me as long as I retain my faculties.
>
> I have also been most carefully studying the care and training of little children among the poor classes. There is much that can aid us in America, for the experience here is surely worth something to us, and there is a work to be done among our cosmopolitan population. . . .
>
> I am invited here [in Vienna] to see the school gardens, the cooking schools and the training schools where girls are taught to be good servants and also for the preparation of good wives and mothers. I am obtaining a few models for the manual labor schools, and seeing all that I can.
>
> If I had a little more time, I would go to Brussels to see the model schools but it cannot be done now.[7]

While Phoebe was preoccupied with setting young people on a useful path, George was consumed with the sport of kings. He had begun racing thoroughbreds in 1887 and his desire was to establish a first-rate breeding farm in California to rival those of his friends Stanford and Haggin. His string of twenty-five horses, racing under gold and green silks, the colors of California, did poorly for several years on the tracks of the East until he acquired a colt named Tournament from Haggin and replaced his "kid-glove" trainer Matt Allen, so-called because he was a natty dresser and put on tight-fitting kid gloves before sponging out his horses' mouths. George was tickled when his well-dressed former trainer was occasionally mistakenly identified in the paddock as "Senator Hearst—worth $50 million," while George stood by in his tobacco-stained suit. A black trainer, Albert Cooper, took over the stable in 1890 and George's racing fortunes improved. Tournament won more money that season than had ever been won by any horse in America in a single year—nearly ninety thousand dollars. George once replied to a *New York Times* racing writer, when things were going badly on the turf, "I get discouraged, man? Bless you, no. I never failed in anything I ever undertook yet, and I'm not going to throw up my hands in a little game like horse racing." Still, the sports writers speculated, "in two years [Hearst] must have spent enough money on his stable to start a good-sized national bank . . . something like $300,000. . . . [despite all his losses] his patience is sublime." Then George paid the largest sum ever realized—forty thousand dollars—for a yearling, King Thomas, who was never to win a race.[8] That was too much for Will, who wryly wired his father on hearing the news,

> Please telegraph me whether or not it is true that you have paid forty thousand dollars for a colt. If you have, I shall let everything here [go] to thunder and come East and take care of you. In the meantime, you had better get a nurse. I mean this.
> I shall leave immediately. It is more important to keep you from throwing away your money than to learn to take care of your business, when, if you keep on like this, you won't have any to take care of. If you insist upon squandering all your money, I will stop working and see what I can do in that line myself. But you simply want to become notorious, I think. I can suggest cheaper methods and some that will reflect less on your intelligence.[9]

If George's racehorses were a trial for Phoebe, her real continuing heartache was her son, who would not give up Tessie, whom Phoebe now openly called a "prostitute." From Europe she implored George,

> I do hope you can induce Will to change his manner of living. I suppose you hear from him occasionally. I never do. How is it possible for him to devote his time and attention to a prostitute and utterly ignore his mother? He will surely have his punishment.[10]

And from London, she asked,

> Do you intend to continue your indulgence? The paper still draws heavily upon you and it will never pay expenses while you supply funds. William will purchase the place at Sausalito and you will pay for it, thereby encouraging his present shameful manner of living. I try not to be utterly crushed by this sorrow, but it is hard to bear.[11]

Will went merrily on his way, spending money as if it were in endless supply. He hated his newly imposed allowance and asked his "Poppy" for "some rocks . . . a small checklet for a few thou." for Christmas. "This dollar limit business is no good," he wrote his father.[12]

He sent Tessie away for a time and devoted all his energies to the Examiner, telling George,

> The Call is practically out of the race, but the Chronicle is fighting tremendously hard, and it does not hesitate to adopt any idea we bring out. . . . It

has altered its make-up until it is almost exactly like ours . . . its matter is so similar that we are not allowed to reap much advantage from our moves.

You bet your life those *Chronicle* people are smart and they are not retarded by any false pride.[13]

The *Chronicle*'s next move (in 1890) was to put up the finest new building in San Francisco with the largest clock face in the world, which was to "be lighted by electricity and . . . visible all over San Francisco and from <u>Oakland</u>," Will wrote George:

This kind of thing has its effect on <u>everybody</u> . . . it had an effect on Grandpa even. He said, "Dear me, that fellow must make an awful lot of money."[14]

Will wanted a bigger and flashier building and a better press, and he argued that the only way to save the *Examiner* was for George to realign his resources to benefit the paper. In the same letter he wrote,

. . . the *Examiner* has been successful not because it has been going to do something in the future but because it has been doing something in the present all the time. Now we are losing subscribers, we are losing advertisements, we are losing prestige. I tell you, governor, we have got to do something.

We have either got to go in and win or we have got to go out of the business. I am doing the best I can. I have sent my girl away and I am working at the paper all the time. I am here at eleven o'clock in the morning and I leave at three o'clock at night when the paper goes to press. . . .

I am sorry we ever got into this business but we are in it, and we have got to stay. You will have to do just as De Young has done—withdraw some of your capital from outside interests and put it into things connected with the newspaper. . . .

Of course, the chief thing of this class is a building—a great big magnificent building that will be the talk of the continent.

He berated George for carrying "letters around that it would be a positive injury for people to see," and for continuing to sink money into his losing racehorses. Will's admonishments fell largely on deaf ears. While he was candid with his father, he had to resort to pleading with a sense of humor, hoping to get his attention.

I am working awfully hard, and getting a little bit tired and a little bit discouraged. . . .

How long do you suppose it will be before we can put up a building—a stunner that will knock [De Young's] endways and make him as sick as he is now making me?

I have been talking it over with Stump and we have cut me down to a thousand a month. We'd like to cut you down a little if you don't mind. Can't you sell that stable pretty soon? You promised faithfully you would sell it years ago. We figured you could sell it for a hundred thousand while if you didn't sell it you would spend a hundred thousand on it—a difference, you see, between selling it and not selling it of two hundred thousand dollars, enough in itself to start the building with. You owe a good deal of money, you know, and if we don't begin saving up, we never will get anything. . . .

You are a good prophet. I wish you would prophesy that Senator Hearst is going out of the jockey business and into city real estate.[15]

The idea of Will's recommending ways to save money must have amused George. Will already had a glint in his eye for another paper—in New York, the "big apple," where he had set up a fancy, redwood-paneled East Coast bureau for the *Examiner.* The *New York Press* reported on 13 October 1889 that

. . . young Hearst . . . has been trying to induce his father to set him up in business here, either by buying some old paper or establishing a new one. Senator Hearst was in New York this summer, watching his race horses. He is a genuine old-fashioned patron of the turf, one of the few honest old standbys. About his son's New York ambition he said to a friend recently:

"There's plenty of money if the boy really has his heart set on it, but I am in hopes he will conclude after a while that one big paper is enough for one man to run."

Plenty of money there surely is, for the Senator's wealth is estimated at $20,000,000.

But by the end of 1890 the *Examiner* would begin to make money. Will's show-business promotional schemes, combined with a muckraking, trust-busting quality and no lack of imagination when it came to "manufacturing" news, would attract the highest circulation in California and show other newspapers in America tricks of the trade that they had never thought of. Personally shy, by his own admission, Will was nothing if not his best public-relations agent. A rival paper, the *Daily Alta California,* called him "a young Napoleon" in a tongue-in-cheek front-page piece about W. R. Hearst in Europe in January 1889. Though derisive, as rival papers were of Will and his "Monarch of the Dailies," the article could only have served to spark interest in the *Examiner.* It had Will meeting the editor of the *London Times* ("Walter") and the Prince of Wales, who was portrayed as a buffoon to Will's Wild West sophistication. To the Prince of Wales Will was quoted as saying, "I understand how you feel—you are a little bashful in the presence of strangers. I used to feel that way myself before I broke loose from my mother's apron strings."

The fictional conversations with the *Times* editor made fun of Will's promotional gimmicks—and of his familiarity with "chippies" and "variety actresses." After all, Will's life with Tessie was an open book in

San Francisco. But there was a hint of jealousy in the derision over his success:

> I soon told Walter who I was, and what a paper I had made of the *Examiner*, and how I usually make things hum. . . . I told him how I had startled the whole country by running special trains to Petaluma and Milpitas, and spending a lot of money on balloon ascensions, tight-rope walkers and oyster suppers, and whooped things up generally . . . the old chap didn't catch on at all.
>
> "What do you run special trains for?" he asked.
>
> "That's for enterprise," said I.
>
> "What are the balloons for?" asked he.
>
> "They prove that you've got the liveliest newspaper," said I.
>
> "What are the tight-rope walkers, the oysters and the other things for?" asked he.
>
> "They show that you've got the largest circulation," said I. . . .
>
> "But wouldn't it be better," he suggested, "to buy news with your money. . . ?"
>
> "Why," I said, "I don't buy news because we can fake it."
>
> . . . he could not repress his admiration. . . .
>
> ". . . such an idea never occurred to me. Young man, you undoubtedly have a remarkable development of the head. If your example should be generally followed, some singular consequence would ensue."[16]

Will went to Europe early in 1889 and saving money was not one of his themes. He declared that he had "art fever" akin to "avarice," and sent his mother a long treatise on how to buy art. It was a commentary on her inability to pass up anything and everything that she wanted.

> Why didn't you buy [Leopold] Ansiglioni's "Galatea?" It is superb. . . . I have a great notion to buy it myself, in fact. The one thing that prevents me is a scarcity of funds, as it were. The man wants eight thousand dollars for the blooming thing and that is a little above my head.
>
> I have the art fever terribly. Queer, isn't it? I never thought I would get it this way. I never miss a gallery now and I go and mosey about the pictures and statuary and admire them and wish they were mine. My artistic longings are not altogether distinct from avarice, I am afraid. . . .
>
> So I want some of these fine things and I want you to have some of these fine things and do you know, my beloved mother, there is a way in which you might get them. If, instead of buying a half a dozen fairly nice things, you would wait and buy one fine thing, all would be well.
>
> As it is at present we have things scattered from New York to Washington . . . to San Francisco, more than a house could hold and yet not among them a half a dozen things that are really superb. . . .
>
> Ansiglioni says it is a great time to buy. The people [of Italy] are heavily taxed; the government is nearly bankrupt and cannot buy up these opportunities [from palaces] itself as it has formerly done, and some wealthy American or Englishman will soon step in and, taking these chances here

and there, will have a collection almost equal to that of some of these national galleries.

I wish I could be the rich American. I wish you could be. How nice it would be if we could exchange all our alleged pictures for two or three masterpieces such as I have mentioned. In price, they are the same but in value, how different.

. . . I am not going to buy any more trinkets. . . . Then when advanced in years I will not have had all that I wanted, but I will have all that I want—which is better. Go thou and do likewise, Mama, dear. If you don't, you will be mad at yourself next time you come abroad. What's the good of more trinkets when we haven't room for those we have? Save your money, Momey, and wait. . . .

I see that some Royal Duke of Spain has gone to America with a fine collection of old masters and will sell them there. Get one. Get a Murillo or a Velasquez. Don't get four or five old masters that nobody ever heard anything about. Get a Murillo or a Velasquez. Of course, get a Murillo and a Velasquez if you can but get at least one good picture and wait again.

> Your wise and reverent son,
> W. R. H.

P.S. If you can get Pa interested, he will do the business. He has a way of doing things when he gets interested that I rather admire.[17]

Indeed, George knew what he wanted when he wanted it. But for Will and Phoebe, Will's advice was hardly heeded. Phoebe's art collection was characteristic of wealthy people of the period who lamented the plight of the common man and woman but preferred to see them depicted in romantic natural settings with idealistic overtones. Her collection consisted largely of nineteenth-century realist paintings of dark and traditional subjects, mixed with portraits of European royalty and quantities of lace, statuary, oriental rugs, tapestries, fans, enamels, miniatures, carved ivories, and other curios, including a Louis XV French sedan chair. It was singularly lacking in "modern" works of art. In a moment of aberration, she had purchased a Monet impressionistic painting, which she realized she did not like. She asked one of the artists whom she patronized, Carl Oscar Borg, to sell it for her. He found a buyer who would pay $3,500 for it, and he urged her to take the offer, knowing, as he told her, that "you did not care for the picture anyway and I am sure the money will be of more use to you."[18]

Will seemed to have inherited by osmosis his mother's buying habits and tastes for the traditional and grandiose, for rare curiosities such as old coins and letters, for "trinkets." Like his mother, he simply could not restrain himself when an opportunity that intrigued him crossed his path. Neither of them relied much on art experts to advise them in their collecting; they bought through dealers, who knew that the Hearsts were free-handed in their purchases. Although they were not duped and came to know good value, their collecting was random and impetuous. As one newspaper put it, "[Mrs. Hearst's] fancies and not the prices dictated every investment."[19]

Much of the collection then scattered about the country would be gathered in the Washington house, a showplace that Phoebe opened to selected guests for charity occasions and in which she entertained grandly. Two railroad cars of her treasures were shipped from California. Guests wandered through rooms filled with paintings by Corot, Sir Joshua Reynolds, Rousseau, Watteau, Millet, George Romney, Van Dyke, Copley, and pastoral scenes by lesser-known German, French, and Dutch painters. Phoebe had a fascination for Napoleon and possessed an eclectic collection of Napoleana, including a miniature of the emperor by his favorite painter, Jacques-Louis David, which Empress Josephine had worn fixed inside the jeweled center of her coronet. Royalty fascinated Phoebe, and she lived like a queen.[20]

The house, at the corner of Twentieth and O streets, had been purchased from former President Cleveland's secretary of the treasury, Charles S. Fairchild, shortly after he had bought it but had lost his post with the change to administration of President Benjamin Harrison. It was a plain, square house, built in 1870, one of the first large houses in the area. With Phoebe's vision and the help of architect Harvey L. Page, it was turned into a thirty-room palace, changed inside and out so that little remained of the former building except some bricks. Turrets and towers were added, along with a red-tiled roof, porte cochere, and a new wing to hold a ballroom. Remodeling took more than a year, in part because of a freight blockade around Washington. Phoebe was proud of the fact that everything new in the house—woodwork, carved and inlaid furniture, embroidery on coverings and hangings—was manufactured on special order from designs by American workers in American shops, much of it in Washington and Baltimore. When someone pointed out that such specially made items cost more, Phoebe replied, "No doubt, but think of the men and women right here who were given employment."[21]

As wagons rolled up, emptying their contents into the Hearst mansion, even sophisticated Washingtonians were dazzled at the prospect of the entertainments that Phoebe planned. She was described in the newspapers as "a handsome woman . . . strikingly of the Spanish type" who "aspires to be the popular society leader in Washington" whose home would be "the scene of . . . open-handed hospitality." Said one society columnist,

Mrs. Hearst is fond of social life, fond of young people, and fond of keeping about her pretty young women as her season's guests. The Senator evidently enjoys having his wife do all these things, and he is proud of her, with very good reason. . . .

Mrs. Hearst admits that she takes the best care of herself, and this she considers every woman's duty. Her complexion is dark, but wonderfully soft and clear; her eyes are dark and expressive, her hair is dark and shining, and worn as smooth as satin. She is slightly below medium height, with slender, graceful figure. Her voice is low, and her manner exceedingly quiet, gentle and easy. . . .

[The Senator's wife] looks scarcely half his age. Taking good care of herself has taken a good many years off her personal appearance.[22]

Considering the trouble she took to hide her frequent poor health and personal unhappiness, she must have enjoyed the compliments. But she did not like the gossip, the innuendos that she was a vain and extravagant woman with a crusty old husband who had lost interest in her and merely paid the bills.

The papers delighted in speculating about the Hearst's domestic relations, suggesting that George was shunted off to a small room in the mansion because he and his wife were incompatible:

The Senator detests society and fashionable entertainments of all sorts. He never takes part in any of it, and finds his amusements outside of the Senate chamber in driving behind good horses and sitting in the back room at John Chamberlain's telling and listening to good stories with a circle of intimate friends.[23]

One paper went farther:

. . . it is hardly fair to say that Senator Hearst has occupied the house . . . for he is not much of a factor in the domestic organization. . . . The Senator has not bothered his head about the matter, except to pay the bills, an easy task for him. He told Mrs. Hearst to . . . build up the house, and when she was ready to move in he would move in with her and that would be all there was to it, so far as he was concerned. . . . When Mrs. Hearst decided to move into a part of the house while the remainder was being finished, "Uncle George," as the Senator is known by all his friends, took possession of the little corner assigned him without a bit of grumbling.[24]

That must have irked Phoebe, for although the two had separate bedrooms, George was well provided for in the way of quarters. He had a large bedroom and den, and an office in the basement. Certainly it was true that he had given Phoebe a free hand in designing and decorating the house, having no interest in such matters and knowing that she would do as she pleased anyway. In that they were entirely compatible.

The mansion was high Victorian in style but had exotic oriental touches that showed Phoebe's desire to stand out from the crowd. The uniqueness began at the entrance with a disguised doorbell rope that frustrated visitors. The bell was attached to a decorative piece of iron filigree in the design of a blooming wild rose to the right of the doorway. Even George, coming home to his new house shortly after the artistic bit of *trompe l'oeil* was installed, could not find his own doorbell. He had to resort to pounding on the huge door panel to announce his arrival.[25]

The next surprise to unsuspecting guests was a clock that chimed German tunes in the carved oak-paneled reception hall. From there they went to exotic room after room, each with a distinctive decorating theme. There was a high-ceilinged music room hung with Aubusson and Gobelin tapestries; a Marie Antoinette-period drawing room; a Louis XVI salon full of hanging embroideries; a library in a tower with walls hung in blue India velvet; a Dutch-style dining room with Venetian leather-covered walls and a table that could stretch to twenty-six feet; a redwood-paneled supper room with a mosaic floor that could seat one hundred; a tapestry-lined ballroom that occupied one-half of the first floor; and a kitchen with "every culinary convenience imaginable," including two Chinese cooks "moving in noiseless preparation," the society pages reported.[26]

There was a plethora of cupids, satin and romantic marble statues, including busts of Phoebe and Will by the Italian sculptor Ansiglioni. The rooms were in rose, blue, or ivory, and the fireplaces had black onyx Mexican mantelpieces. It was a house dominated by the tastes of a "refined and cultivated" woman and always fragrant with the aroma of fresh flowers. Reporters who were privileged to see it called it "homelike" and "used," ready to be occupied at a moment's notice. Filled as it was with artifacts, one writer ironically said,

> There is an entire absence of the usual overwhelming lot of bric-a-brac, but what there is is very rare and priceless. The trail of the decorating fiend is not visible. The house is at once homelike and a marvel of elegant simplicity.[27]

It was Phoebe's dream palace. She had come a long way from the farmhouse in Missouri. Here she swept through magnificent rooms, explaining her treasures to her guests, and gently but firmly commanding a staff of servants, which included a stable master to look after her six high-stepping hackney-bred bay horses and a kennel full of Scotch Skye terriers (a favorite of the English court). The stable was the most modern obtainable, heated by steam and lighted by electricity. She could ride out in a Victoria, a Landau, a theater wagon, or, when she wanted to play the whip herself, a Spider carriage, all trimmed in blue livery with her monogram on silver mountings.

She opened the house to Washington society with a colonial costume ball on 19 February 1889, to commemorate Washington's birthday. The flowers alone were thought to cost twenty-five thousand dollars. Guests came in period dress. The *Washington Post* called it "by far the most brilliant event of the kind ever held in Washington." The party favors included fans handpainted by a beneficiary of Phoebe's in San Francisco, tortoiseshell combs and ostrich feather tips for the ladies; silver medals cut with cocked hats ordered from Tiffany, white kid pen wipers, antique silver whistles, paper cutters, and tiny buckets of California redwood in the form of pin cushions, with a silver bear attached, for the gentlemen.[28]

George, more commonly seen in his scraggy clothes, preferring a card game to a White House dinner, dressed up and dutifully turned out for the ball. But he was bored and out of place. He cornered some newspaper cronies for company, who reported that "Senator Hearst does not appear to find much enjoyment in his wealth."

> Moving uncomfortably and alone through the glittering throng, the master of the house met a well-known newspaper correspondent. Said the wealthy Senator eagerly:
> "Get a few good fellows together and we'll go to some quiet room and enjoy a bottle of wine and some cigars."
> There were whispers in the ears of two other correspondents, and then, led by the Senator, the quartet marched through the big house from parlor to attic. In every room there was a chattering throng or a wrap divesting bevy, or piles of hats and overcoats. With a sigh the Senator turned backward. He descended to the cellar. Beside the coal hole a colored servant arranged a table and chairs and brought wine and tobacco.
> "Now," said the millionaire with a sigh of relief, "we can have a good time here without being interrupted by those idiots upstairs. I can't see the fun in my wife's rackets."[29]

But his wife went on with her "rackets" and her invitations became the most coveted in Washington. They were prized because she was known to have little patience with social butterflies, preferring the cultured set. One society column said "she occupies a peculiar position":

> She is not of the smart set, yet it would only too gladly welcome her to its arms.
> No doubt it would, but Mrs. Hearst being an intellectual woman, prefers the cultured to the smart set. The former is the more exclusive. The "open-sesame" of the cultured set is carried in the head and not in the pocket.[30]

She was "the philanthropic grande dame of the Capital" who

> . . . does not seek prominence in the "butterfly society." Independence of the smart set rules her ways and methods, and she will not tolerate at her

functions any personage whose aspirations do not rise above pink teas and germans.

Mrs. Hearst's guests are chosen from the world of art and literature. Her dinners and receptions are enlivened by exquisite music, by elevating discourses, sparkling conversation. Mrs. Hearst excludes from her gatherings all people whose reputation is in the slightest degree "rapid."

There are men and women in Washington who would sacrifice much to obtain an invitation to one of Mrs. Hearst's evenings at home. The attractions to them would not be her beautiful paintings or the performance of the foremost artists of the day, but simply the stamp of her approval. In a quiet, modest way she has become the arbiter of unsullied elegance at the Capital.[31]

She was "at home" on Thursdays, and the house more often than not was full of guests, usually young women whom she had taken under her wing or was introducing to society in the nation's capital:

Mrs. Hearst . . . always has a number of pretty and pleasant girls staying with her. She is very nice to girls, as, indeed, she is to everybody. She gives more genuine pleasure to more people than any other rich women that I know of, often going out of her way without seeming to do so, to do something pleasant for one, whom, considering how busy she must be, she might well be excused for overlooking.[32]

Her dinners were "perfection" in the eyes of the chosen few who attended:

Her dinners are always small, so that the conversation can be general, and her first care is that everything is cooked just right. Her cook she brought with her from California, and she is obliged very often to send to New York for delicacies not to be had in our markets. Her table decorations are generally of medium height, so that her guests can see each other across the table, and are not obliged to toss their words over a mountain of flowers.[33]

She made sure that her gatherings were never too crowded to be uncomfortable. And she planned her costume so as to stand out despite her diminutive frame, frequently dressed in antique lace, lavender, and magnificent jewels, never worn ostentatiously or in profusion.

Her teas, musicales, and "tableaux" entertainments of readings and concerts were unique and magical, often with surprises. If Will had a penchant for lively entertainments, he learned it from his mother, who delighted in startling her guests pleasantly or transporting them into another world for the hours that they spent in her presence. Her grandest and most novel event in Washington was a lavish eighteenth-century masquerade ball and concert in honor of Florence Bayard, the daughter of the American ambassador to England. The occasion also showed off a newly acquired harpsichord, made in Salzburg in 1760 and reputedly once used by Haydn or Mozart. Two sets of invitations were sent—one hundred thirty to older people for the concert, and sixty to the younger set for a midnight cotillion. All the guests were required to appear in the costume and powdered wigs of Haydn's day, and a number of moustaches and Van Dyck beards were sacrificed for the occasion by gentlemen guests. Four black servants dressed in Moorish outfits—crimson velvet suits and turbans—ushered in the guests, who were treated to a show of splendor. A twenty-piece orchestra played and the colorful costumes were reflected in hanging panels of mirrors, all lit by candles in the music room.

Anton Seidl, the orchestra conductor, dressed as Haydn and caught cold, later reading with amusement his obituary in a morning newspaper. The painter Howard Pyle and his wife came as two old portraits. Phoebe held court in her rubies and diamonds, much as Haydn's patron, Count Esterhazy, might have done one hundred years before.[34]

Phoebe's household budget was close to five thousand dollars a month and she confessed to a reporter that it might be possible for the wife of a congressman to manage "pleasantly and happily, too" on a congressman's five-thousand-dollar annual salary but "I could not undertake to tell how she could do it."[35] Her entertainments were legend and her house was nearly always full. On one occasion she called at a stylish boarding house on Fourteenth Street near I Street to engage rooms for friends, telling the unsuspecting landlady that she had not sufficient accommodations at her own house.

"Is your house full?" asked the landlady.

"Yes, just crowded, or will be," replied Mrs. Hearst.

"Do you keep a boarding or lodging house?" queried the landlady.

"How's that," asked Mrs. Hearst.

"Do you give room and board, or only let rooms?" wondered the boarding house owner.

"Oh, I give both board and room at my house," said Mrs. Hearst, cheerfully, presenting her card. "Good morning," and she swept away to her carriage, into which she was shown by a liveried footman.[36]

Phoebe had a wry sense of humor that did not extend to offending sensibilities. She delighted in being the anonymous benefactress who was found out.

George's days were spent quite differently. When he first got to Washington, his naiveté made him vulnerable. He formed the habit of making the rounds of watering holes and, in true western style, throwing a twenty-dollar gold piece on the bar and inviting everyone present to step up and imbibe. After a few weeks, word got around and all the down-and-out "old judges and majors and colonels in which Washington abounds," as one columnist reported, "got to sending out scouts in order to learn of the jolly Senator's whereabouts":

> As soon as they heard where he was after adjournment of the Senate, they started on his trail, and never let up till they had filled their old skins as full as they could get them at Uncle George's expense.[37]

George somewhat curtailed his free handed spending but he was fond of taking a number of his Senate colleagues in his open carriage down Pennsylvania Avenue to Chamberlain's for an hour or two of sociability before dinner.

When a California congressman died, George wanted to deliver an eloquent eulogy. He hired a journalist to write the speech, for which he paid $2,500. To George's embarrassment, he found out that the words he delivered were not original but had been plagiarized from many other rhetorical obituaries printed in the *Congressional Record* over the previous decade.[38]

George used his own Senate salary to pay one of two secretaries, and he secured positions in government departments for several women whom he had befriended. He delighted in giving his colleagues good tips on mining investments, and not a few of them made nice profits on George's advice. He was careful not to become entangled with female "lobbyists" who were sent to entice members into compromising positions on issues. This was such a common entrapment that at least one congressman made it known that he would not respond to a card sent him by a woman whom a page described as young and handsome. George was a member of the elite senatorial poker club, which one of his colleagues unashamedly said "fairly runs the United States Senate."[39]

His angular head with its frowsy white hair and bald spot the size of a silver dollar (he won a bet on its dimensions and bought the loser a bottle at Chamberlain's) more often than not rested on his long beard while he snoozed in the Senate chambers. "Senator George Hearst borrows half the day to finish his night's sleep," the gossips remarked.[40]

Although he was publicly accused of having bought his seat with his wealth (he was in good company—the Fifty-first Congress contained more millionaires than ever before) and of being the dupe of California party bosses, his critics could not find him corruptible. "No honester man ever represented this or any other State on the floor of the United States Senate than plain, blunt, unpretentious, unhackneyed George Hearst," an opposition paper said. He was derided as being a "cipher," an "easy-going old negative," who at least could not be feared as "brainy" and dangerous. When he was on the Senate floor he was generally silent. In four years in the Senate, he made only two speeches, each less than ten minutes long. Said one political wit,

> . . . really this is a tribute to the Senator's good judgment and excellent sense. He knows that he was not born an orator, and sees that election to the Senate did not make him one. It might be a more nearly correct characterization of his speeches to say of them that they were 10 minutes blissfully short.[41]

He got into some embarrassing situations and was found out. Using the *Examiner* to take his side, he concocted a strike among iron workers, so as to appear sympathetic with the workers and the one who successfully persuaded the federal government to give San Francisco a large contract to build navy cruisers. The *Examiner* again was his tool in editorializing in favor of repealing the Restriction Act on Chinese labor. George had consistently opposed unbridled Chinese immigration. But after he bought a ranch in 1888 in Sonoma County that had a historic mansion once occupied by General William Tecumseh Sherman and some of the finest vineyards in California, the *Examiner* vociferously argued in favor of more Chinese coolies as farm laborers and George made no attempt to stop repeal of the law.[42]

One of George's favorite ploys was to appear ignorant and illiterate when, in fact, he was as smart as a fox. A story that became apocryphal in his lifetime was his misspelling of "burd." It variously was reported to have occurred at the California Democratic convention in 1882, when he sought the gubernatorial nomination, and in Washington. George himself no doubt got plenty of mileage and chuckles out of the story, one version of which was recounted in the press as follows:

> Senator Hearst has been represented as an illiterate man, but . . . he has not played cards among the bluffers of California for nothing, and like many of his brother Senators he is by no means averse to a bet.
> Not long ago he entered a well-known restaurant of San Francisco, and on the blackboard at the back of the bar he saw the word "bird" among the items of the bill of fare. It was spelled "birde," and Hearst at once called up the keeper of the restaurant, who was a noted California character, and said:
> "See here, Blank, that's a devil of a way to spell 'bird.' Don't you know any better than that? You ought to spell it 'b-u-r-d.' "
> "I would have you understand, George Hearst," replied the restaurant keeper, "that I am just as good a speller as you, and I am willing to leave it to the best scholar in the room that you don't know any more about the matter than I do. In other words, I'll bet you a basket of champagne that you can't spell 'bird' the right way."
> "Done," said Hearst.
> "All right," said the man, "and here is a piece of paper for you to put it down in black and white."
> With that he handed Hearst a sheet of brown paper, and Hearst with a stub pencil wrote out the letters:

"The right way to spell it is 'b-i-r-d.' "

"But," said the restaurant keeper, "you spelled it first with a 'u.' "

Senator Hearst threw himself back and looked the restaurant man in the eye. "And," said he, "did you think that I was blanked fool enough to spell 'bird' with a 'u' when there was any money up on it?"

A California colleague in the House of Representatives, Joseph McKenna, related a story about George's clothes. One day he arrived at the Hearst mansion to find George busily engaged in cutting out a clipping from the evening paper. "Some young rascal of a reporter," he said, "declares here that I am the most poorly dressed man in the California delegation." "And pray then," McKenna asked, "why are you trying to preserve so libelous an article about yourself?" George chuckled and said, "Poole of London makes all my clothes. He has the reputation of being the best tailor in the whole world, so I think the joke's on him, and I'm sending him this criticism of my apparel, with my compliments."[43]

Despite exhortations from his business manager, Irwin Stump, that he was overextended financially, George continued to spend money like the millionaire that he was—at the rate of $1 million a year. In the first two months of 1890, his expenses were $150,000, of which $24,000 was paid to Phoebe, $19,000 for the Washington residence, $10,445 for his racing stable, and $40,000 for the *Examiner.* Stump wrote him,

> . . . you are spending money at the rate of near one million dollars per year, more than your income, and while money matters are so tight with Mr. Haggin, it does seem to me that you cannot afford to embarrass yourself by going into new speculations. For God's sake, you have enough already without straining matters to obtain more. Besides all this, you know that the *Examiner* will require a great deal of money in a short time or it must stop . . . you must go slow in your expenditures or you must commence selling property to keep up.
>
> . . . Do not allow all the persuasive eloquence of your friends to lead you into new adventures no matter how seductive or promising they may be.[44]

More troubling than his finances though, was George's health. He had been taken ill in Mexico in 1889. The family physician had gone there to treat him and he had seemed to recover. Will told the press,

> My father has a strong constitution and can stand a good deal more than younger men can. He takes long trips in stages which break me all up, and doesn't seem to be affected by them in the slightest.[45]

Nevertheless, George was not able to regain his old robustness. He went to see a specialist in New York in December 1890. The diagnosis was a "complication of diseases" stemming from "a serious derangement of the bowel"—a polite way of describing cancer.[46] The years of hard living, poor diet, perhaps the arsenic in Virginia City water, and count-less bottles of wine and whiskey had taken their toll.

Phoebe at first refused to accept the diagnosis of cancer. She believed in the power of mind over matter. But George developed kidney trouble and his attending physician, Dr. Charles S. Ward of New York, thought he would die within forty-eight hours. Again he rallied, his tough constitution refusing to give in. He was able to visit with Haggin and Senate colleagues and attend to business matters. On 26 January 1891, Phoebe wrote Janet Peck, who was in a Philadelphia clinic:

> Mr. Hearst is very much better. Is it not extraordinary, after the sudden and serious development of the kidney trouble, he should resist everything and come out of it with a certain amount of a strength? His mind as clear as it ever was and with the prospect of lasting many weeks.
>
> Dr. Ward told me when he came he thought Mr. Hearst would live forty-eight hours. Now he may live a month, his vitality is so great.[47]

But a deathwatch was on across the nation. Will was summoned from San Francisco and Jack Follansbee arrived from Mexico. Phoebe denied to the press that George had cancer and for some weeks the press kept "considerably silent as to the cause of the Senator's illness, for the reason that his friends feared the effect of disclosing to the Senator the real situation."[48] Phoebe was worried that George would see the alarming press reports, and she kept up a cheerful front to friends and the public that George was improving and would recover, claiming the doctors had not told her the illness was cancer:

> Her persistency in claiming that he has no fatal disease has convinced many of her friends that she may be right, although the general opinion is that the doctors have not made a mistake and that Mr. Hearst's seat in the Senate will soon be vacant.[49]

Speculation over his successor was rampant. Six hopefuls announced their intentions to seek the Senate seat. Political writers called it a "disgraceful scramble" that suggested "a band of jackals hovering in the woods around a clearing, waiting for a carcass to ripen," a "ghoulish contest" and "indecent exhibition of greed" in a "grim race between politics and death." It was an inconvenient time for a Democrat to die because the Republican-controlled California legislature ensured Republican domination of the Senate with George's successor. One commentator noted

> . . . that there was Republican legislators in the corrupt State of California who are secretly hoping that Uncle George Hearst will be beaten by death in the struggle now going on in the palace at Dupont Circle.[50]

Some of George's Senate rivals held up action on bills in anticipation of a change in the vote count. Speculation on the size of the estate also filled the papers. Will was assumed to be the instant heir-apparent to a fortune that his father had taken forty years of hard work to accumulate. Lovers of the turf also mourned the imminent loss of one of their favorite patrons, coincidentally soon after the death of another, August Belmont. George recently had been elected president of the new Saratoga track.[51]

George defied them all, however, and rallied three times when doctors had given him up. He offered to wager a California congressman who called to see him that he would get well.

> Senator Hearst declares he is not going to die. He sets his teeth, doubles up his fist, utters a cuss word now and then and defies the grim destroyer. Nothing but his iron will has kept him alive for the last three or four weeks. Three times have the doctors given him up, and three times has the old Senator pulled himself together, disappointing the men of medicine, sat up in bed and begun to tell stories of his pioneer days on the coast.[52]

Hard as he fought to deny the end, he grew worse in February. By then he had accepted his fate and told a reporter who called on him, "I do not fear to die. It is the lot of man. I only regret leaving my family and the good friends who have been with me." George made no complaint during his painful illness, the writer said, "justifying his words that he would 'die as he had lived, and take it when it came.' "[53] "He has been traveling in his mind," Phoebe wrote Janet Peck on 6 February.

> He called me to come as there was something he wanted done, none of the others would do it for him. I told him I would attend to it immediately and not to worry about it any more. That satisfied him and he went right off to sleep. Today he is very weak.[54]

He was "quite bright" at times and Phoebe stayed close by, sleeping little. On 28 February she was called from supper about seven o'clock. George had gone into a coma.

Will and Jack Follansbee were at his bedside, and Phoebe and the doctor each held one of his hands. At 9:10 the great body gave up its fight. So quietly did it happen that Phoebe did not know he was dead until the doctor told her so. He seemed to have fallen asleep.[55]

Senator Stanford called a few minutes later, and word of George's death was sent to the Congress and to the president. A funeral service was held at home on 5 March but it had been decided that the body would return to California. A special funeral train, dyed "Titian red," was provided by the Pennsylvania Railroad Company and included two Pullman sleeping cars, a baggage car, and dining car. Senator Stanford put his private car at the family's disposal for the week-long trip to the West Coast. Eighteen members of Congress—nine from each house—joined the entourage, which left Washington a few days later with the body.

The U.S. government footed the bill for the transcontinental funeral party, which cost $21,322.55—the largest funeral bill to date paid for burying a member of Congress. It prompted introduction of legislation in 1895 (not enacted) to limit the government's contribution for congressional funerals to the cost of embalming the body and sending it home.[56]

That was not the only scandal accompanying George to his final resting place. The funeral party was accused by a "noted Indiana temperance agitator" of being drunk all the way back to Washington on wine donated by California vintners. It made the front page of the *New York Times*, which quoted the temperance lady as having seen privately marked cases of wine and hundreds of empty bottles loaded on and off the Hearst train when the baggage car derailed near El Paso, Texas. "It was said that the Hearst party did not have a drop of water on their train, but drank wine altogether, using orange wine to quench their thirst," the *Times* reported. The congressmen indignantly denied the allegations, saying they were the "reckless gossip of a woman who does not know what she is talking about," and who was angry because railway officials would not let her cars hook up to the congressional funeral train.[57]

George would have enjoyed himself. But in San Francisco his body lay in state for several days until an imposing funeral was held on Sunday, 15 March at Grace Episcopal Church, a parish attended by society "blue bloods." Phoebe saw to it that he was sent off in style. George would have scoffed at the hoopla as one of his wife's "rackets." Thousands of people stood in pouring rain waiting to follow the senator's cortege from the church to the cemetery at Laurel Hill (he was moved in 1908 to a family mausoleum at Cypress Lawn in Colma, south of San Francisco). Some in the crowd were the old miner's comrades and many who had benefited from his easy charity, although they were not among the privileged dignitaries who sat in assigned pews of the crowded church. From every arch and rafter hung streams of flower garlands; palms and evergreens filled the niches. It was a lush scene that showed Phoebe's tasteful hand. She had had the bare church transformed into an arboretum that took one's breath away. Wherever the eye turned "were gems and treasures of the florists's art such as [had] rarely been brought together to do honor to the dead," the *Examiner* reported.[58]

The decorations were in large scale. Two seven-foot white flower crosses banked the altar and in front of the casket was a floral representation sent by the *Examiner* that simulated a front page with a portrait of George. Phoebe left the church on Will's arm. Their carriage led a ten-block-long column in a slow procession to the cemetery. "The strains of the dirges and the long roll of the muffled drums were the only sounds above the patter of the rain," a reporter wrote.[59] Phoebe rode with Will and her parents behind the hearse, which was drawn by four jet-black horses. Twenty-thousand people watched the procession pass and a crowd at the cemetery gates had to be cleared to allow the cortege to enter.

Phoebe and Will were the last to leave the casket. As a handful of earth was flung on top of it, waves of contradictory feelings must have swept over Phoebe: loss mixed with relief; sadness tinged by guilt over their incompatibilities; sweet and bittersweet memories of happy times from the Meramec River to the Sierra Nevada; apprehension of the future coupled with anticipation and a sense of freedom. She was forty-eight years old. It was the end of one life for her and the beginning of another. No one would ever call her Puss again.

She had known intimately the private man, not always accurately described by the public tributes at his death. One political writer had correctly said of George, before he died,

> . . . the man as he is has never been presented to the public in print. His biographers have always been puffers or satirists and the difference between the real Hearst and the Hearst of the newspapers, or of Bancroft's odious publications, is the whole character of the man.
>
> Hearst is neither a saint nor a fraud. He is one of the simplest and shrewdest men you could find anywhere, a contradiction in terms, perhaps, but an inexplicable paradox. He is the only rich man I know or ever read of whose wealth has not accumulated at the expense of others. . . .
>
> I like to regard Hearst as a brave, simple-minded old man who has no guile except such as is needed to keep up his end in a horse trade or catch on to the wiles of those who salt mines to catch tender feet.[60]

George was gullible and got into "a good deal of trouble in his life by sticking to men who did not do him justice," the same reporter said. But "he would sooner die than warrant an unsound horse or sell a blind lead," according to the writer, who told the following story:

> Once I was sent to him by a rich man, and a man he did not like, to buy a horse that he owned.
>
> "The brute is ill-natured," he said, "and unfit for anything."
>
> "That is our risk," I said. "I know all about the horse and his failings, and will buy him without warrant."
>
> "You're foolish."

"Not at all. I'm getting a commission on the purchase. Mr.——did not want to come to you himself."

Hearst thought a few seconds and said:

"If I let him have the horse, and it kills him, it would be a good thing for the State. But, confound it all, I ain't the public executioner. He shan't have the brute."[61]

Phoebe had known those qualities in her husband. George would have been pleased, if sometimes amused, she thought, by the accolades after his death. It was true that he had been an "unaffected" man of "no pretense," whose "shrewdness baffled pretenders," as one obituary said. "The greater the stake and the more critical the emergency, the calmer and clearer of brain he became." Phoebe knew, all too well, and often to her annoyance, that "his heart was tender . . . his capacity for forgiveness was inexhaustible," that he did not "cherish enmities" or grudges. Such a "softness in his disposition," she agreed, had not helped him in politics but had "endeared him in private life."[62]

His California colleague in the House of Representatives, Thomas J. Clunie, called him "gentle as a woman":

No man could talk with Senator Hearst without going away from him feeling that he had learned something. . . .

No man in our great State did more in a quiet, unostentatious manner to relieve distress in California, and in fact several other States and Territories where his extensive interests called him, than did Senator Hearst.[63]

George had looked after his own and supporters' interests as a politican and had done what was expected of him. His attributes as a member of the "club" did not go unremarked. He had gotten what his constituencies—mostly business interests—wanted from him. Said Clunie,

I could name a score of his colleagues who have told me that no Senator could by simply saying "This bill is right, I want it passed," get as many votes for a measure as Senator George Hearst.[64]

The *New York Times* headline at his death remarked on his career "From an illiterate, penniless gold hunter to a popular member of the national legislature and a millionaire," and called it "phenomenal, a career . . . presenting extremely sharp contrasts and almost incomprehensible incongruities." "In the meanwhile," the *Times* said, "only such an amount of culture had attached to him as would necessarily be forced upon a man whose household was presided over by a model wife, who was a society leader, having practically limitless wealth at her command."[65]

When eulogies were delivered in Congress more than a year after

George's death, the "purple prose" was rampant. Senator George G. Vest of Missouri put it bluntly:

> Above all, he knew himself, and put no false estimate upon his powers, either of performance or endurance. Self-constrained, self-reliant, with every faculty trained in the school of practical life and absolute necessity, he wasted no energy upon ornament, but reserved his strength for the real and useful.[66]

If he was not an orator, trained debater nor a "showy man" (which, Congressman James G. Maguire of California said, "placed him at some disadvantage with men of the East"), George's "strong common sense . . . made him not merely an efficient representative of California, but a safe and useful legislator for the entire nation."[67]

Republican Senator William M. Stewart of Nevada, whom George had known in his Virginia City days, remembered that "he had a vein of humor which amused and fascinated the learned as well as the illiterate. . . . He was a good judge of character, and readily distinguished the true from the counterfeit."[68]

Those were the qualities for which George Hearst would be revered and remembered by his peers. He would not be memorialized for the day-to-day frustrations that Phoebe had known, his stubbornness against her wishes, his unwillingness to discipline their profligate son, his dirty clothes smelling of tobacco and whiskey, his roving eye for the ladies, nor for his wry humor and generous indulgences of his younger wife and her ambitions, his gentle love and dependence on her. They had been an odd couple and, for better or worse, there would never be another George Hearst.

11
New Horizons, New Challenges

George's will, which he had made ten years earlier, was short and specific. It left everything to Phoebe, nothing to Will. George and Phoebe had talked about it and agreed that Will had no sense about money and was incapable of managing it wisely. George trusted Phoebe to provide for their son. The estate was valued at some $20 million.[1] And it was tax-free. No one except Phoebe and her legal advisers knew exactly how much she had inherited since the probate record simply stated that the estate exceeded ten thousand dollars. It included more than a million acres of land in the United States and Mexico and some of the richest mines in the world, including the Homestake and Anaconda. It also had debts.

George had bequeathed "to my wife absolutely" all the property "and the profits thereof." He made her executrix and guardian of his son. But there was a catch. If she remarried, everything went to Will. The will read:

> I commend my son, William R. Hearst, to my said wife, having full confidence that she will make suitable provisions for him, but in the event of the marriage of my said wife after my death, I hereby give and bequeath to my son all of my said property that may remain in the possession of my said wife at that date.[2]

Phoebe was given a free hand to manage all the property, invest and reinvest at her discretion, to sell as she deemed best, "and to do all other acts and things she may think best in the management and disposition of said property."[3]

Will could not disguise his shock and anger at the reading of the will. It was embarrassing for a grown man to have to beg his mother for money. He had been accustomed to asking his father for what he had assumed would rightfully be his one day. But his father had had several talks with him about his looseness with money. Now he was faced with going to his mother for every penny until she died or remarried. And Mother did not always approve of what he was doing. He would have to charm, cajole, and placate her for his money. He might even have to change his ways if he were not to be cut off. It had never occurred to him that he would lack for money and he was tired of begging for it. Some years, later, in the wisdom of hindsight, Will would write his mother,

> My father never did a better thing than when he made the will he did. I have admired him for it and have been happy to concur in it, and I have never told you how many times I have been advised by fools and scoundrels otherwise. That is the kind of thing for our own kind of people, and I hope to so live that you will have as much confidence in me as my father had in you. I hope, too, that I will never live to read your will, and that you will live as long as I do and that we both shall be as happy as I am now. Affectionately and gratefully, Will.[4]

But at the time, it was a hard pill to swallow.

George's death had taken its toll of Phoebe's health. She suffered from insomnia and hoped that a camping trip to the California foothills would restore her ability to sleep. She went to the Valley of the Moon and rested in the summer sun, sleeping in tents among oak trees surrounded by vineyards and orchards. She was not far from a railroad, though, which brought her mail and a few friends. There she thought about the rest of her life and began to set her priorities in order.[5]

She was faced with enormous responsibilities. First, she would attend to business matters, learning all that she could about the complicated and vast operations of her husband's empire. Second, she would decide what good works could be done with the fortune that she now controlled. Third, she would try to wean Will away from his mistress and marry him off.

Phoebe secretly desired that he pick a well-born woman, preferably English and with a title, as many rich Americans were doing. She put any number of eligible, attractive women in his way. Gossip columnists delighted in speculating on Will's marriage prospects. He was twenty-eight years old and a worthy catch. A natty dresser, he was tall and slender, with a moustache and blond hair parted in the middle. He looked strikingly like his mother with his narrow lips, high forehead, and facial shape. He had a polite if commanding presence and a healthy demeanor. He did not drink or smoke. He was a confident young man, if a little arrogant and nervous, given to drumming his fingers and swinging his feet.[6]

"No other question is of such intense interest" to his mother than the marriage of her son, "the apple of her eye," said one society writer:

> She would have her son travel abroad, mingle with men of culture and leisure, especially Englishmen, for Mrs. Hearst has a leaning towards England and the English. . . .
> But unfortunately for his ambitious mother, William Hearst is hopelessly

American, hopelessly democratic in theory and practice, and uncompromisingly "down" on aristocratic tendencies. . . .

Mrs. Hearst . . . frankly confesses that her son's choice of a wife will make her a happy woman, or his marriage may prove the greatest sorrow, so much is her heart wrapped up in his future.[7]

Will knew that he had a hard task in choosing a wife who would please his mother. But like his father he put little stock in social standing. His reluctance to choose no doubt also was influenced by efforts on his mother's part to thwart and break up affairs with women whom he liked. There even was a rumor that he had secretly married. A newspaper reported that he had married a Boston girl "with whom he was intimate while at Harvard" (probably Tessie) and had sailed for Europe with her.[8]

Will did return to Europe in 1892, as did his mother with her niece Anne Apperson and other friends. Will met them in England and traveled with them to France, Germany, and Spain. He also went off on a "photographic tour" of France and Switzerland. But he was not alone. Phoebe's niece remembered that he had Tessie and his private secretary, George Pancoast, with him.[9] He did not allude to them, though, in his letters to his mother, which were full of amusing descriptions of sights and experiences. His disdain for "society" is evident in a letter that he wrote his mother from a ship. On the occasion of this letter, he had a Japanese valet along, another source of amusement.

Lady Cunard is on board. She is at my table. She spoke about you and asked how you were. She is a nice little thing but kind of light-headed and chatters loudly with a sort of turkey gobbler by the name of Guinness who makes the soup and a gibbering idiot by the name of Van Alen who doesn't make anything except a holy show himself. Lady Cunard asked me why I didn't go into society and I could have told her that if I had no other reason the present company would furnish enough. She isn't bad, though, she certainly shines intellectually when compared with the men.

In deference to your wishes I took Thomas the Jap along as valet. He has been very valuable so far in keeping my mind occupied looking after him. He comes in every morning about seven o'clock and wakes me up when I want to sleep and I don't see him anymore for the rest of the day. Fortunately I am a natural born American citizen able to look after myself and a valet, too. All I object to is the money he is costing me. He will foot up a thousand dollars before the trip is over and that would enable me to bring home an Egyptian mummy—something intrinsically valuable and which would make fully as good a valet as Thomas in a pinch. Anyhow it wouldn't wake me up in the morning and would stay put.[10]

Will had no patience with nouveau riche Americans who invented blue-blood ancestors, once remarking wryly to Orrin Peck in an amusing letter that he had heard Mrs. Head "has developed a family and a long line of 'dookal' ancestors":

> Think of those bare feet that used to patter around Virginia City, now nearing Queen quality . . . and carrying around a pudgy descendant of a line of imaginary Kings.
> Of course if you haven't got any ancestors, you can kind of think up a better lot than if you are hampered by a bunch of real ones.[11]

He feigned an interest in Florence Bayard, the U.S. ambassador to Britain's daughter whom Phoebe had introduced to Washington society. He sent her "kind remembrances" and took photographs of Joan of Arc's birthplace, which he knew "would please Miss Bayard." He had taken up photography with his characteristic enthusiasm for new toys and photographed every peak and pass in Switzerland and other sights and "unfrequented places" in France and Germany, where he was seeking to restore his health from overwork at the paper, his mother told a friend. She pretended that Tessie was not with him. He had the *Examiner* sent to him and wired back orders from his various ports of call.

He met his mother—without Tessie—in Munich, where, at Phoebe's insistence, he was to have his portrait painted by Orrin Peck. Phoebe was having a small portrait made of her, which she thought a good likeness. She wrote a friend, "I have known Mr. Peck since his infancy and I know he will be able to catch my best expressions (if I have any)."[12] She also remarked that her health had improved—"I have not felt so well for two years"—although her eyes bothered her. As for Will, she urged him to come to Munich for his portrait "before he became too brown from his tramping life," as she liked to think of it. She absolutely refused to meet his mistress and he assured her before going that he would be "alone and [would] give Orrin all the time he wants for a perfectly beautiful picture."[13]

Orrin produced an inspired work, a full portrait of Will, then thirty-one, seated in a chair and looking directly forward with his penetrating steely eyes—a remarkable likeness that showed his self-confidence and concentration, his way of fixing his cold blue eyes on whomever he was looking at, seemingly without emotion. Like the man, the portrait was unsettling but riveting. He did not avert or waver, he did not lie, even to his mother and even when he knew that she was unhappy with him. He told her everything, often things that she did not want to hear. Although he knew that he upset her, Will was brutally honest with her. If she found out something about him and confronted him, he did not deny it.

"I hope you people told Pheobe about Will's purchases even in a general way," Janet Peck wrote Orrin at one point, "for you know she will learn of it from Will who does not conceal anything purposely from her if he happens to want to speak of his doings, believing he has a right to do as he pleases anyway, and she will think you are trying to be secretive which is not a desired state of mind to leave her in."[14]

Will secretly enjoyed shocking his mother. He had not shocked his father, from whom he had inherited his fondness for unaffected women. George had excused his own behavior, and that of his father, as something that they simply had done, but he had told Will that he hoped his own son would have a different moral code, more like Phoebe's and her down-to-earth parents. But dull, straight-laced people bored Will.[15]

His mother suddenly had her own rumor to put down. It was inevitable that speculation would arise about her remarrying. On her return from Europe, she was confronted with a front-page *New York Times* item that suggested she would wed Senator Charles J. Faulkner of West Virginia, a widower and one of the congressional party who had accompanied George's body to California. Her friend Mrs. Anthony wrote Phoebe that she must have been amused by the rumor. Phoebe was not amused. She emphatically denied that she was engaged to marry—her husband's will certainly was a disincentive to do so—and she told the press that "she did not understand how the report could have originated," adding that "similar stories made her wish sometimes that she were a man long enough to punch their authors."[16]

Her more immediate concern was learning the details of the vast business empire that she had inherited. She wanted to "have a personal knowledge of everything connected with it," she told the Homestake superintendent. Her first priority was to hire someone she trusted to keep an eye on her interests. She did not like or trust Irwin C. Stump, George's business manager. She wrote him in July 1892,

> My disappointment and anxiety increases each day with the failure to receive letters from you, and direct and detailed information in regard to my affairs, which I am not overexacting in expecting. Although it is more than two months since I left California, I have had but one letter from you. My business is unquestionably more important to me, and should be to you, than either Mr. Haggin's affairs or political interests.
>
> I can derive but little benefit from a trip abroad while I am harassed with anxieties and uncertainties, in fact, knowing absolutely nothing in regard to my own affairs. I wish to know details even though I may not be expected to use my own judgement in deciding them.[17]

After consulting relatives and trusted friends, she sent for Edward Hardy Clark, a younger second cousin from Missouri, who, with his brother Fred, ran the grocery store in Fresno that their father, Austin Clark, had started. George had loaned young Clark ten thousand dollars, which he had repaid in full with interest—the only person to whom George had lent money who fully honored his obligations after George's death, Stump told Phoebe. That impressed her, and since Clark was experiencing poor health in the hot valley and was thinking of selling the business, she offered him a position in her company to look after her affairs and report to her on Will's spending habits. Clark was put in charge of the San Francisco office and ranches and instructed to learn the mining business. She trusted him and thought of him as a son. He was grateful for the opportunity given him and very loyal to Phoebe. He was no match for Will, though, who came to dominate him. Clark bent under Will's control and became lenient with him, more than Phoebe knew, but she had great confidence in her cousin and he served her well and faithfully until she died, by which time he had become president of the Homestake Mining Company. Stump was put in charge of a new office in New York, but Phoebe became suspicious of him and got rid of him after she discovered that he was sending out agents, unknown to her, to negotiate the sale of Hearst mines. A promoter, Stump tried to sell mining investment schemes and ultimately fell to his death down a New York hotel elevator shaft.[18]

Phoebe also set about deciding what to do to honor George while benefiting others with the inheritance. George had told her near his death that he wanted to establish a school for underprivileged boys where they could be taught useful trades. Phoebe planned a "technical or industrial school for poor boys," which she would build on the 450-acre Pleasanton farm, "where I hope it will be a blessing to numberless children in the future, and be a lasting monument to my husband," she wrote a friend. She contemplated burying George in a tomb nearby the school, which would be a working farm and home for boys eight to sixteen years old. The cost of the buildings was estimated at two hundred thousand dollars and she envisioned the farm-school being self-sufficient from revenues generated by the produce and products of the pupils. The boys would be allowed a percentage of the earnings from their crafts in their last year at school so that they would have something on which to live while looking for a job when they left. Phoebe based her plans on European schools that she and Mrs. Kincaid visited. One newspaper called it "practical philanthropy," crediting Mrs. Hearst with "rescuing from degradation scores of embryo criminals and creating in their stead an honest working class."[19]

If the Pleasanton ranch was not to be a horse-breeding farm—Phoebe had auctioned off George's racehorses two months after his death—it also was never to be turned into a boys' school. Her monument to George's wishes would take the form of charitable contributions to other schools and homes for destitute children, but the Pleasanton site was destined for other things. Will helped see to that. He had his own plans for a large ranch house where he could frolic with his friends.

Meanwhile, Phoebe conceived another monumental idea—a public museum for San Francisco, with her art collection as its nucleus. She announced her intentions before going to Europe in 1892, saying that they would be executed contingent on certain arrangements in the settlement of the estate. The museum was to be located in Golden Gate Park, where she thought it would have the maximum exposure to the public. It would house her enormous art and curio collection, much of which was stored in warehouses in New York, Washington, and San Francisco. Newspapers reported that she intended to give the park an initial $1 million and to leave in her will an endowment of another $1 million so that the museum could be maintained and its collection enlarged. For whatever reasons—possibility the fact that there was indebtedness against the estate—that plan, too, did not come to fruition, and the owners of the opposition newspaper, the De Youngs, would build an art museum on the very site that Phoebe had chosen for hers.[20]

Will, for his part, had bought a 112-foot yacht, the Vamoose, which he kept in New York. It was the fastest yacht afloat, with engines so big that the deck trembled when they ran. Will came up with the idea of running a "blockade" staged by the navy's White Squadron at Charleston, South Carolina, in 1896. The Vamoose shot through the blockade and none of the navy ships could catch her, to Will's delight and the admiral's fury. He raced Vamoose against any challenger and ingratiated himself with the New York Yacht Club and the press by allowing her to be a viewing boat during regattas. He also made it available to his mother. "The Hearsts are odd people in many ways, and they are admirable in many ways," one columnist wrote: they "have not been accustomed to do things by halves."[21]

Will spent a good deal of time in New York and had established the largest East Coast bureau of any western newspaper. He took space in the Pulitzer building, which was ironic, considering that the paper was to become his principal rival, and set up offices paneled in California redwood and furnished in plush red-upholstered mahogany for the comfort of visitors and correspondents. From there he and his staff could send "exclusive" news West by wire and observe the Examiner's growing business in the East. Still, he had his sights set on a New York paper. He considered buying the Times and had talked George into making a bid of $5 million for the Herald the year before he died. When the Herald owner had turned him down, George had made an offer on the Sun, which also was rejected. But Will had not given up his dream.[22]

He was looking for houses for his mother in New York, no doubt hoping that she would purchase one that he also could use. He was anxious to establish himself in the right clubs on both coasts for the purpose of making useful contacts—social amenities were only as good as they were helpful to his enterprises—and he knew his mother could help him. He enlisted her to entertain people for him and on several occasions accused her of being cold to friends whom he had cultivated for the purpose of entree to clubs. On one occasion she rebuked him, saying that his choice of friends was not of her doing.[23]

Will's drawing on the family accounts was a growing thorn in both their sides, and his continuing affair with Tessie did not help his case with his mother. He bought more property in Sausalito so that his view would not be obstructed. He cleverly sent a surrogate to trick the Greek owner of an oyster market—who was holding out for $10,500 for his waterfront property—to sell it for $4,500 on the premise that a competitor was about to set up shop. The competing fishmonger was, in fact, W. R. Hearst.[24]

Will was tiring of having to answer to his mother for his spending money and he made her an offer.

Because of my now being 30 years old, because of the unavoidable annoyance of my present dealings with Mr. Stump, because of a plan that I have in mind, and because of the fact that the request I make would not amount to an increase of my salary so much as a change of the manner of delivering it, I beg of you to instruct Mr. Stump to put to my credit at any bank on the first of each month a definite sum of $2,500.

. . . I think I might properly have now what was doubtless too much for me three years ago.

. . . I should be very happy to be relieved of the inconvenience of dealing with Stump on an indefinite basis. As long as I come to ask him for extra thousand dollars here and there, he will treat me as a child, asking 10 cents for soda water. "Can't you get along with five cents! Soda water isn't very good for you anyhow. Well, come around next month and I will talk to you about it."

There is mixed with this parental patronage an air of business mistrustfulness such as you might meet at a bank where you were overdrawing your account. This is annoying but it is unavoidable I think under the present system.

. . . The plan I "have in mind" is a mighty good one and deserving of a little encouragement. It is to get something laid away; and to get into the habit of laying something away.

. . . I shall feel satisfied with the arrangement and will not demand or desire any extra money. I will not be asking you for a thousand dollars on Christmas, a thousand on my birthday, a thousand for Bell, a thousand for

Shreve; a few thousand now and then for unforeseen expenses. I give you my word to this.

Consequently the amount paid me by the end of the year will not be greater than it is now, but the manner of paying it will, I think, be much improved.

You have always been most kind and generous to me and given me extra money whenever I asked for it but don't you think it would be better for me if I didn't ask for it so often, if I were put now on a more independent and manly footing?[25]

His mother had a different plan, one that involved getting rid of Tessie. Whatever her motives or inducements, the girl became ill and "a mental case," according to Anne Apperson, who then was a teenage member of Phoebe's household. Tessie went away, leaving Will devastated and melancholy (although he was to take care of her financially in her old age). Even Phoebe felt sorry for him. Orrin Peck, the family's favorite court jester, was sent for to cheer Will up. He gave up the Sausalito house, moved to the Palace Hotel in San Francisco with Phoebe, Anne, and Orrin and distracted himself with his other love, the *Examiner*.[26]

He was planning construction of a larger building and leading a fight against the monopoly of the Southern and Central Pacific railroads and their efforts to extend the time for repaying a government loan. In November 1894 he wired his mother,

Paper is winning its anti-railroad fight. Budd, Sutro, Temple, Henshaw, and nearly all anti-railroad candidates elected, resulting in big boom for the *Examiner* and we are gaining circulation about 100 a day.[27]

He also discussed openly his desire to build a newspaper empire. "I hope soon to get my New York paper," he said in one letter to his mother. And in another the same year (1894), he wrote that he was "beginning to get old":

I have made up my mind to work very hard on the paper from now on. I must positively build myself papers in Chicago and New York and, if I have the ability, in London, too.

I am beginning to get old and if this great plan is to be carried out I have no time to lose, and I am going to devote myself to business, first putting the *Examiner* on so satisfactory a basis that it will get along without much attention from me and will produce enough to enable me to buy my first paper elsewhere.[28]

The 1894 Christmas issue of the *Examiner* made news in its own right: it was produced entirely by women. The twenty thousand dollars proceeds from the forty-page issue, mostly from advertising, were donated to charities of the women's choosing, particularly a ward for incurables at the Children's Hospital of San Francisco. Although *Harper's Weekly* commented, before the issue reached the East Coast, "It is a solemn thing for a daily newspaper to devote a whole issue to a joke," other critics said the Christmas issue was "in all respects creditable to the temporary editors," "readable," and a tribute to the "originality" of the publisher. A correspondent to the *Chicago Tribune* wrote:

> Society women reigned supreme in the big red brick office of the *Examiner* tonight. Every room was thronged with chattering, well-dressed, handsome leaders of San Francisco society and the erstwhile male members of the staff were relegated to escort duties and quietly snubbed when they ventured to offer any advice.

The wife of the publisher of a San Francisco periodical, the *Argonaut*, was managing editor, and the wife of a local sugar magnate, Mrs. Claus A. Spreckels, was news editor. The regular staff left the building and the women took full charge, "puzzling their pretty heads over reports of murders, sugar differentials, suicides, currency bills, etc.," reported the *Tribune*:

> Terrible in their lack of symmetry and usage were some of the headlines, but an astonishing amount of perception of the technical details was noticeable. . . . Every line of it was either written or edited by the women, and in all except the mechanical part is the product of feminine hands.[29]

A string of taxicabs was put at the women's disposal so that they could go safely through the city to cover the news, and a suite of rooms at the Palace Hotel provided them a place to rest and refresh themselves with coffee and ice cream. Most of them collapsed there at midnight. But, deferential as the comments were, the hardened male critics admitted that "by looking it over, the way in which women consider that a paper ought to be run may be seen, and newspaper men may be able to get a number of pointers from it":

> There was very little space given to street brawls, doings in Chinatown, the police court and crime in general. A "men's page" told all about masculine fashions, footwear, head wear, gloves, coats, trousers, etc. Interviews with Chicago University football players indicated an interest in the game not confined to men. . . . The views expressed on women's rights were very conservative.[30]

If those views were conservative, the concept was progressive and reflected Will's respect for women and their ability to do a job as well as men. His mother was a powerful influence on Will's views of women as capable equals. Much as he disagreed with her on personal matters, she was his female role model, and throughout his life he supported women's equality. Phoebe may even have inspired the women's issue idea, as the Children's Hospital was one of her charities.

Despite his mother's best efforts and contrivances, Tessie returned and Will took a New York apartment without telling his mother. When she found out, he wrote her,

> I have just received your letter referring to the apartments. I started some time ago to furnish a couple of rooms in New York, but stopped on account of a depression in the money market. I know of no second apartments—am not fitting up any girl's rooms as might be inferred or any other rooms than the two first mentioned.[31]

He also liked to have parties at the Pleasanton ranch, where he retreated with his friends from the busy life of the paper. While Phoebe was in Europe in 1894, Will hired A. C. Schweinfurth, subsequently architect of the *Examiner* office and one of the first to design mission-style buildings that complemented California's mild climate, to build a "country house" on a ridge overlooking Livermore Valley thirty miles east of San Francisco.

Another clash of wills was about to occur between Will and his mother. Phoebe heard about the house in a letter from a friend. By that time, the shell was completed. In the spring of 1896 she went to see it and realized that Will was "appropriating" the property. "I will take the place—it is mine," she told her niece, Anne. "He never said a word to me about building it." She and Will had a showdown in which she berated him for taking over the property and for his wild parties. She took possession of the site and decided to make it into her own summer home. After that Will lost interest in it—"It bored him," Anne said—and he realized that he would have to build his own place on a hilltop somewhere else.[32]

On another front, however, he won her over, as was generally the case. It was the most important transaction of their lives since it affected Will's future. The Anaconda Copper Mine had not been paying dividends because its manager, Marcus Daly, reinvested its profits. Other stockholders, including Haggin, Tevis, and Phoebe, decided in 1895 to sell a one-fourth interest in the mine to the Rothschilds. Phoebe controlled 39 percent of the property and Haggin the majority of other shares. After negotiating with Haggin over the amount of her share, Phoebe agreed to sell her interest, reportedly for $7.5 million.[33]

Phoebe did not abandon her interest in Anaconda, however. She established a free library, dedicated in the summer of 1898, that predated those endowed by Andrew Carnegie. A city official called the Hearst Free Library a "reservoir whence will flow out streams of pure healthful literature to fructify and strengthen the intellectual life of our people." Phoebe's remarks were short and sophisticated, as polished as if written by a professional speechwriter. However, it is likely that they were her own words, expressing her love for the value of books, carefully thought out and written down in her perfect hand. It is one of the few surviving examples of her public speaking. She and Will were honoring George with their gift to the mining town, she said.

> As the absorbing interest of my husband's life was mining, with its collateral industries, and his love for the great West with all the personal friendships in it a joy until his last day, my son and myself sought some way of adding to the pleasure of the people who are spending their lives in the development of the material and other interests of this mining region. We could think of no more lasting and life-spreading influence for good than a library, and we take great satisfaction in giving you what we hope will be a help to all as the years go on.
> In view of the great advance in the arts, with the constantly changing economic conditions, and of the vast discoveries in science, it becomes a necessity of individual and civic advancement to keep abreast of modern thought and investigation, and the library is the common ground for this preparation.
> Then for the solace and intellectual pleasure of those out of the wearing strife of the day's affairs, the library will be a blessing, while for the young, who get their stimulus and life lines through the unconscious tuition of their environment, it will be a potent factor.[34]

She also established a Hearst Free Library in Lead, South Dakota, another "company town." Phoebe genuinely loved books, bought valuable first editions, and had a large library herself. She found great solace in reading—her library was not merely ornamental—and she sent books to others when she thought they would enjoy or benefit from them. Her attentions to the mining towns were not limited to libraries, however. She insisted that monthly musicales be held in them and she established and supported free kindergartens in both towns. She periodically visited them, gliding through the dusty streets like "Lady Bountiful" in her lavender dresses and lace, even donning a miner's helmet to go down into the shafts.

Although the towns were virtually run by the mining companies, Phoebe took a proprietary interest in the welfare of the workers. Besides sponsoring free libraries and kindergartens, she periodically purchased construction bonds to build schools and made annual contributions to the churches. She built a Methodist church in Pinos Altos, New Mexico, with the condition that it have a reading room for miners at the nearby Hearst gold mines. Such benevolence for many years kept the miners from unionizing. Phoebe's firm, if indirect, influence on the mining companies had a definite effect on employee relationships.

Managers and workers alike viewed her as charming and affectionate but strong-minded when it came to her opinions and objectives.

Phoebe had sold the Anaconda stock largely with one objective in mind: "to do right" by her son by helping him purchase his long-dreamed-of New York newspaper. He had pressed her for some time for the money. At one point, she had wired him from Paris,

> How can I know exactly when matters can be arranged? When incorporation is settled, suppose can borrow half a million for you, then sell part as soon as possible and turn part funds to you. Will do right, but feel terribly distressed by your unreasonable urging. Cannot be allowed to have a little rest? My trip cannot benefit when I am constantly worried. I have no news from Stump. Am anxious. Think you should go home this month and see what is being done.[35]

In return for the money, Will signed over to his mother the deed to the Babicora Ranch in Mexico, which his father had put in Will's name.

The sale of the Anaconda stock also allowed Phoebe to free the estate of debts—"I shall not know how to behave," she wrote a friend. Will proposed a partnership with his mother, which she refused. "William declines my offer of which I told you and will probably be unpleasant, but no partnership for me under the existing state of things," she wrote one of the Pecks on 29 September 1895 from Paris.[36]

She grudgingly had to admit that Will was irrevocably a newspaper proprietor and that he might make newspapers profitable with the infusion of a lot of capital. When the Examiner's business manager warned her that the paper was losing $1 million a year, Phoebe replied, "At that rate, William will last 30 years."[37]

So it was that in October 1895 Will bought the New York Morning Journal for $180,000 with offices over a once-popular saloon. Its owner, once-removed, had been Albert Pulitzer, the brother of the man who was Will's most admired peer, blind Joseph Pulitzer, owner of the New York World, which Will set out to rival. He shaved off his moustache ("in accordance with the current fashion in Park Row," a newspaper commented), and promptly changed the name of the paper to The Journal, an emulation of The Times of London that did not go unnoticed. At thirty-two he was the youngest newspaper proprietor in Gotham.

While some considered him "naive," "too erratic to succeed," and playing with "a newspaper toy," others noted that he was "old beyond his years," that he was "not unaccustomed to fighting and rather enjoys the excitement of strife." The commentators also pointed out that he had "money to burn." He quickly backed "his capital with some of the best journalistic gray brain matter" in the country, bringing his top talent from the *Examiner* and wooing away—with high salaries—from all the other papers, particularly the *World*, the best news people in the business. He dropped his newsstand price to one penny, forcing the *World* and others to follow, and began his trademark tricks to attract readers—fireworks to display election results, full texts of dispatches from overseas. He was considered "popular with his army of friends— friends who love Mr. Hearst not for his money or his power, but for himself," a "pleasant young man, modest in appearance and apparel and of engaging address . . . a great clubman," and one who took an active part in the city's gay life.

He had bought the *Journal* because he was inspired by the success of Pulitzer's *World*, and he said, "because it had more circulation than other papers that were offered me. I thought it would be easier to change its reputation, and make that good, than to take a paper with a good reputation and little or no circulation."[38]

While her son was expanding his newspaper empire, Phoebe, at the age of fifty-three, suffered a heart attack in 1895. A famous surgeon, Dr. William Pepper of the University of Pennsylvania, was called in to minister to her. They formed a strong friendship that would have important ramifications. Dr. Pepper was president of the University Archaeology Museum and the personal physician of an anthropologist with the Smithsonian Institution, Frank Hamilton Cushing, who wanted to explore early Indian settlements on Florida's west coast. Phoebe's and Dr. Pepper's relationship was to be a fruitful one for the field of archaeology since she agreed to underwrite Cushing's Marco Island digs.

Will wired his mother, in his self-deprecating, joking way to cheer her up, "Dr. Pepper says you're all right. Be up in a few days. Says you need better son and better business manager, that's all."[39]

Phoebe had become interested in many kinds of cures, particularly homeopathic. She was a patron of Homeopathic Hospitals in Philadelphia and San Francisco. When she became ill in early 1895, she called in homeopathic consultants. Will was skeptical, writing her in a letter addressed, "Dear Mommie,"

> Jennie says she has sent for a real doctor and I am awfully glad. Homeopaths are fine when you are not sick but of no particular use when you are.[40]

She had become ill shortly after another lively speculation that she would remarry. At the White House in January 1895 she had been escorted into dinner by Senator David B. Hill, a former governor of New York and a Democratic presidential contender considered a rival to President Cleveland. Phoebe was given credit for bringing the two men together in a reconciliation meeting. Immediately public "cupids" ascribed them with the ability to refurbish the Democratic party with her money and Senator Hill's political alliances. But romance with another man was elusive for Phoebe, either because she did not want it, protecting her right to the inheritance that afforded her so many opportunities, or because no man could meet her standards. He would have to be as bright as she, intellectually stimulating, and someone with whom she learned and shared interests. Otherwise, there was no need for her to marry. She had everything she wanted and could surround herself with people who stimulated her, at least intellectually.

She and Senator Hill both must have been amused by the talk of their marrying. He was "not a society man in any sense of the word, but "a genuine 'old bachelor,' seeming to have no soft spot in that adamantine heart of his for fair womankind," one commentator said.

> Senator Hill, as is well known, is averse to female society if matchmaking is in the air. . . . the Senator is not a ladies' man. . . . For a long while [he] has been inaccessible to women sending him cards.[41]

Although Phoebe was "a most excellent woman," "modest, attractive and practical, still on the sunnyside of 50," and one of the richest women in America, she was ten years older than the balding Hill. The "imaginary prospective marriage" was a "foolish lie," the more sensible writers concluded. For Phoebe it was another instance when her life was lived in the public eye. How wrong the newspaper writers were, how little they knew![42]

Phoebe's trips to Europe were now truly in the grand manner. The "widow of the California Senator . . . never allows expense to interfere with her disposition to travel by land or sea in the most luxuriously comfortable manner," one newspaper reported. "She has a saloon railway carriage and state cabin on the channel steamer when she goes from London to Paris, or vice versa, and on the Continent, when obtainable, special and exclusive traveling facilities usually associated with royalty," with whom she did, in fact, associate. Her calendar and diary for April through June 1895 included invitations to the duchess of Marlborough's wedding (30 April); a reception at the United States Embassy (2 May); luncheon at "Mrs. Roosevelt's"; a "dinner in my honor at the Embassy," where her friend Thomas Bayard was Ambassador (3 May) and the Derby (29 May). On 5 June "Ambassador Bayard took me to the Tournament" and hosted dinner again at the embassy; and on 6 June she wrote that she "made 10 balls."[43]

Will also was in Europe that year on a buying spree while Phoebe treated herself to some new Paris bonnets. She wrote one of the Pecks,

I have ordered three of the most beautiful and becoming bonnets for myself. They look a little as in former days, fine in color, and make me look very different.[44]

A democrat in heart and spirit, she nevertheless appreciated the advantages that wealth afforded. She wrote Orrin Peck in 1896, while taking a cure for headaches and her eyes in Lisbon,

You are quite right in your remark about the old country (and new country, too) having great respect for wealth—or the appearance of it. If I had my way it would always be with "the right foot foremost," in the best style possible. I'm not a bit proud but I do love the prestige that filthy lucre gives one. And another thing, I do hate to come in contact with common people.[45]

She confided many things to Orrin that she would not dream of saying to others. He was the confidant to whom she could pour out her deepest feelings. And while he was close to Will, ready to accompany him on trips or capers, Orrin was Phoebe's "confessor." With the exception of a daughter, Helen, who married well, other members of the Peck family—Mrs. Peck, Janet, and Orrin—each received a monthly check from Phoebe, who supported Janet's music studies in London and Orrin's life as an increasingly successful artist, thanks in part to Phoebe's giving and getting him commissions. The Pecks owned the quaint White House in Chelsea, built as a studio by painter James Abbott McNeill Whistler, which Phoebe may have purchased for them. The Pecks in return made themselves available to help Phoebe and travel with her, handling ticket arrangements, attending to customs, shipping trunks and art works, meeting her where she wanted them as companions. They were uncomplaining close friends and helpmates. Phoebe addressed Orrin as "My Other Son," and signed her letters to Janet and Orrin, "Your Other Mother." She shared gossip with them (in the same letter to Orrin from Lisbon she said Ambassador Bayard "must be in his dotage to have forgotten himself so far," and she called his daughter "dreadful" and "stuck up") and told them all her woes, sometimes with a wry sense of humor. The doctor in Lisbon had asked if she perceived a loss of memory connected with her headaches:

No doubt his ideas ran in the direction of softening of the brain. I told him I had always been greatly troubled with insufferable attacks of stupidity—which old age had not improved—but that I had not realized any particular gain or loss in memory.[46]

On her return from Europe in 1896 she felt America "in such an unsettled condition, politically and financially, it frightens me." She had to curtail her purchases because "Will's paper has cost such enormous amounts. I feel <u>very</u> poor. Our income is much less, and all investments pay smaller incomes."[47]

That did not curtail her life style, however. When she transferred her household across the country, eight or more servants went along (the Chinese staff and coachman took a "tourist or emigrant train"). The "Spanish house" in California was nearly finished and ready for occupancy in 1897. It was to be a small paradise overlooking a fertile valley and a town called Pleasanton (later the site of a prison that would confine Phoebe's great-granddaughter, Patricia, an independent rebel in her own way, not unlike her Victorian ancestor). Phoebe called it the Hacienda del Pozo de Verona for the wellhead (pozzo) that she and Will had transported from a Verona courtyard. It was the centerpiece around which the hacienda was built.[48]

Originally called the Hacienda del Oso in the plans drawn for Will, the fifty-three-room house designed by Schweinfurth was patterned after Spanish and Mexican buildings that he had seen. Visitors were first titillated by the sight of the white, red-roofed hacienda visible like a Spanish castle from trains passing through Niles Canyon below. From its own train station, Verona, the house was approached by a long winding drive up the hill, past orchards and vineyards and finally masses of flowers leading to wooden gates between round Moorish guardhouses. The landscape abounded in flowers, which also were grown in conservatories and given to organizations, hospitals, and friends for charitable occasions or often to cheer people up.

Botanist Luther Burbank was so impressed with the gardens that he asked if he could send some of his "newest gladioli" to "grow among your other many beautiful plants." After a visit to the Hacienda, he wrote Phoebe,

> . . . Along the way I saw trees which I have not seen before in California, as well as most of those which I have seen here, all thriving side by side in the most friendly manner. Every flower that I saw seemed happy and as if at home. . . .
>
> I noted in all this work that everything had a place and everything had a <u>use</u> besides its ornamental value which is so rarely seen any where else. . . .
>
> Your helpers seemed to be so loyal to you and you to them and at the same time understanding that it was you by whom they were employed. In other words—none of them seemed to "own the place." . . .
>
> I had learned from many mutual friends of the beauty of the Hacienda and when I met you at my place some time ago, I easily saw that you were a most remarkable woman, but I had not the faintest thought even then, of the skill and ability with which you managed this institution.[49]

The large, airy house had numerous towers and a three-story central section connected by corridors to smaller wings on either side. Windows opened onto patios and verandas. The white walls, red-tiled roof, elaborate window-grille work, carved wooden doors, palm trees, grape arbors, colorful striped awnings, and Mediterranean openness suited it to sunny California. "The whole place had a sense of pink and light," a visitor remembered. When Phoebe finished the decorating—which she supervised herself—the rooms would be filled with art treasures, books, clocks, elaborate antique chests, and oriental rugs. Tapestries hung on the walls of a high-ceilinged music room which was capped by a glass skylight. All the guest rooms had views, fireplaces, and sunken marble bathtubs. Forty guests could be housed on a weekend. Later there would be additions, designed by architect Julia Morgan, to accommodate grandchildren, and the first indoor swimming pool in the state, green-tiled to give it an ocean tint. Below the terraces Orrin Peck had a studio. Phoebe even allowed the remaining members of a native Indian tribe to have a village on the estate. And then there was the "Christmas room," lined from floor to ceiling with shelves and drawers filled with gifts that Phoebe collected throughout the year in anticipation of birthdays and Christmas. Several women year-round catalogued, wrapped, and addressed packages at a center table while Phoebe dictated the names of recipients. Careful records were kept so that no one got the same gift in successive years. The list included not only personal friends, numbering 1,020, but employees of the estate and their families, some 200 employees of the South Dakota mines, 110 at San Simeon, and 865 employees of the Mexican ranch in Chihuahua. But there Santa Claus only visited the children who attended school; it was a more persuasive incentive than the compulsory education law.[50]

The Hacienda was a working ranch and Phoebe's office. It was largely self-sufficient, having its own water supply, dairy, carpenter, electric, plumbing, and machine shops, a garage to store thirty-six cars and an eleven thousand-gallon fuel storage tank, an ice plant, crops, and animals. Guinea hens and chickens, cattle, and various fruit and vegetable products were raised and grown for consumption and for market. A private telephone line was installed in 1897 so that Phoebe could conduct her business without having to wait to be switched onto the trunk line by a central office in Pleasanton. The house itself had every modern convenience. It required a small army of butlers, maids, cooks, gardeners, and coachmen to manage and maintain it. But it was not ornate. It was practical, conducive to entertaining and living in the outdoors, unlike the Victorian mansions of the previous decades. It was part of a new California style of architecture, a showplace that rivaled any built by other rich San Franciscans down the peninsula south of the city or in surrounding Bay area suburbs. In that respect, Phoebe did not follow the fashionable trend, in part because the land at her disposal was located across the Bay and inland east of the city. Although it required a ferry ride and train trip to reach the Hacienda (special trains were hired for special occasions), few notables passing through San Francisco failed to visit Phoebe Hearst at her hilltop villa.[51]

The Hacienda would be a place of respite, she hoped, from headaches and other illnesses, although Janet Peck wrote Orrin that the many guests were frequently "petty" and backbiting, making it often "a house with the air full of floating nerves." Phoebe's nerves were not abated by Will involving himself in national politics, as he would be over the next decade. How extensively he would be involved Phoebe could not then imagine. But on his return from the 1895 trip to Europe, Will and the *Journal* took up the battle over free silver versus a gold standard. Initially Will opposed free silver (although the family's silver mines stood to benefit from such a policy) and its proponent, the Republican presidential candidate, William McKinley, who had been one of the congressmen at George's funeral. But the Democrats nominated a free-silver candidate of their own—"cross of gold" campaigner William Jennings Bryan. Still a loyal Democrat in the tradition of his father, Will was convinced to support Bryan, an unpopular stand since the silver issue had bitterly split the Democrats. Phoebe was extremely upset by Will's vitriolic campaign against McKinley, knowing that Will privately supported the gold standard. She asked Edward Hardy Clark, then in the company's New York office (to keep a closer eye on Will's bank account), to try to convince her son to take a different stand. Even Phoebe's alleged former "suitor," David B. Hill of New York, who led the opposition to Bryan at the Democratic convention and whom the *Examiner* had supported in previous political endeavors, failed to change Will's direction. He was inextricably in league with Bryan, an alignment that caused him to be ostracized at his clubs and the *Journal* to lose advertising, as Bryan was to lose the election. Phoebe, whose dislike of politics intensified, nevertheless publicly supported her son, and even agreed to entertain the rather common Bryan, which she did, graciously.[52]

The *Journal*, however, would recover. Will wired his mother on the eve of the election in 1896, "Too bad about Bryan but don't worry about the *Journal*. The orders for tomorrow are nearly nine hundred thousand. I don't know how we can print them."[53]

The *Examiner*, however, was having its own problems, another cross that Phoebe had to bear for her son's actions. Supporters of the Southern Pacific Railroad in the Congress and the press dropped a bombshell on Will that was embarrassing for him and, by association, for Phoebe as well. While Will had been in Europe in 1892 after his father's death, *Examiner* business officials had negotiated a contract for Southern

Pacific advertising in a special issue, the terms of which purportedly required the *Examiner* not to criticize the railroad. In other words, it was "influence money," like that which the railroad openly paid other newspapers. Will had consistently fought the railroad and was lampooning its president, Collis P. Huntington, unmercifully in 1897 when the railroad sought special legislation to allow it to pay its government debt over a longer term than originally scheduled. During Congressional debate over the issue in 1897, Will was castigated by a California Republican as a "blackmailer" who intimidated politicians, a "literary coyote" and "debauchee" who was "licentious" and "erotic in his tastes." Will called the alleged secret agreement between the paper and the railroad a forgery but he personally had cashed the company's check. Whether it had strings attached will never entirely be known. It did not curb the *Examiner's* tongue, however; when it came to choosing sides on railroad issues, Will tended to pick the underdog.[54]

The matter must have caused Phoebe unpleasant moments socially. She was a friend, if not close, of recently widowed Jane Stanford, whose inheritance came from the Southern Pacific Railroad; the two frequently met at board meetings of the Golden Gate Kindergartens, of which they were generous benefactors. Nevertheless, Phoebe was proud of her son's efforts to expose scandals in which the public was being deceived. No matter what her real feelings, she was always outwardly loyal to her son. And it was fierce loyalty. She would be angered by criticism of Will or his papers and defend him, even though she may not have agreed with him. It hurt her to hear him attacked and although his continual financial demands distressed her, Phoebe had great confidence and faith in his abilities. She kept hoping that they would be channeled more responsibly and more in line with her own views and wishes. That was not to be, although she grudgingly conceded that he had learned some things from her, commenting once after looking around Will's New York apartment, "Well, the scamp has good taste, I'll have to say that."[55]

Despite her fierce loyalty and public pride in him, she was troubled, even heartbroken at times, about his ways and impetuous actions. He had at last severed his relationship with Tessie, who had become mentally and physically ill, probably from the impermanent relationship with Will and the constant pressure from his mother. Phoebe's niece Anne Apperson believed that Will, furious when he found out about his mother's meddling in Tessie's first departure, saw to it that his quiet companion of nearly ten years was comfortably provided for with a house in upstate New York and a stipend for the rest of her life.[56]

More than in his personal life Phoebe was disappointed that Will did not fulfill her large expectations for him, after all she had done to prepare him for greatness. She confided to her niece that if only she had had six children instead of this one son, she would have been very happy. More than once Anne saw how upset her aunt was over something Will had done. Anne developed a habit of protecting her aunt from knowing things about Will that would upset her. But Mama usually found them out anyway.[57]

Phoebe's life in the decade following George's death was full of new dimensions that would help take her mind off Will, who she now recognized acted entirely independently of his mother, regardless of his financial umbilical cord. Phoebe began to entertain ideas for philanthropic activities on a large scale, which required a good deal of education and preparation on her part. She was feeling her way, recognizing her philanthropic potential, making her own rules. Her support of Cushing's excavations at Key Marco resulted in the exciting discovery of what Cushing called the "Court of the Pile-Dwellers," prehistoric Calusa Indian settlements. The Episcopal Cathedral in Washington, D.C, was approaching her about a new school for girls. A group of radical-thinking mothers wanted her to help found an organization to improve the quality of public school education. She was funding free kindergartens and teacher training for blacks and whites in Washington. And she was taking a personal interest in the University of California. She was becoming a major source of support for the academic and educational communities.

Phoebe knew the value of education. It meant independence instead of dependence, for women as well as men. It meant the difference between contributing to society and being exploited. Knowledge, indeed, was power. She herself was an example of that. And she believed in influencing an infant in its most formative years. She had fed information into Will's head from the moment he could absorb it, reading to him, coaching him, correcting him, encouraging him, putting him to new tests as quickly as he could take them. The appalling ignorance and vulnerability of masses of people disturbed her. Her personal observations and those of others for her in Europe taught her that there were innovative teaching techniques that could be applied in America, modified to meet the young and vigorously growing country's needs. Early childhood education was not common in America for the working classes. More often, education was sacrificed for employment to augment the family income. A good, free public education, starting at an early age, was the best solution, Phoebe believed, for upgrading the lot of working-class men and women. Even many middle-class young people with potential were unable to afford the costly educations required to make them doctors, lawyers, artists, musicians, architects—a terrible waste, Phoebe thought.

She was always open to a private request for help in sending a bright youngster through school. No one but she ever knew how many people benefited in that personal charity, but they were numerous. Several of her protégés went on to distinguished careers and positions: Donald McLaughlin (son of Phoebe's secretary) became president of the Homestake Mine; Harriet Bradford became dean of women at Stanford University; Dr. Gobind Behari Lal received a Pulitzer prize for science writing; Carl Oscar Borg was a well-known painter of American Indians. One whom Phoebe proposed to help politely declined her offer: Julia Morgan, whose California family could support her, was the first woman to receive a degree in architecture from the Ecole des Beaux-Arts. After seeing her exhausted from supporting herself as an architectural drafter in Paris while preparing for her examinations, Phoebe proposed aiding her. Morgan wrote her 16 February 1899,

> If I honestly felt more money freedom would make my work better, I would be tempted to accept your offer—but I am sure it has not been the physical work which has been, or will be, hardest, for I am used to it and strong, but rather the months of striving against homesickness and the nervous strain of examinations. Now my brother is here, and a place is now at the Beaux-Arts, really mine now it seems, the work ought simply to be a pleasure, whether housekeeping or study.
>
> Your kind words at the depot were so unexpected, so friendly, they gave and still give, more help than you can guess, and I will thank you for them always.[58]

Phoebe's girlhood friend, Clara Anthony, estimated in 1896 that Phoebe was spending fifty thousand dollars a year to send students through school. "I know of whole families of children of whose education and maintenance she has taken the entire charge until they become self-supporting," Mrs. Anthony said.[59]

The importunings for Phoebe's charity were not always practical nor without humor: a man in Lovelock, Nevada, wrote her, in 1900:

> I have a duck egg that was laid this morning and the outer shell is quite badly broken and inside is another perfect egg. I write you thinking that you were collecting curiosities and if you deem this of sufficient worth I will express it to you.[60]

Frequently she imposed a rule requiring her beneficiaries to "pass on" their advantages when they were able to do so. She asked students to whom she gave "scholarships" to do the same for other promising and needy students in the future. She applied the rule particularly to architectural students, who she knew would make good incomes once they were in practice. She corresponded with her students, closely following their progress, and she was not averse to cutting them off if she felt they were abusing her benefactions by not applying them as they were intended or were not making progress, having unrealistic expectations. She could be brutally frank. After receiving a self-pitying letter from a woman whom she had helped in musical studies but who had not recognized her limitations, Phoebe instructed her secretary to tell the woman to stop dreaming and go to work:

> Send a typewritten letter. Use very plain language. Instead of dreaming, she should go to work to help herself and her family. Do something useful. There is plenty of good, plain work to be done. She should be ashamed to say that she is in the same old groove. She is not artistic. She owes it to herself and family to do some sensible, practical work, not to me.
>
> I have no patience with such unrest and complaining, and feel no interest in her. I do not wish to receive letters from her and she need not expect answers. When I think of all the worthy people who have suffered and still suffer for the ordinary necessaries of life, and she complains of not having gained a place in the musical world. The truth is she has not the ability to do the things she constantly expresses a wish to do.[61]

She had strong feelings about women becoming capable workers, doing whatever jobs they did to the best of their ability, and being adequately prepared for the task. In 1886 she had written a friend, whose daughter, Ada, wanted to train for a profession, her convictions in support of women working. Everyone should be prepared for the possibility of having to work for a living, Phoebe felt:

> I believe that, leaving out any consideration as to the motives that prompt one to work, the training and influence coming from well-directed effort to learn a business are calculated to strengthen the character, ennoble the life, and benefit society as well as the individual.
>
> The best life results come from training young people in the direction of their tastes and worthy predilection, and it seems to me that if a daughter greatly desired to fit herself for a special vocation, it would be an indication of how I should plan for her.
>
> The uncertainties of business, the insecurity of investments, the chances and changes in the most prosperous life, make it a duty for parents to fit their children for self-support even if the need never comes.
>
> Indeed, I know some noble girls who are supporting themselves, though their necessities did not urge them, and I am sure that a finer womanhood, full of purpose and refined energy, has grown from their endeavors.
>
> Judge Wright's daughter is in Washington, daily expecting an appointment to the Interior Department, and is happy in the prospect of definite work.
>
> Ada's natural ability and enthusiasm, partly directed into channels of useful, productive occupation, would make her a happier girl and the times of her home staying would be fuller of cheer to you all.
>
> You speak of her never having had a duty, but I think that immunity, meant in all tenderness by you, can not be conducive to a complete and satisfied

life. The very opportunities of travel she has had have no doubt broadened her views of life and its means of helping to best conditions.

I sympathize with her desire to study some art or profession, and am sorry that you feel as you do about it.

She is a lovely girl, and would be an ornament to any profession, always respected for her solid qualities and appreciated for her true worth. . . .[62]

At a time when the prevailing view was that women should be housewives and mothers, or, if they had to work, seamstresses, cooks, laundresses, or beauticians (as a newspaper columnist recommended for those who found themselves untrained and suddenly without income), Phoebe had a larger view of women's capabilities. She supported women through medical school and training for other professional careers and she financed salaries of women professors at the University of California. She dealt with intelligent, professional women every day and employed them on her personal staff. She had no qualms about the equal ability of women to perform as well or even better than men. She realized that women were underutilized and undertrained. But whatever work a woman did, she encouraged the highest standards. In a rare newspaper interview, given the *New York Herald* at Christmas 1894 (the year before Will bought his New York paper), she was described "as a business woman who is naturally much interested in the improvement of the condition of working women in this country." She was quoted as saying:

I wish someone would impress upon the minds of women who desire to or are forced to earn their own living the necessity of doing their work well—of preparing themselves to render excellent service, no matter where they are employed. I become very much discouraged sometimes in trying to aid women who wish to work.[63]

She described problems finding capable secretaries, stenographers, and seamstresses, having hired and dismissed many who could not sew, write, or were indiscreet: "I do wish that young women could be made to feel very keenly that if they would succeed they must learn their business thoroughly."[64]

Phoebe applied those standards to herself. She became conversant with all the details of George's businesses. She visited the mines, descended into the thousand-foot shafts, passing through the tunnels, visiting the stamp mills, the smelters, learning the different terms used in mining so that she could understand the reports sent to her. She familiarized herself with the fruit ranch, the pruning and grafting of the trees, and with the ranching operations at San Simeon, with its seven dairies of one hundred cows each. She understood cattle and horse breeding and was in close touch with her ranch manager, Captain

Murray Taylor, a Virginia gentleman who had lost his plantation during the Civil War and whom George had hired from Haggin to raise horses. She ran her household like a business, keeping account ledgers in minute detail, from the "coin to Chinaman for fare to Verona" ($1.10) to superintendent W. J. Dakin's monthly expenses ($1,000 for the Hacienda in 1906).[65] "If you have good things, you should take care of them," she believed. She personally selected the books for the Lead and Anaconda libraries, saying, "No matter how much or how little a book costs, it is important to know that the print is good and that the book is complete."[66] And, throughout her life, she insisted on opening her own personal mail, although she had two private secretaries. It became an increasingly monumental task, which she performed in the mornings, sitting propped up in bed with its large P.A.H. monogrammed linen, surrounded by pillows, a shawl around her shoulders. When her friends remonstrated with her over that practice, she replied,

> It is a duty which I owe to my friends. How can I tell what they may wish to write me, of the grief and sorrow which may have crept into their lives, and which they would not have anyone else see except myself?
> No, as long as I can see I shall read my own letters.[67]

She was a tough business woman but her appearance was deceptive. The *Herald* article said:

> No trace of her decided executive ability can be detected in Mrs. Hearst's appearance. She has a kind, sweet face, with bright gray eyes. Her hair is dark and but very slightly threaded with gray. Her voice is melodious, and her manner sympathetic. She dresses in excellent taste. Her gowns are stylish, yet not elaborate. The jewelry she wears is always in keeping with her costume.[68]

A large part of her life was spent in the business of giving away her money. A central theme was teaching the poor how to manage better with limited resources. "How wasteful the poor people of our country are," Phoebe told historian H. H. Bancroft for a biography he was writing of George about 1890. "It is extraordinary that generally they so ill understand how to get the most out of the little they possess. They often use the less nutritious food, and discard that which is more nutritious, merely for want of a rudimentary knowledge of dietetics. The life of our social system depends greatly upon healthful and happy marriages; but as a rule our girls are not brought up to be useful and helpful, and a great many men are deterred from marrying by this fact." Education should be practical, she believed. "I think (the poor) should be educated in a way that would enable them to make the most of their present condition and cultivate them to fill any higher station to which they may be elevated. Girls should be taught to do all kinds of useful work. I am indebted to my mother that I am able to sew, wash, iron, mend, and churn. I did not find her discipline altogether agreeable at the time, but I have learned to thank her since, for her teaching has made me independent."

Vocational training was the key to helping the working classes, Phoebe told Bancroft: "I think it would tend very much toward preventing the troubles which are so much feared by us on account of the various nationalities among our laboring people, which do not readily assimilate. It seems that an earnest effort in this direction will be rewarded by an improvement in the children in the next generation. Higher education will always take care of itself; we should look rather to rudimentary and useful training."[69]

Her concern that women could not receive a comparable education to men unless they were financially able to live in comfortable surroundings conducive to study prompted her, in 1891, to set up the first scholarships for women at the University of California, and later to finance residential and social clubs, which she furnished, where student women could live, study, and entertain.

On 28 September 1891 she told the University Regents,

> It is my intention to contribute annually to the Friends of the University of California the sum of fifteen hundred ($1,500) dollars, to be used for five $300 scholarships for worthy young women.
> I bind myself to pay this sum during my lifetime, and I have provided for a perpetual fund after my death.
> The qualifications entitling students to the scholarships shall be high character and noble aims, it being understood that without the assistance here given a University course would, in each case, be impossible.[70]

She placed the awarding of the scholarships in the hands of the faculty and Regents, free from her control, but requested that the awards not be given as prizes for honors in entrance examinations. And, although she did not suggest that they should carry her name, the regents, in accepting, voted to call them the Phoebe A. Hearst scholarships.

The scholarships not only were the first for women but were the first ever offered for undergraduate study at the university. In 1891 only two fellowships were given at Berkeley (each worth six hundred dollars a year), one in Latin and one in philosophy, and three graduate scholarships, two of them for study at Harvard. The Hearst scholarships (five at first, expanded to eight in 1892) were unique. The University Regents hoped they would start a trend, noting in a letter of acknowledgement to Phoebe that "it seems peculiarly fit and pleasing in this instance that, as the University of California was one of the first to throw open its doors to women, a woman is the first to give the University a benefaction for the encouragement of undergraduates." In response to the Regent's resolution of appreciation for her gift, Phoebe wrote them that she was "greatly pleased" and considered "it one of the most beautiful and useful tributes that I have ever known."[71]

The first "Phoebes," as the recipients came to be called, got a monthly check from Irwin C. Stump, who was named a regent for 1892. In her will Phoebe left a permanent endowment of sixty thousand dollars for the perpetuation of the scholarships. Although the amount given students—three hundred dollars a year—remained the same, recipients were no less grateful for the stipend, although it was smaller in value in subsequent years. Many of the women who received the gifts became physicians, dentists, and professionals in other fields, which they said would not have been possible without the benefit of the Hearst scholarships. Phoebe herself was personally interested in her scholarship students and followed their careers, pleased when they were chosen for honorary associations such as Phi Beta Kappa, president of the Associated Women Students, or winner of the university poetry competition, as some were.[72]

Her initiative in setting up the scholarships, a few months after George died, brought her to the attention of the University Regents, who were ever on the lookout for private sources to help build the struggling western university. In 1891, as one newspaper characterized it, the University at Berkeley "was a weak institution with plenty of land, a collection of broken down buildings, beggarly endowments and few students. . . . It was little more than a site and a hope."[73] It was a land-grant college that had grown out of a church missionary academy started shortly after the Gold Rush. It was chartered as a state university in 1868. Tuition was free and it was one of the first American public institutions of higher learning to admit women. By 1891 it had 547 students, 164 of them women. (Interestingly, less than 1 percent of the nation's population were college graduates at that time, although California would soon have nearly 3 percent of its population in college.) The campus consisted of small temporary structures and seven large buildings (only one of which, South Hall, survives today), including a gymnasium, a library and art gallery, mechanical, engineering, agriculture, and chemical buildings. Dirt footpaths wound through pine, eucalyptus, and cypress groves, across a creek, past an orchard, vineyard, and experimental garden. It was an unplanned "farm" that had sprouted on foothills facing the Bay and Pacific Ocean in a town named for George Berkeley, bishop of Cloyne and author of the line, "Westward the course of empire takes its way."[74]

The campus and its library were unlit at night and social activities were few. Women students used a tiny cramped room in North Hall and men used the gym for social events. There was no student union, no theater, no residence halls. Students who did not live at home had to find lodging in university-approved boardinghouses. Phoebe was struck by the disorganized condition of the state's only public source of higher education, which was chronically short of funds and had a meager faculty. The school was self-conscious about its provincialism and isolation from East Coast and European seats of learning, but the state legislature was not particularly sympathetic. A one-cent tax on every one hundred dollars worth of property provided little sustenance. Private benefactors were few. Nevertheless, some far-sighted citizens endowed the young university with a tenacious pride and liberal attitudes that would characterize it in the future. But to Phoebe it was a poor example of a university compared to those with more ancient lineages that she had seen in Europe and the East Coast of America.[75]

Phoebe's willingness to help the only public university in her adopted state did not go unnoticed by those who wanted it to become a leading institution. Another wealthy widow was devoting all of her energy and inheritance to a private university south of San Francisco, in memory of her son and husband, Leland Stanford. Phoebe saw a role for herself in building a public university that would rival the best schools in the country, indeed in the world. It would not be a fashionable school for the rich but a university with practical curricula geared to the needs of the times and open to new ideas and fresh perspectives for the future.[76]

Phoebe Hearst appeared at a time when the tiny university needed financial help. Its supporters grudgingly watched Stanford build the largest endowment of any school in the state with a per-student dollar ratio of two to the university's one, while the university enrollment was increasing each year. With her genuine interest in education, her own ideas and convictions, and her receptiveness to new concepts, Phoebe Hearst could be the school's salvation. As a German professor, whose visiting lectureship at Berkeley was financed by Phoebe wrote, she was "a real lady" with "real millions."[77]

In addition to her scholarships, she began to make other gifts to the university. In February 1896 she contributed $2,700 to light the Bacon Library and Art Gallery and the campus walks. But her visions for the university were bigger, and others saw opportunities to which she lent an interested ear. In that same year she proposed donating a mining building to honor her husband. She hinted that she would be interested in funding more buildings if other donors would match her contributions. She was ready to proceed immediately if the university wanted it. Acting President Martin Kellogg was taken by surprise at her generous, unfettered offer. He stalled, wondering how he could come up with a design on short notice, but he assured Phoebe that if she would return in a day or two, he would present her with more concrete ideas of what they could do with the money. The school had no department of architecture, but it did have an engineering department and, someone remembered, an instructor of descriptive geometry in the drawing department—a man named Bernard Maybeck, who had a degree in architecture from the Paris Ecole des Beaux Arts. Maybeck came up with a preliminary plan for a mining building in twenty-four hours and "a miserable sketch it was," he later recalled. He was afraid that the generous lady would never give money for such a building. But he had an inspiration; he rushed home and over his young wife's protests, removed a pair of plush drapes from a window, grabbed some potted geraniums from the garden and presented the building sketch to Phoebe in a setting surrounded by curtains with flowers in front. She approved the preliminary drawing. "How could she resist?" Maybeck said; "After all, she was a woman."[78]

Maybeck then posed a broader possibility. Where was the building to go, he asked? The campus had no overall plan and it was growing in a hodge-podge way. Phoebe and Regent Jacob Bert Reinstein, a San Francisco lawyer, listened intently as Maybeck unfolded an idea for an international competition to develop a master plan for the university campus. He believed that an objective outsider should do it, one who would not be influenced by pressures from people connected with the university. The competition would attract the best architects in the world. The campus would no longer be a dusty farm but would have direction for the future and become a landmark. "Even if we err toward the brilliant, which is not probable, time will give to the whole that earnestness and seriousness that will awaken love in the hearts of the men that beheld it," Maybeck said.

Phoebe and Reinstein were intrigued. The other regents and the president saw the possibilities of attracting private money to the university from rich people who would be more inclined to endow buildings that were "part of a superb architectural pile that would excite the admiration of the world" than a non-descript pile, university historian William Carey Jones later wrote. Maybeck further argued that such a competition not only would be good for architecture generally, stimulating the best talent in the world, but, if conducted openly and fairly, would give a good name to competitions, which sometimes had been tainted by charges of favoritism among colleagues, to the disadvantage of aspiring new talent.[79]

Phoebe saw an opportunity for using her resources to a large-scale advantage, and in October 1896 she made an offer that startled univer-

sity directors. She would finance all expenses associated with an international competition to produce a plan for the university.[80]

Her letter outlining the proposal suggested that a board of trustees,
consisting of Governor James Herbert Budd representing the state, Professor William Carey Jones representing the university, and Reinstein
representing the regents—all graduates of the university—be con-
stituted to oversee the program. Ratification of a final plan would rest
with the regents, she noted. She wrote Reinstein:

                              Palace Hotel
                              October 22, 1896

Dear Sir,

Referring to the conversation I had last week with yourself and Professor
William Carey Jones, I desire to say that I am deeply impressed with the
proposition now before the Board of Regents to determine upon a comprehensive and permanent plan for the buildings and grounds of the University of California on the site of Berkeley, and heartily approve of the idea.

My son and I have desired to give some suitable memorial which shall
testify to Mr. Hearst's love for and interest in this State, and after having
carefully considered the matter we feel that the best memorial would be one
which would promote the higher education of its people. And I must confess
that the absence of a suitable plan for the university buildings has seemed an
obstacle in the way of carrying out some ideas which we have cherished.

I feel now so imbued with the importance to the university and to the State
of having such a plan that I should be glad to aid in its complete and speedy
realization. I may also say that I am the more anxious for this, as I have in
contemplation the erection on the university grounds of two buildings, one
of them to be the memorial referred to.

I would therefore suggest that I be permitted to contribute the funds
necessary to obtain by international competition plans for the fitting architectural improvement of the university grounds at Berkeley. While I understand from you that such plans can be procured for about $15,000 I desire to
say that the success of this enterprise shall not be hampered in any way by a
money consideration.

I have only one wish in this matter—that the plans accepted should be
worthy of the great university whose material home they are to provide for;
that they should harmonize with and even enhance the beauty of the site
whereupon this home is to be built; and that they should redound to the
glory of the State whose culture and civilization are to be nursed and
developed at its university.

As the full execution of these plans will probably require a long period of
time, and one of constant and assiduous attention, I should like to suggest
that this trust be reposed in a special committee which will represent the
several interests involved. . . .

I believe that the release of Mr. B. R. Maybeck (who has been identified
with the idea of this plan from its inception) from his duties of instruction at
the university, and his presence in the eastern States and Europe would
greatly facilitate a proper understanding of our design among architects. I

would, therefore, further suggest that he be given a leave of absence for one or two years, and I offer to provide for him a reasonable compensation.

> Yours very sincerely,
> Phoebe A. Hearst[81]

Governor Budd, who said the offer took his breath away, called it "noble" and Reinstein said it was "a wise gift" that he saw as the beginning of a great fund-raising drive: More than $4 million would be raised from private sources, he predicted.[82]

So it was not surprising that the following year, in 1897, Phoebe was named by Democratic Governor Budd to be the first woman regent of the University of California, filling the unexpired term to 1899 of the late Charles F. Crocker. Newspaper editorials congratulated the governor for honoring "the womanhood of the state," and some were quick to say that Will's personal friendship with the governor and the *Examiner's* editorial support of him had nothing to do with the unusual appointment. It was a "departure" from previous practice, "a tribute to one of the noblest women of her time and a recognition of the desirability of the influence of cultured, generous, refined womanhood in our higher institutions of learning," one editorial said. "The girls of California," it continued, "ought to have one of their sex on the board of administration—should have had representation on that body long ago. . . . She will dignify the body [and] reflect honor on womanhood generally, which is not the least important of the good things that will accrue from placing a woman in this position."[83]

Commentators mistakenly assumed that Mrs. Hearst would pay for the erection of many new university buildings, misconstruing her offer to fund the competition and one building initially, an editorial error that Phoebe corrected on her copies of the news clippings, no doubt with a wry smile. Although the appointment required some lobbying— one petition came from university women—it was confirmed by the legislature and on 10 August 1897, Phoebe took her seat at her first regents' meeting. It was to be a long and fruitful affiliation for the university—and for her.

Julia Morgan, first woman architect to graduate from Ecole des Beaux Arts, in her Paris apartment kitchen, ca. 1900. She rejected Mrs. Hearst's offer of financial assistance but later became a popular architect for the Hearsts, designing William Randolph's castle at San Simeon after his mother's death. *Courtesy, Julia Morgan Collection, California Polytechnic State University.*

Main house of Hearst's San Simeon complex, showing one of the two towers inspired by a Spanish church at Ronda. Photo, Judith Robinson, 1982.

Hearst ranch house at San Simeon, built in 1875 by George Hearst, still standing in the valley below the "castle" on the Enchanted Hill. Photo, Judith Robinson, 1982.

Hearst Hall, connected by passageway to Phoebe Hearst residence, left, in Berkeley, 1899. At Mrs. Hearst's expense, Bernard Maybeck designed this unusual arched structure to serve as a student social hall. The building was moved to campus a few years later but burned in 1922. *Courtesy of the Documents Collection, College of Environmental Design, University of California, Berkeley.* Photo, G. E. Gould.

Interior of Hearst Hall, with tapestries in alcoves. *Courtesy of the Documents Collection, College of Environmental Design, University of California, Berkeley.*

Wyntoon Castle, Mrs. Hearst's summer retreat in the Sierras, 1902. Designed by Bernard Maybeck, it burned in 1929. Photo, J. H. Eastman.

Bernard Maybeck when he was instructor in drawing at the University of California, Berkeley, 1895. He managed the Phoebe Hearst International Competition for the university, 1899–1900. Maybeck also was a close friend of Mrs. Hearst's. *Courtesy of the Documents Collection, College of Environmental Design, University of California, Berkeley.*

Millicent Willson Hearst as Will's young bride. *Courtesy of the California Historical Society, San Francisco.* Photo, Marceau, New York.

Hearst as a Congressman in 1904, wearing the hat that became his trademark. *Courtesy of the California Historical Society, San Francisco.* Photo, Clinedinst, Washington, D.C.

W. R. Hearst with son George, born 1904. *Courtesy of the California Historical Society, San Francisco.*

Phoebe Hearst in portrait by Orrin Peck. It was given by her in 1904 to the National Cathedral School, Washington, D.C., which she built and hangs today in its Hearst Hall. *Photo courtesy of Phoebe Apperson Hearst Historical Society, St. Clair, Mo.*

Orrin Peck, painter, confidant to Phoebe Hearst and her son and "court-jester" to the Hearst family. *Courtesy of the California Historical Society, San Francisco.*

Will with his mother at her Hacienda. *Courtesy of the Phoebe Apperson Hearst Historical Society, St. Clair, Mo.*

Phoebe Hearst, philanthropist, as she might have appeared at board meetings. *Courtesy of the California Historical Society, San Francisco.*

Apartment house in Paris at Place de l'Alma, with view of the Eiffel Tower, where Phoebe took a floor in 1905. Photo, Judith Robinson.

Three Hearst children on horseback at their grandmother's Hacienda. *Left to right:* George, William Randolph, Jr., and John. The Hacienda was a child's paradise and the grandchildren spent many of their early years there. *Courtesy of the California Historical Society, San Francisco.*

Phoebe Hearst at the Hacienda with all five grandsons: *left to right:* William Randolph, Jr., born 1908; twins Elbert Willson (later changed to David) or Randolph Apperson (Patty Hearst's father), born in 1915; George Randolph, born 1904; and John Randolph, born 1910. *Courtesy of The Phoebe Apperson Hearst Historical Society, St. Clair, Mo.*

Phoebe Hearst *(fifth from right),* in Chinese robe, at YWCA convention she hosted at the Hacienda, 1913. *Courtesy of The Bancroft Library, University of California, Berkeley.*

Phoebe Hearst and entourage at the Hacienda. Orrin Peck is at her immediate right. Others are unidentified. *Courtesy of the California Historical Society, San Francisco.*

Phoebe Hearst in traveling clothes on a steamship pier in rare candid photo. *Courtesy, Phoebe Apperson Hearst Historical Society, St. Clair, Mo.*

Phoebe Hearst signing constitution of the Woman's Board of the Panama-Pacific Exposition, of which she was chair, 1915. *Courtesy of The Bancroft Library, University of California, Berkeley.*

Phoebe Hearst, possibly at the 1915 Panama-Pacific Exposition, San Francisco. *Courtesy of the* San Francisco Examiner.

Phoebe Hearst, seventy-four years old, marching in the San Francisco Preparedness Parade, July 1916, in which a bomb killed ten people. *Courtesy of the San Francisco Examiner.*

Phoebe Hearst with *(left to right)* William Wallace Campbell, eminent astronomer, director of Lick Observatory, and later president of the University of California (1923–30), and Thomas A. Edison, at the Hacienda. In 1916 Mrs. Hearst asked Edison to wire Mount Vernon, George Washington's home, for electricity, causing controversy among the monument's regents. *Courtesy of the Phoebe Apperson Hearst Historical Society, St. Clair, Mo.*

Phoebe Hearst writing letters in bed, which she did in the mornings of her later years, at the Hacienda. *Courtesy of the California Historical Society, San Francisco.*

Phoebe Hearst in rare candid photo, c. 1918. *Courtesy of the California Historical Society, San Francisco.*

Hearst Mausoleum at Cypress Lawn Cemetery, Colma, Calif., where Phoebe, George, and William Randolph Hearst are buried. Photo, Judith Robinson, 1986.

IN MEMORY OF
PHOEBE APPERSON HEARST
FROM HER FRIENDS

Fountain in honor of Phoebe Hearst in San Francisco's Golden Gate Park, the only memorial to her in the city. Photo, Betty Clapp Robinson, 1986.

12
Largesse and Luxury

The turning of the century was a time of new dimensions for Phoebe. She was respected as a strong-minded and advanced woman who was setting an example for those with great wealth. Her philanthropies were much publicized. She was courted for financial favors and for her presence. She was a person with influence. For her, it was a rich time, full of new and rewarding experiences. It was also a trying time. She was occupied daily with the demands on her, but she enjoyed the power she had achieved despite her ill health and concern over Will's activities. He was by that time in his early thirties, and, while still an attentive son, led an independent life, largely in New York. Phoebe divided her time between Washington, California, and Europe.

In August 1897, her fifty-fifth year, Phoebe attended her first meeting of the University Regents; it was held at the Mark Hopkins Institute of Art on Nob Hill in San Francisco. She was escorted into the room by Regent Reinstein and seated next to President Kellogg. A woman reporter sent to cover the event recorded that "one could not but be impressed with the expression of deep thoughtfulness—the realization of the importance of the duties she was assuming . . . the ordeal of taking her seat among the most prominent, influential and honored body of men in the state, co-equal with them in every regard, her vote hereafter to bear the same weight and leave the same impress . . . as theirs." For, although "Mrs. Hearst is only a woman . . . no one saw it." She accomplished the "ordeal" with calm dignity and only an "extreme pallor" gave her away as having just risen from a sick bed. She was smaller than the reporter expected, "her features regular, her complexion clear, almost verging on coldness."

Her thin lips, closed firmly, express determination without severity or harshness, leaving a pleasant smile about the mouth. A sensitive person would look with pity at the heavy circles about the eyes, and wonder whether sorrow or physical suffering had left tell-tale marks, but one look into the clear depths of those wondrous eyes and love takes the place of sympathy. Suffering there may have been, but it has left no sting. A mind at peace with itself and the world was my conviction.[1]

She was dressed in black silk lined in white silk with cuffs and a collar of lace that covered her shoulders and bodice. A bonnet with California violets and drooping lilies of the valley was perched on her head over the high forehead; a wrap, "a confection" of black lace and crepe lined with ivory satin, a white parasol with a heavy gold handle, and white kid gloves completed her outfit—"as dainty and elegant a costume as any woman of Mrs. Hearst's age . . . need want," the reporter noted in detail.[2]

If Phoebe appeared tired, the volume of her activities did not reflect it. The architectural competition consumed much of her time. Although there had been two previous plans for the campus—one by landscape architect Frederick Law Olmsted in 1865 and another by David Farquharson in 1873—none had been as far-reaching as the Hearst competition envisioned, "the most lavishly endowed architectural competition known to history," university historian William Carey Jones wrote. Architects around the world had Berkeley on their minds and drawing boards. The London Times of 10 January 1898 said,

> Not since Aladdin built his famous palace, never since Wren sought and was deprived of the opportunity of rebuilding London according to his own splendid conception, have architects been offered so unique and so transcendent a chance.[3]

The competition was attracting wide attention at home and abroad. The New York Times "Saturday Review of Books and Art" referred to the "Phebe A. Hearst University of California," prompting a letter to the editor claiming that Mrs. Hearst intended to spend $4 million on "a suite of buildings" for the university. The California legislature was so impressed by her offer that both houses unanimously voted a one-cent increase in the state tax to support the university. "It gives us especial pleasure to note that your generosity has contributed to this fortunate result," President Kellogg wrote Phoebe. "In the arguments before the Committees, the Hearst benefactions proved an effective challenge to the State's liberality."[4]

The competition was not without critics, however. They argued that only Americans or Californians should be allowed to compete. Some European architects scorned the pretensions of Americans to build an "Athens of the West." Others feared that the contest would favor Americans. With the exception of the leading English architect, Norman Shaw, however, the eminent European architects who were chosen to judge the entries supported the competition. Maybeck's new wife, Annie, who was to be his helpmate in all his endeavors, wrote from Berlin in 1897 to reassure Phoebe against the contest's detractors:

We feel that all possibility of "wire-pulling," scheming or littleness would be impossible and our University would come to be the thing these men would see it. . . .

Incidentally, each man we met showed or told us we were on the right track. . . .

When one sees how seriously really great men look upon the problem, the attitude of our American architects seems "small" indeed and the difficulty of finding an American jury man worthy to rank with the men we can find here almost insurmountable.[5]

Even the London *Spectator* editorialized on the subject, if derisive of newly rich Americans:

On the face of it this is a grand scheme, reminding one of those famous competitions in Italy in which Brunelleschi and Michael Angelo took part . . . [The endowment of] grand universities shall stand as a protest against the theory that money-making is the end of life. . . .

We indulge the hope that the projected city of learning on the slopes of the Pacific has arisen out of a conviction of this kind. We trust that it has grown out of a desire to identify California in the thought of the world with something else than mines, ranches and newly enriched millionaires.[6]

The Maybecks traveled with Reinstein through the United States and Europe, seeking advice on how to best proceed. The program was drawn up at Maybeck's alma mater, the Ecole des Beaux Arts in Paris. Six thousand programs in English, French, and German, with contour maps and photographs of the site sloping down Berkeley hills with a view across the Bay to its bridgeless entrance, were sent to interested architects. An advisory board of landscape architects was named to see that any new building would conserve and enhance the natural beauty of the place.

Maybeck's rich imagination was evident in his lofty prospectus for the competition, which foresaw a classical plan to rival the Parthenon. The architects were to feel no constraints in their designs.

One hundred and five entries were received—from Japan, South America, every country in Europe, and the United States—and on 30 September 1898 Phoebe and Reinstein arrived in Antwerp for the judging. A carefully selected jury met to narrow the field to finalists. The plans, which were insured for one hundred thousand dollars, were delivered sealed to the United States Consul in Antwerp. The rooms where they were kept were guarded round the clock, and the names of the entrants were not given to the jury. Besides Reinstein, the only nonarchitect, the jury was made up of eminent men in the field: Jean Louis Pascal of France, Paul Wallot of Germany, Walter Cook of the United States, and Norman Shaw of England. For five days the jury studied the plans, each day eliminating a few, sometimes reconsidering them. No plan was eliminated that any member of the jury wished retained.

In the end, eleven plans received unanimous votes and were declared finalists, from which a winner would be chosen in San Francisco. There were four runner-ups who Phoebe made sure did not go entirely unrewarded for their efforts. She personally sent the results, with photographs, to James Creelman, European *Journal* editor in London, whose office forwarded them to New York "with strong request for their publication," Creelman's aide assured her.[7] She had come to appreciate the value of publicity and the far-reaching impact that it could have. She was not unsophisticated in using the press, although she had been angered by it many times.

The Burgomeister at Antwerp hosted a banquet for Phoebe and the jurors, who declared that "Mrs. Hearst had every reason to be satisfied with the result" and "that no architectural competition of which they had had any experience had ever been conducted so perfectly."[8]

The issue of fairness was one that Phoebe and Reinstein worried about; they wanted the competition not to be tainted by bias in any way. Reinstein, on a channel boat returning to England, invited a young American, James Gamble Rogers of Chicago, to join him. Rogers, in his fourth year at the Beaux Arts, had entered the Hearst competition. Reinstein did not identify himself as one of the jurors while the architectural student talked about the competition. Mrs. Hearst, he volunteered, was "a love of a woman" and "the whole thing was great and a perfect success," though he had been a loser. Reinstein said that he had heard such competitions were no good, that juries favored their friends. The student protested that was not the case with the Hearst competition, that "he knew the sentiment about the Ecole des Beaux Arts and about Paris [dominating juries]," but that the thing had been "perfect from start to finish." He pointed out that two of juror Pascal's friends had not been finalists, and that while "the greatness of the scheme had lured the big men all in, [and] the youngsters had a lurking fear that friendships with members of the jury might—would—sway them, the event proved that 'everything was just alright from the basement to the top story,'" Reinstein wrote Phoebe. Only after listening to the innocent competitor did Reinstein give him his card and identify himself. "I learned just exactly the inside of the whole business from one who was strictly in it, talking to one who he thought was simply a pretty good listener," Reinstein said, suggesting that the young aspirant should get "some kind of benefit out of this."[9]

Reinstein's letters to Phoebe were full of humor, learned references, anecdotes, and affection, suggesting that the two were close friends. He wrote of missing her and of being concerned about her health. He was solicitous and deferential. He even dreamt of her, he said, and was grateful for her attentions (Maybeck's arrangements for his travels "were just like Mrs. Hearst's to me"). He sent her a love note that he found on a train, "evidently from some lovelorn swain to his dearest, kindest and best." He carried boxes of things for her to America, and signed his letters affectionately.

> The months of November and December will be extremely pressing ones for me, but after that I shall be quite free—for me—and will then be able perhaps to follow more of your advice and kindly counsel, but only in order that I may be the better able to look after the affairs of some one who has been more than good to me.[10]

The two had a close and respectful relationship, but if it were more than a friendship, it was discreetly hidden. Reinstein was well read, a good storyteller, and wise in the ways of California politics. Although Norman Shaw, English architect and juror, humorously called him "that old wag,"[11] Reinstein was a sympathetic man, and for that, among other things, Phoebe appreciated him. He frequently acted as her spokesman. He tried (without success) to get the London papers to interview him about the competition. And he met with the attorney for Sir Thomas Lipton—"the great philanthropist who is coming to America to try to win back the America cup with a yacht he is having built"—to discuss a global charity idea of Phoebe's: the Hearst Humanity Fund. "Then he will start a Lipton Humanity Fund but it will be merely a copy of yours," Reinstein wrote Phoebe.[12] The fund, though never launched, was in concept what the United Nations and other international charities later would become.

The architectural competition then shifted to San Francisco. The eleven finalists included six American architects, three French, one Austrian, and one from Switzerland. They were invited to California, at Phoebe's expense, to examine the Berkeley site and make adjustments to their plans as necessary. Each finalist received four hundred dollars plus travel expenses (five hundred dollars for the Europeans), and nine went to California. Reinstein thought "these visiting architects seem to me to be a little over-enthusiastic, and I think their impetuosity ought to be restrained by some of us calmer Californians."[13]

The success of the international competition prompted another scheme—a similar competition to plan San Francisco. Phoebe had seen great planned cities, with their wide avenues, parks, historic streets, and monuments. Her Gold Rush city was growing like "topsy" over its hills and valleys, unplanned and disorganized. It boasted several privately owned and unconnected cable car lines and a new $20 million water system, but no plan for future expansion. Some of its citizens, including Jacob Reinstein, worried about its haphazard development. Why not take advantage of the visiting expert architects to hold a competition to lay out San Francisco? The idea appealed to Phoebe and she agreed to support such a project. She authorized Reinstein to announce her intentions. He wrote her in Paris 29 November 1898:

> Some time during this week, probably, I shall give out publicly your intention to have these visiting architects enter into another competition for the laying out of the City of San Francisco on ideal lines, so far as practicable, with the same Jury to judge the plans, and I think that a very great and good result can be had for a very small sum of money, compared therewith, inasmuch as you have already incurred all of the expense necessary to this second competition, except the amount of the money for the prizes, and in my judgment this will not exceed $10,000, and if you intend giving but two prizes, perhaps half of that sum would be sufficient.[14]

Phoebe's inclination to bring European culture to America's West Coast was perceived by some as pretentious, and she was not without detractors, some of whose motives may have been jealousy. While few could fault her generosity to worthy causes, some San Franciscans privately thought her presumptuous. She was then in a position to attract visiting dignitaries to her table, but her fondness for European ways gave the appearance of hautiness in a society accustomed to accepting members with newly acquired credentials. She was revered and admired by most of her peers, nonetheless. She was the first president (in 1888) of an elite women's group, the Century Club, devoted to helping talented women and serving as an intellectual forum for lectures and educational programs. The demands on her for appearances at social and fund-raising events were more than she could fulfill and she turned down more invitations than she accepted. She preferred to help raise money quietly by persuading her rich friends to join her in supporting charitable causes, lending her name to boards of directors but keeping a low profile. Her life at the turn of the century was centered not in the city but largely at the university and the Hacienda, where distinguished visitors to the area—royalty, politicians, performers—were privileged to be entertained. King Albert of Belgium stayed there while traveling incognito, and Mr. and Mrs. Herbert Hoover were guests when he was a young geologist. Phoebe held court from her Pleasanton hilltop, independent from the city's social pack; those who were not privileged to receive her invitations accused her of disdain.

Her impeccable social standing and gentle power of persuasion, however, caught the attention of San Francisco's leading citizens in this new effort to beautify the city. Reinstein invited John MacLaren, a

Scotsman who was designing Golden Gate Park, and sugar king Adolph
Spreckels to give the distinguished visiting architects a tour of the city
in Spreckels' four-in-hand carriage. "I believe that this last plan of
yours, or if you prefer it, of ours, will be universally received by the
citizens of San Francisco and the State of California, with pleasure and
gratitude," Reinstein wrote Phoebe.[15] If the project required appropriating some private property, that did not daunt its supporters. The *Baltimore Sun* editorialized:

> The widow of Senator Hearst, keeping in touch with the spirit of the city's
> life, has recently come forward with a scheme which is enormous in its
> scope. It is nothing less than to make San Francisco, architecturally, the most
> beautiful city in the world. Her project requires the cooperation of property
> owners, but nothing daunts her. First, she contemplates the building of
> conduits and sewers, so as to make San Francisco the healthiest city in the
> world; then, the laying out of an elaborate system of parks and boulevards,
> and then the architectural work.[16]

Although Mayor James D. Phelan, a friend who shared Phoebe's dedication to public service and to beautifying the city, endorsed the idea, the
competition did not come about, and San Francisco continued to grow
without a plan, although one was subsequently drawn up in 1905 by
Chicago architect Daniel H. Burnham, who designed the 1893 Chicago
World's Fair and plans for Washington, D.C., and other cities.

The university architectural competition, though, caused great excitement in San Francisco. The finalists' plans arrived in August 1899
(Phoebe had to use her influence in Washington to have a six thousand
dollar duty on them lifted). The jury met in September, and, after much
fanfare and secrecy, awarded the first prize of ten thousand dollars to a
Frenchman, Émile Bénard, whose code name in the competition had
been "Roma." He had won the Grand Prix of Rome in 1867 for the
design of a fine arts building, which had been reproduced as the art
palace at the 1893 Chicago World's Fair without credit to him. Bénard
was an established architect in France, fifty-five years old, a graduate of
the Beaux Arts, a member of the Paris Jury of Public Works, and with
many notable buildings to his credit. He had not visited the Berkeley
site and was not present in San Francisco to receive his award.

One thousand people were invited to view the finalists' drawings at
the Ferry Building on 7 September. Phoebe stood on a curtained dais,
receiving guests with four prominent San Francisco women, but toward
the end of the evening, the heat, lights, crowd, and her fatigue and
excitement at the triumphal cumulation of the two-year effort were too
much for her and she fainted. She was quickly revived and taken home.
The whole affair had cost her more than two hundred thousand dollars.

Another ten thousand dollars in prize money was divided among the four runners-up, all Americans: Howells, Stokes and Hornbostel of New York, second; Despradelle and Codman of Boston, third; Howard and Cauldwell of New York, fourth; and Lord, Hewlett and Hull of New York, fifth. The American Institute of Architects declared there had been "no shadow of unfairness" in the competition.

Bénard's plan stood out from the others for its grandiose design and classical elegance. It had long avenues, spacious courts, imposing buildings. The New York Tribune said it had "hints of the Acropolis at Athens, but only hints, for his design is original and modern." There was "nothing monotonous" about it, the article concluded, and it harmonized with the live oak-covered environment. It called for fifty buildings in classical Roman Ionic style, grouped by academic discipline, many of them lining a long avenue leading down a slope, crowned by an observatory and culminating in a huge gymnasium with equal facilities for men and women. The other designs had not been chosen, the Tribune said, because they gave too much prominence to dormitories (Howell's); or did not have enough open spaces and trees (Despradelle's); or had buildings too similar in design (Howard's); or required costly grading of the landscape (Lord's).[17]

Bénard, who had never seen the site of his design, demanded that his prize money be sent immediately to him in Paris. Then he set off (on 11 November) for California to see about implementing it. The competition was over, but another series of problems began.

Skeptics wondered about the practicality of executing such a grandiose plan. Cost estimates ranged from $10 million to $100 million. Could the design actually be adapted to the land? Private property would have to be taken; property owners close to the university were worried. The Examiner's principal opposition, the Chronicle, wondered whether the whole scheme might be a white elephant, "a lopsided and fragmentary example of architecture over on the Berkeley hills, which will bear to architecture the same relation that an ancient torso bears to sculpture—a mutilated example of art, carrying with it a suggestion of beauty, but whose complete and finished form will ever remain an unsolved riddle."[18] A great deal depended on Phoebe's willingness to underwrite construction of much of the plan, stimulating the state legislature and other private donors to match her contributions. And a great deal depended on Bénard's cooperation.

That would turn out to be increasingly difficult. Soon after his arrival on 1 December, Bénard set conditions that called for an additional thirty thousand francs for further work to adapt the plan to the landscape, although he had told Reinstein that he believed little revision was necessary. He even drew some quick sketches of revisions while talking through an interpreter to Reinstein and Maybeck. Reinstein pointed out that all the competitors had known that they might have to make modifications before the university accepted a design; and that if Bénard had accepted the invitation to visit the site before the second judging, he might have made the necessary modifications then. In view of Bénard's own admission that he would simply give directions to his draftsman to relocate or scale down certain buildings, Reinstein suggested that the architect might be willing to perform such services at no or a lesser charge. Reinstein told him that the regents, who had the final power to accept or reject the plan, found it "impracticable and too expensive." Bénard accepted the need to alter his design and seemed content for about two weeks; Phoebe had paid his and his wife's expenses to visit California and provided him with an interpreter, draftsman, office, and French-speaking office boy. A central issue, however, was who would oversee the plan's execution. Bénard thought that was to be his role. The trustees tried to explain to him that it was up to the regents of the university to decide which of the top three plans to select and how to implement it. His work concluded with his award of first prize in the competition. Bénard could not accept that. It was then that he "met many evil-disposed persons in San Francisco," Reinstein wrote jury president Pascal, "who prejudiced his mind against Mrs. Hearst and the Trustees. He made complaint against our good faith."[19] The plan's and Phoebe's detractors had gotten his attention and he was saying openly that he had been betrayed. Upset at hearing this, Phoebe arranged a meeting with Bénard at a Berkeley home that she had recently rented. Reinstein, Professor Jones, and the head of the French department also attended.

> . . . and there Mr. Bénard stated that he had interviewed a number of representatives and influential citizens of the State of California, and he had been informed by them, and believed, that the Regents would never adopt his plan because he was a foreigner, and that there was no money to execute the plan, and that he had been basely deceived; that he had been informed by Mr. Pascal that he was to come to this country to make the contract for the execution of the buildings, and not to modify his plan at all; that he had no faith in the enterprise, or in the honesty of anybody connected with it. . . .
>
> There is no doubt that Mr. Bénard was foolish enough to talk to all of the enemies of his plan, and its execution, who had even gone so far as to call upon him or throw themselves in his way in order to produce the very effect desired by them, in order to further their own interests. We, ourselves, had heard various criticisms of the plan, stating that it was inartistic, impracticable, and was not suited to University purposes, and, in fact, that it was wholly bad. Mr. Bénard evidently chose to believe the enemies of his plan, rather than its friends, and his real friends.
>
> At this interview, however, Mr. Bénard showed himself a man who was incapable of listening to reason; excitable even to the point, almost, of

hysteria; and irritable to such a degree as to indicate to all of us who were there that he was not a fit man to intrust with the execution of any work whatever, at least in this country; and he most grossly insulted everybody there present, including Mrs. Hearst, to such an extent that only the fact of his being a guest in that house prevented him from being forcibly ejected therefrom. He shouted at the top of his voice, and raved and stamped about it; said all he wished was to be permitted to go back, and that he had already been made the laughing stock of the world.

But he demanded thirty thousand francs to prepare any new plan, or to make any modifications concerning it, and to this point he steadily adhered from start to finish, together with all his expenses for coming and going from Paris, and for all expenses that were to be incurred here.[20]

Bénard's behavior may have been the result of a genuine misunderstanding on his part or of a temperamental artist or foreigner uncomfortable out of his milieu, but he insisted either on the authority to execute his plan or an additional thirty thousand francs. Reinstein explained to his Paris colleague:

It is perfectly evident to me, as it was to everybody present at all these interviews, except Mr. Bénard . . . that he desired to make an arrangement with the Trustees, or with Mrs. Hearst, by which he was to be charged with the execution of all the work under the new plan; and when he found that it was utterly impossible for us to make such arrangements, inasmuch as that was beyond our duty, or our power . . . he made up his mind that in any event he would get 30,000 francs out of the matter. . . .

But in his effort to secure this result, in the manner and method of doing it, and the positions he took, and the charges he made against all of us, it became entirely clear to us all that he would never be able to succeed in this country, in the carrying out of the work because we are sure the experience of all of us with Mr. Bénard was something absolutely unique and, in my judgement, absolutely disgraceful, for he not only impugned our good faith, but our intelligence and our honesty on every hand.[21]

They paid him his thirty thousand francs, after which Bénard became apologetic and claimed he had misunderstood those who had influenced him earlier. But the Americans had had enough of him and were not about to do further business with him. His "temper, his suspicions, his lack of calmness and judgement, and, in fact, of good American horse sense" made it out of the question for him to oversee construction of the plan he had designed, Reinstein told his Paris contacts. They were glad to be rid of him.

Since the regents agreed to go forward with a plan for construction of new campus buildings, based on Bénard's design, it was necessary to find someone who could manage its development. Maybeck recommended, and, having Phoebe's approval, the regents agreed to hire John Galen Howard of the New York firm that had taken fourth place in the competition. Howard accepted, modified and simplified the Bénard plan—by then called the Phoebe A. Hearst plan—and in December 1901 surveyors began marking out with red and white flags the corners for new buildings. The first was to be the Hearst Memorial Mining Building. Phoebe selected Howard to design it (Maybeck's original design had been greeted with laughter in Howard's New York office).[22] When Phoebe announced to the regents, "I am deeply interested in the subject of mines and mining, and I would be pleased to furnish the means to erect and equip the proposed building," she added a caveat, "with feeling and marked emphasis":

> I must ask permission to choose the architect, for I do not want one who would make such mistakes as have been made on some of our other buildings.[23]

The building site had to be changed because Bénard's design placed it where there was a seventy-foot elevation. Howard, after studying all the major mining schools in Europe, designed a classical structure with a large central hall surrounded by balconies. He called it "masculine" and the *San Francisco Chronicle* termed the building "of little moment beside the great memorial pile Mrs. Hearst will rear" on the campus, but the *Pacific Coast Miner* said that, when built, it would be "the result of the best advice the world can afford . . . unrivalled in its sphere in the world." It cost $650,000 and when dedicated in 1907 was the most modern and expensive mining education facility in the world.[24] A simple plaque on the wall states:

> This building stands as a memorial to
> George Hearst
> A Plain Honest Man
> and Good Miner.

> The stature and mould of his life bespoke the pioneers, who gave their strength to riskful search in the hard places of the earth. He had a warm heart toward his fellow men, and his hand was ready to kindly deed. Taking his wealth from the hills, he filched from no man's store, and lessened no man's opportunity.

Phoebe chose the word "lessened" over the word "diminished" in approving the tribute drafted by President Wheeler.[25]

Howard enjoyed a long and productive relationship with the university, designing twenty buildings between 1903 and 1924 that became the core of the campus, including a Greek Theatre that Will donated—at his mother's urging—which was dedicated to Phoebe. In 1903 Howard was named to head the school's first architectural department. Phoebe paid part of his annual salary for many years and donated a collection of architectural books that was the nucleus of the department library. Maybeck was out of a university job, but he did not lack for commissions; Phoebe helped see to that. The Phoebe A. Hearst Permanent Plan was officially adopted in 1908 as the "basis for future building operations and landscape gardening on the campus," according to regents' meetings. In her lifetime, Phoebe saw eleven granite or concrete structures of the Hearst Plan built, five of them financed by private gifts, including a new library. The regents' secretary wrote her in 1916,

> The great change which is coming over the aspect of the campus . . . the great framework for the completion of the library riveted in place, and the steps, balustrades and terraces installed for the esplanade about the Sather Campanile, gives the members of the University a new appreciation of the inestimable boon to the community which the Hearst Plan has proved.[26]

Years later, Maybeck would credit the university plan as the beginning of "civic planning" for major cities such as New York and Washington, D.C., other colleges and "even real estate tracts." "The Phoebe A. Hearst Plan for the U.C." he wrote Phoebe, "according to Mumford Robinson's book, was the beginning of the modern movement in Town Planning":

> This was, it seems, the apex of a cone which is constantly broadening as time goes on. Since then other universities have followed suit, also a number of cities, including the city of Washington, have had a general scheme worked out. It had also other influences, such as knocking out the theory that symmetry must be, willy nilly.
> Probably you have not realized the reaction of your good deeds, of this and others.[27]

During her years as benefactor to the university, she supported many other projects besides the architectural plan. Shortly after her appointment as regent, Phoebe provided funds for furnishing a women's lounge in a new wooden classroom building (East Hall), where young women could meet, study, and be served tea in the afternoon, at Phoebe's expense. She also formed a charitable entity that provided training in return for wages and employment for women students. Hearst Domestic Industries in Berkeley offered instruction in needlework for women who needed additional income to pay their college expenses. Phoebe also was concerned over the lack of economical but proper and comfortable housing for women students. She purchased and furnished two residence halls, which became social clubs called Enewah and Pie del Monte, and were forerunners of sororities at the university.[28]

Phoebe entertained the senior class at the Hacienda with a picnic each spring. But the lack of social life and of opportunities for students and faculty to mingle led her to an even bigger scheme. In 1899, she rented a house at the southwest corner of Piedmont Avenue and Channing Way in Berkeley, and on adjacent land she commissioned Maybeck to build a large pavilion connected by passageway to her house. Maybeck's independence of spirit, enthusiasm, and sense of drama had endeared him to Phoebe during the architectural competition. Hearst Hall, as the new building was to be known, became the center for student social activities, many of which Phoebe hosted herself: Saturday afternoon receptions, Sunday musicales, Wednesday "at homes," dinner for women three nights a week when men were at military "drill." The building was a masterpiece of modern design and ingenuity. A vaulted wooden structure that set precedents in American engineering and architecture, it was the first to have laminated arches. They were fifty-four feet high, held together by bracings and straps that could be tightened as necessary. Maybeck called it "honest" Gothic. The interior and exterior were sheathed in natural or stained redwood shakes and ornamented in carved wood, a trademark of Maybeck's. From a roof garden strollers could look onto the 140-foot hall through windows filled with wooden spindles that admitted light while adding structural support. Ten tapestries made for Marie de Medici hung in alcoves and paintings by Rembrandt, Murillo, and others adorned the walls. At night, when the windows were illuminated from behind by red lamps and hundreds of lights hung in circles from the arches, the place was like a fairyland. It more than fulfilled Phoebe's love for magical settings that transported one to another world. Maybeck had outdone himself.[29]

Women, however, had no physical education facilities and a sparse athletic program. They were allowed to use the gymnasium only a few hours of the week, when men were at drill. Hearst Hall was the logical building for the women's gym, and a few years after its construction, Phoebe bought land closer to the campus and the entire hall was moved to the new site. The building had been constructed in five sections in anticipation of its removal to a permanent location on the campus, but during the move one section broke loose and rolled into a ditch. Maybeck, who was watching the move wearing a long black overcoat and his personally designed trousers that reached nearly to his armpits and flapped around his ankles, ran to investigate. He found that his sturdy construction had not even warped; the section was hauled up and moved on its way. Hearst Hall was transformed into the women's gym, and physical education, which Phoebe advocated, became a requirement for women students. Maybeck designed an arched passage and a women's basketball court with openings for trees through the bleachers.

The outdoor court had a twelve-foot high fence to prevent male spectators from seeing the women play; they were allowed to compete only before their own sex.[30]

In 1899 California's new Governor Henry T. Gage, a Republican, annulled Phoebe's appointment as regent, causing an outraged reaction. Gage argued that women were out of place on the board. The San Francisco Argus editorialized that

> The question is rather whether there should not be a fair proportion of females upon the governing board of an institution which harbors so many of that sex, in order that its interests may be properly represented in the general councils. It is unaccountable that Mr. Gage should have committed such an error of judgement. . . . To the world at large it must seem the rankest ingratitude to endeavor to humiliate a lady of such generosity, liberal mind and public spirit. . . .[31]

The public pressure was so great that Gage reappointed her.

It was a time of big changes for the university, which had grown to nearly three thousand students by the turn of the century and was fifth largest in the United States. President Kellogg, nearing seventy, resigned in 1899 and the regents launched a search for a new president. Reinstein, en route across the country from Europe, interviewed candidates. Phoebe was in Europe during much of that year, but, Reinstein wrote her in March, the regents did not want to decide on a president until she returned and could offer her views on the subject. A leading candidate was a professor of philology and Greek at Cornell University with a reputation not only as a teacher but as a liaison between students and faculty. He had another, more dubious reputation, however. In a letter saying he was "looking forward greedily to your return," Reinstein wrote Phoebe of the dilemma:

> I saw President Harper [of the University of Chicago] for a few minutes about President of the University. He deprecates Professor [Benjamin Ide] Wheeler's appointment and corroborated certain facts or perhaps charges that I had heard made against Professor Wheeler's manhood and told me that the proof or evidence was "ample and convincing."[32]

The regents would not act until Phoebe had met with Wheeler on her return from Europe. She did so and approved of his appointment and of four conditions that he astutely set forth before accepting the post. "Saw Mrs. Hearst. She agrees with me entirely. Desires acceptance," he wrote in a postscript dated 1 July 1899 on his letter to the regents stating his conditions: the president would be the sole communicator between faculty and regents; he would have final authority over faculty appointments; the board as a unanimous unit would support the president in matters regarding the faculty; and the president would have full authority over officers and employees of the university. The regents agreed to his conditions.[33]

Wheeler had a guardian angel in Phoebe Hearst. They were to become a team that for the next twenty years would preside over a "golden age" at the University of California. The student enrollment and faculty would treble, much of the Hearst Plan would be built, and twenty new departments would be established. Wheeler was a skillful fund-raiser and lobbyist with the legislature, and, with Phoebe's help in underwriting portions of salaries, he would be able to attract faculty members who in the past had gone to richer eastern institutions. A typical example was that of the French department head who, in 1909, was offered a comparable job at the University of Chicago for one thousand dollars more a year than his four thousand dollar salary at Berkeley. The professor was very much tempted by the offer even though he liked Berkeley. President Wheeler wrote Phoebe:

> We hunted three years for a man. There is a great lack of material in this field. We believe that in getting Professor [William A.] Nitze we got positively the best man in the country, and our judgement has been confirmed immediately by the action of Chicago.
>
> I cite the conditions of this case to you somewhat in full in order that you may appreciate the difficulties under which we are laboring here in securing first-rate men for teaching positions.[34]

In many such cases, Phoebe paid the difference in salary and the professor remained at the university.

Phoebe's relationship with Wheeler was close, personal, and complementary. She trusted his judgment and recommendations. He consulted her on minute details, including seating arrangements and programs for special ceremonies, courted her with deference and respect, treated her as an equal irrespective of her sex. She in turn wrote checks for his favored projects, entertained him and his wife frequently at the Hacienda, and treated them much as part of her family. "You do these things so quietly and fit them so neatly to the needy spot where no help would ordinarily come, that they have fourfold value to one who knows what they mean," Wheeler wrote Phoebe in 1902. He even helped her make up weekend guest lists when important visitors were expected at the Hacienda, recommending professors and those who would be "appropriate" company. During their reign the university grew into one of the nation's foremost academic institutions, enlarging enrollment to nearly ten thousand students, five campuses, an extension division, summer schools, graduate schools, and research programs. Self-government by students and faculty also was introduced.[35]

Phoebe's benefactions to the university were not always large. She brought the Minetti String Quartet to the campus in 1897 and opened her Berkeley home for concerts and art lectures, to which faculty members and students were invited. Other gifts included a medical library, which she donated with Mrs. William Crocker, and $7,400 worth of equipment for an anatomy laboratory. She gave money to Lick Observatory, not only for its operation but also for expenditures to distant parts of the globe for astronomical observations (her two thousand dollars in 1893 sent a professor to Chile to observe a solar eclipse). She bought rare books for the library and paid for publishing others, including a complete works of Cervantes in Spanish prepared by a university professor. Each volume sold for more than five hundred dollars, which Phoebe turned over to the library for the purchase of more books. She paid for collections of portraits of Indian tribes, and gave her good friend, historian Henry Morse Stephens, one thousand dollars to purchase books and manuscripts in Spain in 1910, including documents describing early voyages and explorations by Spanish explorers to California.[36] When members of the Class of 1910 wanted to build a bridge over Strawberry Creek and needed funds for an architect, they appealed to President Wheeler. He told Phoebe about it and she agreed to donate five hundred dollars to the project, anonymously. The gift made the difference between a utilitarian footbridge and one with a classical arch. The class secretary then asked Wheeler if the "unknown friend who has promised to bear the last $500 of the estimated cost of $1,500 . . . will permit his or her name to be used" on the arch's inscription. Phoebe, thinking it was small enough recognition not to be overbearing, wrote "Yes" on the letter. It is the only inscription on the campus commemorating a donation by her to the University of California.[37]

Besides the Mining Building, Hearst Hall, and a swimming pool (1915), other structures erected on the campus with the help of Phoebe's contributions included an anatomy building; an anthropology building designed by Howard (1904); a hydraulics model basin; a metallurgical laboratory (1885); and the president's house, for which Phoebe broke ground on 12 May 1900.[38]

Subjects of intense interest to Phoebe, though, were archaeology and anthropology. Through her friend, Dr. William Pepper, at the University of Pennsylvania, she had become a student of the subjects. She had a personal fascination with American Indians, whose cultures were rapidly disappearing.

Dr. Pepper died unexpectedly in 1898 while visiting the Hacienda for his health. It was a deep and personal loss to Phoebe. She considered him "one of the best friends of my whole lifetime." "His beautiful helpful sympathy has encouraged me in many ways," she wrote a friend of the Pepper family, "and I know that the same benign influence went out to all who came near to him."[39] To Mrs. Pepper Phoebe wrote of her shock at the death, crediting Dr. Pepper with saving her life after her heart attack:

> That rare life has done its work so well that its influence will go on, and the world be more and more blessed for its having been. It was a comfort to me and my household to try to bring health to the friend who had saved my life and whose wise counsel and judgement helped me to solve many serious problems.[40]

Her words might serve as a tribute to her own legacy in archaeological studies. The University of Pennsylvania benefited from expeditions that she underwrote in the 1890s to settlements of southwest Indian cliff dwellers (part of the excavated material was exhibited at the 1893 Columbian Exposition in Chicago), the Florida pile dwellers, and the Etruscans. But Phoebe's allegiance shifted to the University of California by the end of the decade, and she began to finance major archaeological expeditions in Egypt, Peru, Europe, and North America. In 1899 she agreed to fund a five-year "dig" in Egypt headed by Dr. George A. Reisner, a noted American Egyptologist. The excavations were conducted systematically in a way that no such expedition had been before. Previously excavations in Egypt had been treasure hunts with little regard for scientific recording of the sites and of historical information about them. For the first time photography was used extensively to show tomb interiors as they were found and careful card files were kept with drawings showing the location of bodies and identifying artifacts in tombs before the items were removed and the site destroyed by the excavation. Reisner later wrote in his report on the work that at one group of prehistoric cemeteries "the bodies were wonderfully well-preserved so that it was possible not only to recover the exterior physical characteristics but many internal organs and tissues, contents of intestines and many of the harder products of disease." The excavations produced information and rare finds from a two thousand-year period extending from early predynastic times to the end of the New Kingdom.[41]

Another significant find from Upper Egypt (which Reisner purchased) was a quantity of papyri manuscripts stuffed as wrapping in human and crocodile mummies. They contained medical formulae never before known, which were intended for use by practising physicians and included incantations for cures. At the time, they were the oldest medical documents on record and they became known as the Hearst Medical Papyrus.[42]

Not only was the scientific quality of Reisner's expedition extraordinary but the time was opportune for it. It was still possible to excavate in productive sites and to remove legally many of the antiquities found in Egypt. Reisner got the confidence and support of his native diggers and methodically worked his way across all parts of Egypt, finding and opening tombs, the discoveries from which he was required to share with Egypt and the University of California. Artifacts began to arrive at Berkeley by the boatload.

Reisner's reports were so enthusiastic and the finds so extraordinary that Phoebe could not resist the temptation to go and see the work for herself. In February 1905, at the age of sixty-three, she made a month-long trip (not her first) to Egypt, traveling by boat up the Nile to Aswan and by camel and donkey to the digs and the Pyramids of Gizeh, where the party stayed at a camp in stone and mud huts with no modern conveniences and a plethora of wind and sand. If "a little trying at times," she wrote Janet and Orrin Peck, it was "all very good discipline," and "good for me no doubt to be without conveniences and then I appreciate my blessings. . . . It was amusing, too." But the discomfort did not dampen her rapture at seeing the results of her largesse unearthed before her eyes.

> . . . The work is splendid. We saw a tomb opened where they found two statues. If you had seen me hanging over the edge of the place looking down to see the figures as they were uncovered, you might have thought it right to class me with excavators. I was more excited than any one.[43]

The Pyramids and the Sphinx during the full moon were "enchanting"—she sat for a long time and gazed at them—"far better than by daylight." Although she was spending ten thousand dollars a year on the Egyptian excavations, she complained that she could not afford a fine Dahabeah (Nile boat), which she would have liked to live on for the winter. She suspected that she might never see Egypt again.

Reisner provided a feast of appreciation for his native diggers, with fireworks that they thought were a fantastic meteor shower. Phoebe later honored Reisner at the Hacienda with a feast that rivaled many of her galas. The Hacienda was transformed into a scene evoking Arabian nights. The courtyard was covered with a deep blue canopy and hung with hundreds of small lights to resemble an Egyptian sky; servants were dressed in tassled red fezes and gold-embroidered blue pantaloons with lavender sashes; the fountain tinkled among masses of lotus blossoms, and a hidden orchestra played arias from "Aïda." The male guests also donned fezes and were given duplicates of a ring with a cartouch bearing the name of a Pharoah, the original of which Phoebe owned. "The dark skin of the attendants and the picturesque dress . . .

accentuated the artistic effect of the environment," a flowery account in the *Examiner* related.[44]

Phoebe fulfilled her fantasies through theatrical settings, but as a practical matter, she followed the progress of her expeditions closely. There were numerous others besides Reisner's. She retained the services of the best scholars in the field, and, as university archaeologists later stated,

> While not excluding the importance of her powerful monetary support, it is still necessary to affirm other qualities of this remarkable woman. What set her apart from many other benefactors of her era was her determination not merely to surround herself with beautiful and unusual objects, later to be given to a public institution, but to provide the substance and impetus for research by contemporary scholars in anthropology and related studies. The effect of such advanced thinking by an assured and capable person upon a then comparatively small academic institution on the Pacific Coast is incalculable.[45]

Her patronage brought the university valuable ethnological and archaeological collections from California and Peru as well as Egypt. Another major expedition begun in 1899 was that of German archaeologist Max Uhle, a pioneer researcher of the Incas. His six years of field work and excavations of grave sites laid a foundation for understanding the Incan empire. He wrote Phoebe in careful detail about his findings and sent back ten thousand artifacts covering a period from 1000 B.C. through early Spanish colonial times. Uhle also conducted an excavation in 1902 of a shell mound on San Francisco Bay, resulting in the university's first major publication on Indian sites in the region.

In other Hearst expeditions Professor Alfred Emerson in 1901 was sent to Europe with ten thousand dollars to purchase classical Mediterranean antiquities; he returned with one of the largest and most valuable collections of Greco-Roman statues ever gathered in America. Captain Sydney A. Cloman received funds to purchase prehistoric weapons and Spanish armor in the Philippine Islands, and Dr. Philip Mills Jones in 1900 began journeying through California and New Mexico studying Indians, a subject dear to Phoebe's heart. Jones's work was expanded by Alfred L. Kroeber, who was recruited from Harvard. Kroeber was named head of a new department of Indian anthropology, which Phoebe also supported. Kroeber and his assistants were to make "a vigorous effort to rescue the fading remnants of Indian lore, religion and languages before it is too late," including phonographic records of tribal dialects, a newspaper reported in 1901. It was a new kind of undertaking and produced one of the world's finest repositories, bearing Kroeber's name, of information about American Indians.[46]

The university assumed responsiblity for the expeditions under the aegis of a new department of anthropology, which Phoebe agreed to fund in 1901 at the rate of fifty thousand dollars a year. She told the university that she wanted it to be "free of all expense" for the research expeditions as well as administrative costs for the department. She expressly requested that it not be known as her department, preferring that the university receive credit for the explorations and researches. Meanwhile, all of her expeditions were generating crates of treasures that needed a home. In 1899 Phoebe had told the university that she would build a museum for the artifacts, and a temporary fireproof structure was built where the collections were stored and inventoried.

Ten years later, in 1911, the museum itself opened in San Francisco. Thousands of people flocked to see the tangible objects of ancient cultures—Indian artifacts (and later, Ishi, the last surviving Yahi Indian), the Tebtunis papyri, Attic vases—all from Hearst expeditions. "The cost of collecting these works of uncivilized man in California, Egypt, Peru and other places has been somewhere in the neighborhood of $1,000,000, and the collection is worth many times that sum," the *Examiner* reported. "It is one of the four best collections in the United States and the best west of Chicago. In its California Indian exhibit it surpasses anything in the world."[47]

It had not been collected without difficulty and, at least on one occasion, embarrassment to Dr. Kroeber. He and his assistants were threatened by the chief of the Ukiah Indians with felony charges for robbing and desecrating Indian graves. The skeletons and personal obects of the chief's mother and sister had been shipped to the university, along with beads and ornaments. Although Kroeber accepted full responsibility and offered to return the skeletons and heirlooms, the tribe retained a San Francisco law firm and threatened prosecution of the anthropologists.[48]

The university took financial responsibility for the anthropology department in 1908, but Phoebe continued to be its principal benefactor, providing for the physical maintenance of the building that housed her collections and for the publication of research findings. She also continued to contribute to the museum collection, ultimately leaving a bequest of important archaeological and art works that adorned her home. Her initial contributions (some sixty thousand items) stimulated gifts to the museum from other sources, forming the nucleus of what became one of the world's finest archaeological collections, the Robert H. Lowie Museum of Anthropology, renamed in 1992 for Phoebe Hearst, at the University of California. It was the legacy, as grateful university anthropologists later wrote, of "the huge project first envisioned by Mrs. Hearst—the gathering together of objects, rare and common, of beauty and of practical use, from any place or time which has felt the activity of the human spirit. It is in large part due to Mrs. Hearst that the Lowie Museum today is truly a museum of man, and not simply a museum of 'primitive' man."[49]

Phoebe's gifts to the university became legend in her lifetime. Rarely did the regents' minutes fail to show some gift from Mrs. Hearst, ranging from small housekeeping and emergency funds to large sums. It is not possible to ascertain exactly how much she gave the university but it clearly exceeded a million dollars during her twenty-two years as a regent. The university under her benevolent hand and Benjamin Ide Wheeler's guidance grew in physical and academic stature. She knew that the benefits from her gifts would not end after she was gone, but she hoped her example would stir others to match her gifts.

When a state controller in the early 1900s argued that, because of Mrs. Hearst's generosity, the university did not need the appropriation sought by President Wheeler from the legislature, Governor George C. Pardee (1903–7), himself a regent, said.

> I sit on the Board of Regents and am forced to blush for my State.... Time and time again matters of seemingly vital importance come up. We cannot find the money to attend to them. It simply isn't on hand. Then Mrs. Hearst sits down there in her quiet way, nods her head and says softly, "I will attend to that." We are making our university depend on charity.[50]

Another regent commented, "I really cannot see how we could have managed at all if it had not been for Mrs. Hearst." Her fellow regents presented her with a small token of their esteem—a loving cup—and a newspaper editorial said,

> Through her intelligent and faithful effort she has won the appreciation, confidence, admiration and affection of her associates on the Board of University Regents and the good will of the people of the State at large.[51]

Arthur Brisbane, Will's leading editorial writer, in 1915 called Phoebe a "spiritual mother" to the university, referring to her personal efforts to bring students together and to acquaint them with members of the faculty.[52]

In 1914, Regents Secretary Victor Henderson wrote in the *University of California Chronicle*:

> Including what Mrs. Hearst has given for buildings and for the museum, this one good citizen has from her private purse expended more than the vast, populous, and wealthy state of California has given to the University for buildings, permanent or temporary, in the 50 years since California chartered its State University.[53]

And in 1925, when University President William Wallace Campbell was acknowledging receipt from Phoebe's estate of the sixty thousand dollars to be used for scholarships, he wrote,

> Let me assure you that more than the normal amount of interest is attached to this payment, for it is realized by the President, the Regents, the Faculties, and many of the present-day students that the late Regent Phoebe A. Hearst was the best friend the University of California ever had.[54]

The university was not the only large project that occupied Phoebe in those years, however. Despite her heart attack, she returned to an active life that younger, healthier people marveled at. Her inner energy gave her physical stamina.

But her stamina did not come without spiritual help. The numerous demands made on her, chronic weak health, and her continual conflicts with Will had taken their toll. She sought ways to find some peace of mind. While intellectually seeing herself as part of a larger universe, Phoebe nevertheless personalized her sufferings. It was hard for her not to blame others for her unhappiness. Her letters, to the Pecks in particular, constantly referred to her tiny shoulders bearing great weights.

She had not been a devout nor consistent worshiper at any particular religious altar, although she had been raised in the Cumberland Presbyterian Church. Its strict austerity bored her and she had determined as a young woman not to raise her children or grandchildren under such humorless and stark tenets. Although she had buried George in the Episcopal Church, she had not found one religion personally satisfying. Most were too narrow for her broad-minded views of life and death, which were based on extensive readings in various religions and philosophies. The books that she kept in her sitting room and bedroom at the Hacienda included Bertha Conde's *Human Element in the Making of a Christian*; Mary O. Stanton's *System of Practical & Scientific Physiognomy*; Susanna Cocroft's *What to Eat and When* and *Let's Be Healthy in Mind and Body*; Robert Barclay's *An Apology for the True Christian Divinity*; Anna P. Simpson's *Problems Women Solve*; James F. Clarke's *Common Sense in Religion*; May W. Sewall's *Women, World War and Permanent Peace*; Emanuel Swedenborg's *Divine Love and the Divine Wisdom*; ten volumes on mental efficiency, Stanton Coit's *Is Civilization a Disease?*; James H. Snowden's *Can We Believe in Immortality?*; William E. Ritter's *War, Science and Civilization*; and a volume by Anton F. Haddad, *The Maxim of Bahaism*. Her poor health led her to explore ways of curing herself and to study mystics' experiences. Moreover, her interest in archaeology and anthropology made her curious about immortality.[55]

So it was not surprising that near the turn of the century she became interested in the Bahai faith. It was not necessary to disavow other faiths to be a follower of Abdul Baha Bahai (1844–1921), son of the Muslim sect's founder, who espoused unity of all religions, universal education, world peace, equality between men and women, and an international language and government. Bahais stressed simplicity in living and service to the suffering. Even if she did not live simply, the philosophy otherwise appealed to Phoebe. It was consistent with her own worldly views.

In 1898 she led a group of fifteen Americans to meet Abdul Baha Bahai in Syria. Phoebe had with her Robert Turner, the black butler, to take care of her and handle travel arrangements, as he always did. At dinner the first night, Abdul Baha saw that no place was set for Robert, who expected to serve. The Bahai rose and seated Robert in his place. Abdul Baha himself served the guests, in keeping with the meaning of the word Bahai—servant of God. Robert Turner and Anne Apperson also became followers of the faith, as did other close associates of Phoebe's. She entertained Abdul Baha at the Hacienda, for which he gave her a Persian rug in appreciation.[56]

Bahai followers were the subject of some derision in America and newspapers publicized Phoebe's association with Persian "mystics." A 1901 pamphlet espousing the religion contained two letters of support allegedly signed by Phoebe, and several estranged members of the faith tried to extort money from her. She first ignored news accounts of the matter, but finally found it necessary to deny any association with the pamphlet, having the *Examiner* print a telegram from her saying that she had not dictated nor had any knowledge of the letters, and that "The article printed in the [San Francisco] *Bulletin* concerning letters purported to have been written by me is absolutely false." But she continued to be a supporter of the faith although publicly denying it. Bahai preachings for world peace and women's suffrage attracted many educated American women to the movement, a number of whom Phoebe counted as friends.[57]

Her philanthropic activities, meanwhile, expanded. Her commitment to the kindergarten movement made her a logical supporter of a new idea that evolved from it: the National Congress of Mothers. In the summer of 1895, Mrs. Theodore W. Birney, a Georgia belle, Washington socialite, and mother of nine children, presented the concept at a mothers' meeting in Chautaugua, New York. Her enthusiasm was infectious and a number of influential women took up the cause, including Mrs. Adlai Stevenson, Phoebe's friend Mary Kincaid, and others. Their objective was to encourage the establishment of community mothers' meetings, without regard to class and without membership fees, where women could share ideas, hear lectures, discuss problems of motherhood, improve their role as parents, and influence education in schools. The concept was controversial; detractors feared that such organizations would meddle in the sanctity of family life and the management of public schools.

While recovering from her heart attack, Phoebe learned from a mutual friend that Alice Birney wanted to meet her. Against Dr. Pepper's advice, she arranged a luncheon at her Washington home to which Mrs. Birney was invited. Anne Apperson, who was present at the luncheon, remembered that her aunt was impressed with the idea of a National Congress of Mothers and immediately offered to underwrite all expenses of setting up the organization.[58] She had a condition, however, for her financial support: that men and fathers also be involved. "They are just as interested in children as mothers," she said. The women agreed and the genesis of the Parent-Teacher Association (PTA) was born in Phoebe's living room. The first National Congress of Mothers was convened 17 February 1897 in Washington. Phoebe provided a secretary, donated stamps, envelopes, and stationery for invitations to the meeting, her cook prepared food for the organizers, and her carriages transported committee members about town. She hired a hall to accommodate approximately fifty delegates who were expected to attend, and paid for lecturers and the opening luncheon. But more than two thousand women and a few male delegates turned up, throwing the carefully laid plans into chaos. Phoebe asked acquaintances to house visitors in their homes when hotel facilities ran short, and the meetings were moved to a large church and auditorium. She convinced her close friend Frances, President Cleveland's young wife, to host the opening luncheon at the White House.[59]

Phoebe's expenses for the founding and first convention of the Mothers' Congress exceeded thirty-two thousand dollars. It was a cause that she joined with conviction, in spite of opposition to it as being "radical." As it evolved into the PTA (the organization's name was changed in 1908 to the National Congress of Mothers and Parent-Teacher Associations), it would continue to have critics. More academically inclined groups, such as Sidonie Gruenberg's Child Study Association and the American Association of University Women, looked down on it as simplistic and dilettantish, and the Rockefeller Foundation refused to lend support.

In its formative stages, the objectives of the Mother's Congress were unclear—attendees at the first meeting kept asking what it all meant. Alice Birney articulated the rationale in a pamphlet that she circulated. The "physical and mental evils" of contemporary education were high on her list of concerns:

It is proposed to have the Congress consider subjects bearing upon the better and broader moral and physical, as well as mental training of the young, such as the value of kindergarten work and the extension of its principles to more advanced studies, a love of humanity and of country, the physical and mental evils resulting from some of the present methods of our schools, and the advantages to follow from a closer relation between the influence of the home and that of institutions of learning.

Of special importance will be the subject of the means of developing in children characteristics which will elevate and ennoble them, and thus assist in overcoming the conditions which now prompt crime, and make necessary the maintenance of jails, work-houses and reformatories.[60]

Ironically, the intent of the Mothers' Meetings, to strengthen ties between home and school, was considered by critics as interference in both places. What the "evils" of education were was not entirely clear, but "reform" was on the mothers' minds. Said Alice Birney's pamphlet:

Parents' meetings will be an inevitable sequence to the Mothers' Clubs, and the agitation of this subject is already educating public opinion to a sense of the unspeakable injustices meted to the unborn and helpless through the false standards of morality which prevail today.

The effort was aimed at helping both women "of leisure and means" and those without, although the tone of the organizers was patronizing of the lesser-privileged and working mothers. Nevertheless, participation in the clubs was to be without regard to social status, fathers were to be invited, temporary nurseries were to be provided for mothers who could not leave their children at home, and meetings were to be scheduled to accommodate working women, who should find the meetings "refreshing, uplifting and helpful as possible." Rich women would pay fees to be used to buy books for mothers' libraries. A recommended reading list included *Children's Rights* and *The Republic of Childhood* by Kate Douglas Wiggin; *Education of Man* by Frederick Froebel; and *The Children of the Poor* and *How the Other Half Lives* by journalist and social reformer Jacob Riis. The average mother, Birney said, was "but indifferently equipped with knowledge for the moral, mental and physical training of childhood." "What a satire upon our boasted wisdom of today," she wrote, "when dead languages and higher mathematics take precedence over that knowledge which should stand pre-eminent in a woman's education." She urged ladies of leisure to "give less thought and time to current literature and fashion journals" and to read instead the enlightening books that would awaken mothers' hearts to all the needs of childhood. "The finer sensibilities of children are often ignored," she believed.

Her enthusiasm, indeed, was infectious, and Phoebe caught it. The time also was right for the movement, Mrs. Birney perceived. "I knew at the start it could not fail. It satisfied a need that was beginning to be felt all over the country. . . . I believe its work will become a determining force in every home in America," she said in a newspaper interview in 1898.[61] The movement "stands irrespective of creed, color or condition for all parenthood, childhood, homehood," she said; "One of its greatest aims is to cultivate the spirit of centralization in the home, a spirit which the growing tendency of the age is to weaken if not to totally destroy."[62] When skeptics argued that mothers needed no organizations in which to learn instinctive maternity, Mrs. Birney replied that the mothers' meetings gave the "progressive woman every opportunity to improve herself. . . . She is encouraged to take more scientific interest" in, and to become better educated about, the business of child raising. Some saw it as a fad but Phoebe and Alice Birney knew that it was not. The future of the human race would be improved by better child care just as a breed of racehorses could be improved, Mrs. Birney replied to a reporter's question.[63] While other women were gaining notoriety for agitating for suffrage or temperance, the Mothers' Congress ladies were given cautious praise in the press for pioneering the idea of better motherhood, and their first convention was termed "the greatest representation of women ever held in this country." Phoebe was called the godmother of the movement.[64]

At the same time that she was involved with the Mothers' Congress, Phoebe also was occupied with three other demanding projects: the founding of the National Cathedral School for Girls in Washington; the restoration and preservation of George Washington's home, Mount Vernon; and the creation of the Washington Memorial Institution, aimed at combining federal and private university resources to form an educational entity in the nation's Capitol that George Washington had envisioned.

Congress chartered a National Cathedral Foundation in 1893 but the educational facility originally intended had not been established. The Reverend George William Douglas, rector of Saint John's Church in Washington, asked Phoebe that year if she would be one of five donors to a fund of one hundred thousand dollars to found a school for girls under the aegis of the proposed cathedral. Perceiving the opportunity, not long after George's death, to do something for a cause that personally interested her—the education of women—and no doubt realizing the advantage of controlling the project, she told the reverend, "Dr. Douglas, one person can do this work better than five and the amount you name is insufficient. I will give $175,000 for the school."[65]

Phoebe envisioned a school that would have the best possible facilities and educational opportunities for young women. Here was a chance to design a school from the beginning. A department for higher education also was intended. The school would fill a void in Washington, which lacked a good educational institution suitable for daughters of congressmen, government officials, and military officers.

But it would be six years before the cornerstone was laid. Discouraging obstacles nearly ended the ambitious undertaking but Phoebe held to her offer. In 1895 she was presented to Queen Victoria of England and returned to face a host of problems with the school. Land that cathedral trustees wanted to purchase was unsatisfactory to the new bishop, Henry Y. Satterlee, and to Phoebe. Satterlee did not want to tell her of his unhappiness with the site, but Phoebe volunteered her own opinion. "Bishop," she said, "the first time that I saw this ground where they were going to put my school I was sick at heart. I went again the next day and that was enough." Satterlee persuaded her to tell the trustees that, which she did, emphatically. The matter appeared at an impasse. Some of Phoebe's friends advised her to withdraw her offer to build the school. Bishop Satterlee and Phoebe held to their desire for a more imposing location on a three hundred-foot rise called Mount Alban, but its owner would not reduce the price to one the school could afford. Phoebe selected another site, but it was even more expensive. She and Bishop Satterlee became determined to get the Mount Alban land, thirty acres in what was then the outlying area of Washington. To reach it one had to go down a deep ravine, across Rock Creek, and up a hill. Satterlee wrote Dr. Douglas on 31 January 1898, "the Cathedral Board, Mrs. Hearst and I all think it combines all the qualifications for a Cathedral Close." Satterlee showed other potential donors the hilltop and in the spring of 1898, while persuading one benefactor of its merits, he dramatically dropped an acorn to the ground where he prayed the cathedral altar would stand. It would, but not without much prayer and persuasion on his part.[66]

Although a site had not been purchased, plans went ahead for the school. Phoebe increased her gift in 1897 to two hundred thousand dollars to meet the cost of an architectural competition. The five plans submitted were shown first to her for a decision and she picked the one labeled "fireproof." The cathedral trustees also agreed on the building designed by Robert W. Gibson, president of the Architectural League of New York City and architect for the Albany Cathedral and Saint Agnes' School in Albany, New York. An earlier design for the school had been dismissed when builders estimated the cost of construction would exceed three hundred thousand dollars. Still, there was no place to put the school and cathedral. Satterlee lobbied, cajoled, and used his influence with members of Congress to convince the cathedral board to back a fund-raising effort for the Mount Alban property.

Ironically, the Spanish-American War, in which Will was to play a significant role, turned out to be an advantage to Phoebe's school project. Property values dropped and the prospect for purchase of Mount Alban rose. Phoebe went with the bishop to view the site. While they were there a man came up to the carriage in which Phoebe was sitting and told Bishop Satterlee, who was standing by the carriage wheel: "Mrs. Hearst is reported as being a very generous woman; I wonder if she would not help us." She heard the exchange from behind the carriage curtains, to her amusement. In December 1897 the Mount Alban property owner offered to sell the land for $224,000. The bishop prayed a good deal and took tea with rich Episcopalian parishioners. His persuasion worked. Thanks to gifts from Cornelius Vanderbilt, James Pierpont Morgan, and others, and an eight thousand dollar interest-free loan from Phoebe, one hundred thousand dollars was raised for a down payment on the Mount Alban site in 1898. Bishop Satterlee, remembering the difficulties of raising the sum, later wrote:

> Then I thought of Admiral Dewey at Manila, and how for the sake of his country he had taken his life in his hands; how, if he had been beaten at Manila, there was absolutely <u>nowhere</u> for his fleet to go; how they would be portless, coalless, homeless, disabled. Then I felt, "If Dewey can do this for country, surely I can take a different kind of risk for <u>God</u>."[67]

Dewey was elected a trustee of the cathedral fourteen months later, and a Cross of Peace was the first monument erected on the new cathedral grounds.

On Ascension Day, 9 May 1899, in a driving rain, the cornerstone to the Hearst School was laid. It was inscribed, "For Christ and his Children. That our Daughters May Be as the Polished Corners of the Temple." A portrait of Phoebe, along with a journal of the Diocese of Washington and a church almanac, were deposited in the cornerstone. Phoebe was not there to see it, but Bishop Satterlee attributed the building almost entirely to her. "I gladly testify that it was the generous gift of . . . Mrs. Hearst, and her persistence in holding to her offer, which kept the Cathedral Board together in the trying period, 1895 and 1896," he later recorded. "I cannot express my debt of gratitude to you for the way in which you have stood behind me at moments when my courage almost failed," he wrote Phoebe when the purchase of the land had been finalized.[68]

The difficulties were not over, however. The chairman of the building committee suddenly died. There was a succession of strikes, delaying construction (Satterlee said, "The workmen now are the tyrants"). The contractor misappropriated school funds to pay off bad debts. The male architect failed to provide female amenities—there were no linen closets, no housekeeper's office, no space for servants' rooms, no students' parlor, and no closets in the girls' rooms. When the newly named principal, Lois Bangs, asked the architect, "Where will the young ladies keep their clothes?" he replied that the young ladies would have only two dresses, one on their back and the other in a chest under the bed. He also placed the windows too high for the students to look out (a distraction, he thought), and put the refrigeration room directly above the furnace room. There was no heat above the main floor. The elevator did not work. And there was no money left for furniture.

Then there was the question of a name for the school. In December 1899 Phoebe had told Satterlee that she did not think it appropriate to call it the "Hearst School," which Satterlee diplomatically recommended. Both recognized that it might put off other donors to the school. Satterlee recalled in his memoirs, "I went to her and said that if [it were] the 'Hearst School,' she ought to endow it, for the name would prevent anyone else from endowing it. She said: 'I never dreamed of endowing it, and your point is well taken; I fully agree with you.' I then suggested it might be called the 'St. Phoebe School,' but she objected strongly to that name, saying 'Call it simply 'The Cathedral School'; and we then and there agreed it should not be 'The Hearst School.'" Ultimately it was called the National Cathedral School.

The school opened to some fifty students on 1 October 1900 with a curriculum not unlike that taught in men's preparatory schools, except that art was a required subject—an indication of Phoebe's influence. Women should not only develop powers of perception and knowledge but should cultivate an understanding and love for the beautiful, she believed. There were other places where her influence was evident, although she did not interfere in the running of the school nor in its curriculum. Comfort for the girls was a primary consideration. Each was to occupy a single room with the "opportunity for a degree of private life and quiet thought," the first catalogue stated. Students were to cultivate an appreciation of dignity and the ritual of home life. The school motto was "Noblesse Oblige." Still, there were problems. Miss Bangs and her coprincipal, Mary Whiton, were too strict for the girls' and their parents' tastes. Phoebe and Bishop Satterlee stayed discreetly out of that debate, and in the end the school won over the daughters and their highly placed parents, including then-Vice President Theodore Roosevelt.

A portrait of Phoebe by Orrin Peck was unveiled on the evening of 12 November 1904 and hung on the stair landing between American flags. Phoebe had presented it to the school at Miss Bangs's request. Again,

Phoebe was not present, but in her portrait she resembled a commander-in-chief swathed in a high collar of ermine and jewelry; her eyes looked directly at the viewer, giving the impression that she was a presence to be reckoned with. Orrin had captured the mother on canvas as accurately as he had the son.

Phoebe was proud of the results of her persistence, although she made few visits to the school after it was completed. The last was in 1916, when, frail and unwell, she spoke with members of the graduating class and so charmed them that they unanimously elected her an "honorary member," a custom of graduating classes thereafter. It was a gratifying tribute to the former school teacher.[69]

Higher education was the goal of another project in which Phoebe was involved—the Washington Memorial Institution. Its objective was to fulfill George Washington's wish, expressed in messages to Congress, in his will and in letters to Adams, Jefferson, Hamilton, and others, that the government provide for education in the nation's Capitol. Washington had worried about the effect of foreign education on the youth of America. Congress authorized a program in 1892 and again in 1901. The Washington Memorial Institution was not to be another university—since Washington's time, many had been established throughout the nation. But it was intended to foster higher learning by utilizing the scientific and other resources of the government in Washington for advanced study and research in cooperation with universities and other resources. It presaged the National Academy of Sciences, the National Institutes of Health, and other subsequent government entities. Phoebe was one of two women named to a prestigious board of the institution, whose members included Alexander Graham Bell, a regent of the Smithsonian Institution; Nicholas Murray Butler, then professor of philosophy and education and later president of Columbia University; and presidents of Johns Hopkins, Yale, Chicago, and other universities. She represented the interests of the George Washington Memorial Association, with which she was affiliated and which sought to establish a suitable memorial to the nation's first president. The insitution's organizers wanted it to be independent of government support or control. Nicholas Murray Butler noted in 1901 that the government appropriated the astounding sum of "not less than three million dollars annually for scientific investigation and the application of its results. This sum would almost maintain the three great urban universities of the country—Harvard, Columbia and Chicago—for a year." Of the new institution he wrote:

There will be students of history, of diplomacy, and of social science as well as of the physical and natural sciences. No degrees will be offered or conferred by the Institution; it will be an aid and adjunct to universities, but not a new university or a torso of one. Through the existence of the Institution, the educational resources of the government are practically added to those which are now possessed by the several universities of the country, the smallest and the largest alike. To that extent a new governmental endowment of higher education becomes available for students throughout the United States.[70]

Phoebe also supported restoration of George Washington's Virginia river-front home, Mount Vernon, which was in great need of repair in 1889 when she was appointed vice-regent from California to the Mount Vernon Ladies' Association of the Union. She served for twenty-nine years and took a personal if long-distance interest in the monument and its staff. At Christmas for many years she sent a check to be divided among the servants (the equivalent of about one week's pay, which differed between blacks and whites). And for five years she sent one hundred dollars to support two Washington sisters, the last of the family born at Mount Vernon.

Both Phoebe and Will collected Washington memorabilia. Phoebe's first gifts to Mount Vernon, in 1890, were three water colors of the Washington ancestral home and church in England—Sulgrave Manor, Washington cottage, and Great Brighton Church. In 1892 she donated a bookcase that once had been at Mount Vernon and later in the Lee family at Arlington, and a Windsor chair that she believed had been used by a faithful slave sitting at General Washington's bedside the night that he died. The chair had been given to the slave, Christopher, and Phoebe had traced it to his granddaughter, from whom she had purchased it in Washington, D.C. In 1893 she gave a vase purchased at a Philadelphia sale of Washington relics.[71]

And in that same year, with the pomp and circumstance that she loved, she arrived at Mount Vernon for the annual regents' meeting with the Infanta Eulalie of Spain, aunt to the infant King Alphonso XIII, aboard Will's yacht Vamoose. She had borrowed it to bring the Infanta in style to the historic house. They raced down the Potomac River, passing the official boat chartered by the State Department to convey the Infanta's party, and after the formalities at the monument, Phoebe invited the regents for a late afternoon cruise on the river. She was one of the few would could talk with the young princess, who spoke only Spanish and French. On another occasion, she made the Vamoose available to the U.S. ambassador to England, Thomas F. Bayard, for a meeting with President Cleveland. Bayard wrote Phoebe on 25 May 1893, "It was a great indulgence and pleasure that your kindness enabled me to offer to the President and his hard-worked associates in the State and Treasury Department. Thanks to your provident kindness we had an excellent lunch which Robert made most comfortable and all in all the trip was without alloy."[72]

Phoebe made numerous contributions to Mount Vernon. She offered to contribute one thousand dollars toward construction of a separate house for the resident superintendent in 1909 but was turned down. She bought a new farm wagon, cart, and surrey in 1912. And she made annual unrestricted donations of $50 to $250. But it was her larger gifts—of brick, mortar, and wiring—that substantially aided in the preservation of the monument. Although she attended fewer than a dozen annual meetings of the association, she never failed to startle the other regents with the largeness of her gifts, the most important of which were a sea wall, the draining of a mosquito-ridden swamp, and the monument's first telephone line and electricity.

For years the Potomac River, particularly during spring high tides, had eroded the land below the plantation house, causing several major landslides and threatening the mansion. The need for a retaining wall was long known but the funds were not available until Phoebe made them so in 1898. She sent a check for $2,500 to start the construction and modestly asked that she be permitted to continue paying for the half-mile-long wall until its completion, which was not until 1914.

The sea wall complemented another major ecological project made possible by Phoebe—the draining of a swampy area that Washington himself called the "Hell Hole" and that was responsible for the Mount Vernon "sickness"—malaria, an inescapable occupational hazard of the plantation's workers since the eighteenth century. In 1893, after regretting that "illness, exacting business cares and absence of several months from America" had prevented her giving much attention to the association, Phoebe asked for approval to finance draining of the marsh. The regents were impressed that she seemed undeterred by unknown costs of her projects since no one realized at the time the extent of the undertaking. It went on until 1912, when the plantation was at last rid of its malaria-producing swamp and fifteen acres were recovered for farming use.

Always intrigued by new gadgets and inventions to make life more comfortable and efficient, Phoebe arranged for the first telephone communication between Mount Vernon and Washington in 1891. She even agreed to pay the telephone charges (two hundred dollars a year) in advance for three years. One of the telephone's first functions was to carry the sad news of a generous regent's death. And some of the women objected to the "unsightly" poles and wires that had to be installed.

That was nothing compared to the lively debate in 1916 over whether to install electricity in George Washington's home, disturbing the pristine historic recreation of the plantation. The resident engineer argued that the kerosene and coal-oil lamps then in use were no less incongruous than Edison electric bulbs, which were less of a fire hazard and thus more attractive to insurance companies. Besides, they could be removed when not needed, and the wires and low-voltage battery to light them would be hidden. Phoebe offered to pay for installation of the system. Her friend, Thomas Edison, went to Mount Vernon and personally supervised the project. It was accomplished at a cost of more than $2,700, but the regents insisted that the electric lights be turned off except for cleaning and association meetings.

Phoebe also paid for an iron shelter house on the wharf (in 1890) to protect visitors as they stepped off the tour boat (then the principal route to Mount Vernon). There is no accouning of the total amount of her contributions to Mount Vernon but they exceeded twenty thousand dollars. When she resigned for ill health in 1918 (regents were appointed for life), Mount Vernon was considerably restored, thanks in large part to her generosity. She also contributed to rebuilding the rotunda at the University of Virginia, which had been destroyed by fire, and to a church where George Washington worshiped in Pohick, Virginia.[73]

Many regents enjoyed Phoebe's hospitality in California, and on one occasion she tactfully arranged, without the regent's knowledge, for a dowdy southern woman of aristocratic family but post-Civil War poverty to be outfitted in an entirely new and modish wardrobe while visiting the Hacienda.[74]

Such were her ways and they became legend in her lifetime. No one whom she smiled upon, admired, or felt sympathy for escaped some attention from her, however small it might be—a token Christmas gift purchased in Spain months before, a hospital bill paid, a daughter or son's college tuition taken care of, a bunch of fresh flowers sent from the Hacienda gardens to a sickroom. Her capacity to keep track of small details and to perceive individual needs was remarkable, given the number of large projects and activities with which she was involved. Psychologists might say that she had an insatiable desire to be loved and wanted. Or that she was frustrated at having no daughter and at not being able to control an independent son. As a living, breathing fairy godmother, though, she had few peers. Two examples indicate her quiet, often unsung or unknown personal philanthropy.

She learned through friends that a poor San Francisco woman who eked out a living by sewing to support her nonworking husband and children needed a new sewing machine, her rickety old one having given out. The woman felt that she could not earn enough to make monthly payments on a new machine. On a day when Phoebe left

California for the East, a new sewing machine mysteriously arrived at the woman's house, accompanied by a receipted bill. Only by chance did she afterwards learn the identity of her benefactor.[75]

Phoebe also arranged to help out the Carter family of Virginia who had fallen on hard times after the Civil War and were forced to sell their art treasures and take in summer boarders. Phoebe was one of them in 1892. Recognizing their desperate plight, she had Will buy, in Paris, the family portrait of Robert "Councillor" Carter, painted in London (it was then thought) by Sir Joshua Reynolds when Carter and his bride had lived there from 1749 to 1751 (the painting was actually by a contemporary of Reynolds, Thomas Hudson). The money from the sale went to the family. Will wired his mother 17 May 1892 from Paris: "Bought Reynolds seven thousand fine portrait historic person doubly valuable. Please write. No letters, nothing. Will." The painting, for many years crated and stored at San Simeon, later was bought back from Will by a Carter descendant. It was typical of Phoebe's *modus operandi* that she helped out those in her social strata so as to not embarrass them.[76]

Phoebe's keen business sense is evident in her support of an inventor and active suffragist, Kate Bridewell Anderson, during World War I. Mrs. Anderson had demonstrated her "Note-a-Phone Musical Blocks" for teaching children and the blind at the 1915 Panama-Pacific Exposition in San Francisco. She wrote Phoebe from Modesto, California, in 1917, saying that a German firm had stolen her patents and that she was too poor to take action to collect the royalties due her. In return for Phoebe's paying her way to a suffrage demonstration in Washington, Mrs. Anderson offered to deed Phoebe an interest in the invention. By 1918 Mrs. Anderson had issued stock in hopes of raising money to manufacture the "Note-a-Phone" and to sell it to the Red Cross so that blind war veterans could use it as a learning tool and a source of income as a cottage industry. She wrote Phoebe 16 June 1918:

> If we do not succeed in selling the stock, would you advise me to give the patent rights to the Red Cross for the duration of the war? . . . I would like to be instrumental in making it work for our soldiers, both as amusement and recreation in the camps and back of the front line trenches.

On the back of the letter Phoebe instructed her secretary to send Mrs. Anderson money and to tell her, "Better to keep your patents—don't give them up to anybody for anything."[77]

Her practical sense always ruled her giving, and in the new century practicalities would cause her to curtail her philanthropy.

13
Political Pitfalls and Progeny

Many of Phoebe's most significant projects were accomplished in years when Will himself was having an impact on the American scene, of illustrious or infamous merit, depending on one's point of view. He credited himself—and was blamed by others—for starting a war with Spain. He championed the cause of independence for Cuba and sent two correspondents, Richard Harding Davis and illustrator-writer Frederick Remington, to check out the situation for the *Journal* after the rival *World's* correspondent had been jailed by the Spaniards. Remington wired Will: "Everything is quiet. There is no trouble here. There will be no war. I wish to return. Remington." And Will shot back the now-famous reply:

"Please remain. You furnish the pictures and I'll furnish the war."[1]

Will firmly believed in the cause of the Cubans seeking independence and his newspaper began to apply pressure on President McKinley to oppose Spain. Then he found a cause célèbre to rally public opinion in support of the oppressed Cubans. The pretty daughter of a rebel who had been sentenced to a penal colony by the Spanish was herself caught in the act of trying to free her father and arrested. Another *Journal* correspondent, George Eugene Bryson, came upon Evangelina Cosio y Cisneros in prison, and, taking poetic license with the facts of her arrest, told the world that she had been imprisoned for defending her chastity against a lustful Spanish colonel. Will then launched a national campaign for her freedom. Despite the trumped-up allegations, the women of America sent petitions to the Queen Regent of Spain for Evangelina's pardon with such names as Clara Barton, Julia Ward Howe, President McKinley's mother, and Phoebe Hearst, all duly published in the *Journal*. Will acknowledged to his mother during the publicity, "We got and printed your Cisneros communication today. The case is one in which we have every one's sympathy and the paper is growing nicely."[2] In a daring act, he engaged one of his more adventurous writers, Karl Decker, to "liberate" Miss Cisneros from her dungeon, which was accomplished with the help of bribes to the guards. She was smuggled out of Cuba in a sailor's uniform, and Will, while not admitting publicly his role in the plot, staged a New York welcome for her with bands and fireworks. Phoebe could only have been proud of her son's headline, "Evangelina Cisneros Rescued by the Journal."[3]

The portent of war became evident when the U.S. battleship *Maine* (which had been launched in San Francisco in 1890) sailed into Havana harbor in January 1898. Three weeks later it blew up under mysterious circumstances and Will exploited the disaster as Spanish war-mongering treachery. He sent the yacht *Anita* to Cuba with a group of congressmen to report on the concentration camps instituted by the Spanish government. He reported that Assistant Secretary of the Navy Theodore Roosevelt saw the war picture clearly while President McKinley did not (Roosevelt repudiated the report). And he published a stolen letter written by the Spanish minister in Washington that expressed contempt for McKinley. Congress in April 1898 declared war on Spain. And Will went to war. He offered to equip, arm, mount, and serve in a cavalry regiment to fight in Cuba. When that was not accepted, he offered to give his 138-foot yacht, *Buccaneer*, to the navy, armed and manned by sailors at his expense, with him in command or second in command. He was thirty-four years old and commander of his own growing empire. Why not have an army and navy? The government accepted the *Buccaneer* but refused to give Will a naval commission. So he chartered a steamship, the *Sylvia*, loaded it with a floating printing press and newspapermen, brought along Jack Follansbee, who spoke Spanish, and several cameras, and went to the war zone himself, much to his mother's trepidation. He wired her on leaving:

> Goodbye Mother dear. . . . Take good care of yourself. You are much more likely to get sick than I am to get injured and your life and health is just as dear to me as mine is to you.
>
> Your loving son.[4]

From Cuba Will wrote his mother:

> I am at the front and absolutely safe so don't worry. Since poor Marshall was shot the General made strict rules limiting newspaper men to certain localities that are well within the lines so that there is no opportunity for any of us to get hurt even if we wanted to.
> The landing of troops, guns and horses is most interesting and the march to the front impressive. I have interviewed Admiral Sampson, General Shafter and General Garcia. The last named gave me his headquarters flag which has seen much service and is riddled by bullets. He said the *Journal* had been the most potent influence in bringing the United States to the help of Cuba and that they would always remember the *Journal* as a friend when friends had been very few.
> I have been greatly interested in everything and of some service to the hospital ship providing them with ice and delicacies which they lacked. I

think the standing of the paper will profit by my being here. Other proprietors are safely at home—and I will be soon. I hope you are very well and not at all alarmed about me for honestly there is no occasion.

Lovingly,
Will[5]

It secretly must have pleased his mother to know that her son showed the kind of altruism and thoughtfulness, even in war, that she had instilled in him. She read the dispatches that he filed with mixed feelings of anxiety and pride. Will was in the thick of battle, going near the front on horseback, his Panama hat with a colorful ribbon on his head, a revolver on his belt. In one battle shells flew over his head and he reported "that a shrapnel ball passed clean through one of the cans of pressed beef which our pack mule was carrying" for lunch.[6] In that battle, one of his best reporters, James Creelman, was shot in the shoulder. Will comforted him at a makeshift military hospital and wrote down details that Creelman dictated of the battle that he had seen from closer vantage. Will's dispatches from Cuba and his offers to the U.S. government won him grudging if sometimes derisive praise as a patriot from papers whose publishers were not so adventurous, including the *New York Times*.

In the often florid language that poured out of him as if it had been pent up for years, Will wrote that the Spanish "fought like devils," and that their last holdout was "a perfect hogpen of butchery." On the eve of the Santiago battle he reported:

> . . . From where I write this, we can see dimly on the sea the monstrous forms of Sampson's fleet lying in a semicircle in front of the entrance to Santiago Harbor, while here at our feet masses of American soldiery are pouring from the beach into the scorching valley, where smells of stagnant and fermented vegetation ground under the feet of thousands of fighting men rise in the swooning hot mists through which vultures that had already fed on corpses of slain Spaniards wheel lazily above the thorny, poisonous jungle.[7]

He sent the Spanish flag that Creelman had captured to the *Journal*, where he hung it in his office. He reported of the meeting between the Cuban General Garcia and the American General Shafter that

> the gallant old Cuban soldier turned out his half-naked regiment of patriots to salute him, and with tears streaming down his bronzed face took the American commander by the hand, saying:
> "I thank you and your soldiers for coming down here to help me fight enemies of my country. We will serve with you and take your orders without question."[8]

Will's adrenaline was running high. But his finest hour was yet to come: the personal capture of some Spanish prisoners driven to the water's edge. When he saw them, he jumped overboard from a dispatch boat reviewing the destroyed Spanish fleet, swam ashore, and informed the Spaniards that he was going to take them aboard his boat to the American admiral, for which the Spaniards were grateful and Will received a receipt.

He had redeemed himself in his mother's eyes. Her friend Clara Anthony wrote her sympathetically, in terms she liked to hear:

> I don't wonder you could not give Will up just yet. . . .
> I believe Will could do something fine and great should he really break from all trammels and traditions of his present life and throw himself into a great developing movement like a big war.
> My dear, he has in him the same great elemental forces that have moved you, and are still working—and if a blast of dynamite could extirpate most of his present advisers and he be allowed to be himself, he would develop as God meant he should.
> I hope I'm not barbarous but I would like to see Jack Follansbee for one break his ugly neck, and every other fawning sycophant that exploits Will follow suit. You know I believe in Will, and I see possibilities in him that he doesn't know he possesses. . . .
> I love Will so much I want to see the crown of a splendid manhood upon his head—and he doing the world's work in a grand and ennobling way as his mother is doing.[9]

Despite his triumphs and personal sense of accomplishment at bringing on the war, Will felt that he had missed opportunities that would have helped him in another way: he had a desire to run for public office. But the public and the Democratic party were not as fond of nor as tolerant of his excesses and eccentricities as was his mother. He wrote her a curious letter after the war, which sounds genuinely deprecating rather than tongue-in-cheek, as his self-deprecations usually were. He also was jealous of Roosevelt's glory.

Monterey, Cal.

Dear Mama,
      I guess I'm a failure. I made the mistake of my life in not raising the cowboy regiment I had in mind before Roosevelt raised his. I really believe I brought on the war but I failed to score in the war. I had my chance and failed to grasp it, and I suppose I must sit on the fence now and watch the procession go by. It's my own fault. I was thirty-five years of age and of sound mind—comparatively—and could do as I liked. I failed and I'm a failure and I deserve to be for being as slow and stupid as I was. Outside of the grief it would give you I had better be in a Santiago trench [dead?] than where I am. However, I don't suppose it gives you any particular joy to read this kind of thing, so we will change the subject. . . .[10]

He would indeed run for office, after cajoling his mother into supporting his campaigns, but first he took a long trip to Europe and to Egypt, following in Phoebe's footsteps to view Reisner's digs. Ever the concerned son, he wrote her jestingly from Paris in 1899:

> I hope you will find everything all right for I hate to have so many things worrying you. I am enough. The old money isn't worth the trouble of fretting over (and maybe I ain't) but you think I am. . . .
> Don't worry over anything, and if you need me telegraph and I will come home and do the worrying.[11]

And from Cairo, he wrote:

> <u>Please</u> don't overwork and wear yourself out unnecessarily. There is no <u>reason</u> for doing it, Mama. You want to do a lot in the world before you die and you can accomplish most by taking care of yourself and working moderately for many years rather than using yourself up all at once.[12]

Cairo, he wrote, "is a sort of Mexican village, the ownership of which is disputed between gentlemen in divided skirts and mosquitos. The mosquitos would certainly win against any other set of people but the gentlemen in divided skirts seem to hold their own."[13] The Egyptian government had "little appreciation of the value of its monuments, and allows the Nile to undermine them, tourists to deface them and the Arabs to loot them at will," he wrote Phoebe from a *dahabeah* on which he was traveling up the river. He did not see the work of his mother's projects in the same light as that of other excavations, which he considered were looting Egypt of its treasures. Hers, he thought, were an opportunity to build the University of California's museum collection, while trying to preserve Egypt's antiquities.

> The Egyptian government allows anybody who will excavate at their own expense to take away a large quantity of the antiquities found. It struck me that if you wanted to supply the Egyptian room of your museum that this was a good and cheap way. You are sure to find interesting stuff and you may find really important stuff, New Papyri, Missing Kings, etc.[14]

In a later letter, he said:

> My idea is to <u>please</u> the Museum people and the authorities. Everybody else comes and wrecks and ravages Egypt. If we, while excavating and hunting for things, still try to preserve the monuments and benefit the museum people, we will be on a different place and will I am sure be put in the way to get really important things such as no museum in America has.[15]

His mother's act in Egypt was a hard one to follow, although he bought a number of antiquities for the museum.

I am going to write a book about the conquest of Egypt by Mrs. P. A. Hearst. In Cairo the dragomen sailors and waiters besieged me with recommendations from Mrs. P. A. Hearst, on the boat I am entertained with tales of the generosity of Mrs. P. A. Hearst and here at Luxor I am overwhelmed with antiquity dealers (guaranteed) who were the particular favorites of Mrs. P. A. Hearst. The wide swath you cut through Egypt is still distinctly visible. Seriously you must have had a great time and everybody speaks of you with so much admiration and affection that I am very proud to be my Mother's son.

Affectionately,
Mrs. P. A. Hearst's Son.[16]

He took a proprietary interest in the Reisner expedition and started making suggestions to the eminent archaeologist and to his mother about where to dig, urging them to beat others to the sites, particularly Nubia. He even offered to finance additional digs. Will assumed that he would "inherit" his mother's projects. Reisner—whom Will called "a very honest, energetic little gentleman who has determination (which is excellent) to the point of obstinacy (which is not so good)"—at first was cool to Will's suggestions but later became enthusiastic over time. Will fancied himself an instant expert on the subject. His newspapers had taught him some tricks on how to beat others at their own game. To his mother he wrote:

In Egyptology as in everything else the great idea is to do something new and "sensational" and not laboriously potter over what has been done before. I want to see your plans very successful and I expect to proceed with them when you leave them to my hands, so I am really interested and have thought a lot about this and am convinced there is a great opportunity at this moment in this newly opened territory.[17]

Phoebe had agreed not to interfere in the management of Will's papers but he was not so inclined when it came to her affairs.[18]

She heard that he had bought a palace in Italy. En route home he assured her it was not the case. "Ah, Mommy, you ought to know by this time that you can't trust any newspaper but the Examiner," he wrote her from Rome.[19] But the prospect of his buying palaces was the least of his mother's worries then. He had decided that he wanted to buy another newspaper, and mother would have to foot the bill. It was more than she could bear. She wrote to Orrin Peck from Paris in May 1899:

I have been feeling greatly depressed and did not feel like writing. Will is insisting upon buying a paper in Chicago. Says he will come over to see me if I do not go home very soon. It is impossible for me to throw away more money in any way, for the simple reason that he has already absorbed almost all. In a few months there will actually be no money, and we must then sell anything that can be sold to keep on. It is madness. I never know when or how Wm. will break out into some <u>additional</u> expensive scheme. I cannot tell you how distressed I feel about the heavy monthly loss on the <u>Journal</u>. And then to contemplate starting another nightmare is a hopeless situation. I have written and telegraphed that <u>no</u> argument can induce me to commit such a folly as that of starting another newspaper.[20]

Orrin replied, pandering to her fury,

I cannot understand's Will's demand. As you say, it is madness.

He doubtless wishes to control the press of the U.S. That's alright but the main thing is to get the present established *Journal* under control. It's like dashing along a mad road with runaway horses and trying to harness in another. I see the situation is most desperate and makes one simply ill.[21]

But she acquiesced to Will again. Her financial affairs were not as dreary as she indicated. The Homestake mine was paying handsomely (producing some $6 million in gold a year), as was the Cerro de Pasco copper mine in Peru, in which she had a substantial interest. By that time she had "loaned" Will close to $10 million since George's death in 1891. She wanted to "do right" by her son but his uncontrolled spending on ventures that lost money made her nervous.

Still, he won her over again. In the end, he did not buy a Chicago paper—he started one. His desire to enter politics in a big way led to his cutting a deal with the Democrats: starting a party organ would be considered a contribution to the party; in return he was made president of the National Association of Democratic Clubs, which put him in the public eye. He was on his way, he hoped, to fulfilling his dream of matching, or surpassing, his father. On 2 July 1900, William Jennings Bryan started the presses of the *Chicago American*, a few days before he was nominated as the Democratic presidential candidate. And Will himself had his sights set on the White House, using Congress, a mayoralty, or the governorship of New York as his stepping stones. Phoebe was not just bankrolling a paper—she was supporting a political machine. Will wrote his mother a thank-you letter: "I went home full of gratitude for your great generosity and kindness in letting me go into this political contest."[22] He saw it as an opportunity to boost his papers' sales, as well:

Brisbane is sure the nomination will do the paper an <u>immense</u> amount of good. He says just think how it would help the <u>World</u> if Pulitzer were nominated and elected Governor of the state of New York. Would there be any doubt in our minds as to how that would dignify the <u>World</u> and raise it in public esteem, especially if he gave a good administration? The <u>World</u> would be the mouthpiece of the Democracy and we would feel that the <u>Journal</u> was unutterably insignificant and would doubtless seek another political field. That is a fair way to look at it.[23]

Will did not like feeling insignificant, and he would do anything to help his *Journal*, which was losing more than three hundred thousand dollars a year at the turn of the century. He made his friend and confidant, Arthur Brisbane, its publisher and told his mother in the same letter that they thought they would increase advertising enough to cover the losses and "show you a profit on the *Journal* the next year," adding: "Please keep this letter. I think this will be one time that my financial predictions will come true. Your affectionate and grateful son."

He begged his mother to entertain Bryan to help advance Will's own standing in the party, even though she did not approve of him:

> I know you don't like Bryan and don't approve of his politics, but he is coming to California and this gives us an opportunity to approach him in a way in which he is rather susceptible—socially. He is really a fine man, although an extreme radical. His wife is a very nice woman, and I think you will be much interested in them. Anyhow, there is something which I know you always considered—the opportunity to make your offspring solid with a power in politics . . . it is very important that he should be very close to me and to the *Journal*. . . .
>
> If you can entertain him in such a way as to give him and Mrs. Bryan a pretty good time in California, and make them remember in after years pleasant days spent there, you will do more than I can do with the support of the *Journal* to get Bryan's close friendship.
>
> It might be a good idea to send a [railroad] car to Odgen and bring him out on that, entertain him for a few days at the hacienda, and then send him up to the Yosemite, give him a dinner when he gets back, flowers for Mrs. Bryan, and some memento of the trip to her or the children. Can you conveniently do this?
>
> When Bryan was here Mrs. Belmont completely won him over . . . by social attentions. I have just been up to Newport. Mrs. Belmont is a charming hostess. I can imagine how she won Bryan. . . .[24]

It was a challenge that Phoebe could hardly refuse, to match the Newport socialites. With unhappy resignation she had to accept the fact that she had another politician in the family. But the fruit that Will sought would turn sour before he attained his goal.

He had garnered the dubious sobriquet of king of yellow journalism, as he was depicted on the cover of the *New Yorker* magazine 12 September 1901. But he also had built a reputation as a trust-buster, fighting for the little guy against big business and monopolies, which, Will told a newspaper, he viewed as "industrial feudalism on the lines of the old military feudalism and for the same purposes—the exploitation and control of the many by the few." They were "criminal industrial combinations" based on "unsound piratical finance," Will genuinely believed.[25] President McKinley was a tool of the trusts, he felt, and the

Hearst papers were vociferous editorial critics of the president, going to the extreme in a *Journal* editorial on 10 April 1901 of saying, "If bad institutions and bad men can be got rid of only by killing, then the killing must be done."[26] Although Will ordered the reference to "killing" taken out in later editions, the national finger of shame was pointed at him when, on 6 September 1901, a young anarchist with an unpronounceable name shot President McKinley, saying that he was "an enemy of good working people."[27] Will was personally appalled and quickly ran an editorial in all his papers deploring the deed. But the press vilified him as the perpetrator of the dastardly act. He was hanged in effigy; his life was threatened; his papers were boycotted. He was asked to resign from private clubs and he even carried a gun. For his mother as well as himself it was another shock to be borne with dignity and a stiff upper lip. But it was difficult when even her friend and partner in great works, Benjamin Ide Wheeler, publicly condemned Will by allusion saying, "The miserable wretch who fired the shots is not of his own making. Every encouragement of disorder, every wanton criticism of men in public office had helped to make him what he is."[28]

Phoebe felt betrayed at Wheeler's joining in the outcry against her son, but she did not stop her gifts to the university. She did, however, refuse to entertain in her home certain people who had led efforts to expel Will from the Pacific-Union Club in San Francisco. It was a grueling time for her but her loyalty to Will in this, his greatest public challenge, did not waiver.

Despite the national condemnation, Will continued to believe that he could be elected to high office, which, he felt, would have the added advantage of helping his papers' circulations. And he was not without support. In the McKinley debacle, the *New York Post* and other papers editorialized in Will's defense, the *Post* stating:

> Ever since President McKinley was shot a fortnight ago, there has been a tremendous manifestation of popular indignation against yellow journalism and particularly against its worst exemplar in New York city. Like all sudden outbursts of rage, this has been largely indiscriminating and much of it has been quite beside the mark.
>
> The theory, which has been seriously advanced, that Czolgosz was led to assassinate President McKinley by reading a certain daily newspaper, is without a particle of evidence, and is an affront to common sense. . . .
>
> Freedom of legitimate discussion must be maintained. If any editor or any public man feels persuaded that a President is working harm to the republic, he must have the right to say so plainly and emphatically.[29]

With financial support from his mother and from his growing newspaper empire, Will plunged ahead in his campaign for political office.

In a 1906 interview for *American Magazine* that he granted historian Lincoln Steffens about why he wanted to run for public office, he said:

> . . . my early ambition was to do my part in newspapers, and I still propose to do a newspaper part. But when I saw mayors and governors and Presidents fail, I felt that I'd like to see if I couldn't do better. I'd like to go into office, any office almost, to see if I can't do the things I want to see done.

Steffens asked, "Mr. Hearst, would you be content to stick to journalism if you could find men to do those things in office?" "Yes," Will replied. Steffens commented that he "saw Mr. Hearst took a personal view of history and that he saw himself doing in our day what the men he admired did in theirs. So I put to him this question: 'Then your ambition is to personify the modern American democratic movement— not to hold office, but to express the new spirit, and thus be to it what Jefferson and Jackson and Lincoln were to theirs?' He glanced up at me a moment; then he nodded. 'That is my ambition,' he said."

Steffens, while conceding that "Mr. Hearst sees plainly the superficial evils that confront democracy in the United States," believed that he did not typify the movement he represented and had set "a startlingly high standard" by which to be judged. "Imagine Abraham Lincoln editor of the Hearst newspapers," Steffens remarked.[30]

In 1902, when he owned six newspapers, Will was elected to Congress and contemplated a run for the presidency in 1904. His mother did not campaign for him in any of his political forays, although he enlisted her to entertain influential people and to write checks for his campaigns. He ran as a "radical" all-American "conservative," espousing, he told a newspaper, "the preservation of those qualities, rights and principles of proved value to the American people," as well as Socialist views and the government takeover of corporate monopolies.[31] They were views that reflected his parents' influence and genuine concern for the underdog. With his wealth it was easy to be independent and outspoken, and Will recognized the independence that his money gave him. Like his father, in Congress he kept his mouth shut; unlike his father, he did not go along to get along. He was aloof, alienated his colleagues, and was not accepted into the "club." He thus was largely ineffectual in gaining support for his legislation, which included an eight-hour work day, nationalizing certain industries, a variety of pro-labor measures, a graduated income tax, and popular election of U.S. senators. He supported a Panama Canal, and, in his mother's mold, better public schools and vocational education for blacks.

But before Will took his seat in Congress, he did what his mother had simultaneously anticipated and dreaded for years: he married. He knew that before seeking higher office he needed to be a settled family man, not the playboy, stage-loving bachelor that was his public image as he approached his fortieth year. So he picked a pretty dancer and vaudevillian's daughter, Millicent Willson, whom he had been squiring, with her sister, Anita, for seven years. Their affair had been flamboyant: he had given Millicent a hansom cab with a white horse in which she drove around New York City, and he had taken the sisters with him to Cuba, to his mother's distress. Millicent was half his age, as his mother had been when she married his father. But he was afraid to tell his mother (he told his Grandmother Apperson first, unknown to Phoebe) and to take his Brooklyn-born bride home until she was more refined. The story was later told that he sent her to a finishing school in New York and asked them to turn her out in six months. The headmistress told him that it would take longer to ready Miss Willson for Phoebe's salon but Will was not accustomed to waiting, and the job was hurried up.

Even with her Brooklyn accent polished, Millicent did not satisfy Phoebe, who was crushed that her "dear Boy" had chosen a showgirl to be his wife. His mother had hoped that this aberration would disappear as Tessie had, and she had been openly disapproving. "She was in a state of fury about them most of the time—couldn't mention their names," Anne Apperson remembered of her aunt, who had gone after Will tooth and nail to give up this liaison with the Willson sisters. Will's marriage announcement was more than she could bear and Phoebe took to her bed, her aspirations for a high-born, refined daughter-in-law dashed. She had always hoped, like most mothers, that Will would marry someone with whom she could share things, someone she could respect and care for as she wanted to continue caring for her son.

But Will finally severed the umbilical cord the day before his fortieth birthday, 28 April 1903, when he and Millicent were married in a small ceremony that some thirty people attended at Grace Church in New York. It was a beautiful spring day. Orrin Peck "was an ideal best man," Will wired his mother, and Anita attended her sister. Will forgot to bring the bride's bouquet. The bishop who performed the ceremony told Millicent he would help her "keep tabs on the Groom." And someone tried to serve Will with a summons before they sailed on the *Kaiser Wilhelm II* for a European honeymoon.

Phoebe was not there to witness it, claiming illness forced her to stay at the Hacienda. Like her own wedding, Will's was not well recorded on celluloid; he avoided his own newspaper photographers at the church and a blurred print was the only public photographic testimony to the marriage. Phoebe sent her daughter-in-law a magnificent brooch of emeralds—which Will said was the "climax" of the day—and faced the hard fact that she no longer controlled her son's life. In his marriage he had defied and hurt her as in no other act. Her niece believed that it broke Phoebe's heart. But she was to accept the new member of the family with cool grace (she threw a magnificent birthday party for her at the Hacienda not long after the marriage) and in time would find that they were allies with common interests: Will and children.[32]

Will wrote his mother an amusing description of the wedding after his honeymoon party arrived in Paris in May.

. . . The day of the wedding was very fine. The San Francisco papers had published something the day before so before I was dressed in the morning reporters began to call for news. I got out with Orrin and went to the Holland House and we sat around in our frock coats and white ties waiting for the time. We went to the church a little before eleven. Millie was there. She had been crying a little with excitement, and happiness, too, I think. Orrin and I went back of the chantry and waited for the sound of a little bell which gave us our cue.

The chantry was very beautifully decorated with colored roses and apple blossoms. Our wedding was cheerful and not to be mistaken for a funeral. Some thirty of our friends were present. The bell rang, Orrin and I stepped out to the altar. The bishop looked very grand and solemn. Anita came up with Millie and her pa. They didn't have any bouquet. I had forgotten to bring it, Millie didn't mind. She stepped up alongside me trembling and frightened. The bishop married us. Then he kissed Millie quite a smack and patted her on the head and told her he wanted her to come and see him when she returned and that she and he would "keep tabs" on me. Then I kissed Millie and the audience applauded. The bishop hushed them and appeared to be rather shocked but wasn't. We went away after shaking hands with everybody. All seemed pleased. . . . The bishop said "Hearst you are the right sort" so I guess he was pleased too.

After the marriage a few of us went to the Waldorf. We had not intended to have a wedding breakfast but we had to have some kind of breakfast as not many had eaten anything yet. I hadn't for one. We therefore decided to have a spread and I told Oscar all about it. He got the Astor dining room ready and made it very beautiful in surprisingly short time. We had our breakfast.

Presents and reporters arrived alternately. I went down stairs and sent you a long telegram. I hope you got that. Then Millie and I went up stairs to Falk and got photographed to please the reporters. When we got back everybody had been drinking toasts and were in the usual wedding breakfast condition. We had had bouillon and now had ice cream. I don't know what happened between. It didn't happen to us.

Now it was three o'clock and time to go to the steamer. We drove to the docks. A man tried to serve me with a summons and Carvalho wouldn't let him. We got aboard the boat and somebody pelted us with rice. . . . People began to suspect they had a bride on board. Then Benny brought your beautiful Brooch. It staggered me and Millie was just knocked all of a heap. She didn't know whether to laugh or cry. She had presence of mind enough to pin it on. She said she only wished she could have been married in it. Orrin said Mrs. Spreckels was on board. Millie said she didn't care, she guessed Mrs. Spreckels didn't have an emerald brooch like that. I sort of surmised she didn't either from the way she stared at it at dinner later. . . .

> Millie wants to add a line to tell you how fine she thinks you have been. I tell her you are finer than that when she shall come to know you,—and I think you will find that she is nicer than you can imagine, when you know her better. We are all pretty nice folk, aren't we?[33]

Millie thanked Phoebe for her wedding telegram and the brooch and "for having made us so happy and for everything. I hope you will come abroad for Will is very anxious to have you come and I am too." From London she had telegraphed Phoebe, "We will try hard to make you as happy as you have made us."[34]

Will and Millicent took Orrin and an entourage on their honeymoon in Europe. Despite repeated invitations to his mother, Phoebe rarely, if ever, joined him in travels again. He wrote her detailed and picturesque letters from his travels, like one from seeing an eclipse in Spain:

> The Spanish faces got more worried than ever for with the darkness and the wind and rain and the uncanny cold it did kind of look as if the end of things might be at hand and a Spaniard must hate to go to judgement. . . .
>
> All of a sudden it was gone and then there was a second or so before we realized the mystery and the beauty of the spectacle. . . .
>
> There seemed to be a wonderful calm and peace and we really appeared to be transported away from the earth and to be in the presence of the machinery of the universe. . . .
>
> The total eclipse was over. I was sorry. I had dropped out of the skies back on earth again.
>
> I had come back from my strange world to the one that I was familiar with—and not to the most attractive part of it either. . . .
>
> I am sorry that you have not been with us this summer. We have seen so many things that you would have enjoyed. Milly has missed you nearly as much as I have. Please don't wander off again. Try a trip with us next year and I am sure you will have a good time.

> Your affectionate son,
> Will[35]

On his honeymoon Phoebe encouraged Will to take "a good course of Treatment" at Marianbad for his rheumatism and stomach trouble and urged Orrin to take one "to get rid of some flesh." Will seemed to have inherited his mother's hypochondria and penchant for chronic complaints with unexplained causes. Phoebe had not yet met her new daughter-in-law and would not until they returned from their extended wedding trip. It took them to Mexico, where they visited the family's Babicora Ranch and had an audience with President Porfirio Diaz, who had entertained Phoebe and was still grateful for George Hearst's services years before. For her part, Phoebe was occupied with two other marriages—those of nieces Agnes Lane and Anne Apperson, who married a member of the university medical faculty, Dr. Joseph M. Flint.

Wondering about her household without the young women, Phoebe wrote Orrin, "I shall find it strange to adjust my life to such different conditions. Agnes and Anne married and gone. For a change, I shall think of myself a little."[36]

She had gone to Japan and India in the fall and winter of 1903 while another indulgence was under construction—a retreat in northern California at the base of Mount Shasta. She had visited the rustic lodge of her lawyer and friend, Charles Stetson Wheeler, who had acquired property along the McCloud River at Horseshoe Bend for hunting and fishing. Edward Clark also had bought a small property near by, which he named Wyntoon after the California tribe of Wintu Indians. Phoebe had become enamored of the place with its clear, fresh air, sparkling river, and peaceful remoteness from civilization. She could escape in the mountains from the importunings and other demands placed on her. She asked Wheeler if she could lease part of his property to build a summer home. He was loath to sell any of his land but deferentially agreed to a ninety-nine-year lease on the understanding that the Hearst house would be very modest. But a small cabin was not what Phoebe had in mind, and Wheeler privately was furious when he realized the scope of her plans at a ceremonial cornerstone laying in 1901. She hired her friend Maybeck to design the house, which more closely resembled a Rhine River castle than a cabin, with its volcanic rock towers and turrets, stained-glass windows and Flemish tapestries of hunting scenes (removed from Hearst Hall) on the walls. Maybeck's design took into consideration the climate, the danger of forest fires, and a desire to keep the tall trees, six of which were in a semicircle, towering over the medieval "castle." The bedrooms were in a five-story tower high above the river to minimize the sound of tumbling water, and the tapestries kept the living room from being damp, along with a freestanding fireplace that an adult could stand in. Maybeck's fancifulness and imagination paralleled that of Phoebe's and her purse. Newport summer cottages could not compare to her one-hundred-thousand-dollar romantic retreat, which blended with the "dishevelled harmony," as Maybeck called it, of the rugged mountain woods.[37]

It was another magical world, like the Hacienda, where Phoebe could retreat from reality. While it was under construction, she wrote Orrin in Munich asking him to order a "large gothic chandelier for my large room at McCloud (I should say "Wyntoon"). The one that came is too small." She had asked Clark if she could use the name Wyntoon and he, of course, agreed. Whatever Mrs. Hearst wanted, she got.[38] A cottage for overflow guests, The Gables, also was built at The Bend, as well as a Honeymoon Cottage; a separate building housed the kitchen for the complex. Phoebe spent summers at Wyntoon after it was completed in

1904 and liked having young people as guests. She ordered a fence installed along the river to protect youngsters from falling in, for there soon were to be more children in her family.[39]

One year after his marriage, on 10 April 1904, Will became a father and Phoebe a grandmother. Millicent gave birth to a son, who was named George Randolph after Will's and Millicent's fathers and Will's grandfather. After seeing the baby's photograph, Phoebe said that he had "not the Apperson or Hearst head. It is decidedly like Millicent."[40]

Will wrote fond and boastful accounts of his first-born while complaining of his own health problems: "If I didn't have the family constitution I would be well along with nervous prostration or locomotor ataxia. . . . Anyhow, the baby is well and don't seem to worry much. He will have his little troubles in time, I suppose. . . . He is a smart little thing, if I, who am chiefly responsible for his abilities, do say it myself. Milly also admits it." Will weighed 210 pounds, suffered from rheumatism, and had some bone removed from his nose: "Say, Mommie, your son and heir is getting on the antique list and I suppose I have got to reconcile myself to a Grover Cleveland contour," he wrote his mother in early 1905. He went to Mt. Clemens, Michigan, to take a "cure." "I have found a place that beats Carlsbad all to pieces," he wrote Phoebe. "The waters are nastier, the place is duller, the food is worse. . . . All I am afraid of is that I may lose my own diseases that I am used to and acquire somebody's else's that will be new and unfamiliar and perhaps embarrassing."[41]

Will's chief preoccupation, though, was running for president. He felt unfulfilled in his desire for public acclaim. He had written his mother, on his election to Congress, from which he was absent a great deal during his term (1903–7) while running for other offices:

> There is nothing the matter with me except that I am getting old rapidly and I haven't succeeded in accomplishing anything yet. I hope to make a dent on the public attention when I get to Congress. I must connect pretty soon or I shall be on the shelf.[42]

He got a taste of the White House on a visit there in 1905 while a member of Congress. Theodore Roosevelt, with whom he shared no great affection, was president. Phoebe recently had had an audience with the pope, for which she had gotten up at four in the morning to get a good seat. "Come home and see the President of the United States," Will told her; "He is just as important and easier to get a look at."

"Millie and I went to the White House reception the other night and we found that there is some slight delay and difficulty in seeing the President," he went on. After an intolerably long receiving line that wound from "one of those long dairy farm wings that have recently been built," up stairs and through numerous rooms, "underneath the moose, elk and bear heads that are fixed to the Italian renaissance woodwork and over gothic tapestry, all of which is so appropriate in a public building in America," he wrote sardonically, "a country which drew the inspiration of its Republican idea and also of its architecture from the classic times and has no association in spirit or history with medieval Europe" and "reminds you of nothing American except the shoddy pretensions of some of our would-be American aristocrats . . . we began to approach the Imperial presence":

> The I.P. was smiling broadly and evidently hugely "delighted" with himself and his recent immense majority . . . for everywhere were the evidence of his greatness, even in the dining room where the trophies of his prowess as a hunter hung and the testimony of his taste and judgment adorned the walls.
> The I.P. was very nice to Millie anyhow. He said, "Why Mrs. Hearst I am so glad to see you!!!" He didn't appear quite so pleased to see me. He's a peculiar man.

Will's disdain for social pretensions, symbolized by the lorgnette, showed in his continuing saga of the event:

> Mrs. Roosevelt was very pleasant and dignified and made a very good impression. Opposite the President were a lot of invited guests roped in. They belonged largely to the class of vulgar rich who seek to conceal ill-breeding and stupidity behind an affectation of self confidence that amounts to brazen effrontery. The women stared at the passing line from behind the barrier of ropes and through diamond-studded lorgnettes. I despise lorgnettes. They are bad enough when they shield blinky, squinty eyes but oh, the insolence of diamond-studded lorgnettes behind which ignorance and vulgarity take refuge. There is nothing to compare with it in hardihood unless it be the brutal indifference of the tenderloin lady who is "drunk and glad of it."
> I have determined to buy a folding telescope and the next time a lorgnette is leveled at me I am going to ostentatiously draw out my telescope, aim it, focus it and stare back.

The evening concluded with the black doorman "shouting loudly and persistently for 'Senator Hearst's carriage' and I couldn't explain to him that I wasn't Senator Hearst. He preferred it that way."[43]

Will's antipathy to Theodore Roosevelt stemmed from both political and personal scorn. He thought Roosevelt phony and duplicitous, a figurehead created by clever public relations and brought to power by the money from the businessmen whom Roosevelt pretended to scourge. Their rivalry peaked when Will obtained, through surreptitious means of his own, letters from the files of John D. Archbold, executive vice-president of the Standard Oil Company, which revealed extensive political influence and manipulation. Roosevelt denied being controlled by "big business" and commanded Will to the White House in 1908, "about something important." "I don't know what it is all about," Will wrote his mother wryly on 16 November, "but I doubt if it is a matter of importance. I imagine he only wants to be pleasant and keep the papers friendly. . . . It is a singular thing that no matter what people begin to talk about with me, they always touch on Standard Oil letters before they get through. I suppose Roosevelt will touch on Standard Oil letters. Maybe that is the important thing he wants to see me about. He is mentioned in some of them." [44] Phoebe herself received an invitation to "a smoker and reception" for Colonel Theodore Roosevelt to be held at the male-only Faculty Club at the University of California 23 March 1911 (members could invite women and no doubt an invitation had been extended to the university's principal patron as a courtesy). She wrote to her secretary on the back of the invitation, "How surprised they would be if I should attend!" [45]

Will's feelings about Roosevelt were ferociously expressed in a letter to "A.B."—presumably Arthur Brisbane—in 1909:

> Roosevelt is . . . a creation of newspaper notoriety, a past master of the science of advertising and promotion. A man who is sustained on stimulants must continue to take stimulants or collapse. A man who has been built up by advertising must continue to be advertised, or disappear.
>
> If Ferrero is the Salome dancer of history, Roosevelt is the Anna Held of politics. They must both be in the papers, and Roosevelt will advertise Ferrero as long as Ferrero will advertise him.
>
> Ferrero says that Roosevelt is the modern Augustus, and Roosevelt is pleased. If Roosevelt were really great or even really well informed, he would not be pleased. If he had any ambition beyond continuously getting in the newspapers, he would not be pleased.
>
> Augustus amounted to nothing great. He was important merely as the heir of Caesar. He spent his life neatly tagging and pigeon-holing the enormous inheritance of power and glory which Julius Caesar had left him.
>
> Caesar's was the creative mind which composed, and Augustus' was the codifying mind which collected the scattered leaves of the composition.
>
> Caesar constructed the edifice and Augustus swept up the chips.
>
> Roosevelt is neither Julius Caesar nor Augustus. He is an unimportant person in an unimportant period.
>
> The empire is yet to come. [46]

Will's views of imperial leaders were equally disdainful, although a good king was not necessarily harmful, he thought. He wrote his mother, on post cards from Spain and Portugal in 1910, just after the Portuguese revolution deposed its young King Manuel,

> I can't see how a country can run down so. I guess the trouble is with the Kings. Kings are a sort of permanency. If a country draws a good one, the result is immensely beneficial but if it draws a bad one it has to suffer under a selfish and stupid government until the miserable old failure dies. Two or three bad kings in a succession put a country on the bum. Kings are all right

if a country has the recall and can fire a King who isn't making good. Most of 'em I guess would get fired as Manuel was, but the occasional good one could spend his life working for his country and do a lot of good. You see, I'm a third-termer.[47]

Will had hoped in vain to serve some terms in the White House himself. He campaigned on a Socialist, for-the-people theme, but the presidential nomination was not to be his at the Democratic National Convention in July 1904. Even the man whom Will had supported in two previous elections, Bryan, favored another candidate. Nevertheless, Will looked for other political opportunities while building his newspaper and magazine empire. He was "the Chief" or "W.R." to all except his wife and mother, from whom he still asked favors, including rest and recreation for his overworked employees. On one occasion he wired Phoebe that his business manager, Solomon Carvalho,

is worn out and ill. He has been much overworked. Wish you would invite him and his wife and babies to Washington for couple of weeks and give them a good quiet time with a very few agreeable people. Please don't have a lot of queer people.

Carvalho is our most valuable asset.[48]

Phoebe fired back:

I have known for a long time that Carvalho was your most valuable asset, in fact about the only one, and feared he could not bear the great strain and responsibility. It is you and not your mother who should have made his position more endurable. I can invite them here after the fourteenth to spend one week. . . . As to my having queer people you seem to forget that you have the special collection to whom you devote much time and prefer to travel with.

Mother[49]

Her love-frustration with her son was by then a deep theme in her life and was expressed in a poem written in her fine hand and found among her papers. The unknown author could have been herself.

The Two Mothers

For foundling arm, warm breast and life's sweet tide
What does thou to thy mother make return?
Some madcap girl can win thee from her side;
Few tears at best has thou above her urn.

Only to Earth, thy mother, art thou just
To her thou givest all within thy power.

Thy life, thy breath, thyself—a pinch of dust
To star her bosom with a summer flower.[50]

She had bankrolled Will's presidential efforts in 1904 with a million
or more dollars and supported his other political aspirations, although
he was perceived as "buying" the office. The *Boston Traveler* reported 1
June 1904 that the "self-made candidate had succeeded in inducing his
mother to advance him another million, or at least a very large sum of
money. . . . But in a few days came whisperings that Mrs. Hearst had
said when she gave up that contribution to her son's campaign fund it
would be her last. . . ." The paper added:

> It seems a pity that the name of Mrs. Phoebe Hearst has to be drawn into
> this wretched business. She is a woman well beloved throughout the length
> and breadth of the land for her munificent generosity, her endowment of a
> great university, her aid to schools, and her open-handed help of all charities
> and good work. The millions who respect and admire her will hope that her
> fortune has not been impaired by the wild-goose chase of the presidency
> which her energetic and peculiar son has just finished. No one blames her for
> standing by her son and giving him a chance to test his theory that the
> presidential nomination of a great political party in this country can be
> purchased like any commodity, and that the presidency itself is within the
> reach of a man with a long enough purse who will go after it on the plan of
> smashing every man who has a dollar and giving a dollar to every man who
> has none.
> Mrs. Hearst's friends here, some of them very well advised as to the state of
> her affairs, say she will not be embarrassed by the losses of the estate in the
> political field.[51]

Phoebe was more angered by such reports than "embarrassed" by the
financial loss. But she was relieved when Will told her, wrongly, that he
was through with politics for the time being. Enroute to Europe in 1907,
she wrote Orrin,

> Will says most positively he will not be a candidate for any office for many
> years. The next Presidential election will be a rough fight. I feel thankful that
> he will not be in it. The one following—four years later—may be more
> favorable for him.[52]

Will did run for other political offices, which always eluded him. He
fought Tammany Hall for the mayoralty of New York City in 1905 and
1909 and lost a bid for governor of the state in 1906, when he took an
independent stand, believing that the Tammany-dominated Democratic
party had robbed him of the mayoralty. He came to be known as a
"myth" and an "enigma" to the public, as he often was to his mother.[53]
Losing was a bitter and disillusioning blow to Will who wrote Phoebe
from Mexico City after one defeat,

I was beaten, and beaten by alleged democrats. The corporations control the Democratic machine quite as much as they do the Republican machines and anyone who is really opposed to the corporations must count upon opposition from the machines of both parties. On the other hand, the rank and file of the parties do not vote with equal independence and the situation will not be solved until they do.

Then he thanked his mother for her financial support: "I am greatly obliged to you for having helped me and regret that I did not win out for the satisfaction of all but I couldn't do it and I am pretty much worn out in the hard fight I made."[54]

Will knew that he often made his mother unhappy but he used his wit, charm, and her forgiving affection for him when she was upset. He frequently admitted how bad he was but promised to repent and reform. "The old people seem so much better than the young people," he once said to her. "Perhaps the young people will improve in time. . . . I think some of us, however, will have to improve a whole lot in a comparatively short time. I guess I'll begin tonight." He once referred to himself as her "very old baby," and on the way home to the Hacienda for Christmas with his family one year he wrote, "Christmas comes but once a year but when it does it brings me and a lot of other trouble. However, I know you don't mind me—or at least have gotten used to me." He admitted that his business prowess was lacking. Promising to pay off business debts and "the poor people who have been so unfortunate as to sell us things during the past few months," he said sardonically in 1908, "we shall have to be careful about paying some of them. I am afraid the shock might be fatal in certain cases." He began to have heart trouble and a doctor in Los Angeles told him to slow down and take a rest. "He said American businessmen had no sense,—that they know how to take care of their money but not of their health. I told him that I didn't know how to do either." He exhorted his mother to take better care of herself and not to work so hard, "<u>without pay</u>"—"be a good Christian sciencer"—adding in one letter:

When you write send <u>me</u> a letter occasionally. Everything comes to Millicent and all I get is a short note telling me how bad I am. It needn't be so <u>short</u>. That theme might fill up a long letter.[55]

All had not been well for Phoebe on the financial front in the year of Will's presidential campaign, 1904. She and Haggin had lost a mining suit involving $1 million. And the directors of the Homestake mine, which had been paying Phoebe up to six hundred thousand dollars a year in dividends, had decided to rebuild its plant, plowing half its earnings back into the mine. Furthermore, the Cerro de Pasco mine in

Peru, in which Phoebe had invested with a number of other venture capitalists, required several million in assessment for the purchase of a railway and more mines.[56]

Suddenly, without warning and to the astonishment of all her charities, even while Will was campaigning for the presidential nomination, Phoebe announced that she was stopping all of her philanthropic activities. The news shot like a thunderbolt across the nation and made headlines. "Mrs. Hearst Withdraws Aid," the *New York Times* declared on its front page 28 May 1904. Another dispatch said that "she broke into tears as she declared her financial condition prevented further benefactions."[57] By that time, her philanthropy was far-reaching and numerous agencies were entirely dependent on her, including Hearst Domestic Industries for women students at Berkeley, the kindergarten teacher college, kindergartens, and settlement houses. The regents and faculty at the University of California were flabbergasted, although President Wheeler was sedate in his comments about the reasons for Mrs. Hearst's surprising action. He told the press, as he no doubt had been told by Phoebe, that the financial demands on her business affairs were the cause of her retrenchment. Others, however, laid the blame at the failure of Californians and the public to rally around Will's presidential bid. Speculation was rampant over her mysterious rationale.

> Consternation reigns at the State University of California. Mrs. Phoebe A. Hearst, who for so many years has poured a stream of golden treasure into the coffers of the institution, has suddenly withdrawn her hand. No explanation is given. The president and board of trustees are as much in the dark as the janitor who superintends sweeping of the spacious floors.
>
> Of course, the ulterior motive specialists are explaining in the usual way. Some see in the woman's action a manifestation of pique of California's failure to cordially espouse the political ambitions of her son. Others declare that she is indignant over the general indifference of the people of California to an institution which has been the recipient of so much aid and which is so deserving of recognition.
>
> It is more likely, however, that the gossipers and theorizers do not know what they are talking about. Certain it is that anything like censorious criticism of Mrs. Hearst by the people of California will strike most people as extremely unbecoming. If Mrs. Hearst feels that she has done enough, that is her business.[58]

The latter explanation hit closest to the truth. Phoebe felt that it was time for other patrons to take up some of her causes and for many of her charities to become either self-supporting or seek other donors. In that respect, she was a forerunner of future foundations, which would concentrate their efforts on seed money and encourage recipients to plan for long-range support that would not require annual donations from one or a few sources. Her action, however, seemed precipitous, not giving her beneficiaries time to plan for alternative support. But her motives were clear in her own mind and she had warned many of her charities for years that she would not be a lifelong source of sustenance, including the University of California. Disillusioned, she expressed her views in several letters to those whom she cut off, noting in one to the director of the Kindergarten College in Washington, D.C., which Phoebe had founded and supported with $16,000 annually: "My experiences . . . taught me that the people who had money lavished it upon themselves and not upon good works.[59]

The truth was that Phoebe desired to encourage her charities to seek other patrons. She picked no favorites but withdrew her support across the board and across the nation. She was tired of the ceaseless importunings and saw no end to them. Of an editorial in the *San Francisco Leader* 11 June 1904, she wrote across the top: "Not bad." It best explained her motives.

> We have very little respect for some of our esteemed contemporaries, but we did not think that they would throw mud at Mrs. Hearst because they don't like her son. Every one who knows what leeches settlements and industries and such like can become is not surprised that Mrs. Hearst began to cut them out of her work. They were undertaken with the hope that they might become self-supporting, but self-supporting they can never become. If Mrs. Hearst wishes to turn her beneficence in other directions, the general public are too much indebted to her even to comment on the fact.

She was not entirely ruthless in cutting off her beneficiaries. For the West Berkeley College Settlement and the San Francisco Settlement Association she purchased the lots where their buildings stood and turned the land over to the settlements. She wrote the San Francisco Settlement directors:

> I am making many changes in my business in order to lessen my responsibilities and obligations as far as possible, so that I may leave my business for another year or two, spending the time in travel.[60]

The director of the Berkeley settlement, after receiving word of the property gift from Edward Clark, told the press that "Mrs. Hearst did not withdraw her benefactions on account of financial losses, but because she felt that she was being imposed upon by certain charitable institutions, and as she had withdrawn her support from some she felt compelled to treat all alike."[61]

But no institution was more "paralyzed by shock" than the University of California. The immediate impact was to close several departments and to phase out the Hearst archaeological expeditions, including George Reisner's in Egypt. Reisner subsequently went to Harvard. Hearst Hall and the clubs and associations that depended on Phoebe's generosity were also without visible means of support, although it had always been understood that eventually they would become self-supporting. Only the Mining Building and twenty-one permanently endowed scholarships were spared the ax. There were rumors that Phoebe had quarreled with the powers in the university, thus her decision not to build a mansion in Berkeley. In truth, she simply was sending a message to all whom she had supported—and to other potential donors to charities—that she was no longer the sole "Lady Bountiful" with limitless coffers from which they could draw.[62]

Nevertheless, the reduction in her philanthropies did not sit well with critics, who saw her continuing to bankroll her son's political pursuits. The *Wilkes-Barre* (Penna.) *Record* editorialized on 27 May 1904:

> If [shrinking financial resources] is the truth, it presents a peculiar condition of affairs in the finances of the Hearst family. The mother is compelled to abandon a charity established by herself, while the son is waging a campaign for the Presidential nomination on a scale of extravagant expenditure never before witnessed in the history of the country.

Fiscal constraints, of course, were not the only reasons for the drastic change in Phoebe's philanthropic activities, although they served as an excuse. She had taken a tough stand, albeit after long and painful consideration. She had no one to advise her in her vast philanthropic network. She made decisions based on her own initiative, perceptions, and knowledge of how her beneficiaries operated. There was no foundation to carry on her activities—she *was* a one-woman foundation. Phoebe was not to end her giving but in 1904 she had made a hard decision to make a point and she stuck with it.

Phoebe decided to return to Europe and take an apartment in Paris, where she would live much of the time. She even offered to resign from the University Board of Regents, saying that she planned to spend only three months a year in California in the foreseeable future. The board unanimously refused to accept her resignation and President Wheeler wrote her on 20 April 1904,

> I honestly think, as I believe the Regents generally do, that you can do more work and be of more service to the University during the three months of your presence here, joined with the touch with University affairs you are able to maintain at a distance, than most of the Regents are able to render.[63]

Phoebe agreed to remain a regent but she was determined to get away. She no longer had parental ties to California. Both of her parents had died, her beloved father in 1900 at age ninety-one and her patient, stoic mother on 21 January 1904 at eighty-seven, while Phoebe had been in the Orient. She craved distance from the cares and demands of her in America and to be "free from the dozens of people who <u>want</u> things that I cannot do." "I am anxious to steer clear of S. F. as much as possible," she had written Orrin, "for the vampires will be waiting for me and I will be importuned to assume the responsibility of sustaining every 'nere do well' in the town." "I have decided to run away and shirk all I can," she wrote Janet Peck: "I want to go to some quiet place that will not be expensive where I can be quiet and control my time." She found that environment in Europe and in the baths at Marienbad. She was to spend much of the next several years in Europe.[64]

14
War and Suffrage

In the spring of 1905 Phoebe took a magnificent apartment in Paris at 1, Bis, Place de l'Alma, overlooking the Seine and the Eiffel Tower across the river. There were twenty rooms, including grand and petit salons, on the third floor of a year-old building that boasted an elevator, garage, electricity, and telephone services. Phoebe thought it very French in Louis XVI style. After getting the landlord to come to her terms and agree to put in two extra bath tubs, she rationalized the expense by figuring that giving up rooms that she kept on the top of the Hearst Building in San Francisco would free them to be rented for what she paid in Paris. The Washington house had been sold to the Italian Embassy and some of its furnishings shipped to Paris. "I feel that it will be a great comfort to have a little home to go to when abroad, instead of being in hotels, and I don't think it will be more expensive," she wrote Janet Peck 7 February 1905. She confided to Orrin that although she felt it best "to be a safe distance from the U.S. at least half of every year" to "get rid of as many burdens as possible," she would still receive visitors. "You may feel sure I will be <u>neighborly</u> but <u>not</u> with an English accent." She was reluctant to bring her loyal black butler Robert over because "He does not know French and will <u>never</u> learn. . . . I want to have as few servants as possible. They are so troublesome and unreliable in Paris."[1]

Her eyes continued to bother her and she took treatments for them, but her spirits were good. Will arrived in Europe in May with Millicent, her sister, Anita, Mrs. Willson, little George, a chauffeur and two cars in which to travel to Spain and elsewhere on the Continent. He also bought a 60-horsepower Morris car and told his mother that he wanted John Singer Sargent to paint her portrait and one of him with his family. Phoebe liked the idea and was ready to sit if the popular painter would agree and could fit her into his schedule. "I am not growing younger, and do not care to wait very long," she wrote Janet four days after her sixty-third birthday in December 1904.[2] Although Sargent was a mentor to Orrin Peck, the portraits were not done.

Phoebe had reconciled herself to Millicent, writing Janet shortly before George had been born, "She is very nice in her home and quite a number of people like her. . . . Will is very happy and Millicent is a good wife."[3] But the rest of the Willson family grated on her, particularly Mrs. Willson, whom she could not stand. She told Janet before the family's arrival in Paris in 1905, "Old Mrs. W. is coming. If I cannot see the baby often without associating with her, I will not see him often. I just won't."[4]

Millicent's father, the former vaudevillian hoofer George Leslie Willson, was only slightly more acceptable. Will found ways to make him appear useful and put him on the payroll, a pattern that the family would continue for those who married into it. He bought a London paper in his father-in-law's name (the Weekly Budget in 1911) and encouraged him in an "invention" that Willson contrived for newspaper presses. A relative of Phoebe's, Ethel Whitmire, was sceptical, writing, "I think that he must have paid somebody a very good price for the idea as I don't believe that he ever had one."[5]

Will also acquired, in addition to the Budget, Nash's magazine, bringing his colorful style of journalism and comics to the British. Will was stimulated by the challenge of attracting an English audience to new ways. "They are doubtful how to take the comics," he wrote his mother. He was publishing stories by popular American writers such as Jack London, as well as large spreads of illustrations that the English mistook for advertisements. Still, the magazine was gaining readers by "over four thousand a month." "It is higher class stuff than the English magazines print and the people appreciate it":

> Everybody tells us we must change more to the English style but I don't think so. I think the English will like this style as soon as they get used to it. . . .
> You know, most Englishmen are like the Englishman in the play called "Excuse Me." He is told a joke in the first act and he laughs in the second act. I believe our work will tell in the second year. . . .
> We are going to succeed Mummy and when you come over with me next time we can read our own papers.[6]

Will continued to ask his mother to "come with us on some of our trips," which were increasingly flamboyant, his party often "as much of an attraction to the inhabitants as they were to us." But Phoebe declined to join him. He wrote her nostalgically from the Cunard liner Mauretania:

> Do you remember when we were some ten days on one trip and came in with salt all over the smoke stack and things generally mussed up? You and I were children then. Perhaps I was particularly so but you weren't so very

aged yourself. Now I am a pop with a son about as old as I was then and you are a <u>grandmama</u>. Well, we've seen a lot of things in our day and I am hoping we will live to see a lot of things <u>yet</u>.[7]

Phoebe's pleasant respite overseas was to be shattered in the spring of 1906 by events nearly halfway around the world. On 18 April a powerful earthquake struck California. The subsequent fire in San Francisco destroyed the Hearst Building and many of Phoebe's prized possessions, including much of her silver and rugs, which were either stored there or kept in her two-floor apartment in the Spanish-style building. The Hacienda was spared major damage except for its chimneys, and personal papers in a safe survived destruction of the Mills Building in San Francisco. Berkeley was less devastated. "The Hearst Mining Building issued forth without a seam or crack of any sort," Benjamin Ide Wheeler wrote Phoebe. The campus was a refugees' camp, and "Hearst Hall an excellent hospital. . . . Two babies have been born there and three more are likely to be born within the next day or two," he reported.[8]

Phoebe's friends warned her that she would be shocked on seeing the city. Her former Chinese chef lost his business and wanted to return to Phoebe's household. The beautiful Golden Gate Kindergarten in North Beach was lost, as were many of her friends' homes (including the Head's on Nob Hill, where she had once lived) and businesses. The *Examiner, Chronicle* and *Call,* all of which lost their buildings, published a joint four-page issue the day after the earthquake with the banner headline, "San Francisco In Ruins."

Will went to San Francisco and wrote his mother,

> We are not as badly off as most people so we have no right to complain. We have not escaped, however, as of course you know from Edward. . . . everything in the building . . . has gone. . . . The paper loses disastrously. The insurance will partly restore the plant but the income is wiped out for a long time. . . .
>
> When you see poor old San Francisco it seems as if you had come back to earth after thousands of years and were seeing the places you had lived in during a previous existence.

He was particularly struck by their long periods of separation at that time, adding to his earthquake accounts:

> I am awfully sorry you can't come out. It seems as if we were fated never to be with each other and some of these days we will die without having had more than a speaking acquaintance—or rather a writing acquaintance. . . .
>
> I am getting kind of aged and so are you and we ought to stop working and worrying and have some fun together before we die. Then there is the baby. I

want him to know his grandma. He knows the picture and kisses that but it can't be very satisfactory just licking the varnish off a photograph. I think he would prefer the real article and I think you would prefer the real baby. He is no slouch baby.

> Affectionately, your exiled son,
> Will[9]

A dear friend wrote Phoebe, "I know how painful it would be for you to see the ruins of our dear San Francisco. . . . I was glad that you were far away."[10] Another friend wrote, a year later, "Your heart will be heavy within you when you look out on the poor old city, but much of the old spirit that made San Francisco is still there, and I think you will feel as L. W. Harris did when he wrote, 'The damndest finest ruins ever gazed on anywhere.'"[11] "Nothing is left but the indomitable courage of both men and women," wrote Mrs. Charles Stetson Wheeler. "This is the Spirit of San Francisco—nothing else save ashes! ashes! ashes!"[12] Now was the opportune time to implement Phoebe's idea of planning a new San Francisco. Jacob Reinstein, who was a member of the Reconstruction Committee, wrote her of his efforts to revise the idea, but the rebuilding and design of San Francisco were not to be done under Phoebe's patronage.[13]

Will quickly offered support of relief efforts. "How nobly Will took up the relief work," a friend wrote Phoebe. "He goes at things as if he were inspired. I think you have given him the inspiration. Today he is the most talked of man in the nation, and the best-loved, except by those who fear him. . . . I still hope to see him at the head of the Government, but whether he ever attains the office of President or not, he will go down in history as a greater man than any other of his time. I do rejoice with you in the greatness and goodness of your son," she told Phoebe.[14] They were words that Phoebe liked to hear, even if she knew they were not entirely true. Will was then running for governor of New York and "for political reasons" had slipped off to Europe under the pretense of seeing his ailing mother. A telegram sent shortly before the earthquake from the Hearst London Bureau to the Paris Bureau advised the staff:

> For political reasons Chief's mother is ill and he is sailing to see her in Paris. This will save a lot of false reports to New York. Notify mother so she won't deny story to newspapers.[15]

Phoebe returned to New York in June to attend to business matters but elected not to go on to San Francisco, returning to Europe instead. She offered to rebuild the Golden Gate Kindergarten, which was done. But her generosity now had bounds. She wrote her friend Alice Booth MacDonald:

It had been difficult to realize especially at a distance . . . the awful disaster that came to our dear country and city. Only now that details are coming to me do I begin to grasp the enormity and horror of the destruction and suffering. At first I felt as if I must go home at once, but reasoned the matter out that I could do little if there. I would give all I could to the destitute anyway. As my resources had been diminished, it seemed best to stay in my little apartment and spend as little as possible.[16]

She went to London for the season, attending Ellen Terry's fiftieth anniversary on stage, but her heart was in San Francisco. The American ambassador's wife, Mrs. Whitelaw Reid,

. . . sent me her box for the Opera "Siegfried." I could not enjoy it, as I looked over the house and saw such gorgeous jewels on many women who appeared to live only for pleasure. My thoughts went far away to the destroyed city and suffering, anxious people in what was San Francisco and I felt that things were strangely wrong in many ways. My heart ached so that I wished I had stayed at home.[17]

As a small sacrifice, she gave up five weeks treatment at Marienbad— "I could not consider that after such terrible distress at home, and heavy losses as well," she told Alice.

She was trying to improve her health. Will, who was beginning to foresee his mother's mortality, wrote her:

You ought to get well and you ought to be in a dry climate. . . . I am afraid you will not get well in a damp climate like Europe, and you must get well and not allow this trouble to become chronic. . . .

You see, I am talking to you like a dutch uncle. It's all very well for Dr. Flint to talk abut your living until you are 95 but I want to see you live until you are 95 and have a good time and good health besides. Hence the lecture.

Now I suppose you want some news.[18]

The news was not particularly good. George, Jr., had malaria and Will himself had escaped from a runaway coupe. "I jumped out just before the thing hit a lamp post and went to smash. I didn't get off altogether. I fell on my right arm and sprained it badly and injured the something-or-other nerve that runs over the shoulder so I have been an invalid too for the past month."

Little George, whose portrait Phoebe had commissioned Orrin to paint, was to be plagued by a stammer and lingering malaria and "attacks" of diabetes, requiring a strict and special diet that he did not adhere to. And he soon was to have playmates. In 1907 Will took an apartment in the Clarendon at 86th and Riverside Drive. His family was expanding. In 1908 another son, William Randolph, Jr., arrived, and in 1910 John Randolph was born. Will recounted to his mother how George took his brother William Randolph's arrival:

He wasn't jealous a bit. He looked the baby over very carefully and patted it when it cried and named it at once his "Brother Weeyum."

We tried to excite his jealousy a little by telling him he would have to give brother Weeyum some of his toys but George said placidly "all yite I'll give him my horse and my Punch and Judy." This was pretty liberal and all we are afraid of now is that George will grow up an easy mark and want to give all he has got away to somebody. . . .

. . . George refuses to call the baby William <u>Randolph</u> Hearst. George evidently thinks that the Randolph belongs to <u>himself</u>. . . .

Will nevertheless spread the name liberally among his sons. And he thanked his mother for taking "such a motherly interest" in Millie—"She is an <u>awfully nice girl</u>," he said.[19]

Baby William, though, nearly died from an obstruction in the lower stomach until new doctors properly diagnosed and treated the infant. Will called those who failed to identify the problem "professional prevaricators" for continuing to reassure the parents that the baby was well. Will was continuously sceptical and derisive of doctors, who he told his mother "don't seem to know much anyhow."[20]

The grandchildren were to become both a source of mutual affection and conflict between their parents and grandmother. Phoebe took a position of protective custody, offering to care for the grandchildren at the Hacienda for months at a time in the hope that the healthy outdoor environment and her educated and cultural influence—to which she feared they were not exposed at home—would enrich their upbringing. She at last had the expanded family that she had so long desired, and she took a proprietary interest in every facet of the grandchildren's lives, including their schooling and nursemaids. Millicent and the Willsons, she felt, were not up to providing the children with a stimulating, intellectual environment, and a tug-of-war developed between mother and grandmother over who kept the children. Grandmother prevailed for much of each year and in other ways, as letters to Phoebe from Ethel Whitmire testify. Miss Whitmire was a Missouri relative who acted as a secretary and companion to Phoebe and nursemaid to Will's family. After accompanying the grandchildren back to New York on one occasion, Ethel Whitmire wrote:

My dearest Liebe,

. . . We went out to Seagate this afternoon. John and William went in wading and John found a shell which he insists that I send to you . . . not an hour has passed that he hasn't said, "I wish I was at the Hacienda." He misses you and asks if you are on the train. There is a fence between theirs and the adjoining home at Seagate and he keeps wanting to chop it down. He says, "There are no fences in California," rather a large statement, but I suppose that he feels the restraint. . . .

Millicent is dismissing both Harris and the other man because they do not want to wear liveries. . . . [21]

Another letter (on the eve of World War I) reveals the low esteem in which she and Phoebe held Mrs. Willson, as well as Will's desire to have a German-speaking nanny for the children, his obsession with moving pictures—and his mother's perfume.

> . . . Millicent is looking for a new maid. The nurse who takes Emmy's place came this morning. W. R. wants her to speak nothing but German to the children. . . .
>
> Mrs. Willson waddled down (to breakfast) at the last minute. The old lady is good, I suppose, but somebody ought either to give her a dose of poison or a good education. I don't know which would be best. She is perfectly impossible with the children, means well but <u>doesn't know</u>. William acts like a wild Indian with her, John won't do anything she says and George of course has his own way. . . .
>
> P.S. On Saturday we had the moving pictures of the play at San Simeon. W. R. is going to send you a film. . . .
>
> Millicent had on some gardenia perfume and W. R. said "What, where is Conchita? Has she come back? Now go and get some of my mother's cologne." I knew that you would be amused to hear him say that. He said he bought up some in Munich because he knew that it would be impossible to get more, perhaps for four or five years.[22]

Will had an obsession with the children's learning German. "They have to learn German—and then Spanish and the way to learn it is by natural conversation and not by study. Well thank Goodness I wasn't so much worry to you when I was a child," he wrote his mother with tongue-in-cheek in 1913; "I was studious and dutiful and unusually bright as far as I can remember,—and I learned German so well that I can run a German paper without ever knowing what is in it."[23]

The children adored their Grandmother Hearst and the Hacienda, the magical playground of unlimited delights where they spent much of their time. Their divided loyalties popped out of their candid little mouths at inopportune moments, and Ethel Whitmire recorded their remarks for Phoebe's enjoyment. When Will and Millicent failed to meet the children at the train on one occasion, Miss Whitmire wrote,

> . . . John said, "Where is Mommy and where is Poppy?" Mrs. Willson said, "Why, in bed, of course"—whereupon John answered, "Same old story, nothing new!" They were in bed recuperating from a German dinner which they had given the night before and had gone to bed at 3:30 a.m. after a <u>delicate</u> supper of frankfurters, goose, red cabbage, and goodness knows what else! John's greeting to his mother was—"Well, I'm glad to see you but I'm sorry that I ever left the Hacienda." Millicent said, "Oh, but think of all you have here—moving pictures, ball games, etc." John said, "Oh, that's nothing. I like the Hacienda best." George broke in and said, "Well, I like it at the Hacienda, too, and I didn't want to leave." Their mother made several prom-

ises of early returns and then said that they would all go out to Seagate until Monday. . . .

Millicent is making a strenuous effort to secure a higher type of girl (at your suggestion) and is also trying to get a man for George. . . . I think that what she needs and what she wants in such a person are two vastly different things. She is on the right track, however, thanks to your advice, which she has evidently, as last, taken. . . .

They have seen [the film of the Spanish play] and say that you are the best actress of all. W. R. inquired very carefully about you. He also asked many questions about George's illness. . . . I . . . spoke of his diet here and his own inattentiveness and W. R. said that he would talk to George very seriously and that he would make it a point to have him watched and would give strict orders as to his diet, etc. Millicent said that he had never had such an attack here. . . . I said that no matter what had happened that it was very evident that he had had many severe attacks and that he must be taken especial care of and his diet carefully watched. I think that they both will give more time to certain details after this.[24]

Will's own letters and telegrams to his mother in the early years of his family are full of fatherly humor and concern for his absent children. "Letters . . . tell what a glorious time George is having. Don't spoil him or he may grow up to be as bad as I am," Will telegraphed his mother.[25] She took George to see the Great White Fleet sail into San Francisco Bay in May 1908. That same spring "Baby William" was sent to his grandmother's while his parents went to Germany for six weeks so that Will could rest up for the New York mayoral campaign the next year.

They sailed on the Lusitania—"She is a full grown boat and looks as if her bow might arrive in Liverpool while her stern was still in sight of New York," Will wrote his mother.

It is the first fast steamer I have been on that doesn't vibrate and by rights being the fastest, it ought to vibrate the most. It is double framed and armor clad and ready for war service at any time and still is an effective and valuable aid to commerce in time of peace. I wish our people had the sense and our politicians the honesty to spend money in this way and build up at one and the same time a navy and a merchant marine.[26]

On their return he wrote, "Millie is much worried about Brother William and I think it would be a good idea if you could send us a telegram every Sunday telling her all about the children. It does not cost anything to sent it over the special wire, and it relieves her mind."[27]

The babies stayed with their grandmother, and in November 1908 Will wrote his mother,

. . . Milly interrupts to ask if you will not please have some pictures taken of Brother William and George and send them to her. She is getting very lonesome for the children and I suppose we will have to go West soon.[28]

A pattern had been set and they would have a hard time keeping the children from their doting grandmother.

Will was repeatedly exhorting his mother to bring the children back to New York. "Come on soon. . . . Don't forget to bring the children. Milly thinks she misses 'em," he wrote in 1908. The following year he wired, "I am greatly disappointed at your not coming East and I think you are more interested in your insignificant grandchildren than you are in your own handsome and gifted child."[29]

In 1912 Will was to wire her from Paris:

> You have had the children for five months. Milly would be fearfully disappointed if they were not home on arrival. You promised to come and we expected you but if you are not coming please send children anyhow. We have to see them sometime.[30]

At the Hacienda they could ride ponies and dog carts, swim in the pool, play in the giant sandbox with its removable top, the gymnasium, or newly built Boys' House that architect Julia Morgan designed as an addition to the Hacienda complex. But there also were other memorable events in their young lives. In 1913 George unveiled a monument in New York City to the *Maine* at a celebration organized by his father, who proudly took responsibility for raising the money through his newspapers to erect the statue. He had collected the money in 1905 and had been criticized for not producing the monument for eight years.[31] The criticism did not dampen Will's spirits at the dedication. "We cannot all be heroes," he told the crowd, "but we can be grateful for heroism. We are not all privileged to lay down our lives in the services of our country but we can all love and honor and remember the men who have made such splendid sacrifices."[32]

He had wanted his mother by his side but she was not there:

> There is a big dinner at our house for Sec'y of Navy and Admirals of North Atlantic Fleet, and we want you to be here with us and help us to do everything properly.
> You can take George back with you to the Hacienda as we won't be able to leave until latter part of June.[33]

The tug-of-war was tightening. In exasperation the next year, he wired his mother:

> Don't you think I show considerable confidence by leaving my children away from me half the year which most parents don't do? I must continue, however, to take some natural interest in them, to ask information and make recommendations for their welfare. I hope those learned San Francisco doctors will approve.[34]

In an act reminiscent of his father's pranks, young George had shot off a pistol owned by Will's valet, George Thompson, "missed killing himself by half an inch." Their father thought the children's pranks rather amusing, although he made occasional statements about disciplining them and worried about injuries. "The old man whom John shot in the eye [with a toy gun while on a train] is not recovering as quickly [as the children from train sickness]. He is a cranky, unreasonable old man and complained about John's innocent amusements. He can't see a joke—in fact he can't see anything just now," Will told his mother from a train returning East in 1913. He told her not to spoil George "or he may grow up to be as bad as I am." "Don't let George get too independent," he wired her. "A little licking once in a while will do him lots of good. . . . Please tell George his Mama sends love. Tell him Papa sends him a good walloping if he don't behave." There was little such discipline, however.[35]

From a distance Will did show concern about his "ambitious progeny," however. One Fourth of July he wired Phoebe,

> . . . Hope you all have a jolly Fourth. Warn the children not to be gay with firecrackers and please don't let them have airguns yet. Paper only the other day had news items to the effect that two children had been wounded and one blinded by these airguns. Let them throw rocks at the birds. The exercise will do them good.[36]

When George was nearly swept downstream in the McCloud River while visiting his grandmother at Wyntoon, Will urged her to give the boys "a severe warning about the river. . . . George is something of a jackass, almost killed himself with a pistol and he might do other foolish things and lead William into them."[37]

He begged his mother to send William back to New York and to join them for the winter in 1915. "We don't hear from you very often. We get grapes and all sorts of nice things but we would like a letter, especially one telling us when you can come on."[38]

For a major family event was about to occur. Millicent had become pregnant again. "Milly has decided to have a little girl," said Will, also hoping for a daughter to carry on her famous grandmother's name. No one desired it more than Phoebe, who was still longing for the daughter she had never had. She ordered baby clothes handmade, wadded, and tied in anticipation of a granddaughter.

Will telegraphed her in October, "We think Phoebe or Elbert, we can't tell which, will arrive about Christmas and we want you surely to be here for the festivities. . . . Cheer up and come on soon."[39] The three boys put sugar on the windowsill of their Riverside Drive apartment to attract a baby girl stork (salt was for boys). But to everyone's surprise, on

2 December the day before Phoebe's birthday, twin boys were born to Millicent. At the Fairmont Hotel in San Francisco, Phoebe received the following telegram from Will:

> New York, N.Y. 5:55 a.m.
> Dec. 2, 1915

> We cannot call them Phoebe because they are not of that persuasion but we could call them Phoebus and Apollo for just at sunrise two of the loveliest boys you have ever seen were born to Mr. and Mrs. William Randolph Hearst.

> W. R. Hearst[40]

The boys were named Elbert Willson and Randolph Apperson Hearst. Phoebe would not have a namesake until the birth of great-grandchildren whom she would never know.[41]

Elbert's name was later changed to David Whitmire when the little boy was doing poorly in school and Millicent decided that it was the name that held him back.[42]

The night of the twins' birth, Will sent his mother the following telegram.

> George, full of sentiment, looks lovingly at the twins but said that what he wanted most to know was how his Mama was. William was more matter of fact and said he thought boys were better to play with than girls as they would not muss up the place with dolls and dishes and other useless things. John looked the twins over very critically and did not seem much encouraged by their personal appearance. Finally he said more hopefully perhaps they would look better with their hats on.

> Now for my part, I can not get used to the little things. They look so funny lying together on their little bed doing almost the same thing at the same time in the same jerky little way—for all the world like two miniature song and dance artists.[43]

The twins were to begin their stays in the West a year later, when their father implored his mother,

> . . . Please do not allow Randolph to stand on his feet for a month or so yet. Little Geo. and your big son William both had their ankles weakened somewhat by standing up too soon. You have an ambitious progeny but they should not be allowed to overdo it.[44]

On Thanksgiving 1916 he wired "Randolph Hearst or Willson Hearst, Examiner, San Francisco":

> Get up early and eat your bacon and eggs with your lonesome front teeth and meet us at Oakland Friday morning. This is Thanksgiving Day and you

ought to be thankful that you have such a dear devoted Grandma, such kind nurses, such nice noisy brothers, such a handsome father, and such a loving mother. Here is long life and much happiness to you and to all. Now rise up on your hind legs, drink a bumper of imperial granum, look embarrassed and make a proper speech in reply. Say as Tiny Tim said, God Bless us every one.

Pop[45]

And in 1918 Will had to admit to his mother that "George looks perfectly fine, he enters school Thursday, feels more interested and has developed very much, thanks to you."[46]

Their grandmother was fond of playing hide-and-seek with the boys in her music room. Will worried that his aging mother might be overdoing it herself. When the older boys were sent to southern California to recuperate from whooping cough, Will wrote his mother solicitously:

It is advisable for them to be in the warm southern part of the state and it is just as advisable for you to be there. You must take a rest and take care of yourself and it is impossible to do that in the neighborhood of San Francisco where so many people have so many opportunities to impose on you. The benefits that have resulted from your trips east have been due not so much to change of air or scenery as a relief from wearing conditions which tire you out without you realizing how exhausting they are. You must be more careful for your own sake and for our sake. . . .[47]

1915 indeed was a big year for Phoebe. While war was erupting in Europe, San Francisco was rising from its ashes. In a political coup, which Will and the Examiner helped bring about, San Francisco won over New Orleans to host a world's fair and celebrate completion of the Panama Canal. It was expected to attract commerce and confidence in the Golden Gate city. Will's long-time advisor, Andrew Lawrence, then publisher of the Chicago Examiner, when honored for helping bring the fair to San Francisco, credited his boss's "powerful engines of publicity" for the feat.[48]

In fact, Will had dreamed of a world's fair in San Francisco since 1891, when the Chicago World's Fair was being planned. At that time he had commissioned San Francisco architect Willis Polk to draw up plans for a fair that Will envisioned being held at the turn of the century. He had publicized the plans in the 25 December 1891 issue of the Examiner but was unable to garner support for it from other civic leaders. It must had goaded him that his archrival, M. H. DeYoung, brought some of the Chicago displays to San Francisco for the midwinter fair in 1894. Will's enthusiasm for a celebration of California's greatness, nevertheless, was much evident with the 1915 fair, and a manifestation of his passion for stimulating the construction of monumental architectural projects. Not only did he lobby through his papers for San Francisco as the site over New Orleans, but he was one of forty-two businessmen who put up twenty five thousand dollars each as seed money for the fair. And he was instrumental in bringing the original Liberty Bell to be displayed, one of the fair's most popular attractions, along with Will's massive printing press, which won the Palace of Machinery's grand prize.[49]

The fact that the exposition was paid for almost entirely by private citizens was unique. The federal government had subsidized previous world's fairs in the United States. That was not the case with the Panama-Pacific International Exposition, for which funds were raised largely by San Franciscans. No one was in a better position to raise money and act as official hostess than Phoebe Hearst, who was then seventy-three years old. She was named honorary president of the Woman's Board. Her friend Helen Peck Sanborn was president. Orrin Peck was commissioned to paint a picture for the host hall, and Bernard Maybeck was hired to design the Palace of Fine Arts, which surrounded a pool and climaxed a long mall built on 650 acres of filled marshland along the city's marina.

it was the most beautiful and best-planned of the great fairs that America had hosted since Chicago's "Great White City" of 1893. It was a fairyland—nicknamed "Dream City"—of the kind that Phoebe loved but she hoped that this one would have more permanency than other fairs. She expressed her views to the chairman of the exposition commission:

> My deep interest in our exposition leads me to communicate with you and to express the hope that the Government will make an exhibit which will be not only of temporary value but of permanent benefit to the people of this country. We believe the exhibits should be confined to a few subjects of great public interest in the department of social economy. It should have a definite purpose and its effect should be far-reaching.[50]

One of her passions was that Maybeck's splendid pavilion—built of plaster and steel (most other temporary buildings were of plaster and wood)—become a permanent museum to house an art collection, starting with her own. It was a dream that she had cherished since George's death. The beautiful Maybeck building in fact would be preserved as a landmark after falling into ruins—the only building of the great fair to survive at the site—but Phoebe's museum would never materialize. After the fair she lent enough of her collection of paintings, oriental rugs, Persian manuscripts, and tapestries to fill fourteen galleries for an exhibit at the Palace of Fine Arts in 1916, and she paid for the donation of many of the fair's artifacts and exhibits to the University of California.

Phoebe's duties as chair of the Woman's Board were numerous and she rose to the occasion. She lent four Gobelin tapestries to the California building, along with rugs specially made in Scotland, around which the reception room was designed, with furnishings in the red travertine colors that dominated the tapestries and fair buildings. She also provided the Woman's Board with rent-free offices in the Hearst Building. A woman columnist described the California building as "in perfect taste, with dignity and harmony. . . . Beside its chaste and exquisite beauty, even the New York building looks garish."[51] The Californians were showing the world that they had come of age.

Unlike women's boards at other expositions, the Panama-Pacific board was not merely a welcoming committee. It was formed in 1911 to help lobby and raise money for the fair and was composed of enterprising western women accustomed to responsibilities. It also generated controversy, as did many organizations with which Phoebe associated. The men who ran the fair accused the women of having too much fiscal independence, and labor unions and those not included in the board's elite social events complained that it was snobbish, undemocratic, and discriminatory.[52] The Woman's Board, in order to raise money, incorporated and sold shares of stock at ten dollars each. Phoebe bought five thousand dollars worth.[53] The women ran their board with businesslike efficiency and sponsored events of their own choosing, particularly those benefiting women who traveled to the fair. They forced the men to allow women for the first time to attend all the banquets. Besides sponsoring formal receptions and managing the California building, the board held luncheons and teas for "crippled and dependent old people, dependent mothers and children who are charges of our large charitable organizations" and for participants in the *Examiner's* Children's Pets Competition. In her final report Helen Sanborn said that the pet exhibition chair lady "succeeded in working up such an enthusiasm that a most wonderful exhibit of crawling, walking and flying creatures was gathered together." The pet competition evidenced Will's love for animals. But the Woman's Board was proudest of its work in establishing a permanent statewide Travelers' Aid society—a favorite project of Phoebe's, the inveterate traveler. More than one hundred forty thousand "young girls, little girls, old people, the general public . . . were cared for," Helen Sanborn reported, and "our wonderful Exposition was not marred by the loss of a single girl." A society columnist wrote, "There have been no distressing stories to take away the joyousness and gladness that made California a true land of sunshine against the sinister background of a world at war."[54]

It was indeed a paradise far from the front. The exposition also celebrated women's equality and gave women a status not afforded at previous fairs. The June 1915 *Ladies Home Journal* took note of the fact: "The management has realized that in our daily life man's work and woman's work, whether alike or different, are found side by side, each supplementing and completing the other. This is especially true in this age of the new housekeeping."[55]

Helen Sanborn put it in stronger terms in describing the work of the Woman's Board:

> There is no woman's building at the exposition, as the men and women of California are accustomed to working together. Women's work is placed in the various departments of the exposition and not displayed or judged as women's work.[56]

The *Pioneer Mother*, a sculpture and one of a number of works of art to survive the fair, was a central theme. It was given by the women of San Francisco with a large contribution from Phoebe, who helped select the sculptor, Charles Grafly, and who, with Senator James Phelan, was appointed to approve the model of the statue at Grafly's Gloucester, Massachusetts, studio before it went to the foundry. Phoebe asked him to modify the woman's bonnet and make the boy less conspicuous.[57] It was unveiled 30 June 1915 in front of Maybeck's Palace of Fine Arts by five-year-old John Hearst while a real pioneer woman, Pattie Lewis Reed, the last surviving member of the ill-fated Donner Party, fondled a doll that she had carried across the plains and cuddled through that dreadful winter.

The fair was a genuine celebration of the high-spirited West. Actress Ina Claire sang "Hello, 'Frisco" over the telephone from Boston to inaugurate a line between the two cities. Gold Rush dance-hall girl Lotta Crabtree (by then age sixty-eight) performed; octogenarian composer Saint-Saens conducted concerts of works he had written for the occasion; and Lincoln Beachey, famous as the "upside-down flyer," culminated a daredevil aviation show by spiraling to his death before fifty-thousand spectators. There were nightly fireworks and search-lights; seven acres of gardens; model kitchens, homes, schools; and exhibits of how food was produced, minerals extracted from the earth, and consumer products manufactured. With eighteen million people attending, it was one of the few expositions to turn a profit, despite the world war in progress. Many of Phoebe's causes were prominently featured, including the National Congress of Mothers and the Young Women's Christian Association.

The grandest party that she had ever organized, Phoebe delighted in the responsibilities and the opportunity to play official hostess to the world. Will pushed her around the fair in a rolling chair, past his giant printing press that produced the *Examiner* before the public's eyes. She playfully told his photographer, Joe Hubbell, who was taking moving pictures of her at the Hacienda, "Not too close, I'm an old lady."[58] From her suite at the Fairmont Hotel she directed the social events of the Woman's Board and made sure that her friends and those whom she admired were honored, including Dr. Zelia Nuttall, an archaeologist; Mrs. Percy Pennybacker, president of the General Federation of Women's Clubs (of which Phoebe was a founding member); and favored politicians and heads of state. On one of the rare occasions when she spoke publicly, she introduced Mrs. Thomas A. Edison at a luncheon in her honor. The King of Sweden made Phoebe his honorary commissioner to represent his country at the exposition. She entertained nearly every weekend at the Hacienda and sometimes at Wyntoon for three years before and during the exposition. Guests were provided a special boat and train for the two-hour trip from the city to Verona station. Her personal guest list numbered some ten thousand during that period, including former President and Mrs. William Howard Taft; Missouri Congressman and Speaker of the House, Champ Clark, who rubbed elbows with Arthur Brisbane and Edwin Markham (poet to Will's newspapers, of "Man with the Hoe" fame); the Maybecks, ambassadors, and generals. For Phoebe it was a culmination of a lifetime of cultivating powerful and talented friends through worthy works.

"She never lent her name without her participation," an account of the Woman's Board related. "No righteous cause ever suffered defeat because of a lack of financial support. But far and above all that was the value of the presence at all important deliberations of this gentle, low-voiced, discriminating, kindly, generous woman."[59]

The fair honored her as one of the world's most distinguished women, along with social reformer Jane Addams; Dr. Nuttall; Katherine Davis, a member of the New York Police Commission and a leader for prison reform; a Chinese doctor; and a Japanese scholar. At Phoebe's award luncheon, she protested, "But I am not distinguished." To which the hostess replied, "Then you have succeeded in deceiving a great many thousands of people, the members of the Woman's Board included." Phoebe, dressed in a heliotrope-colored brocaded gown and chinchilla furs, rose and told the guests, "All of my friends, you can see that I am not distinguished in any sense except in not being able to make a proper speech commensurate with the kindness and honor which you have conferred upon me."[60] Her shyness was genuine but her heart was touched.

Will also felt triumphant, writing for the fair's commemorative publication, "The Panama Pacific International Exposition demonstrated very clearly and conclusively that this great United States of ours has reached an art and architectural development equal to its material development."

When the nine-month fair closed on 4 December, the lighted fantasyland was plunged into darkness at midnight while fireworks and rockets lit the sky. The noise of war in Europe was very far away but it would soon dominate life in San Francisco as it did elsewhere. That and another war were having a profound affect on Phoebe's life.

In Mexico Porfirio Diaz had been overthrown in a revolution that had begun in 1910 and would continue until 1917. The Hearsts' vast land holdings, including the million-acre Babicora Ranch, were continually threatened and attacked by revolutionists, led by the notorious Pancho Villa's soldiers. Will, after meeting with a Mr Crockett, an American businessman just returned from the area, anxiously wired his mother 16 September 1914, urging that they transfer back to the United States their superintendent, a man named Hayes whom Villa personally hated:

> [Crockett] seems to be somewhat disturbed about the attitude of the Consti-tutionalists towards our ranch people. . . . He said that he did not think Villa was unwilling to let our cattle go out but he thought Villa wanted to put a tax of ten dollars a head on the cattle instead of five dollars a head. He said he was afraid we would have to pay that tax if Villa should demand it and his personal opinion was that it would be a good thing to get the cattle out at this time when prices were good even if we had to pay that additional tax. . . .
> We hear from all sources that Villa hates Hayes and is made antagonistic to our ranches because of Hayes. [Bring him to the United States to manage property but do not] have him representing our properties there when he is venomously hated by Villa who is the absolute dictator of northern Mexico.[61]

But in the winter of 1915, Villa forces took over the Hearst ranch lands and a number of employees, both Mexican and American, were killed. Hayes, along with other employees, was captured and held prisoner. One wrote Phoebe from his prison cell of atrocities by the revolution-aries. They were later freed, but the movement in Mexico was to na-tionalize mineral resources and turn land over to the peasants. A diary sent to Phoebe from the manager of the Hacienda de San Jose de Babicora, reporting on the events between 7 December 1915 and 20 January 1916, told her that Villa's troops were killing livestock for food, taking grain, corn, and horses, and had burned a house. "Americans are fleeing," the ranch manager, P. Simpson wrote. "Villa is near Madera with 4,000 men . . . announced that he was confiscating the Babicora Development Co. . . . Women all suffering headache from lack of coffee. They can't get along without it." On 29 December the "Villistas" offered amnesty, but on 7 January Simpson wrote that more than four thousand head of cattle, along with thirty-nine mules and horses, had been taken, and seventy hogs killed; the house was "cleaned out." The Santa Ana ranch, another property, was given by Villa to a musician and orders issued for gringos to be killed and their cattle given to neighbors. By 10

January Carranza was approaching and five thousand head of cattle had been taken from the Santa Ana ranch.[62]

Phoebe protested to the U.S. government, using her influence in high places. She sent a telegram to Secretary of State Robert Lansing, noting that

> The reason assigned for this action by the de facto Government is that the Babicora Development Company has sold cattle and supplies to the United States authorities to provision and care for the military forces of the United States.
>
> I vigorously protest against this unlawful action on the part of the de facto Government, and I appeal to you to inaugurate immediately an inquiry to ascertain the facts regarding the alleged appropriation of the company's property.
>
> As a citizen of the United States, I suggest to you that it is the duty of this Government to take measures to prevent the de facto Government of Mexico from disregarding and overriding the rights of American citizens who own property in the Republic of Mexico.[63]

Despite the revolution, the Babicora ranch stayed in Hearst hands, although some of the overseers and vaqueros died defending the land. Phoebe was a benevolent absentee landlord whose Mexican employees were encouraged not to enslave themselves to the landowners by indebtedness and to educate their children (a practice made more attractive by the promise of Phoebe's Christmas gifts to children who attended school). Many of the Mexican workers became tenant farmers. Prize cattle and horses were sent from San Simeon to the Babicora to be crossbred and raise the quality of the stock, which was considered among the best.[64]

The European conflict put Phoebe into the public eye in another dramatic and bloody way. After the sinking of the *Lusitania* in 1915, America was shaken out of its neutrality. By 1916 the talk was of "preparedness" against invasion. In San Francisco there also was growing labor agitation, blamed on union leaders who were suspected of being "Communists" and "Wobblies." An ad hoc group calling itself the Pacific Defense League, which was backed by the city's business community, conceived that a parade for American preparedness would be a show of force against union shops and Communist sympathizers. Non-union employees were urged to march or face dismissal from their jobs. There were threats, attributed to anarchists and labor agitators, of violence against the marchers.

Phoebe was asked to lead a women's section as a representative of Pioneer Women of California. The suffragists also wanted her to identify with them in the parade. She was averse to public demonstrations, seventy-four years old, and unwell, but she tentatively agreed to march.

She also was not going to be intimidated. When "Preparedness Day," 22 July arrived, she might have been put off by the unusually hot weather even if the threats to the lives of the marchers had not already frightened her away. But they had the opposite effect.

Dressed in white, as all the women were, a small flowered hat on her head, flag in one hand and parasol in the other, Phoebe led the procession up Market Street, a diminutive but determined old lady. Suddenly, several blocks away near the Ferry Building on the waterfront, a bomb exploded at 2:05 P.M. Ten people were killed and forty others injured. Someone rushed to tell Phoebe the news and to warn of possible further danger. "I hoped you would not march today, Mrs. Hearst. It is so hot, do you think you can stand it?" the courier (likely an employee of the *Examiner*) asked. "Well," Phoebe said, putting her head a little to one side as she tended to do, "I did think it was too hot for me to march, but this morning at breakfast I had eight letters telling me that if I marched I would be blown to atoms—so, of course, there was nothing for me to do but march."[65]

She denied appearing as a suffragist, writing the editor of the *New American Woman,*

> As for my participation in the Preparedness Parade, I did just what thousands of fine thinking women have done in all the larger cities of our nation, and I am thankful that my physical strength proved equal to the emergency.[66]

Two union organizers—Tom Mooney and Warren K. Billings—were convicted and sentenced to death for the bombing. It would take a campaign led by one of Will's editors, Fremont Older, to expose a trial with perjured testimony to save the two from hanging (ultimately Mooney and Billings were pardoned). Arthur Brisbane wrote Phoebe afterwards,

> I had just been seeing, on a business matter at the request of your son, a very cold-blooded individual—Thomas F. Ryan.
> He told me, very earnestly, that the most impressive sight he had seen in years was yourself in the great procession in which you appeared in spite of threats and of personal hardship.
> Life is disappointing at best to those who look upon the world intelligently as you do.[67]

The war presented a particular dilemma for Phoebe. Although she had marched to show her support for "preparedness" and was a member of the Council of Defense, she agonized over the wasteful loss of young lives. She read daily with sadness the accounts of her beloved Europe torn to pieces, the beautiful cities, monuments, and museums from which she had learned so much destroyed forever. War was antipathetic to her nature and she did not "hate" the Germans, having pleasant memories of Germany and friends there. She had spent happy hours with Orrin Peck in Munich and appreciated the country's culture. She joined the Anti-War Society of California and sent $100 to support a petition to Congress asking that a national referendum be held on whether Americans wanted the United States to enter the war.[68]

But after it did, on 6 April 1917, Phoebe vigorously supported the war effort. She ordered khaki yarn by the gross, paying women to knit for the soldiers, and outfitted hundreds of "comfort kits" for them. Her philanthropy continued, although she wrote one French woman in Oakland, "War conditions make it impossible to aid people as in former years." Still, she added, she would like to know more about the woman's request, saying, "In all cases I must make investigations."[69] Her *modus operandi* was different from John D. Rockefeller's, who had set up a foundation and himself was giving $70 million to war relief, exclusive of the sums allocated by the foundation. Phoebe continued to manage her giving personally.

Her contributions were substantial and, she thought, patriotic, requiring sacrifices on her part. She sold property to raise money for more than one hundred thousand dollars in Liberty Bonds, giving many thousand-dollar bonds as gifts. She told one importuner in 1918,

To raise these sums I have had to sell property [that formerly brought] in three times as much in income as the bonds purchased with the proceeds. . . .

I have done my utmost to meet these times of changed stress, with every possible sacrifice, readjusting all my own plans to a greatly reduced income and a fourfold increase in demands that are made upon me.[70]

She also was not well and was taking digitalis for her heart. Dr. Ray Lyman Wilbur, an eminent San Francisco physician who by then was president of Stanford University, attended her, as did her good friend Dr. Philip K. Brown, whose sanitorium Phoebe had helped finance for teachers and professionals in need of rest. She understood that need and she knew the meaning of the word *stress*. Dr. Brown, whose daughter was Phoebe's godchild and whose wife, Helen Hillyer, was a Bahai devotee with Phoebe, wrote her in 1917,

You can't go on living on stimulation and it must be that a break will come if you do not heed the warnings. Will you not therefore take 4 or 5 days of rest in bed and what digitalis you need to help you and then expend only such strength as you have to spend without the need of the heart support? Do this for all of us, for we love you and long for a continuance of your sweet strong help and all the light and joy you scatter on your way.[71]

She continued an active, busy life as a member of war committees. But she noted with apprehension the ominous spread of the wartime influenza epidemic, the "Spanish flu," clipping a newspaper article headlined, "S. F. To Give Influenza Hard Fight—How To Keep Free From Fatal Disease."

Her closest contact to the war was her nephew, Randolph Apperson, who volunteered for the army and spent more than a year as a sergeant in a truck company in Oklahoma. Phoebe sent him weekly boxes of fruit—apples, oranges, grapefruit from the Hacienda groves—and candy, blankets, socks, and sweaters. He wrote her long letters describing his miserable life in the cold and the boondocks, derisive of draftees, whom he called "slackers." He wanted to go to France and see the real war: ". . . Of course, I know you would hate to see me have to go but Auntie you don't know how anxious all of the fellows are to get over there and do a little of the big task."[72] After the armistice he was not ashamed to say that he was glad he had not been sent to Europe.

However, much of Phoebe's work during the second decade of the twentieth century was not related to the war. She was occupied with several other major projects—the development of the Young Women's Christian Association and Mills College in Oakland.

She had supported the work of the YMCA and YWCA some years before and had been a generous benefactor to both associations. In 1911, when the YWCA's summer retreat site, the Capitola Hotel in Santa Cruz, burned down, she took a personal interest in the YWCA's camps, which she had attended on several occasions. She realized that the public did not fully understand how many different activities the organization sponsored. They were not limited to religious exercises and Christian missionary programs, for which she never had great enthusiasm. She did like the idea of getting the women out of doors in a stimulating setting, and conceived the notion of educating the press and the public to the YWCA's objectives through a masterful public relations event. She would host the three hundred delegates to the 1912 YWCA summer camp on the grounds of her Hacienda and invite reporters and influential citizens to attend various activities at the ten-day gathering. The project also gave her an opportunity to create a "play land" in a beautiful setting. As a biographer, Winifred Black Bonfils wrote: "She loved to take a tent and make it livable and attractive."[73]

Part of the agenda to the summer meeting for 1912 was to plan for a permanent campsite. Phoebe suggested that the money usually paid by the delegates for expenses at retreats—a dollar a day or ten dollars each—be turned over to the YWCA as a down payment on a permanent camp. She would pick up all the costs of the 1912 meeting. The proposal was accepted and Phoebe went to work.

She selected a site on a slope several hundred feet above the Hacienda in a grove of old oaks. A large platform was erected and covered by the tent used for Hacienda picnics and Fourth-of-July barbeques. That was the dining room, capable of seating three hundred fifty people. Seventy-three small tents were put in the shade of the oak tree. Each tent held four camp cots, a little dressing table, and other furnishings. Other large tents on platforms were erected for meeting rooms. A kitchen, refrigerators, and a big barbeque pit were installed and the steward of the Bohemian Club in San Francisco was hired to cater the affair. Electric wiring and a water supply for baths and sanitary facilities were installed. Poison oak was cleared out and the picturesque camp on the "Hill of Contentment," overlooking the Livermore Valley, was ready for inhabitants by 17 May.

Automobiles and other conveyances were hired in nearby Pleasanton to transport the guests up the long road from Verona station. Arrangements were made with Pacific Railway to supply special trains to and from the city to accommodate the newspaper writers and influential guests. Phoebe insisted that food and meat be bought from local farmers and that temporary workers be hired from neighboring towns. The Hacienda itself was to house ministers and leaders of the association.

Each day of the conference a certain number of its delegates—college girls from the West Coast, China, Japan, and American Indian tribes— were invited down to the Hacienda for luncheon, dinner, or tea, and the same number of conference leaders staying in the house went up to "tent hill" to dine. The girls were given freedom to roam the grounds and the house with its books and art, billiard room, music room, Victrolas and aeolian harp, tennis court, glass-domed swimming pool, hot houses, gardens, and trails. To them it must have been paradise. After daily meetings they produced nightly entertainments. For those performances, Phoebe opened her large cache of costumes from all over the world and was photographed in a Chinese robe at one event. Reporters were given special facilities and covered the conference daily. On several occasions groups of sixty or seventy friends and acquaintances of Phoebe's were entertained at barbeque luncheons on the hill and attended meetings at which the YWCA's objectives were explained. An invitation from Mrs. Hearst was sometimes more of a summons.

Nothing was spared to make the delegates comfortable. A young man from southern California, who was engaged to one of the girls, sent Phoebe five dollars, asking that flowers be delivered to his fiancée every other day. Phoebe saw that they were. When it rained in the midst of the camp-out, Phoebe woke at 3:00 A.M., worried about the tents' leaking and the girls' catching cold. In the morning she ordered three hundred umbrellas, rubbers, sweaters, comforters, and blankets. The umbrellas and sweaters were to be souvenirs taken home by the girls. An embargo on camp fires was lifted and the conference went on happily in the outdoors. The camp's doctor later reported that the girls had never been healthier, which she attributed to the excellent food they were given. One delegate, expressing the girls' thanks in a prettily drawn card, wrote that "blessing beyond the power of words to measure have come from the Hacienda Conference. Encouragement and inspirations have been given the Pacific Coast Territorial Committee in facing difficulties by the stimulating example of the way one woman has met a large situation in such a large way."[74]

But an incident marred the bucolic event. Three of the local men hired to work at the camp could not resist stealing from the bountiful supply of goods around the place. One of them talked another into taking sweaters, for which the first paid fifty cents. He gave a red one, size 40, to a waitress with whom he kept company at a "sporting house" in a nearby town. The men also got into the wine cellar and were caught drunk by the night watchmen. Soap, blankets, umbrellas, a typewriter, even a tent also were found missing. When two men confessed, Phoebe suggested that they should be arrested to scare the third suspect into admitting to the thefts. As all of them looked to the Hacienda for employment, they confessed, hoping to be reinstated in their jobs.[75]

Will had a typically sardonic view of the event, writing his mother in humorously derisive tones about the missionary-minded girls swarming about the place. His mother telegraphed back, "Your ideas of the girls are as far wrong as the information concerning my health. There were many beautiful and clever women at the conference. Very few intend to work as foreign missionaries."[76]

Phoebe donated all the lumber, beds, furnishings, bedding, towels, dining room and kitchen equipment, cutlery and utensils—some twelve thousand dollars worth—to the YWCA's permanent camp. That was to be located along the coast in Pacific Grove after a field committee, of which Phoebe was a dominant member, selected the site in 1913. She rallied her influential friends to support the project. The Pacific Improvement Company (predecessor of Del Monte Properties) donated thirty acres of land valued at thirty thousand dollars, with the stipulation that another thirty thousand dollars worth of improvements be made within ten years. Julia Morgan was engaged to design buildings for the site. A name contest was held in which "Pine-Hearst," "Gitche-Gumee," and "Che-Mek'-a-ta," an Indian phrase meaning "Happy Meeting Place," were considered. A Stanford student, Helen Salisbury, was awarded first place for "Asilomar," a derivation of the Spanish words for a refuge or asylum by the sea (Asilo al Mar).[77] The first building erected was the Phoebe A. Hearst Social Hall, a wooden structure that blended with the rustic setting and was paid for with funds largely contributed by Phoebe. Subsequent buildings designed by Miss Morgan comprised a beautiful retreat in a setting that later became a state conference center open to the public.[78]

The other project that attracted Phoebe's attention in those years was the only women's school on the West Coast, Mills College. It had grown from a Christian seminary, founded by Susan and Cyrus Mills in 1852, to a liberal arts college with two hundred fifty students and had moved to unincorporated and undeveloped land in Oakland in 1871. Susan Mills had tried for years to interest Phoebe in the school, comparing, somewhat self-pityingly, the two women's work for education. She had written Phoebe in 1908, "I doubt whether any other two women have had as much personal interest in the welfare of the education of young people as you and I. I am now eighty-two, and must soon drop my work."[79]

In another letter in 1911, she said,

> You and I have worked for many years for the young people of California. You have done a great work, and will be recognized more and more. Mine has been humbler, and I have had much less money, but have given myself personally.[80]

The following year, in 1912, she wrote, "How I wish I had all the money I need to do the many things that I should like to do. You know I spend very little for myself. I have given everything I had to the work of this college."[81]

Susan Mills was not to attract Phoebe's largesse, possibly because her interest had been focused on the University of California. It was not until Aurelia A. Reinhardt, a dynamic widow with two sons to support, took over Mills in 1916 that Phoebe's interest perked up. The two women were much alike—sensible, straightforward, progressive, and concerned abut the future of women. Phoebe endowed a chair in American History and donated books for the department and the college library. But her real interest lay in the possibility of financing a plan for the Mills campus as she had done for the university. In that, Bernard Maybeck's savvy hand was evident. He and Aurelia Reinhardt understood fund-raising.

In 1917 Phoebe commissioned Maybeck to do a campus design, which Dr. Reinhardt enthusiastically supported. Maybeck reported to Phoebe in copious letters written either by himself or his wife. Annie. He wanted the plan done "so that any new building will drop into its place and never look new and raw," Annie wrote Phoebe 19 December 1917.

Now this plan is something like the two Ben made for the University as a basis for the competition, except that in the case of Mills it had to be a little more definite. In the case of the U.C. he was drawing to interest architects while in this case he tried to appeal to all sorts of people. . . .

All the drawings must be worked up to interest the layman who may have money to give. Ben finds it a wise thing to color everything—the layman does not care for the black and white architectural drawing.

It is what is called a preliminary sketch . . . a guide to the architect who may build for Mills in the future, to encourage the possible donor by showing and explaining how the money can best be used, and to arouse in Oakland and private interests to do their share in streets, approaches, railroads, etc. What happened to the University after the general plan was adopted may be expected to happen in a smaller way to Mills.

Surely a good girls' school is needed here and with a good plan and such a leader as Mrs. Reinhardt it ought to be a success. Already this last year she has more than doubled the attendance and has persuaded the directors to raise $150,000 for dormitories. She is impatiently awaiting the show drawings so she can raise the money she needs now. . . . The 300 students now there may easily become a thousand very soon if the College is ready for them. . . .

Ben has caught Mrs. Reinhardt's enthusiasm.[82]

Indeed he had. Aurelia Reinhardt was ready to make the small school into a modern institution, responsive to the needs of the time. Even though the trustees' finance committee chairman had gone East, she pushed the board to accept Maybeck's "general method of attack" before the school recessed for Christmas so that the students could "take enthusiasm and college loyalty home with them on their Christmas vacation [and] interest parents and friends" in endowing future buildings. The board voted unanimously in favor of the general plan.[83]

Maybeck had persuaded the trustees that Mills could be as famous as the university in having a campus that could grow in an orderly way, but in contrast to the philosophy of the university competition, he believed that the Mills plan should be flexible and blend with the eucalyptus-covered hills and stream beds of the college site. It should be "a subtle guide, leading the unsuspecting girls of Mills to hunger for ideals, like fine music stimulating to great deeds."[84]

Mills needed to acquire some additional land and lay out a plan into which buildings could be added as money became available, long after the designer was gone. Maybeck wrote Phoebe on 15 December 1918:

Mills has no money and I shall be dead before anything worthwhile will be done. . . .

Whatever may happen, this is certain: that having a definite scheme carefully worked out, it will prevent Mills from becoming a hodge-podge and the men who will change [it] will do so because at that time there will be another development that we could not foresee [sic], and it would be a pity, don't you think, if they made no progress.[85]

His proposal was not without problems. One skeptical trustee asked him what he intended to do to keep the mud off the young women's feet next winter. Most of his proposed avenues ran through existing buildings on the campus, many of them designed by Julia Morgan.[86] His scale for the small college was larger than life—a formal garden imposed on a forest landscape. Although much of his plan did not come to reality, it influenced the campus for all time, determining outlines for roads and buildings and preserving the topography with its woods and creek. He did convince the trustees to start planting shrubs and trees and to irrevocably shape the campus to his outline. Thus, many natural elements today are vestiges of Maybeck's elegant design for a "Garden of Eden" in Oakland.

Ultimately another architect was hired (in 1922) to work with Maybeck's plan and to consult him on its implementation. If not exactly as Maybeck would have had it, a harmonious campus evolved that fulfilled his and Phoebe's good intentions. The art building in particular was erected on the site designated by Maybeck.

The Maybecks had a close and fond relationship with Phoebe, not marked by the ingratiating attitude that many of her beneficiaries and protégés took. The Maybecks were genuine friends with whom she talked candidly. They shared a sense of humor about life and people in high or influential positions, whose arrogance they gently made fun of. Phoebe liked to have the Maybeck family around her; they entertained her and she had long conversations with Ben. Both he and Annie "had great respect for Mrs. Hearst and William Randolph—they felt they were doing great and important things," Maybeck's daughter-in-law, Jacomena, remembered. "And Mrs. Hearst liked him—his courtliness, his Frenchness, his gentle manners. He was extremely courteous, he stood up when women entered the room and kissed their hands. He was a charmer, he spoke French and had lovely manners. He was very persuasive. He knew how to flatter," she recalled.[87]

Phoebe liked his unconventionality, his standing out from the crowd in his beret and baggy pants and Chinese-style striped shirt while working, his handmade suits and cummerbund in the salon. Phoebe identified with his eccentricity, his sense of drama combined with propriety. "He was just as proper as she was," Jacomena said, "but he had a magic pencil." He could create fanciful environments for Phoebe's amusement. "Why not live like a Queen or King?" he thought, even if you were not one. They both liked to dress in costumes and to transport themselves into other worlds. "I know that your imagination is so full of poetry that it is needless to wish you a Merry Christmas," he wrote Phoebe in 1902.[88] Annie told her in a letter in 1912, "Ben worked on Hearst Hall and Wyntoon with just one idea in mind—to try to help you to have a good time."[89]

Maybeck felt guilty about taking Phoebe's money. He wrote her in 1901:

> We seem to feel that it is sacrilege to take anything for what we do for you, and that we ought to work for you in the same spirit that Michael Angelo worked for the Church of Rome; if we did, you would not be satisfied.[90]

If Ben had a reluctance to taking a fee, Annie did not: "Whenever Ben finds a man who is actually willing to build the least bit as he [Maybeck] thinks a house should be built, he is so grateful that away goes the fee—that is, if I am not there to prevent it."[91] Phoebe paid Ben a retainer of one hundred dollars a month to do various work when he was not on a university salary in 1897, but Annie said, "It does not feel just right to receive one hundred dollars per month for about 'four bits' worth of work and we have had attacks of conscience very often. We have a feeling that we would like to be paid by some enemy or some 'soulless corporation,' so that our work for people with ideals may be love work. . . . We ask only that you use us and our time—put us to work and let us do it for fun."[92]

Phoebe rewarded them with commissions and unpretentious gifts—grapes from her vineyard (Ben was a plump vegetarian), chrysanthemums from her garden, a case of instruments for Ben, a player piano at Christmas in 1910. It turned their "shack into a Paradise," Annie wrote. Ben played while the family danced around him. "When Ben smiles, we all dance," Annie said, "and music sends his barometer up."[93] "My children have been taught to know Santa Claus, fairies, brownies, ghosts, etc., as 'imaginary' beings. I have a suspicion that they believe you to belong in the same fascinating list," Annie wrote in a thank-you letter to Phoebe.[94]

Another subject at the turn of the century attracted Phoebe's attention but not her active involvement. That was the campaign to give women the right to vote, which she had watched from a distance most of her life. She was a reluctant suffragist. She had made the best of her Victorian situation, recognizing its limitations for women, yet she was anxious that future generations of women should be capable of caring for themselves, not dependent on men for their lives and their livelihood, like so many of her acquaintances—and, indeed, herself. She had always thought of herself as equal to men in intellectual tasks, but she had not taken a public stand in favor of suffrage, eschewing politics as men's work and demonstrations as unbecoming to sophisticated women. Her innate shyness kept her from public speaking and appearances, and she perceived that she was influential without the privilege of voting. Still, there was no greater champion of women's independence and equal education than Phoebe Hearst. The active suffragists were itching to get her name on their letterheads. She had been besieged by all the suffrage leaders for money and overt support but she would not march or speak out in favor of the movement. After the two met on a ferry from San Francisco to Oakland in 1896 Phoebe had given Susan B. Anthony money while not joining her National American Woman Suffrage Association. Of the meeting, Susan Anthony wrote another progressive California woman and supporter, Jane Stanford:

September 21, 1896

My dear, dear Mrs. Stanford:
   . . . I must tell you that on Saturday p.m. 4:00—as I went on the Ferry Boat—a lady said—you don't recognize me, Miss Anthony—and before I could call her name, she said "Mrs. Hearst"—She was going out to her new home—near Pleasanton—had invited a large number of friends to go out with her to share Sunday—and therefore had a special car attached to the train and invited me to take a seat in with herself and guests—which I did—
   On the boat as well as in the car—she was very free in her talk—told me of her many experiences since she became manager of her estates—which have done much toward making her see and feel the need of woman's possessing political power—as well as financial freedom—I am sure she will grow into the full realization of the importance of woman's enfranchisement—So I am profoundly thankful that you did not accede to my wish—She spoke of you and your great and grand enterprise—and told me of her own plan to help women educationally—

Susan B. Anthony[95]

Phoebe wrote Anthony in 1898, congratulating her on her biography.

Hacienda del Pozo de Verona
April 7, 1898

Dear Miss Anthony,
   I am glad that your biography has been written while you are alive and able to give absolute accuracy to the history of a movement that is to impress itself so vitally upon the future of our country.
   While I have never been an advocate of woman suffrage, I regard with deep respect your heroic life and entire devotion to the cause you have consecrated to it.

Yours very sincerely,
Phoebe A. Hearst[96]

In a 1911 letter to another suffragist she said,

   I feel that the day when women will vote is sure to come but I have always held myself apart from the organizations that were working for suffrage because the methods did not appeal to me.
   While I have not been willing to join the forces of those who were—and

are—working for suffrage, neither have I wished to take any active part, however small, on the other side.

I prefer to take no part for or against this struggle and for that reason do not wish to allow my name to be used as you suggest.

This is my attitude now. I will not say that I may not favor one or the other side later on, but, for a very long time, I have felt as outlined in this letter, and I do not feel at this time that I can make any change.[97]

At last Phoebe quietly joined the movement. California suffragists called hers an "eleventh-hour conversion" when she agreed to be named as a supporter of the 1911 constitutional amendment giving California women the vote.[98] She wrote educator Caroline Severance,

I share your feeling about the benefit our State will receive through the right of its women to the ballot. I decided to unite with those who were working to obtain it after considerable thought, and have great hopes that the results will justify all our expectations.[99]

By 1913 Phoebe had come out publicly for suffrage and the Hearst newspapers took up the cause. "The Hearst papers in New York, Chicago, San Francisco, and Los Angeles have done much towards forcing the American press to represent the suffragettes in the proper light," a Canadian newspaper said in 1913.[100] Another reported that Phoebe had sent a letter of support to a suffrage reader.

There has been some dispute between suffragists and antis as to how Mrs. Phoebe A. Hearst stood on the subject. The question is definitely settled by the following letter from Mrs. Hearst, lately received by Mrs. Stearns:

> Hacienda del Pozo de Verona
> Pleasanton, California

Dear Mrs. Stearns:

In reply to your inquiry, I will say that I was not in favor of suffrage until the campaign in California was well on, and then certain information came to me which convinced me that the time had come—here, at any rate—when women should have the right to vote.

I felt convinced then that women would unite in favoring certain work tending towards the betterment of conditions affecting women and children particularly, which men heretofore could never be relied upon to favor when it came to the test of the ballot.

I must add, however, that, while I am a suffragist, I have no sympathy whatever with the tactics of the militant suffragette.

> Very sincerely yours,
> Phoebe A. Hearst
> Jan. 2, 1913[101]

As late as 1916 she wrote to someone seeking her political support for the presidential candidacy of Republican Charles Evans Hughes, "You are mistaken about me being the principal sponsor for this women's party movement, nor did I approve or support the 'Special Train' movement in any way more than to lend my name as a suffragist and Hughes supporter. No doubt the women in charge had the best intention, but they, and we all, have much to learn yet." A secretary, to whom Phoebe had dictated the letter, had crossed out an earlier version that added, "for I had nothing whatever to do with the forming of the 'National Women's Party,' which was originally called 'Congressional Union for Woman Suffrage,' but I do approve and lend support to suffrage and some of the things they are trying to do." By that time, she had been chosen by the newly formed National Women's Party as one of two vice-chairs.[102]

Her own experience had taught Phoebe that women really were equal to men in most tasks. She wrote an article at the time of the 1915 World's Fair entitled "California as a Field for Women's Activities" that expressed her thoughts about the role of women:

> In California women have been recognized since pioneer times as physically and intellectually qualified to occupy high positions of trust and responsibility in connection with public affairs, and have discharged the duties of such positions with popular recognition of their efficiency as well as with popular approval of their devotion and energy.
>
> In California enterprises women have always participated not only as owners, but as directors and managers, and have certainly attained as high percentage of success in such affairs as men have. It is no surprise in California that a woman should decide to direct her own business affairs. On the other hand, it is rather expected that she will manage them, for during the several recent decades of rapid development of the finance and industry of the State women have made good in such undertakings.
>
> The enfranchisement of women in California was the logical result of the foregoing demonstration. It was not a whim or sentiment of men, for whims and sentiments were generally against it. It was an irresistible evolution from California experience and it stands as a surety to coming women that they will be free to act in public affairs and in their own business and that they will be appreciated and judged just as men are in similar undertakings.[103]

It was clear that the ability of the female vote to influence government policies and programs affecting women and children had been a major factor in persuading Phoebe to overtly champion suffrage. She had seen another milestone in her life.

15
Mortality and Immortality

Although the war in Europe was drawing to a close in 1918, it had caused Phoebe much personal anguish over the hostile publicity leveled at her son. He had been accused of being pro-Germany and anti-England. The former was a mistaken interpretation of Will's pacifism and isolationism—an unpopular position in a nation at war. He had published a German-language newspaper, the *Deutsches Journal,* some years before. But with the outset of World War I, he had favored a military draft and the sale of Liberty Bonds, which he patriotically advocated through his newspapers. Perceiving that Germany was winning, he despaired of sending young American boys into the jaws of the Huns or to the bottom of the sea in ships sunk by U-boats. He thought American involvement a fruitless and "bloody sacrifice" that served only to prop up a dying Empire-preserving England. America, he believed, should be prepared for invasion, arm itself, and let the Germans come to it. Let Europe take care of itself, had been his position.

He was accused, however, in a bitter mayoral campaign in New York from which he withdrew, of being "the spokesman of the Kaiser." There were hints that he was a liaison of German spies, the result of a meeting with a man who Will publicly stated had sought his help in getting newsprint, which was hard to come by in war-torn Europe. The Secret Service tailed Will; a congressional committee investigated him; a federal agent even was installed as butler in the Hearst household. His newspapers lost circulation and were boycotted, burned, and banned in some places.[1]

A friend wrote Phoebe:

> I have been intensely interested in the Becker accusations against Mr. Hearst. It certainly looks like he would come out with flying colors. I have always said when I have heard him accused, that the strongest proof of his loyalty was the fact they could prove nothing against him, with all the Secret Service department working to the limit trying to trap him.[2]

In spite of the anti-Hearst feeling, the mayoral candidate whom Will supported won in New York and Millicent was made chair of the women's division of the Mayor's Committee on National Defense. She was busy and active in charity and civic work. When the wounded men returned to New York for a "Heroes' Day" welcome, she appeared at her husband's side to present the mothers of boys who had been killed a little medal designed by Will. She donated a ring that was auctioned for five thousand dollars, the proceeds from which went to purchase buses to transport the wounded veterans about New York. "I never saw anyone want buses as badly as Millicent does," Ethel Whitmire wrote Phoebe.[3]

The Hearsts appeared to be the happy parents of a happy family—good publicity for a man, then fifty-four, who was still considering running for high office. Few except his closest friends, including Orrin Peck, knew that there was trouble in paradise. Will had noticed a vivacious Ziegfeld chorus girl with blonde hair and a slight stutter, the daughter of a New York politician. She called herself Marion Cecilia Davies and she had appeared in a memorable 1917 Follies that Will had attended.[4] He wasted no time in meeting her. He was determined to keep his acquaintance with the woman some twenty years his junior a secret, especially from his aging and unwell mother. But Phoebe had her own "secret service" in the form of loyal family retainers and relatives, like Ethel Whitmire, who lived with the Hearsts and helped care for the children. Little escaped Ethel's keen eye and all was reported in detail to Phoebe, her benefactor. It is unlikely that any comings and goings of Will's were not known to his mother.

If Phoebe learned about Marion, it was another in a lifetime of disappointments concerning her son. Though she would not have chosen Millicent as a daughter-in-law, Phoebe tolerated her and believed in the viability of marriage and family. She recognized from her own experience the necessity of working hard to preserve both. She could not countenance an extramarital affair, although she had known her own frustrations—and possibly the indiscretions of her husband—in a marriage that had had its difficulties. Still, marriage was a bond that two people made and endured. Even Will had said to his mother (in 1912), commenting on a highly publicized divorce involving a woman cited as a "protégé of Mrs. Phoebe Hearst" and based on facts "given out at the Hacienda":

> Why should they allow some folly to break up their married life? Ninety-nine couples out of a hundred could find technical grounds for divorce if they had not sense enough to overlook them. The number of ladies and gentlemen fit to cast stones are comparatively few. Please spank them and tell them to make up.[5]

But Will again had taken up with the kind of woman his mother disapproved of, a showgirl, in the sort of liaison that he seemed to court to spite his mother for her consistent opposition to his choice of women friends. Phoebe continued to believe that she was right in discouraging such friendships.

Yet she kept up her outward loyalty to Will, never doubting his genius and capability of becoming a great man. To her friends and contemporaries Will was "Phoebe Hearst's boy," and as such he was ever the dutiful and adoring son.[6] To Phoebe, he was still "my dear boy." At one point toward the end of her life, she carefully wrapped her letters to him and wrote on the envelope, "My letters to my dear boy. He may care for them when I am gone. P.A.H."[7] Her influence over his life had created a complex relationship between them, complicated by his strong personality and resistance to his mother. The fact that his father had not been at home during much of his son's formative years possibly had made him a mother's boy, insecure with women.

But the one woman he could always count on to stand by him was his mother, and she did so in the dark war years in which he was vilified as a German sympathizer. It pained her privately to see him ostracized by those in the social strata where she herself was entertained and admired. Phoebe also shared Will's anti-war sympathies and she was an unequivocal patriot, as she knew Will was. The thought of her son as a traitor was inconceivable. The two were a unique complement to one another. Arthur Brisbane had told her once,

> Many mothers get glory and public approval from the works of their sons. Your son is helped in public esteem by his mother's work—and you are honored by the splendid public fights that he has made—a rare combination.[8]

Phoebe spent Christmas of 1918 in New York with Will and his family. On her seventy-sixth birthday, he wired her, "We are rejoiced to hear that you will be here for Christmas. . . . May you have many happy birthdays and spend more of them with us." In another telegram, he added, "Leave a little before the 17th if you can. George will like to see the Christmas shops and you don't want to be so tired after your trip that you won't enjoy Christmas."[9]

She was to make it a special Christmas for Will. One morning not long after her arrival at his apartment on the corner of Eighty-sixth Street and Riverside Drive, she went downstairs to the sitting room, where Will read the papers. She had been talking with Edward Clark. She asked Will how his affairs were going and he told her "pretty fair considering the war condition," but that he had had to borrow some money and might have to borrow some more. He said his newspapers were probably in as good condition as any others. Phoebe then asked him if the notes he owed her were a detriment or hindrance to his credit and Will said, "I suppose they might to a certain extent." Then she told him that she intended to cancel all his indebtedness to her. Will replied, "Mother, I would like to pay it." She would not accept that, but she had a caveat, and knowing Will's cavalier tendencies toward money, she emphasized what she wanted him to do in return:

> I don't expect you to pay it; I don't want you to pay it. I intend to cancel it, but there is one thing that I seriously do want you to do, and that is actually agree to pay and pay to me $300,000, which I want for a definite purpose to construct a building to house my collections at Berkeley. I want you to consider that a serious business obligation and agree to pay that and pay it.[10]

Phoebe considered the cancellation of his obligations to her the turning over of his half of the inheritance. She had given Will more than $14 million since George's death in 1891. She was paying off business loans of some $2 million herself in 1918 and she told Will that he should be careful not to call on her for further help because she would not be able to give it to him. She also wanted him to share in her work at the University of California by contributing to a wing of the proposed art and anthropology museum, to which she intended to donate her personal collections. She often had told her attorney and friend, Charles Stetson Wheeler, of her desire to have a wing of the museum, saying "I want Will to build that." Will gave her a promissory note for $300,000, payable in three years.[11]

Despite a cold that she suffered in New York, Phoebe felt better than she had on two previous Christmas holidays; she went about with her usual energy, shopping, dining, and lunching with friends, going to the opera. On New Year's Eve afternoon she drove with her maid to New Haven to visit Anne and Dr. Flint, then professor of surgery at Yale University. She told Anne that she planned to spend next Christmas at Wyntoon, a treat that she had long promised the grandchildren.[12]

But on her return to New York her cold became worse and it appeared that she had been struck by the insidious Spanish influenza that the doughboys were bringing home and that a servant at the Hacienda had contracted on a trip to San Francisco shortly before Phoebe left California. Randolph Apperson, still in the army, had written his "Auntie" 11 December 1918,

> Sister writes me that there is an influenza epidemic started at the Hacienda and Mary Walsh had to go in the city and brought it home and spread it all over the place. It is always a brainless person that has to do a thing like that and the Hacienda has been so free of it up to now.[13]

Mary's trip proved to be fateful for Phoebe. She was one of half a million Americans who were said to have caught the disease; fifty thousand cases had been reported in San Francisco and more than seven thousand people had died of it in California. Phoebe rallied, however, and was well enough to attend a luncheon given by a friend late in January. But she had a relapse and was confined to her bed at Will's home during the first weeks of February. On 12 February, with the Edward Clarks, the older grandchildren, and others in her entourage, she left New York in her private railroad car for California. She was well enough on 14 February to dress and attend a Saint Valentine's Day celebration during the trip. The train arrived at the Hacienda on 18 February at one o'clock in the morning, but Phoebe was up the next day and began to improve in health. She laughingly said to her house-keeper, Marie Bernhardt, "Look, Marie, I have all of my teeth left, and that is a good sign that I will live to a very old age."[14]

She asked Edward Clark to draw up the necessary papers to cancel Will's notes. She had decided also to return to him the Babicora deed and stock, valued at $1 million, which she had been holding in trust for him since "buying" it in 1898 to give him money. According to George's will, it was his, after all. "Am arranging the matter we discussed, and also something more which I think will please you," she wired Will. On 27 February 1919 she wrote him:

My dear Son—

I am fully alive to the fact that the demands and difficulties occasioned by the War have put a severe strain upon your finances. I can also see very plainly that during the next few years you will, in all probability, have to use your credit to a very considerable extent.

The notes which you and your various corporations have given to me in the past, and which I now hold, amount to a total of upwards of one million, eight hundred thousand dollars ($1,800,000). The existence of these obligations would naturally embarrass and hamper you in making representations to your bankers.

The indebtedness which these various notes represent have never been treated by me or really looked upon by me as strict business transactions. I let you have the money because I wanted to help you over difficulties.

I have concluded that the best way to help you in the present situation is to make an out and out gift to you of all the moneys in excess of three hundred thousand dollars ($300,000), which I have thus advanced to you or to your corporations. . . .

Your affectionate mother,
Phoebe A. Hearst[15]

While recovering from her illness, she daily signed papers at her desk and dictated business or social correspondence from a couch or chair placed in the sunshine; her secretaries read to her and she saw visitors. But late in March she again became seriously ill, and her physician, Ray

Lyman Wilbur, as well as the local doctor who treated the Hacienda staff, were summoned. They were alarmed. Until then they had expected her to recover, counting on her parents' longevity—which she herself kept pointing out—to keep her alive for some years hence. Will insisted, on hearing of his mother's relapse, that a nurse be engaged; she arrived on 19 March. On 26 March a change for the worse occurred. A tubercular lesion of long standing opened in Phoebe's lung and brought about complications in the form of pneumonia. It was then that she said to Dr. Wilbur, "I will depend upon you as an old friend to tell me at any time you think I am going to die." "So I was under a responsibility to tell her," he later remembered.[16]

That was the last week in March. A few days later, a blood vessel broke, spreading tubercular pus through the fragile body. "Until that happened, there was a good prospect of her getting well," Dr. Wilbur recalled. "Of course, when that happened, there was no such prospect and I, kindly as I could tell her as a layman could understand it, then told her that there was a distinct change in her condition." Phoebe, too, up to that point had thought she would recover. She was making plans to open Wyntoon in the summer and hiring three Chinese cooks to go there in June, engaging a tutor for her grandsons, talking with President Wheeler about her museum wing and her desire to build a house for him on land that she owned in Berkeley where he and his wife could live after his imminent retirement. She also was discussing with her local doctor, who had been in Cuba, arrangements for opening a health center for the Mexican ranch hands. But by the end of March she had become discouraged about her illness. She asked her secretary, Margaret Clark, if she thought Will should be sent for. Mrs. Clark said, "Yes." On 26 March they telegraphed him and he set out the next day, arriving at the Hacienda with Millicent on 31 March.[17]

Their presence created tension, Anne Flint recalled, although Phoebe rallied somewhat with Will's arrival. "Will and Millie brought guests up by the houseful," which Anne thought disrespectful to her aunt. "Don't let that woman (Millicent) come into my room," Phoebe told Anne.[18] Other close friends were welcome at the bedside. Helen Peck Sanborn remembered that Phoebe clung to her friend's hands as if it were for the last time.

On 13 April at 4:30 in the afternoon, in her room overlooking the valley and California hills that she loved, Phoebe fell asleep and quietly died of pneumonia. Will and eleven-year-old William Randolph, Jr., were among those at her bedside. The powerful little woman who had so ruled and influenced their lives was at last still.

Ironically, it was not her heart, which had troubled her all her life, but complications from the wartime plague that had killed her. She died on

Dr. Wilbur's birthday and two weeks before her son turned fifty-six. She was seventy-six years old.

For three days, as Will's tribute to his mother, converge of Phoebe's death and funeral filled the *Examiner.* Obituaries throughout the country, including one in the *New York Times*, were lavish in their praise, particularly of her womanliness. "One of the nation's most womanly women," one said. Others called her "a great-hearted gentlewoman of the old school," "a true woman of God who lived by the Golden Rule and not the rule of gold," and one who "spoke of the great good which would come to the women of the world and our own country with the right of suffrage," "a steadfast supporter of the ballot for women." Benjamin Ide Wheeler said, "She was herself gifted not only with exquisite taste but with a singularly clear and powerful mind."[19]

Civic leaders in San Francisco set about gathering funds for a suitable but modest monument to Phoebe, who, they said, "would never have approved of a costly or elaborate memorial for what she considered her duty as a citizen." It was decided that a public drinking fountain would be fitting, not of "great proportions or of great cost, but one that will daily remind those who knew her, as well as the stranger within our gates, that there once dwelt among us this modest and great-hearted woman who was also a noble citizen." Even the elevator boy at the Fairmont Hotel contributed to the fund. The drinking fountain was erected in Golden Gate Park and today is the only monument in San Francisco to Phoebe Apperson Hearst.[20]

Her funeral was a state affair. She would have been publicly embarrassed at the florid tributes but she would have smiled in private satisfaction at their outpourings. Like George's, the funeral was held at Grace Episcopal Cathedral in San Francisco. The governor of the state was an honorary pallbearer. Presiding was the Episcopal bishop, William Ford Nichols, a personal friend of Phoebe's. The church ceremony followed private services for the family and friends at the Hacienda. A separate musical service for those not invited to the funeral was held in the Civic Auditorium. Flags in San Francisco were lowered to half-staff—the first such tribute ever given a woman by the city. But the ceremonies were marred by another, ironic sadness. Phoebe's good friend Professor Henry Morse Stephens, head of the University of California history department, dropped dead at the ferry depot after leaving the service. When her casket was lowered into the vault, William Randolph, Jr., cried out, "Goodbye, grandma."

Historians would look for deathbed words of acrimony between Phoebe and Will, but William Randolph, Jr., remembered that there were none. Phoebe had made her peace with Will and with the world, and if she had bitter thoughts, she kept them to herself. She left the bulk of her estate, whose total value could not be calculated, to Will. In all, the estate included $91,000 in cash and more than $8.5 million worth of properties in California and Mexico, among them the Babicora Ranch, the Hearst Building at Third and Market streets in San Francisco, the Hacienda, Wyntoon, San Simeon Ranch, and a fruit ranch near Palermo in Butte County, California. The rest of her estate was in mining and other stocks. The inheritance tax was close to $1 million.

Phoebe's affairs, typically, were in careful order. She had made her will in 1911, writing it out in longhand for twenty-two pages. She had changed it only once, in 1917 (a correction was made in 1918). Trust funds of fifty thousand dollars were set up for her brother, Elbert, his wife, Elizabeth, and nephew, Randolph Apperson. They were not given money outright for a period of years but allowed to receive the income from the trusts, which were to be managed by her trustees, Will, Edward Hardy Clark, and Frederick Sanborn (who died before Phoebe and was replaced). The arrangement showed a certain distrust of Elbert to manage money. Anne Apperson Flint was given Wyntoon, a Cadillac valued at twenty-five hundred dollars and a legacy of $250,000. Will was "furious" that Anne had gotten Wyntoon, and he refused to give her back certain artifacts from the place that Phoebe had loaned to the exhibition at the Palace of Fine Arts in San Francisco, as well as some items that Anne had given her aunt and that were at the Hacienda. Will bought back Wyntoon for $198,000 in 1925 but the bitterness between the cousins lasted all their lives. Anne said that her aunt had "terrible regrets" on her deathbed for not having done enough for her niece.[21]

Others who received legacies included her cousins Edward Clark, who got one hundred thousand dollars, and Richard Clark, twenty-five thousand dollars. She took care of her long-time servants and faithful employees with bequests of one thousand to five thousand dollars for each person. Gifts to remote cousins and several close friends, some of ten thousand or fifteen thousand dollars, were canceled in the 1917 codicil to her will for reasons unknown; she may already had given them money or property while she was living or simply changed her mind about the bequests.

In other changes made in 1917 she declared that her legal and voting residence was the Fairmont Hotel, San Francisco, and she reduced bequests to friends and relatives by several thousands dollars each. The most dramatic change, however, was the stipulation that the Hacienda should be sold and the profits divided equally among her grandchildren. No one in her family was to live there after she was gone. A few years later it was sold for $125,000 and eventually her magnificent home was turned into a country club. The stables and servants' quarters were destroyed by fire in 1959, and the house burned to the ground in 1969.

In the 1917 will she also canceled a gift of one hundred thousand dollars to the University of California Mining School and one of half a million dollars for the museum or wing that she had wanted built to house her art and archaeological collection. She expected Will to build it in her honor; that did not happen and the archaeological museum later built at the university did not bear her name, although another structure would. After Hearst Hall burned in 1922, Will in 1925 gave the university, in honor of his mother, a magnificent classical gymnasium building and pool designed by Bernard Maybeck with Julia Morgan doing the construction drawings. The complex initially was intended to include a museum, which ultimately was not built. Phoebe left the university the sixty-thousand-dollar trust fund for women's scholarships and a large quantity of art, including the marble bust of herself by Ansiglioni, five Aubusson and other tapestries, eighteen oriental rugs, her collection of American Indian blankets and baskets, and a collection of serapes from Mexico. The rest of her art collection went to Will (some of it was sold by him to pay business debts in 1937).

At the reading of the will four days after her death, the mother's and son's fiscal separation was finalized. Will no longer would have to ask his mother for money or approval. But he was not to be psychologically free of her strong hand, even after her death. He was denied many of her properties, but not his beloved ranch. The Hearst Building in San Francisco was given to her grandsons, Wyntoon to Anne Flint, and the Hacienda property was to be sold. He resolved then to build his own, more spectacular castle on a higher hill than any his mother had dominated. It was almost as if he were shaking his fist at the heavens and saying, "I'll show you, mother." It would be a place of wonder and make-believe beyond any that Phoebe had ever inhabited. He asked Julia Morgan, shortly after his mother's death, to make some drawings. He wanted "something a little different" from what others were building in California, he told her. She sketched a rough design of a castle with two towers similar to an old church that he admired in Ronda, Spain.[22] Will liked the sketch and told her to go ahead with the design of a palace to be built on the Enchanted Hill (La Cuesta Encantada), overlooking the Pacific Ocean at San Simeon. He would construct it for the rest of his life. He had written his mother in 1906, while on a camping trip to San Simeon with his family,

> I am exceedingly fond of the ranch as you know. . . .
> I am going to save up and build a cabin down there just big enough for you and Milly and the baby and me. Then I suppose you will go to Abyssinia and stay a year and a half.

He thought the ranch "the loveliest spot in the world." "You reproved me for not liking the Hacienda better," he wrote his mother in 1917; "I do like the Hacienda and realize that it is a delightful place; but I am out here to jam as much health into my system as possible. . . . It seems to me that anything that can be done anywhere is all assembled and ready to be done on the ranch." In the same year he also wrote her:

> I love this ranch. It is wonderful. I love the sea and I love the mountains and the hollows in the hills and the shady places in the creeks and the fine old oaks and even the hot bushy hillsides—full of quail—and the canons full of deer. It's a wonderful place. I would rather spend a month here than any place in the world. And as a sanitarium! Mother, it has Nauheim, Carlsbad, Vichy, Wiesbaden, French Lick, Saratoga, and every other so-called health resort beaten a nautical mile.[23]

Will had other problems with his mother's will. He was appalled to find that he had to pay $949,101 in inheritance taxes. There was a lengthy dispute with the U.S. Internal Revenue Bureau over the estate tax. The tax collectors charged that Phoebe had given her son legacies in contemplation of her death in order to avoid paying some of the tax. That amount in question was a paltry $8,261, but it was several years before the executors prevailed and convinced courts that Mrs. Hearst had no intention of dying when she did and certainly not of shirking her tax obligations.[24]

At the time of Phoebe's death, newspaper headlines reported "Doughboys Come Home" (California regiments that had fought at Argonne marched up Market Street April 22), "Germans Called to Versailles," "Free Ireland Fund Growing," "172 Miles an Hour Attained by Flier," "Divorce is Theme of Daring Play." President Woodrow Wilson announced that Austria-Hungary no longer existed as a nation.

Phoebe Hearst had seen a civil war, a Spanish-American war and a world war to end all wars. She had traveled from mule-drawn wagon to luxury motorcar. She had watched the development of the aeroplane, the telephone, electric lights, and moving pictures (in which her son had a consuming interest). She had marveled at it all and changed with the times, moving forward with curiosity, interest, tolerance, and a consistent concern that people look out for their sensibilities above all else. She would not see the Jazz Age, short skirts and bobbed hair, the jet rocket or the atom bomb. But she would not have been surprised at such wonders. Her era had ended and she had made the most of it. She had said to her friends that life had gotten richer and sweeter as she had grown older.

An astrological chart that she had commissioned in her lifetime showed her to manifest the strong characteristics of Mars as ruling planet. Astrological interpreters said that it made her a domineering, aggressive person with great initiative, one who liked to control other people's lives, who expected others to conform to her expectations and withheld her love until they did. In that, and other interpretations, the chart accurately described her. "She was not a martinette," her grandson remembered, "but if she wanted something, she got it. When she gave an order—'Go to bed'—you went."[25] According to one interpreter of her chart, she adored attention and was concerned for her appearance, evidenced by her elaborate dress, but she had a wry, satirical sense of humor that allowed her to laugh at her own self-centeredness—and to make jokes at others' expense. The chart showed that she placed a great importance in her progeny, and, as with others, expected they would do the right thing and be responsible. In fact, she appreciated people who were serious and consistent in fulfilling their responsibilities. She could be piqued when she felt that others were not handling matters to her satisfaction, and would take on the tasks herself. She had a genius for seeing other people's talents and assets and for putting them to advantage. Her great enthusiasm, persuasiveness, and emotional energy made others around her appear weak. She was good at convincing others that they wanted what she wanted.

Phoebe understood the importance of tradition and the security that money provided for a stable position in the world. She was suspicious of those who were overly generous to her, but she valued social mores. Her astrological chart indicated that she was difficult to educate because she had a mind of her own, which was true; she did better teaching herself knowledge of a practical sort. She had a remarkable memory for details. She emulated intellectuals but preferred to demonstrate her convictions through deeds. The chart suggested that she married someone who made money in an unusual fashion and had financial surprises. It also implied that she may have married more for practicalities than for love, although she was idealistic about the commitment. She also may have been sensitive about sexuality and may have felt repressed or sexually inadequate, if the chart were to be believed.[26]

She certainly was a woman with conflicting drives. She wanted many friends but was not often open about her thoughts and feelings. While she had a great sense of responsibility and duty, she sometimes resented the demands placed upon her. She needed continual stimulation, yet she frequently complained that she lacked peace and quiet. When frustrated or depressed she could become ill. The chart indicated that she may have had a strained relationship with her mother, and sought freedom from her family because she felt that she was different and did not quite belong to it. Indeed, she was different. Whatever else her marriage brought, it gave her freedom from a constraining lifestyle. She had created and ruled her own family dynasty.

In short, she was a person of tremendous power who thrived on challenge and crisis, who lived a fulfilling and rewarding life and brought joy to many other people's lives.

Phoebe often told the story of the little boy who had written her a letter, after hearing about one of her elegant parties, saying that he wished she would not spend so much money on company because he was afraid that one day she would go to the bank and find all her money gone. She was fond of reading the boy's letter at dinner parties, telling her guests, "You see, I am not without a good practical friend to advise me."[27]

Abbreviations

Brooks biography	Adele S. Brooks, "Report on Letters, Records, Certificates, Documents, and Papers of All Descriptions Belonging to Mrs. Phoebe Apperson Hearst"
Clark transcript	Edward Hardy Clark, "Reminiscences of the Hearst Family"
Flint interview	Anne Drusilla Apperson Flint, transcripts of interviews with W. A. Swanberg
GH Papers	George Hearst Papers, Huntington Library
GH Letters	George Hearst Letters, Bancroft Library
McLaughlin transcript	Donald H. McLaughlin, transcript of interview with Harriet Nathan
PAH Papers	Phoebe Apperson Hearst Papers, Bancroft Library
Paul Reminiscences	Almarin Brooks Paul, Reminiscences
Peck Papers	Peck Papers, Huntington Library
Orrin or Janet Peck Papers	Orrin and Janet Peck Correspondence, California Historical Society
Peck Family Letters	Peck Family Papers, Bancroft Library
WRH Papers	William Randolph Hearst Papers, Bancroft Library

Note on Editorial Principles

Much of the material was drawn from original letters in several manuscript collections, principally at the Bancroft Library, University of California, Berkeley; the Huntington Library, San Marino, California; and the California Historical Society, San Francisco. Undated letters were matched by their subjects to events in the Hearsts' lives. George Hearst's handwritten letters often contained misspellings and grammatical errors, which are retained in the text. Where a word in any letter was undecipherable, it has been left blank with a question mark. Most of the correspondence I examined was handwritten but many of William Randolph Hearst's (WRH) communications in the Bancroft collection—both handwritten and telegrams—had been transcribed to typewritten copies. Phoebe Hearst's handwriting was clear but many of her letters were written on transparent paper, horizontally on one side and vertically on the other, making them difficult to read. To the extent possible, the original language and emphases in letters has been retained, including underlined words. The Hearst family communicated in later years by many telegrams, possibly via a private wire for the Hearst newspapers. As they communicated frequently, many wires or short notes, particularly from William Randolph Hearst, are not fully dated.

The Hearst family began to give papers from its archives, largely in San Simeon warehouses, to the Bancroft Library in 1972. As additional material is given to the library, it is catalogued by the year it is received, which accounts for numerous citations for Hearst papers at Bancroft. The Phoebe Apperson Hearst (PAH) Papers, to which there is a key to arrangement, are organized alphabetically by author of incoming correspondence and by general subject matter. George Hearst letters are identified both in the key to the PAH collection and in other Hearst collections. Most of the newspaper articles cited are from that collection. They were not organized but were loosely placed in boxes. Many of the newspaper articles are identified by a clipping service, which Mrs. Hearst apparently used. The author examined material in approximately 150 containers of the growing Hearst collection at the Bancroft Library.

The Bancroft letters are identified as PAH and WRH Papers. George Hearst Papers cited separately are from the Huntington Library. Peck Papers also are identified by their location—the Bancroft, Huntington, and California Historical Society libraries. Material from Hearst San Simeon State Historical Monument and the Phoebe Apperson Hearst Historical Society was not organized. Other library collections are catalogued by the names and citations used here.

Notes

Preface

1. Postcard from William Randolph Hearst (WRH) to Phoebe Apperson Hearst (PAH), "from the train," undated, Phoebe Apperson Hearst Papers, Bancroft Library, University of California, Berkeley; hereafter cited as PAH Papers.

Introduction

1. Phoebe Hearst Brown, godchild of PAH, interview with author, 14 March 1982, San Francisco.

2. Adele S. Brooks, "Report on Letters, Records, Certificates, Documents, and Papers of All Descriptions Belonging to Mrs. Phoebe Apperson Hearst," prepared after PAH's death, PAH Papers. Hereafter cited as Brooks biography.

3. Clara Reed Anthony to a Miss Ramirez, 1896, PAH Papers. A lifelong friend from Missouri, Mrs. Anthony was the daughter of Dr. Silas Reed, physician and mining colleague of George Hearst's. She wrote of PAH, "She has a masculine grasp of financial affairs and superintends her vast estate with the ease that comes of an orderly and well-balanced mind."

4. PAH to Orrin Peck, 3 May 1899, Peck Papers, Huntington Library, San Marino, California.

5. PAH to Daniel G. O'Connell, 16 October 1916, PAH Papers.

6. Dwight Bentel, draft history of George Hearst (1946), William Randolph Hearst Papers, Bancroft Library, University of California, Berkeley; hereafter cited as WRH Papers.

7. Arthur Brisbane to PAH, 10 June 1915, PAH Papers.

8. "Phrenological Character, Wm. R. Hurst [sic], Prof. O. S. Fowler, Phrenological Author, Editor and Lecturer, Boston, 18——," WRH Papers.

9. Arthur Brisbane, column, 1934, King Features Syndicate, PAH Papers.

1. Missouri Years and Apperson Family Roots

1. PAH to Eliza Pike, PAH Papers.

2. I shall spell her name Phoebe. Although she signed her name both "Phebe" and "Phoebe," her name came to be spelled commonly with an "o."

3. Billie Louise Owens and Robert James, *Sons of Frontiersmen: History & Genealogy of Rowland, Whitmire & Associated Families* (Canon City, Colo.: Master Printers, 1976), 45.

4. Ibid.

5. Ibid., 51–52, 61–62, 77; George Leland Sumner, "Historical and Genealogical Newberry County, South Carolina," 1950, private publication, p. 95.

6. Eva Turner Clark, *Jacob Clark of Abbeville, South Carolina, and Some of His Descendants* (New York: Downs Printing Co., 1926), 91–94; Vera Apperson English, *The Apperson Family in America* (Pelham Manor, N.Y.: 1977), p. 267.

Randolph shows up most often subsequently as a Hearst family name, but it is not clear exactly why. Phoebe's paternal great-grandmother was Isabella, or, one record states, Elizabeth Randolph of Virginia. Four of Phoebe's five grandsons and numerous other descendants would carry the name. William Randolph Hearst, Jr., one of her grandsons, thought it was because his father, as he put it, "had a love affair with the name. He just liked it."

7. Records at Hearst San Simeon State Historical Monument, San Simeon, Calif; letter from H. B. Apperson, 17 April 1897, in PAH Papers.

8. Mrs. Mabel Reed to Ralph Gregory, undated, Phoebe Apperson Hearst Historical Society, St. Clair, Mo.; Ralph Gregory, "To Dedicate Memorial to Famous Franklin County Woman Sunday," The Washington Missourian, 1 August 1963.

9. H. S. Forte, Pen Pictures from the Garden World: Santa Clara County (Chicago, 1888).

10. Owens and James, Sons of Frontiersmen, 62; Winifred Black Bonfils, The Life and Personality of Phoebe Apperson Hearst (San Francisco: J. H. Nash, 1928), 4. Missouri genealogists also list two other daughters born to the Appersons—Jennie and Bessie. Jennie was said to be beautiful and to have moved to St. Louis; Bessie to have been buried in an unmarked grave in Sullivan, Missouri. Nothing else has been found about Phoebe's sisters nor is their existence corroborated. Other biographers say that a third child died as an infant.

11. "Memoriam, Phoebe Apperson Hearst, Vice-Regent for California," Mount Vernon Ladies' Association of the Union, Mrs. John Julius Pringle, Vice-Regent for South Carolina, Minutes of the Council, 13 May 1919.

12. Ibid.

13. "A Schoolmarm at Meramec Iron Works," Rolla (Mo.) Herald, 17 January 1895, copy in Phoebe Apperson Hearst Historical Society, and notes taken by Dr. Clair V. Mann, Rolla, Mo., 5 October 1972.

14. The Missouri Transcript, 12 March 1897, copy in Phoebe Apperson Hearst Historical Society.

15. Mrs. George Eastham to Ralph Gregory, 3 March 1962, Phoebe Apperson Hearst Historical Society. Phoebe helped the academy out of debt in later years.

16. "Schoolmarm," Rolla Herald.

17. Springfield (Mo.) Daily News, 10 June 1933; Ralph Gregory to Mrs. Eastham, 6 May 1961 and 13 March 1962, Phoebe Apperson Hearst Historical Society.

18. Poems from "Album of Love," written by Phoebe Apperson and R.W. Apperson, early 1860s, Sullivan, Mo., from family records of Louis Martinelli, Colfax, Calif., grandson of Ellen Patton Bowles and son of Margaret Bowles Martinelli, Phoebe Apperson Hearst Historical Society.

19. "Schoolmarm," Rolla Herald.

20. Ibid.

2. George Hearst and Marriage

1. Fremont Older and Cora Older, George Hearst, California Pioneer (Los Angeles: Westernlore, 1966), 13. Published originally in 1933 by William Randolph Hearst for private distribution only.

2. H. T. Cook, The Hard Labor Section (1923; reprint. Greenwood, S.C.: The Attic Press, 1979), 23.

3. Ralph Gregory, "George Hearst in Missouri," Bulletin of the Missouri Historical Society, January 1965, 76–77.

4. George Hearst autobiography, George Hearst Letters and Autobiography, 1877–1890, Bancroft Library, University of California, Berkeley; hereafter cited as GH Letters.

5. Gregory, "George Hearst in Missouri," 76–77.

6. Clark, Jacob Clark; W. V. N. Bay, "A Brief Sketch of the Life of the Hon. George Hearst," PAH Papers. See also Older and Older, George Hearst, 33. (The latter names George's brother as Philip.)

7. W. A. Swanberg, Citizen Hearst (New York: Scribners, Paperback, 1961), 4.

8. GH autobiography, GH Letters.

9. Edward Hardy Clark, "Reminiscences of the Hearst Family," transcript of interview by Wesley Cook, 1967, Bancroft Library, University of California, Berkeley. Hereafter cited as Clark transcript.

10. Swanberg, Citizen Hearst, 4; and Older and Older, George Hearst, 29.

11. Gregory, "George Hearst in Missouri," 77.

12. Bay, "Brief Sketch," PAH Papers.

13. W. W. Allen and R. B. Avery, California Gold Book (San Francisco, 1893), 340.

14. Bay, "Brief Sketch," PAH Papers.

15. "Death of Senator Hearst," New York Times, 1 March 1891, 1; and Bay.

16. Bay, "Brief Sketch," PAH Papers.

17. Gregory, "George Hearst in Missouri," 77; and records from Phoebe Apperson Hearst Historical Society.

18. Deposition of George Hearst, Hearst v. Holligan et al, 120, U.S. Circuit Court, S. Missouri District, 1873, p. 132.

19. Gregory, "George Hearst in Missouri," 79.

20. GH autobiography, GH Letters.

21. Ibid.

22. Deposition of George Hearst, 1873, 139.

23. GH autobiography, GH Letters.

24. Ibid.

25. Ibid.

26. "George Hearst. B. J. Watson Tells a Story of Early Days," Nevada City Herald, 18 January 1889.

27. GH autobiography, GH Letters.

28. Allen and Avery, California Gold Book, 331–32; "George Hearst," The Resources of California (San Francisco, 1885), 16–17; and GH autobiography, GH Letters.

29. Almarin Brooks Paul Reminiscences, 1878–83, California Historical Society, San Francisco, 195–201. Hereafter cited as Paul Reminiscences.

30. Sam Henderson, "The First Citizen Hearst," Golden West, July 1974; and Catherine J. Webb, History Reconstructed: Stories of Tallman, Ianthus, Horace, and Samuel Rolfe, (Berkeley, Calif.: Privately printed, 1978), p. 99.

31. GH autobiography, GH Letters.

32. Gregory, "George Hearst in Missouri," 81.

33. Ibid., 81–83.

34. Swanberg, Citizen Hearst, 5; Rockwell D. Hunt, California and Californians, vol. 4, (Berkeley: Type-Ink, 1926), 46; "He Envied Titled Ones," New York Times, 26 June 1886, and "Death of Senator Hearst," New York Times, 1 March 1891.

35. George D. Lyman, The Saga of the Comstock Lode: Boom Days in Virginia City (New York: Charles Scribner's Sons, 1934), 53, 74; T. A. Rickard, A History of American Mining (New York: McGraw-Hill, 1932), 98.

36. PAH Papers.

37. Allen and Avery, California Gold Book, 332–33.

38. GH autobiography, GH Letters; see also John S. Hittell, The Commerce and Industries of the Pacific Coast (San Francisco, 1882); Henderson, "The First Citizen Hearst"; John S. Hittell, "Honest George Hearst," American Magazine, 21 March 1891; "Notes on the Life of George Hearst," Hearst Papers, Hearst San Simeon State Historical Monument, hereafter cited as Hearst Papers/SS; and Webb, History Reconstructed, 116. The Comstock Lode received its title from a miner who was one of the first to obtain a claim on the vein; Virginia City was named after his native state.

39. Allen and Avery, California Gold Book, 333.

40. Telegram from GH and William M. Lent, Virginia City, 13 May 1860, to Joe Clark, B. F. Sherwood and Col. Heydenfeldt, reporting the death of U.S. Army Major William M. Ormsby and calling for arms at the beginning of the Paiute War, California Archives, PAH Papers.

41. Lyman, Saga of Comstock Lode, 136, and Paul Reminiscences, 217–27.

42. Lyman, Saga of Comstock Lode, 79–80.

43. George Hearst Papers, Huntington Library, San Marino, Calif.; hereafter referred to as GH Papers.

44. Evan Dollarhide History, Biography Collection, California Historical Society, San Francisco.

45. *San Francisco Daily Evening Bulletin*, 1 August 1860.

46. Gregory, "George Hearst in Missouri," 83–84.

47. Ibid., 85–86. Hearst later sued the two men for the title and a lengthy and bitter litigation ensued between 1873 and 1876, pitting former friends and prominent citizens against one another. The case was dismissed in September 1876 in the U.S. Circuit Court, Missouri District (except for the setting aside of a quit-claim deed that meant little to George Hearst), and ultimately went to the U.S. Supreme Court. But George never regained title to the lands.

48. William M. Lent to GH, 5 October 1860, GH Papers.

49. Ibid., 8 June 1861, PAH Papers.

50. J. W. Dickinson to GH, 17 October 1860, PAH Papers.

51. Joe Clark to GH, 10 February 1861, PAH Papers.

52. See also Gregory, "George Hearst in Missouri," 84.

53. "Union Refugees in Missouri," *Harper's Weekly*, 28 December 1861, 818.

54. William Hearst to GH, 6 May 1862, PAH Papers.

55. William Lent to GH, 27 August 1862, PAH Papers.

56. Ibid., 7 October 1862.

57. "He Envied Titled Ones," *New York Times*, 25 June 1886.

58. Crawford County Marriage Contract Book A, Nos. 1, 4, 5, Steelville, Mo.; Minutes of Mount Vernon Ladies Association of the Union, Mount Vernon, Virginia, 13 May 1919. The eulogy by the Mount Vernon Ladies Association states:

Pioneer miner and forty-niner George Hearst met, fell in love with and addressed Phoebe Apperson. He was her senior by twenty-two years and she refused him, but he was not to be discouraged. An old uncle who lived in the family was greatly interested in her and spoke to her, telling her she should think well before disregarding the devotion of such a man—a strong, noble character, whose love any woman should be proud to win. She ended by accepting him. When the successful suitor told the old man of his engagement, this *deus ex machina* told him he ought to make a settlement on the young teacher that would relieve her from want in the event of his death, as he had succeeded in diverting her from her chosen profession, and, though George Hearst was not a rich man at this time, this settlement was made without the knowledge or sanction of this fiancée.

59. *Springfield* (Mo.) *Daily News*, 10 June 1933; Gregory, "George Hearst in Missouri," 84nn. 25 & 26.

60. *Springfield* (Mo.) *Daily News*, 10 June 1933; ibid; see also Leo C. Menestrina to Ralph Gregory, 1 December 1962, Phoebe Apperson Hearst Historical Society.

61. GH autobiography, GH Letters.

62. Hearst deposition, 1873, 136 and 147.

63. Ibid., 144. Passport from Headquarters Executive Department, Missouri (original in papers of Mrs. Phoebe Hearst Cooke). Passport (No. 1806), signed by George E. Leighton, Major, 12th cavalry, acting A.D.C., in St. Louis, 2 September 1862, permitting George Hearst, "a citizen of the state of Missouri, subject to military duty and not intending to avoid the performance of the same . . . to pass to _____ in the state of California without interruption; to be absent for the space of _____ days. By order of the Governor of Missouri." The passport, lacking a photograph, describes Hearst as "age 41, size 6, weight 145, eyes gray, hair sandy, nativity Missouri."

3. Early San Francisco Years

1. "Phoebe Apperson Hearst," Station KMBC radio script, San Francisco, June 1961.

2. Phoebe Hearst Browne, a god-child to Phoebe Apperson Hearst, interview with author, 14 March 1982, San Francisco; Older and Older, *George Hearst*, 122.

3. Bonfils, *Life and Personality of Phoebe Apperson Hearst*, 13.

4. Lawrence Ferlinghetti and Nancy J. Peters, *Literary San Francisco* (San Francisco: City Lights Books and Harper & Row, 1980), 37.

5. Ibid. 12. See also "The Approach to San Francisco," *Harper's Weekly*, 6 June 1857, 360–61.

6. T. H. Watkins and Roger Olmsted, *The Mirror of the Dream* (San Francisco: Scrimshaw Press, 1976), 98.

7. Ibid., 100.

8. KMBC radio script.

9. Charles Lockwood, "The Transcontinental Connection," *San Francisco Examiner & Chronicle*, 22 April 1979, 60.

10. Anne Drusilla Apperson Flint interview with W. A. Swanberg, 20 February 1960. Unless otherwise noted, Mrs. Flint's observations are from this and one other unpublished transcript (18 January 1960), kindly lent me by Mr. Swanberg, and will hereafter be cited as Flint interview.

11. Ibid.

12. William Lent to GH, 27 August 1862, PAH Papers.

13. Ibid., 7 October 1862.

14. Ibid., 24 November 1862.

15. Ibid., 20 January 1863.

16. Swanberg, *Citizen Hearst*, 9–10, referring to Mrs. Fremont Older, notes and letter dated 9 December 1866.

17. William Lent to GH, 13 October 1863, PAH Papers.

18. Swanberg, *Citizen Hearst*, 8.

19. William Lent to GH, 15 January 1863, PAH Papers.

20. Ibid., 20 January 1863.

21. Older and Older, *George Hearst*, 173.

22. KMBC radio script.

23. Older and Older, *George Hearst*, 159, 211.

24. Ibid., 138.

25. Swanberg, *Citizen Hearst*, 11, quoting the *Sacramento Bee* in John Bruce, *Gaudy Century: The Story of San Francisco's Hundred Years of Robust Journalism* (New York: Random House, 1948).

26. "He Envied Titled Ones," *New York Times*, 25 June 1886.

4. Mother and Miner

1. GH to PAH, 14 September 1864, PAH Papers. All of George's letters are quoted verbatim and I have made no attempt to correct his grammar, punctuation, or spelling. "Feet" presumably refers to shares of silver stock.

2. Ferlinghetti and Peters, *Literary San Francisco*, 28.

3. PAH Papers.

4. Watkins and Olmsted, *Mirror of the Dream*, 101.

5. PAH Papers.

6. Lyman, *Saga of Comstock Lode*, 368, referring to *San Francisco Bulletin*, 11 November 1859, 2.

7. Notebooks, PAH Papers.

8. Ibid.

9. PAH Papers.

10. Pp. 223–24.

11. Older and Older, *George Hearst*, 131.

12. Bonfils, *Life and Personality of Phoebe Apperson Hearst*, 22.

13. Older and Older, *George Hearst*, 139.

14. PAH Papers.

15. Ibid.

16. Older and Older, *George Hearst,* 139.

17. *California Gold Book,* 333.

18. *The Great Diamond Hoax and Other Stirring Incidents in the Life of Asbury Harpending* (Norman: University of Oklahoma Press, 1958), 116.

19. *California Gold Book,* 338.

20. Hunt, *California and Californians,* 4:45.

21. As told to the author by Carroll E. B. Peeke, 31 August 1982, San Francisco.

22. Ken Murray, *The Golden Days of San Simeon* (Garden City, N.Y.: Doubleday, 1971), 3.

23. Swanberg, *Citizen Hearst,* 12–14.

5. High Times, Low Times

1. Older and Older, *George Hearst,* 11.

2. PAH to Eliza Pike, 16, 17, 25 June 1864, PAH Papers.

3. Swanberg, *Citizen Hearst,* 12.

4. Ibid., 12–13, refers to Mrs. Fremont Older, notes, letters; and Edmond D. Coblentz, *William Randolph Hearst, A Portrait in His Own Words* (New York: Simon and Schuster, 1952), 8.

5. Swanberg, *Citizen Hearst,* 13–14; Coblentz, *William Randolph Hearst,* 10–12.

6. Swanberg, 14.

7. 2 July 1865, PAH Papers.

8. Inventory of Chestnut Street house, PAH Papers.

9. Notes from diary kept by PAH in 1866, Phoebe Hearst Cooke papers, private collection.

10. PAH to Eliza Pike, 18 September 1866, PAH Papers. Ellen Patton married Caleb Bowles in 1868 and named two of their three children after George and Phoebe Hearst. Bowles bought a farm near San Simeon. Despite George's suit against the Patton heirs for loss of his Missouri land, Ellen and Phoebe remained lifelong friends. Patton descendants claim that Dr. Patton originally lent George Hearst money for his trip to California, for which Hearst put up his property deeds as security, in anticipation of sharing gold rush spoils with Dr. Patton. From a recorded account by William F. Patton to the author, Sacramento, 9 November 1982.

11. "The Resources of California," a monthly publication, San Francisco, January–February 1885, 17 (in catalogued Hearst files, San Francisco Public Library).

12. GH autobiography, GH Letters.

13. Allen and Allen, *California Gold Book,* 341.

14. *Mark Twain's Autobiography,* (New York: Harper & Brothers, 1924), 2:13–15. Emphasis is Twain's.

15. GH to PAH, 12 March 1868, PAH Papers.

16. Flint interview, 18 January 1960.

17. GH Memorabilia, PAH Papers.

18. Mrs. Blanche Hill (first wife to George Randolph Hearst and mother of Phoebe Hearst Cooke) to author, 1 April 1982.

19. GH memorabilia, PAH Papers.

20. Ibid.; and GH to PAH, 21 March 1868, PAH Papers, and records at Hearst San Simeon State Historical Monument.

21. Ann Miller (former curator, Hearst San Simeon State Historical Monument) to author, 23 June 1982.

22. Don Jesus was administrator of the San Miguel Mission (1841–43) and justice of the peace at San Luis Obispo in 1846. He was captured by Americans in battles with the Mexicans but was paroled. When Colonel John C. Frémont captured an Indian servant of Don Jesus' and shot him as a spy, Don Jesus broke his parole and was arrested by Frémont and condemned to death. Señora Pico, her fourteen children, and many San Luis Obispo Spanish-Californian women threw themselves at Frémont's feet and begged for Don Jesus'

life. When Frémont's own officers joined the request, Frémont granted a pardon to Pico, who became a lifelong and useful friend to Americans. After the war with Mexico, in which Don Jesus helped secure California for the United States, he lived on the Piedra Blanca Ranch, serving as assessor of San Luis County and as a member of the California assembly (1852–53).

23. Older and Older, *George Hearst*, 169–73. The Mexican government bought the Babicora ranch for $2.5 million in 1953; see Swanberg, *Citizen Hearst*, 631.

24. James Van Ness to GH, 20 May 1865, San Luis Obispo, PAH Papers.

25. Ibid., 17 October 1865. Graves was another agent of GH's.

26. Ibid., 28 November 1865.

27. 20 October 1866, PAH Papers.

28. James Van Ness to unknown person, 17 February 1869, PAH Papers.

29. James Van Ness to GH, 18 September 1869, PAH Papers.

30. 2 February 1870, PAH Papers.

31. PAH Papers.

32. PAH Papers. A "wharfinger" is a manager.

33. James Van Ness to unknown person, 31 May 1866, PAH Papers.

34. Thomas Edwin Farish, *The Gold Hunters of California* (Chicago: M.A. Donohue, 1904), 215.

35. GH autobiography, GH Letters.

36. Older and Older, *George Hearst*, 137–38.

37. Bay, "Brief Sketch," PAH Papers.

38. PAH Papers. "Leland" may have been Leland Stanford.

39. PAH to Eliza Pike, 18 November 1866, PAH Papers. "Queen Emma" was from Hawaii; Mrs. Montieth was a seamstress. Alice was a maid.

40. Ibid., 9 December 1866.

41. Ibid., 20 February 1867.

42. Ibid., 29 March 1867.

43. Ibid., 19 June 1867.

44. Ibid., 21 July 1867.

45. GH to PAH, 27 August 1867, PAH Papers.

46. PAH to Pike, 15 September 1867, PAH Papers.

47. Ibid., 8 December 1867.

48. GH to PAH, 11 December 1867, PAH Papers.

6. Travels and Tribulations

1. PAH to Eliza Pike, 7 June 1868, PAH Papers.

2. Ibid., 10 June 1868.

3. Ibid., 5 July 1868.

4. Ibid.

5. Ibid.

6. Ibid., 29 July 1868.

7. Ibid., undated.

8. Harpending, *The Great Diamond Hoax*, 117.

9. Lent had trouble raising money to pay his indebtedness. In a letter to George Hearst Lent wrote (in jest) that he had "offered Ralston [owner of the Bank of California] Mrs. Lent to secure a loan. [Ralston] said it was 'not his business to have anything to do with a married woman.'" William Lent to GH, 21 January 1868, PAH Papers.

10. Harpending, *The Great Diamond Hoax*, 114.

11. Farrish, *The Gold Hunters of California*, 215–19.

12. Allen and Avery, *California Gold Book*, 334–35.

13. Older and Older, *George Hearst*, 155.

14. Ibid., chap. 22.

15. Farish, *The Gold Hunters of California*, 216–17.

16. Allen and Avery, *California Gold Book*, 335–36.

17. Farish, *The Gold Hunters of California*, 217–18.

18. Older and Older, *George Hearst*, 143, 162.

19. "He Envied Titled Ones," *New York Times*, 25 June 1886.

20. Forte, "George Hearst," in *Resources of California*, 16–17.

21. Hittell, *Commerce and Industries of the Pacific Coast*, 301.

22. Harpending, *The Great Diamond Hoax*, 114–16.

23. Oscar T. Shuck, *Bench and Bar in California* (San Francisco: The Occident Printing House, 1888), 247–49.

24. PAH Papers.

25. B. A. Haggin to GH, 12 November 1872, PAH Papers.

26. Daniel Cohen, "Charles Tiffany's 'Fancy Goods' Shop and How It Grew," *Smithsonian*, December 1987, 58.

27. Box 64, PAH Papers.

28. Thurman Wilkins, *Clarence King: A Biography* (New York: Macmillan Co., 1958), 172.

29. GH autobiography, GH Letters.

30. Alonzo Phelps, "George Hearst," *Contemporary Biography of California's Representative Men* (San Francisco, 1882), 2:9–10.

31. "As Told in Corea," by Frank G. Carpenter, (Washington, D.C.) *Evening Star*, 11 May 1895, quoting General Clarence Greathouse, "foreign advisor to the King of Corea" and a former associate of California miners; lawyer for George Hearst.

32. GH to PAH, 30 January 1869, PAH Papers.

33. Ibid., 11 November 1869.

34. Ibid., 18 December 1871.

35. PAH to GH, 14 July 1868, PAH Papers. The Chestnut Street house had been rented.

36. Ibid.

37. Ibid., 30 July 1868.

38. Ibid., 19 August 1868.

39. Ibid., 17 September 1868.

40. Ibid., 29 September 1868.

41. Ibid., 4 October 1868.

42. Ibid., 10 October 1868.

43. Ibid.; and PAH to Eliza Pike, 2 and 27 November 1868.

44. PAH to GH, 29 November 1868, PAH Papers.

45. PAH to Eliza Pike, 27 November 1868, PAH Papers.

46. Ibid., 10 February 1869.

47. Ibid., 8 January 1869.

48. Ibid. Lillie Hitchcock's marriage to Benjamin Howard Coit was the social highlight of 1869. He was a handsome Arizona mining man and later a "caller" on the San Francisco Stock Board. The couple soon separated (Coit died in 1885) and Lillie became a devotee of the San Francisco Fire Department, played poker, smoked cigarettes, and spent much of her life in Paris after 1903 when a deranged relative took a shot at her in a San Francisco hotel. When she died in 1929 she left funds for a statue to commemorate the Volunteer Fire Department and to beautify the city, which led to construction of Coit Tower on top of San Francisco's Telegraph Hill. See: David F. Myrick, *San Francisco's Telegraph Hill* (Berkeley, Howell-North Books, 1972), 75–6.

49. Ibid., 10 February 1869.

50. Ibid., 8 May 1870.

51. Ibid., 26 January 1870. Ellen Patton Bowles was Phoebe's friend from Missouri.

52. Ibid.

53. Ibid.

54. Brooks biography. Alice Booth is not the same as a maid mentioned in chapter 5.

55. PAH to Eliza Pike, fragment, 8 August 1870, PAH Papers.

56. Ibid., 26 January 1870.

57. Ibid., 13 November 1870 and 10 August 1872.

58. Ibid., 10 August 1872.

59. Ibid., 28 August 1871.

60. Ibid., 13–19 November 1870.

61. Ibid.

62. Ibid., fragment, 22 May 1871.

63. Ibid.

7. Europe and Beyond

1. PAH to Jeannie Peck, 15 April 1885, Peck Papers, Huntington Library, San Marino, Calif. Mrs. James Peck was the mother of Orrin and Janet Peck, whose acquaintance Phoebe made on her maiden voyage to San Francisco. See Chapter 3.

2. PAH to Eliza Pike, 8 February 1873, PAH Papers.

3. GH to PAH, 31 March 1873, PAH Papers.

4. PAH to Eliza Pike, 26 September 1873, PAH Papers.

5. PAH to GH, 28 July 1873, PAH Papers. The Monitor and Caribo were mines.

6. Ibid., 25 March 1873.

7. Ibid., 1 April 1873.

8. Ibid., incomplete, [April?] 1873.

9. GH to PAH, undated and incomplete, PAH papers. GH noted his collar size was 15½.

10. Ibid., 17 July [1873?].

11. Ibid., undated and incomplete, [1873 or 1874?].

12. PAH to GH, undated and incomplete, [April 1873?], PAH Papers.

13. PAH, 11 May 1873.

14. GH to PAH, 27 May 1873, PAH Papers.

15. Ibid., 30 May 1873.

16. Ibid.

17. PAH to GH, 17 May 1873, PAH Papers.

18. Ibid.

19. Ibid.

20. Ibid.

21. PAH to GH, 5 June 1873, PAH Papers.

22. Ibid., 15 June 1873.

23. Ibid., 5 June 1873.

24. Ibid., 15 June 1873.

25. Ibid.

26. Ibid., 5 June 1873.

27. Ibid., 15 June 1873.

28. Ibid., 3 August 1873.

29. Ibid., 29 June 1873; 13 and 28 July 1873.

30. Ibid., 28 July 1873.

31. Ibid., 5 June 1873.

32. Ibid., 15 June 1873.

33. GH to PAH, 20 June 1873, PAH Papers.

34. Ibid., 19 August 1873.

35. PAH to GH, 29 June 1873, PAH Papers.

36. Ibid.

37. Ibid.

38. Ibid. and 28 July 1873.

39. Ibid., 8 August and 18 November 1873.

40. WRH to GH, 13 October 1873, WRH Papers.

41. PAH to GH, 28 July 1873, PAH Papers.

42. WRH to GH, 23 October 1873 (postscript by PAH), WRH Papers.

43. PAH to GH, 8 August 1873, PAH Papers.

44. Ibid., 2 September 1873. Clarence Greathouse was a friend and lawyer.

45. Ibid., 16 August 1873.

46. Ibid., 20–23 September 1873.

47. Ibid., 16 August 1873.

48. Ibid., 23 August 1873.

49. PAH to Eliza Pike, 26 September 1873, PAH Papers; PAH to GH, 2 September 1873, PAH Papers.

50. PAH to GH, 20–23 September 1873, PAH Papers.

51. Ibid.

52. WRH to GH, 13 October 1873, WRH Papers; PAH to GH, 5 October 1873, PAH Papers.

53. PAH to GH, 14 October 1873, PAH Papers.

54. Ibid.

55. Ibid.

56. GH to PAH, 4 October 1873, PAH Papers.

57. Ibid., 19 December 1873.

58. PAH to GH, 21 November 1873, PAH Papers.

59. Ibid., 3 December 1873.

60. PAH to GH, 21 November 1873, PAH Papers. WRH to GH, 15 November 1873, WRH Papers.

61. Some years later they bought the well head and had it shipped to California. It became the centerpiece of the Hacienda del Pozo de Verona, over which they would fight for possession, and a symbol of their fondness for the same things. The well head would finally reside at Willie's own mountain-top palace at San Simeon. It was a prominent reminder that their trips together to Europe were orgies of culture and consumption.

62. PAH to GH, 3 December 1873, PAH Papers. Willie was taking German, French, and arithmetic lessons.

63. Ibid.

64. Ibid.

65. PAH to Eliza Pike, 10 December 1873, PAH Papers.

66. PAH to GH, 15 December 1873, PAH Papers.

67. Ibid., 20 December 1873.

68. PAH to Eliza Pike, 10 February 1874, PAH Papers.

69. GH to PAH, 31 January 1874, PAH Papers.

70. Ibid., 10 January 1874.

71. GH to WRH, 8 February 1874, PAH Papers. Mrs. Peck's boy is Orrin.

72. R. C. Chambers to GH, 7 January 1874; PAH Papers.

73. GH to PAH, 31 January 1874, PAH Papers.

74. Ibid., 8 February 1874.

75. Ibid., 10 [March?] 1874.

76. Ibid., 28 February 1874.

77. Ibid., 10 [March?] 1874.

78. PAH to Eliza Pike, 10 December 1873, PAH Papers.

79. PAH to GH, 20 April 1874, PAH Papers.

80. PAH Papers; "Arrived today. Well. Rough voyage. Leave here Wednesday night."

8. Prosperity and Politics

1. "Life of George Hearst," unpublished page proofs prepared for "Chronicles of the Kings, 1887–1890," 376, Hubert Howe Bancroft Papers, Bancroft Library, University of California, Berkeley.

2. Coblentz, *William Randolph Hearst*, 13 (referring to a column written by WRH).

3. PAH to Eliza Pike, 27 December 1875, PAH Papers.

4. Ibid.

5. PAH to Eliza Pike, 24 and 29 September 1876, PAH Papers.

6. Swanberg, *Citizen Hearst*, 20.

7. PAH to Eliza Pike, 5 January 1877, PAH Papers. In this letter PAH curiously changed the salutation to "Mrs. Pike" instead of "Eliza."

8. Ibid.

9. WRH Papers.

10. WRH to GH, 12 January 1879, WRH Papers, and PAH to GH, 5 February 1879, PAH Papers.

11. Coblentz, *William Randolph Hearst*, 15–16.

12. Ibid., 15–19.

13. "Mr. Hearst Order to Leave France, Articles in His Newspapers," *London Times*, 3

September 1930. With characteristically sardonic humor, Hearst told the press when ordered to leave France for having published articles in a German nationalist newspaper suggesting that the World War I peace treaties were, as he put it, "generally regarded as being extremely prejudicial to French interests":

I have no complaint to make. The officials were extremely polite. They said I was an enemy of France, and a danger in their midst. They made me feel quite important. They said I could stay a little while longer if I desire, that they would take a chance on nothing disastrous happening to the Republic. But I told them that I did not want to take the responsibility of endangering the great French nation; that America had saved it once during the War, and I would save it again by leaving. . . .

The whole affair reminds me of the story of the rather effeminate young man who went to call on his best girl and found her in the arms of another young fellow. The effeminate youth went into the hall, took up his successful rival's umbrella, broke it, and said, "Now, I hope it rains." You see, for the French national policy of "revenge" to be completely successful, we will have to have rain.

14. Coblentz, William Randolph Hearst, 8, 13–15.

15. Thomas Barry Diary, May–August 1879, photocopy, Bancroft Library, University of California, Berkeley.

16. Ibid.

17. Thomas Barry to PAH, 11 August 1879, PAH Papers.

18. Ibid., 17–27 August 1879.

19. Ibid.

20. PAH Papers.

21. WRH to PAH, September [?], 1879, WRH Papers.

22. Ibid., 21 September 1879.

23. Ibid., 27 September 1879.

24. Ibid., undated, 1879.

25. Swanberg, Citizen Hearst, 25 (referring to Oliver Carlson and Ernest Sutherland Bates, Hearst, Lord of San Simeon [New York: Viking Press, 1936], 39). The text quoted here was not found in WRH Papers or Letters.

26. WRH Papers.

27. Coblentz, William Randolph Hearst, 20–21.

28. PAH to Eliza Pike, 27 December 1875, PAH Papers.

29. Brooks biography, pt. 1, chap. 5.

30. Swanberg, Citizen Hearst, 26.

31. "Society Notes," San Francisco Chronicle, 19 September 1880, 2-1.

32. Flint interview, 18 January 1960; Swanberg, Citizen Hearst, 19–20.

33. Julia Altrocchi, Spectacular San Franciscans (New York: E. P. Dutton, 1949), 252.

34. John Tebbel, The Life and Good Times of W. R. Hearst (New York: E.P. Dutton, 1952), 25–26; Bonfils, Life and Personality of Phoebe Apperson Hearst, 54. The mob attack was likely part of labor unrest during the 1877 depression.

35. Carol Roland, "The California Kindergarten Movement: A Study in Class and Social Feminism," Ph.D. diss., University of California, Riverside, 1980, 95–96, referring to Sarah Cooper, The Reasons Why (San Francisco, 1882). The deacons' charges were that Cooper was "un-Presbyterian in principle and practice and in life," and that she associated with atheists, an allusion to Cooper's cousin, Robert Ingersoll.

36. Mrs. Sarah B. Cooper, Tenth annual report of the Hearst Free Kindergartens, Golden Gate Kindergarten Association, 1889, 42; Eleventh annual report, 1890, 34–37, San Francisco Public Library.

37. Ibid.

38. "The Listener," Boston Traveler, 13 September 1899; "Kindergartens," San Francisco Daily Report, 21 December 1883; "A Noble Mission," undated newspaper article, PAH Papers.

39. Ibid., "Work among Needy Children," The Evangelist, 1896.

40. By 1901 kindergartens were part of the Washington, D.C., system and in 1913

California law required school districts to conduct a kindergarten wherever twenty-five parents petitioned for one.

41. *Oakland Saturday Night*, 10 August 1901. "Practical results" referred to the training of twenty-four black kindergarten teachers.

42. "Work among Needy Children."

43. PAH to Sarah Cooper, 26 May 1889, quoted in Tenth annual report, Golden Gate Kindergarten, 1889, 43.

44. PAH to Sarah Cooper, 29 July 1889, PAH Papers.

45. Ibid., January 1890, quoted in Eleventh annual report, Golden Gate Kindergarten, 1890, 35.

46. Ibid.

47. Twelfth annual report, Golden Gate Kindergarten Association, 1891, 57–58.

48. Roland, "The California Kindergarten Movement" 144–46, 167–68; *San Francisco Examiner*, 12 December 1896.

49. Jerome A. Hart, *In Our Second Century* (San Francisco: The Pioneer Press, 1931), 82–83.

50. Ibid., and A. James McCollum, "William Randolph Hearst," lecture presented to the Family Club, 30 August 1973. *Examiner* owner was William S. Moss.

51. GH autobiography, GH Letters.

52. GH to PAH, 16 December 1882, PAH Papers.

53. Ibid., 21 December 1884.

54. Maggie Hamilton to PAH, 13 October 1881, PAH Papers.

55. Flint interview, 18 January 1969.

56. WRH to PAH, [1882?], WRH Papers.

57. Altrocchi, *Spectacular San Franciscans*, 252.

58. *Brooklyn* (N.Y.) *Standard-Union*, 11 September 1901.

59. PAH diary, 9–20 January 1882, PAH Papers.

60. Ibid.

61. Ibid.

62. WRH Papers.

63. WRH to PAH, undated "On The Train" [1882?], WRH Papers.

64. Coblentz, *William Randolph Hearst*, 22.

65. Swanberg, *Citizen Hearst*, 30–31.

66. Former Hearst employees to author, oral interviews, 1984.

67. WRH to GH, 19 April 1883, WRH Papers.

68. Coblentz, *William Randolph Hearst*, 23.

69. PAH to WRH, 5 May 1884, PAH Papers.

70. WRH to PAH, April 1883, WRH Papers.

71. Ibid., 5 June 1883.

72. PAH account book, 1883, PAH Papers.

73. WRH to PAH, 5 June 1883, WRH Papers.

74. Ibid., undated [spring 1883?].

75. Ibid.

76. Ibid., April 1884.

77. Ibid., undated [spring 1883?].

78. Ibid., 5 June 1883.

79. WRH to GH, 5 January 1884, WRH Papers.

80. WRH to PAH, undated [1884?].

81. Ibid.

82. Ibid., March 1884.

83. Ibid., 27 April 1884.

84. Ibid.

85. Ibid., undated [1884].

86. PAH to WRH, 20 April 1884, PAH Papers.

87. Ibid.

88. Ibid., 5 May 1884.

89. Ibid.

90. Ibid., 30 April 1884.

91. Ibid.

92. Ibid., 5 May 1884.

93. "Uncle George," *Oakland Daily Tribune*, 10 January 1891.

94. "The Political Outlook," *Daily Alta California*, 2 June 1882, 2-1.

95. *Chico Enterprise*, 9 June 1882, quoting *San Juan Times*.

96. Ibid., quoting *Sacramento Bee*.

97. "Hearst for Governor," *Chico Enterprise*, 2 June 1882, 1-1.

98. *Oakland Daily Tribune*, 10 January 1891. He used the *Examiner* as his platform in that fight. Fourth and Townsend was the address of the Central and Southern Pacific Railroad office.

99. "General Stoneman Nominated for Governor," *Daily Alta California*, 24 June 1882, 1–4.

100. PAH to WRH, 10 November 1884, PAH Papers.

101. WRH to PAH, undated ["May——the don't know"], 1884, WRH Papers.

102. "Hearst's Boodle Fight," *New York Times*, 11 January 1887, 1.

103. "Rich Congressmen," *Washington, D.C., Evening Star*, 25 March 1893.

104. "Hearst's Boodle Wins," *New York Times*, 19 January 1887, 1.

105. "Mr. Hearst and the Senate," editorial, *Daily Examiner*, 12 May 1883, quoting editorial "Not True," *Oakland Independent*.

106. "A Serenade. George Hearst Congratulated by the Iroquois Club," *San Francisco Call*, 21 January 1887, 1–4.

107. "Chronicles of the Kings," Hubert Howe Bancroft Papers.

108. Flint interview, 18 January 1960.

109. WRH to PAH, undated [possibly early 1890s, shortly after GH's death in 1891], WRH Papers.

9. Challenges and Disappointments

1. PAH to WRH, 12 May 1884, PAH Papers.

2. Ibid.

3. Ibid., 13 May 1884.

4. Harvard records, July 1884, WRH Papers.

5. PAH to WRH, 10 November 1884, PAH Papers.

6. Ibid., and 15 November 1884.

7. PAH to GH, incomplete and undated [1884?], PAH Papers.

8. Alfred A. Wheeler to WRH, 15 March 1885, WRH Papers.

9. "Is W. R. Hearst Married?" undated newspaper article [1888 or 1889?], PAH Papers.

10. WRH to PAH, undated [1884 or 1885?], WRH Papers.

11. Ibid.

12. Ibid., undated [1884 or 1885?].

13. Ibid., undated [1884 or 1885?].

14. Swanberg, *Citizen Hearst*, 44.

15. WRH to GH, 4 January 1885, WRH Papers.

16. Ibid., 29 January 1885.

17. Ibid.

18. Ibid.

19. WRH to PAH, undated [spring 1885?], WRH Papers.

20. J. H. Rathbone to "little Willie," 23 August [1885?], WRH Papers

21. WRH to PAH and GH, telegram, 4 October 1885, WRH Papers.

22. Flint interview, 18 January 1960.

23. Orrin Peck to PAH, undated [March 1885?], Orrin Peck Papers, California Historical Society, San Francisco.

24. Oliver W. Huntington, Chemical Laboratory, Harvard College, to GH, 11 November 1885, PAH Papers. Mr. Huntington was thanking GH for his gift of minerals.

25. Swanberg, *Citizen Hearst*, 41.

26. PAH to GH, 22 October 1885, PAH Papers.

27. Ibid.

28. Ibid., 28 October 1885.

29. Ibid., 12 November 1885.

30. Ibid.

31. Swanberg, *Citizen Hearst*, 37–38.

32. PAH to GH, 12 November 1885, PAH Papers.

33. Ibid., 22 October 1885.

34. Ibid., 29 January 1885; fragment, undated [1885?]; 15 April 1885.

35. Ibid., 12 April 1885.

36. WRH to GH, 23 November 1885, WRH Papers.

37. PAH to GH, 4 January 1885, PAH Papers.

38. J. P. Oliver to PAH, 6 February 1886, PAH Papers.

39. WRH Papers.

40. William Randolph Hearst, Jr., to author, 22 December 1981. His son, William Randolph Hearst III, was a Harvard graduate; David Hearst's daughter, Millicent, was the first to obtain a college diploma.

41. WRH to GH, 25 or 26 January, 1886, WRH Papers.

42. GH to WRH, undated [1886 or 1887?], WRH Papers.

43. WRH to GH, undated [1885 or 1886?], WRH Papers.

44. Ibid., undated [1886 or 1887?].

45. "Miss Eleanor Calhoun," *The Washington Herald*, undated; "Daniel Rochat, *Atlanta Constitution*, undated, from PAH Papers; and "Eleanor Calhoun," *San Francisco Call*, 5 February 1887, from California Section, California State Library, Sacramento.

46. PAH to Mrs. [James] Peck, undated [early 1887], Washington, D.C., Peck Papers.

47. Flint interview, 18 January 1960.

48. Janet Peck to Orrin Peck, undated [1892?], Orrin Peck Papers. Anne Apperson was sixteen when the letter was written. Miss Egan was Phoebe's secretary.

49. PAH to Orrin Peck, 22 December 1886, Peck Papers.

50. WRH to PAH, undated [1886], WRH Papers.

51. Ibid., undated [1886?].

52. Ibid., undated [1886].

53. Ibid.

54. WRH to PAH, undated [1886], Chihuahua, Mexico.

55. PAH to GH, 19 February 1887, Phoebe Hearst Cooke Papers.

56. WRH to PAH, undated [1887], WRH Papers.

57. Older and Older, *George Hearst*, 209.

58. Swanberg, *Citizen Hearst*, 44 (letter probably written in January 1887).

59. WRH to PAH, undated [1887], WRH Papers.

60. Bancroft, "Life of George Hearst," unpublished proof sheets prepared for *Chronicles of the Kings*, 408–9, Hubert Howe Bancroft Papers.

61. WRH to GH, undated [1887?], WRH Papers. Mike DeYoung was an owner of the *San Francisco Chronicle*, a major rival newspaper.

62. Ibid., undated [1887?]. Stump was GH's business manager.

63. Coblentz, *William Randolph Hearst*, 34–35.

64. "Wm. R. Hearst," *New York Journalist*, 29 December 1888, quoting John Russell Young, 2; A. James McCullum, "William Randolph Hearst," lecture, 30 August 1973, to the Family Club, San Francisco.

65. WRH to GH, undated [1888?], WRH Papers. The S.P. was the Southern Pacific Railroad.

66. Bancroft, "Life of George Hearst," 408.

67. GH autobiography, GH Letters.

68. PAH to GH, 21 July 1888, PAH Papers.

69. Ibid., 7 August 1888.

70. Swanberg, *Citizen Hearst*, 39.

71. Charlotte Newbegin, owner of Tillman Place Bookstore, San Francisco, to author, 24 October 1986, based on anecdote told her by her late husband.

72. PAH to GH, 21 July 1888, PAH Papers.

73. Ibid., 11 August 1888.

74. Ibid., 20 August 1888.

10. Love, Death, and Independence

1. PAH to GH, 15 March 1889, PAH Papers. The house was on a triangular lot at the intersection of New Hampshire, 20th, and O Streets on the south side of Dupont Circle. It later was used as the Italian Embassy, and was torn down in 1964 to make way for an office building. See James M. Goode, *Capital Losses* (Washington, D.C.: Smithsonian Institution Press, 1979), 93–7.

2. Ibid., 2 August 1889.

3. Ibid., 27 August 1889.

4. Ibid., 25 August 1889.

5. Ibid., and 13 and 30 September 1889.

6. Mary W. Kincaid to GH, 28 August 1889, PAH Papers.

7. PAH to GH, 16 September 1889, PAH Papers.

8. "Racing News and Notions," *New York Times*, 2 March 1891; *Boston Courier*, 29 June 1890; *Chicago Times*, 30 November 1890; "Pastime of Millions," *The Thoroughbred of California*, April–August 1950.

9. WRH to GH, telegram, 28 June 1888, WRH Papers.

10. PAH to GH, 28 September 1889, PAH Papers.

11. Ibid., 16 October 1889.

12. WRH to GH, undated [1889?], WRH Papers.

13. Ibid., undated [1889?].

14. Ibid., undated [1889?].

15. Ibid., and undated [1889?].

16. "A Young Napoleon Abroad," *Daily Alta California* (San Francisco), 15 January 1889, 1.

17. WRH to PAH, January 1889, WRH Papers. Phoebe was a benefactor to the sculptor Leopoldo Ansiglioni, with whom she became acquainted on one of her European trips, and commissioned several works—busts of herself and Will as well as a statute of Galatea, according to three 1879 receipts and a letter dated 24 June 1879 in the PAH Papers. She gave the sculptor permission in 1882 to sell the Galatea to an Englishman (it now is on display at Avery Hill Park Winter Garden, England) and commissioned another for herself. In November 1889 she was still subsidizing the sculptor and may have purchased the second Galatea statue then, which ultimately went to her Hacienda in California. In 1922 Will moved the statue to San Simeon where it is displayed on the Main Terrace. See *Friends of Hearst Castle*, newsletter, August 1989, excerpting a paper by Robert Pavlik, Historian, San Simeon Region, California State Parks.

18. Carl Oscar Borg to PAH, 22 September 1918, PAH Papers.

19. "Washington Chat," *Council Bluffs* (Iowa) *Daily Nonpareil*, 17 June [1890?].

20. "To be Shown for Charity," *Washington, D.C. News*, 26 March 1895.

21. *Philadelphia North American*, 8 August 1892.

22. "A Californian in Washington," *New York Sun*, 22 February 1890; "New Washington Homes," *New York Sun*, 9 February 1890.

23. *New York Sun*, 9 February 1890.

24. *Springfield* (Mo.) *Republican*, 10 June 1890.

25. "Some Homes under the Administration," *Demorest's Family Magazine*, October 1890.

26. Ibid., and *Philadelphia North American*, 8 August 1892.

27. "Slipped on Sawyer's Rugs," *Chicago Herald*, 15 December 1890.

28. "Social Events," *Washington Post*, 20 February 1889.

29. "Senator Hearst's Ideas," *Tombstone* (Ariz.) *Prospector*, 6 May 1889; *Los Angeles Times*, 25 April 1889.

30. "She is not of the Smart Set," *San Francisco Town Talk*, 16 February 1901.

31. "Special Correspondence of *The Sunday Republic*," undated newspaper clipping, PAH Papers.

32. "Another Thursday house . . . ," *Burlington* (Vt.) *Free Press*, 7 February 1889.

33. "Dinners and Dinner Givers," *St. Louis* (Mo.) *Post Dispatch*, 3 February 1889.

34. "Washington Social Life," *Philadelphia Ledger*, 2 March 1895; "Anton Seidl's Illness," *New York Daily News*, 1 March 1895; *Boston Globe*, 17 May 1895; "All in the Gayest Mode," *Chicago Tribune*, 25 March 1895.

35. "The Opinion of a Millionaire's Wife," *Denver Times*, 15 March 1890.

36. "Mrs. Hearst's Boarding House," *Hutchinson* (Kans.) *News*, 2 May 1889.

37. Robert Graves, "Washington Gossip," *Topeka* (Kans.) *Capital*, 8 June 1890.

38. Ibid.

39. "Senator Hearst," *San Francisco Examiner*, 26 March 1892; Graves, "Washington Gossip."

40. "Senator George Hearst of California . . . ," *New York Public Service*, 15 March 1890; "Flies in the Senate," *Savannah Times*, 25 June 1890.

41. "Hearst and Waterman," *San Bernardino* (Calif.) *Courier*, 1 June 1889; "The Menace of Brains," *New York Evening Telegram*, 10 January 1889; *Denver Times*, 10 April 1890.

42. "Hoodwinking and the Strikers", *San Francisco Californian*, 16 June 1890; *New York Tribune*, 30 December 1888; "A Narrow Escape," *San Francisco Chronicle*, 5 April 1890.

43. "Senator Hearst . . . represented as an illiterate man," St. Paul (Minn.) *Globe*, 23 February [1889 or 1890?], PAH Papers, regarding "Burd" story; Isabel McKenna Duffield, "Washington in the '90s," *Overland Monthly*, October 1929, 318 (she was the daughter of Rep. Joseph McKenna, later U.S. Supreme Court Associate Justice (1898–1926), appointed by President McKinley).

44. Irwin C. Stump to GH, 22 March 1890, PAH Papers.

45. "He Is Much Improved in Health, and Is Able to Get Around," *San Francisco Evening Post*, 1 June 1889.

46. "Vanquished at Last," *San Francisco Examiner*, 1 March 1891.

47. Peck Papers.

48. "Senator Hearst has Cancer," *Fort Wayne* (Ind.) *Gazette*, 7 January 1891; *The West End*, 10 January 1891; "Cheerful and Hopeful, Mrs. Hearst Denies Reports of the Senator's Dangerous Condition," California Associated Press, 14 January 1891, PAH Papers.

49. "The Case of Senator Hearst," *Grand Rapids* (Mich.) *Democrat*, 9 February 1891.

50. *Chicago Herald*, January 28, 1891; *Gainesville* (Ohio) *Signal*, 31 January 1891; *Des Moines* (Iowa) *Leader*, 12 February 1891; *Chicago Post*, 10 February 1891.

51. *New York Evening Telegram*, 27 December 1890; *New York Truth*, 8 January 1891.

52. Unidentified news clipping, 27 January 1891, PAH Papers.

53. "A State's Loss," unidentified news clipping, Society of California Pioneers Library, San Francisco.

54. 6 and 18 February 1891, Peck Papers.

55. *Examiner*, 1 March 1891, and "Death of Senator Hearst," *New York Times*, 1 March 1891, 1.

56. "Cost of a Funeral Trip," *New York Times*, 29 March 1891, 16; "The Subject of a Congressional Inquiry," *Philadelphia Times*, 28 February 1892; *Utica* (N.Y.) *Press*, 26 December 1895; "Congressional Funerals," *New Orleans Times-Democrat*, 28 January [1895 or 1896?], PAH Papers. Sen. William A. Peffer of Kansas in 1895 introduced a bill (S. 236) "to provide for proper disposition of the remains of deceased members of the Senate and House of Representatives who die at the capital during sessions of Congress." In floor debate on the bill, to which there was strong opposition, Peffer inserted into the *Congressional Record* an editorial from the *Springfield* (Mass.) *Republican*, "Peffer on Funeral Junkets," which called the Hearst funeral trip "probably the worst junket of the sort for years." 20 January 1895, 53rd Congress, Third Session, *Congressional Record*, 798.

57. "No Water in Their Tanks," *New York Times*, 27 March 1891, 1; "Water, Water Somewhere," *New York Times*, 28 March 1891, 1.

58. "Senator Hearst's Funeral," *San Francisco Examiner*, 16 March 1891.

59. Ibid.

60. "Uncle George," *Oakland Daily Tribune*, 10 January 1891.

61. Ibid.

62. "The Dead Senator," *San Francisco Call*, 12 March 1891; and undated, uncited obituary, PAH Papers.

63. "Announcement of the Death of Senator Hearst in the House of Representatives," Rep. Thomas J. Clunie, 28 February 1891, from *Memorial Addresses on the Life and Character of George Hearst* (Washington, D.C.: Government Printing Office, 1894), 14.

64. Ibid.

65. "Death of Senator Hearst," *New York Times*, March 1, 1891, 1.

66. Senator George G. Vest, "Eulogies in the Senate," 25 March 1892, from *Memorial Addresses*, 25.

67. Representative James G. Maguire, from *Memorial Addresses*, 56–7.

68. Senator William M. Stewart, from *Memorial Addresses*, 27.

11. New Horizons, New Challenges

1. Based on "The Annual Average Purchasing Power of the Dollar," Bureau of Labor Statistics, U.S. Department of Labor, 1985; the estate would have been valued at more than $200 million in the 1980s.

2. George Hearst's will, filed 29 April 1880, San Francisco.

3. Ibid.

4. Coblentz, *William Randolph Hearst*, 26–27; Brooks biography.

5. Brooks biography.

6. Flint interview, 18 January 1960.

7. "The Brides of the Season," *Denver Times*, 19 July 1889.

8. "Is W. R. Hearst Married?" undated [1892?], PAH Papers.

9. Swanberg, *Citizen Hearst*, 75.

10. WRH to PAH undated, aboard R.M.S. *Lucania*, WRH papers.

11. WRH to O. Peck, undated, Orrin Peck Papers.

12. PAH to Mrs. Hester Holden, 7 September 1892, PAH Papers.

13. Ibid., and WRH to PAH, letters and telegrams, 6 and 26 August 1892 and undated, WRH Papers.

14. Janet Peck to O. Peck, undated, Orrin Peck Papers.

15. Flint interview, 18 January 1960.

16. "Mrs. Hearst's Emphatic Denial," Pierre (S.D.) *Capital*, 23 January 1893; *New Haven Palladium*, 24 January 1893; "Senator Faulkner to Wed Mrs. Hearst," *New York Times*, 20 January 1893.

17. PAH to Thomas J. Grier, Homestake Mine superintendent 1884–1914, [1893?]; and PAH to Irwin C. Stump, 3 July 1892, both in PAH Papers.

18. Clark transcript; PAH to Thomas J. Grier, [1893?], PAH Papers; PAH to Irwin C. Stump, [1893?] PAH Papers; "Irwin C. Stump Killed by a Fall," unidentified newspaper article, New York, 29 October [1890s?]; Flint interview, 20 February 1960; Mildred Fielder, *The Treasure of Homestake Gold* (Aberdeen, S.D.: North Plains Press, 1970), 154.

19. PAH to Mrs. Latham, 18 March 1892, PAH Papers; "A Philanthropic Woman," *New York Journal America*, 11 February 1893.

20. "Mrs. Hearst Aims to Give City a Museum," *San Francisco WAVE*, 6 February 1892; "Mrs. Hearst's Museum," *Boston Traveller*, 27 February 1892; *Boston Weekly Journalist*, 15 December 1892; "Mrs. Hearst's Gift," *Syracuse Herald*, 29 January 1892; and PAH to Thomas J. Grier, [1893?], PAH Papers.

21. *Washington Capitol*, July 15 [1892 or 1893], and John A. Heffernan, "Newspaper Folk Regret 'Cap' Thompson's Death," unidentified and undated newspaper clipping, WRH Papers; *New York Recorder*, 26 October 1891; *Harper's Weekly*, 20 August 1892; *New York Times*, 15 August 1892; *New York Sun*, 29 February 1893; *Brooklyn Eagle*, 20 August 1893; *San Francisco Chronicle*, 1 September 1893.

22. *Illustrated American* (New York and Chicago), 22 October 1892, WRH Papers; "Washington Stories," *Baltimore News*, 7 August 1893, WRH Papers.

23. WRH to PAH, two undated letters, one from New York and one from the California Limited, Santa Fe Railroad, both in WRH Papers.

24. *San Francisco WAVE*, 18 February 1893.

25. WRH to PAH, undated [1893?], WRH Papers.

26. Flint interview, 18 January 1960. When Will learned later that Tessie, nearing seventy, needed money, he arranged to have a generous monthly check sent to her (Swanberg, *Citizen Hearst*, 541).

27. WRH to PAH, telegram, 8 November 1894, WRH Papers.

28. Ibid., November 1894.

29. *Harper's Weekly*, 29 December 1894; "Society Women are in High Glee," *Chicago Tribune*, 25 December 1894; "The Women's Paper," *Utica* (N.Y.) *Herald*, 27 December 1894.

30. *Utica* (N.Y.) *Herald*, 27 December 1894.

31. WRH to PAH, undated [1894?], WRH Papers.

32. WRH to PAH, undated [1894?]; and telegram, 4 February 1895, WRH Papers; Flint interviews, 18 January and 20 February 1960; *The American Architect and Building News*, 2 May 1896, 46.

33. Swanberg, *Citizen Hearst*, 75; "The Anaconda Mines," *San Francisco Argonaut*, 21 October 1895; *Leslie's Weekly*, 23 July 1896; *Boston Advertiser*, 13 November 1896; *San Francisco WAVE*, 5 October 1895. News reports varied, saying Mrs. Hearst's revenue from the sale ranged from $3 to $10 million.

34. "The City's Formal Thanks for the Gift of Mrs. Hearst," *Anaconda Standard*, 12 June 1898, 14.

35. PAH to WRH, telegram, [1893–95?], WRH Papers.

36. Peck Papers, Huntington Library; and "Brief in Support of the Showing That Certain Transfers to William Randolph Hearst Were Not Made in Contemplation of Death," in the Matter of the Estate of Phoebe A. Hearst, U.S. internal Revenue Bureau, First District of California, 21 May 1921, 8–9, 21–22, 24, Charles S. Wheeler Papers, Bancroft Library, Berkeley.

37. Dwight Bentel, draft history of George Hearst (1946), WRH Papers; and George Rascoe, former *Examiner* artist, to author, 12 July 1982, San Francisco.

38. "A Napoleon of Journalism," *In the Public Eye* [c. 1895], 547–48; "Now Known as 'The Journal,'" *San Francisco Call*, 10 November 1895; "Mrs. Hall's Budget, A Millionaire Proprietor and Editor," *St. Joseph* (Mo.) *Herald*, 7 December 1895; "We are Here to Stay," *Youngstown* (Ohio) *Telegram*, 8 November 1895; "One Cent World," *New York Fourth Estate*, 15 February 1896; *Printer's Ink*, 4 December 1895; *New York Town Topics*, 16 April 1896; *Scranton* (Penn.) *Truth*, 13 November 1895.

39. WRH to PAH, telegram, 16 January 1895, WRH papers.

40. WRH to PAH, [February 1895?], WRH Papers. Jennie was Mrs. Peck.

41. "Mr. Hill and Mrs. Hearst," *Syracuse Post*, 7 January 1895.

42. *Salt Lake Tribune*, 5 January 1895; *New Bedford* (Mass.) *Journal*, 5 January 1895; "Hill and the President," *Richmond Times*, 6 January 1895; and undated newspaper articles, PAH Papers.

43. PAH diary, April–June 1895, PAH Papers, and *Springfield* (Mass.) *Union*, 17 August 1895.

44. PAH to member of Peck family, 29 September 1895, Peck Papers.

45. PAH to Orrin Peck, 8 April 1896, Peck Papers.

46. Ibid.

47. Ibid , 26 May 1896.

48. The wellhead was moved to San Simeon, where it can be seen today.

49. Luther Burbank to PAH, 5 October 1912, PAH Papers. Burbank lived in Santa Rosa, California.

50. "At Hacienda del Pozo de Verona," *Santa Cruz Surf*, undated article, PAH Papers; Jacomena Maybeck, daughter-in-law of architect Bernard Maybeck, to author, 12 March 1985; Porter Garnett, "Stately Homes of California," *Sunset Magazine*, April 1914, 843–847; William E. McCann, "History of Rural Alameda Co.," 1937, 217–219, book collections, California section, California State Library. The house was 740 feet long.

51. Oscar Lewis, *Here Lived the Californians* (New York: Rinehart & Co., 1957), 236; Bonfils, *Life and Personality of Phoebe Apperson Hearst*, 114–17.

52. Janet Peck to O. Peck, undated, Janet Peck Papers; Flint interview, 20 February 1960; Swanberg, *Citzen Hearst*, 99–106; Arthur Hargrave, *The Family Story*, (San Francisco: The Family, 1978), 2–8. When the board of directors of the Bohemian Club in San Francisco—of which Will was a member—banned the *Examiner* from its clubrooms over the Hearst position on McKinley, fourteen *Examiner* employees who were members of the club resigned and started their own club—"The Family."

53. WRH to PAH, telegram, 4 November 1896, WRH Papers.

54. Swanberg, *Citizen Hearst*; Rep. Grove Lawrence Johnson, *Congressional Record*, January 8, 1897, 54th Congress, Second Session, 592–93.

55. Flint interview, 18 January 1960.

56. Ibid.

57. Ibid.

58. Julia Morgan to PAH, 10 February 1899, PAH Papers.

59. Clara Reed Anthony to a Miss Ramirez, [1896], PAH Papers.

60. A. S. Bailey, Lovelock, Nevada, to PAH, 27 March 1900, PAH Papers.

61. Note by PAH on letter from Gladys Worden to PAH, 26 June 1906, PAH Papers.

62. PAH to Mrs. Butterfield, 17 August 1886, PAH Papers.

63. "Business Women, Take Notice," *Chicago Times*, 25 December 1894 (from *New York Herald*, "A Business Woman, Lessons for Young Women from the Life of Mrs. Hearst").

64. Ibid.

65. "Statement of Mrs. P. A. Hearst's Personal Account for the months May, June, July, 1906," PAH Papers.

66. "Business Women, Take Notice," *Chicago Times*.

67. Ibid.

68. Ibid.

69. Bancroft, "Life of George Hearst," 377–79.

70. J. R. K. Kantor, "The Best Friend the University Ever Had," *California Monthly Journal*, November 1969; Brooks biography.

71. George T. Marye, Jr., chairman, Committee on Internal Administration, University of California, to PAH, 14 April 1892, PAH Papers; and PAH's personal note on back of letter from Martin Kellogg, Acting President, University of California, 20 October 1891, with Board of Regents' Resolution of Appreciation, adopted 13 October 1891, PAH Papers.

72. H. Henderson, secretary to University of California president, to PAH, 17 April 1911, PAH Papers.

73. *Utica* (N.Y.) *Observer*, 4 October 1901.

74. "An Example to Millionaires," *San Francisco Examiner*, 4 June 1899.

75. Verne A. Stadtman, ed., *The Centennial Record of the University of California, 1868–1968* (Berkeley and Los Angeles: University of California, 1968).

76. Editorial, *San Francisco Examiner*, 11 March [1905?], PAH papers.

77. "Needs of the University," *San Francisco Examiner*, 19 January 1901; "An Example to Millionaires," *San Francisco Examiner*, 4 June, 1899; and Ludwig Boltzmann, "Summer in Berkeley—1904," *Westways*, September 1976.

78. "Gifts for Lands and Buildings," 11, University of California Archives; and Annie Maybeck to PAH, 20–21 September 1918, discussing Mills College Plan and Maybeck's presentation to a Red Cross committee, referring to Maybeck's method of convincing clients of his designs' merits:

> I suppose he must have put in a eucalyptus tree or a pink geranium or some other of his hypnotizers for the committee went wild and determined to have the building. . . . For some reason when anyone is exposed to a "Maybeck" idea he either has a violent attack or he is absolutely immune.

79. Esther McCoy, *Five California Architects* (New York: Praeger Publishers, 1975), 6.

80. Kantor, "The Best Friend the University Ever Had."

81. PAH to Jacob Bert Reinstein, 22 October 1896 ("The International Competition for the Phoebe Hearst Architectural Plan for the University of California," 1900), University of California Archives.

82. "Mrs. Hearst Promotes Higher Education," *San Francisco Examiner*, 25 October 1896.

83. "Regent Phoebe A. Hearst," *The Expositor*, (undated), PAH Papers.

12. Largesse and Luxury

1. Adelaide Marquand, "Mrs. Hearst's First Session," unidentified article, 11 August 1897, PAH Papers.

2. Ibid.

3. McCoy, *Five California Architects*, 6.

4. "Mrs. Hearst's University Plan," *New York Times*, 16 January 1898, 7; "Mrs. Hearst and the University of California," *New York Times*, Saturday Supplement, 5 February 1898; Bonfils, *Life and Personality of Phoebe Apperson Hearst*, 96–105.

5. Annie Maybeck to PAH, Berlin, 8 March 1897, PAH Papers.

6. William Warren Ferrier, *Ninety Years of Education in California, 1846–1936* (Berkeley: Sather Gate Book Shop, 1937), 320–21; "Talk of Replacing the Old Buildings with New Ones," *Oroville* (Calif.) *Mercury*, 30 July 1897, 3.

7. S. M. Williams, *New York Journal* London Office, to PAH, 5 October 1898, PAH Papers.

8. J. B. Reinstein to John M. Carrère, 31 October 1898, quoting Mr. Pascal and jurors, PAH Papers. Carrère (1858–1911) was an American architect (in practice with Thomas Hastings, New York), who designed the New York Public Library and U.S. Senate and House office buildings.

9. J. B. Reinstein to PAH, 19 October 1898, PAH Papers.

10. Ibid., 31 October 1898.

11. Norman Shaw to PAH, 20 October 1899, PAH Papers.

12. J. B. Reinstein to PAH, 19 October 1898, PAH Papers.

13. Ibid., 29 November 1898.

14. Ibid.

15. Ibid., 2 December 1898.

16. "Praises Mrs. Hearst's Plan," unidentified newspaper article, 21 December 1898, quoting *Baltimore Sun*, PAH Papers.

17. "An Acropolis of Letters," *New York Tribune*, 10 September 1899.

18. "The University Plans," *San Francisco Chronicle*, 17 September 1899, 18.

19. J. B. Reinstein to Theodore A. Lescher, Paris contact for the competition, 13 February 1900; Reinstein to J. L. Pascal, undated [c. February 1900], PAH Papers.

20. J. B. Reinstein to Theodore A. Lescher, 13 February 1900, PAH Papers.

21. Ibid.

22. McCoy, *Five California Architects*, 6.

23. "Mrs. Hearst's Latest Gift" and "Mrs. Hearst will Construct Mining Department Building," unidentified and undated newspaper articles, PAH Papers.

24. PAH to B. I. Wheeler, 16 February 1901, PAH Papers; "Ready to Erect Mining Department Building," *San Francisco Chronicle*, 1 February 1901; "Our College of Mining," *Pacific Coast Miner*, 15 May 1901; "Gifts for Lands and Buildings," 18–19, University of California Archives.

25. Benjamin I. Wheeler to PAH, 13 January 1908, PAH Papers.

26. Victor H. Henderson to PAH, 15 August 1916, PAH Papers.

27. B. Maybeck to PAH, 2 December 1913, PAH Papers.

28. Kantor, "The Best Friend the University Ever Had."

29. McCoy, *Five California Architects*, 9.

30. Ibid.; "Gifts for Lands and Buildings," 16, and "Centennial Records of the University of California," 32, University of California Archives. Hearst Hall was destroyed by fire in 1922. William Randolph Hearst commissioned Maybeck to build a replacement to honor his mother. He designed a beaux-arts structure with a domed auditorium, gymnasium, courts and pools, a museum and gallery to house Mrs. Hearst's art and archaeological collection, which had been given to the university. A scaled-down version of the building was erected in 1925, designed by Maybeck with construction drawings by Julia Morgan.

31. "Ingratitude to Mrs. Hearst," *San Francisco Argus*, 15 February 1899.

32. J. B. Reinstein to PAH, 26 March 1899, PAH Papers.

33. B. I. Wheeler to Regents, 24 June 1899, PAH Papers.

34. B. I. Wheeler to PAH, 24 February 1909, PAH Papers.

35. Victor H. Henderson to PAH, 26 June 1905, and B. I. Wheeler to PAH, 16 Nov. 1902, PAH Papers.

36. Ibid., 19 November 1910, and 3 May 1911, PAH Papers.

37. Ibid., 14 September 1910, PAH Papers.

38. "Centennial Records of University of California," University of California Archives.

39. PAH to Mr. J. B. Leonard, 17 August 1898, PAH Papers.

40. PAH to Mrs. William Pepper, 2 August 1898, William Pepper Papers, Van Pelt Library, University of Pennsylvania.

41. "Report of Dr. G. A. Reisner on Work in Egypt, 1899 to 1905," R. H. Lowie Museum of Anthropology, University of California, Berkeley. More than 17,500 catalogued items were excavated or purchased by Reisner, including a stela (relief sculpture) of Wepemnofret, son of King Cheops, found at Gizeh, now part of the university's collection.

42. V. M. Frederikson and A. B. Elsasser, "Ancient Egypt, An Exhibition at the Robert H. Lowie Museum of Anthropology of the University of California, Berkeley, 25 March exhibition catalogue, 23 October 1966," University of California, Berkeley.

43. PAH to Orrin Peck, 9 February 1905, and PAH to Janet Peck, 7 February 1905, Peck Papers.

44. "Historic Splendor of Ancient Egypt," *San Francisco Examiner*, 19 September 1902.

45. A. B. Elsasser, "Treasures of the Lowie Museum, An Exhibition at the Robert H. Lowie Museum of Anthropology, University of California, Berkeley, January 2–October 27, 1968," exhibition catalogue, University of California, Berkeley, 8.

46. "College Chronicles, Success of the Archaeological Expeditions Sent out by Mrs. Hearst," *Oakland Saturday Night*, 31 August 1901.

47. *San Francisco Examiner*, 3 September 1911.

48. "Indian Graves Robbed for Science," undated newspaper article, PAH Papers.

49. Elsasser, "Treasures of the Lowie Museum," 14.

50. Unidentified and undated newspaper editorial, PAH Papers.

51. Unidentified and undated, PAH Papers.

52. "One Woman's Work for Education," unidentified reprint from *New York Evening Sun*, 1915, PAH Papers.

53. Cited in Kantor, "The Best Friend the University Ever Had," 30.

54. Ibid.

55. "List of Books from the Hacienda," undated, PAH Papers.

56. Ramona Brown to Mrs. V. Eastham, 3 August 1969 and 21 July 1969; and Eastham to Ralph Gregory, 5 October 1969, founders, Hearst Memorial Historical Society, St. Clair, Mo.

57. "In the Social World," *Oakland Saturday Night*, 9 March 1901.

58. Flint interview.

59. Voncille McCord Eastham, "PAH and the PTA," *Missouri Parent-Teacher*, February 1973, 18–20.

60. "National Congress of Mothers," pamphlet, [1896], PAH Papers.

61. "Congress of Mothers," *Washington Post*, 13 March 1898.

62. "The Mother's Great Work," *New York Times*, 20 December 1896.

63. "Will Save the Children Through Mothers' Hearts, Rich and Poor Women Will Meet in the Same Clubs and Walk Side by Side for the Common Good," *New York Journal*, 20 December 1896, 3.

64. "Mothers' Congress" (letter from Mrs. Alice Birney to her sister), *Atlanta Constitution*, 27 December 1896, 8.

65. Mary Kay Lewis, ed., *Polished Corners: A History of the National Cathedral School for Girls* (Washington, D.C.: Mount Saint Alban, 1971), 5.

66. Henry Y. Satterlee, private record, "History of the Cathedral of St. Peter and St. Paul" (c. 1900–1901), archives of the National Cathedral School, Washington, D.C., 8, 10; and Lewis, Polished Corners, 249.

67. Satterlee, "History of the Cathedral," 13, 19–20.

68. Ibid., 10–21; Bishop Henry Y. Satterlee to PAH, 17 August [1898?], in Bonfils, "Life and Personality of Phoebe Apperson Hearst," 78–79.

69. Lewis, Polished Corners, 11–28, 62; Satterlee, "History of the Cathedral," 33–35, 40–49.

70. Nicholas Murray Butler, "The Washington Memorial Institution," The American Monthly Review of Reviews, July 1901, 56–59.

71. "Washington Relics at Auctionry," Philadelphia Inquirer, 11 December 1890.

72. T. F. Bayard to PAH, 25 May 1893, PAH Papers.

73. Elswyth Thane, Mount Vernon: The Legacy (Philadelphia: J. P. Lippincott, 1967), 11, 51, 63, 77, 84–87, 113, 153, 164–65, 178–79, 180–81; Minutes, Mount Vernon Ladies' Association, 1890–1919; and Clara R. Anthony to a Miss Ramirez, [1896?], PAH Papers.

74. Thane, Mount Vernon, 84–85.

75. "A Story about Mrs. Hearst," San Francisco Town Talk, 4 March 1901.

76. WRH to PAH, telegram, 17 May 1892, WRH Papers; "Oatlands," Historic Preservation, National Trust for Historic Preservation, March–April 1978, 52–63; Virginia Historical Society, to which the painting was a bequest from Mrs. Louise Anderson Patten, a Carter descendant who purchased it from WRH 28 December 1940.

77. Mrs. Kate Bridewell Anderson to PAH, 1 March 1917 and 6 June 1918, PAH Papers.

13. Political Pitfalls and Progeny

1. Swanberg, Citizen Hearst, 127, citing James Creelman, On the Great Highway (Boston, 1901), 177–78.

2. WRH to PAH, undated [1897?], WRH Papers.

3. Swanberg, Citizen Hearst, 146–50.

4. WRH to PAH, [1898], WRH Papers.

5. Ibid., [1898]. Admiral W. T. Sampson commanded the U.S. Navy blockade fleet; General William Rufus Shafter commanded the U.S. Army force; General Calixto Garcia was the Cuban rebel commander. Journal correspondent Edward Marshall was shot through the spine while accompanying the Rough Riders in a skirmish. See also Swanberg, Citizen Hearst, 154–59.

6. "How Our Troops Captured El Caney, W. R. Hearst, Editor of The New York Journal, Graphically Describes the Bloody Battle and Brilliant American Victory," Philadelphia Press, 4 July 1898.

7. "Situation at Santiago, Exact Condition of Affairs as Personally Seen by W. R. Hearst," Bangor Commercial, 1 July 1898.

8. Ibid.

9. Clara Anthony to PAH, 20 June [1898?], PAH Papers.

10. WRH to PAH, [1898 or 1899], WRH Papers.

11. Ibid., Paris, 1899.

12. Ibid., Cairo, 1899.

13. Ibid., Cairo, 1899.

14. Ibid., from Dahabeah Nitocris, [1899–1900].

15. Ibid., "just back from Egypt," 1900.

16. Ibid. from Dahabeah Serapis, Luxor, [1899–1900].

17. Ibid. Hearst had a lifelong interest in archaeology. In 1923 he offered to pay paleontologist Roy Chapman Andrews $250,000 outright for an exclusive story on his expedition's discovery of dinosaur eggs in Outer Mongolia. See Douglas J. Preston, "A Daring Gamble in the Gobi Desert Took the Jackpot," Smithsonian Magazine, December 1987, 102.

18. PAH to Mrs. Caroline Maria (Seymour) Severance, 19 September 1907, Severance Collection, Huntington Library, San Marino, Calif.

19. WRH to PAH, 1900, WRH Papers.

20. PAH to O. Peck, 3 May 1899, Peck Papers.

21. O. Peck to PAH, [1899], Orrin Peck Papers.

22. WRH to PAH, [1899 or 1900?], WRH Papers.

23. Ibid.

24. Ibid., 29 August 1899.

25. "The 'Conservative' Trusts," Lockport (N.Y.) Union-Sun, 3 February 1904.

26. Hart, In Our Second Century, 171.

27. Leon F. Czolgosz, 28, shot McKinley in Buffalo, New York, 6 September 1901; the president died 14 September. Czolgosz was executed for the assassination.

28. "Benjamin Ide Wheeler Points Out Responsibility for Crime," San Francisco Call, 7 September 1901.

29. "Responsibility for Yellow Journalism," New York Post, 21 September 1901.

30. Lincoln Steffens, "Hearst, The Man of Mystery," American Magazine 63 (November 1906): 1–22.

31. Lockport (N.Y.) Union-Sun, undated, PAH Papers.

32. Flint interviews, 18 January and 20 February 1960; Swanberg, Citizen Hearst, 206–14; "Editor Hearst Weds in New York," San Francisco Chronicle, 29 April 1903. The bride's father was identified as George H. Willson, president of The Advance Music Co. of N.Y.

33. WRH to PAH, Hotel Wagram, 208, Rue de Rivoli, Paris, May 1903, PAH Papers. Solomon Carvalho was WRH's business manager. The Bishop was Henry Codman Potter.

34. Millicent Hearst to PAH, telegram, 5 May 1903, PAH Papers.

35. WRH to PAH, White Hart Hotel, Lincoln, [1907], WRH Papers.

36. PAH to O. Peck, 9 July 1903, Peck Papers.

37. Richard Longstreth, On the Edge of the World (Cambridge: MIT Press, 1983), 344–45, 379, 399; W. W. Murray, "Wyntoon," Siskiyou Pioneer 3, no. 1 (1958): 13–20; Bernard Maybeck, "House of Mrs. Phoebe A. Hearst in Siskiyou Co., Cal." Architectural Review, January 1904, 65–66; Kenneth H. Cardwell, Bernard Maybeck (Salt Lake City, Utah: Peregrine Smith Books, 1983), 52–55.

38. PAH to O. Peck, 9 July 1903, Peck Papers; Clark transcript, Bancroft Library.

39. WRH later purchased the property and more land, which became a tree farm. In 1929, the Castle burned to the ground; WRH in the 1930s built a Bavarian village, designed by Julia Morgan, at the site, which today is owned by the Hearst Corporation.

40. PAH to Janet Peck, 21 November 1904, Rome, Peck Papers.

41. WRH to PAH, undated [April 1904?]; and undated [early 1905?]; and from Park Hotel, Mt. Clemens, Michigan, [1904 or 1905?], PAH Papers.

42. WRH to PAH, undated [c. 1902], WRH Papers.

43. Ibid., undated [early 1905].

44. Ibid., Washington, D.C., 16 November 1908.

45. PAH Papers.

46. WRH to A.B., 21 March 1909, WRH Papers. Guglielmo Ferrero was a popular historian and Anna Held was a well-known actress.

47. WRH to PAH, postcards, [1910?], WRH Papers.

48. WRH to PAH, telegram, 3 April 1901, WRH Papers.

49. PAH to WRH, telegram, [April 1903], WRH Papers.

50. PAH Papers.

51. "Waste of Millions," Boston Traveler, 1 June 1904.

52. PAH to O. Peck, 14 January 1907, Peck Papers.

53. "Persons in the Foreground, the Apostle of Social Discontent," Current Literature 41 (September 1906): 270–72. "Hearst is now a man of forty-three, and one of the least known, in his personality, of any man in public life. 'Hearst is an enigma,' one politician is quoted as saying to another in the mayoralty campaign. 'No,' was the reply, 'Hearst is not an enigma; he is a myth.' When he was elected to Congress, it was supposed that this mythical person would reveal himself. He has now served two terms and his appearance on the floor of the House of Representatives is almost as rare an occurrence as the appearance of Timothy Sullivan the Big, and he was present at the late session, so they say, less than two hours in all."

54. WRH to PAH, undated [1905?], PAH Papers.

55. Ibid., "just about to leave on the Lusitania," 1908; from Hotel Alexandria, Los Angeles, 14 March 1910; Southern Pacific postcard, undated; from Hotel Alexandria, Los Angeles, undated; telegram, New York, 1 May 1908; letter from Paris, [1907?]; and letter re: "In about 10 days, if all goes well, there will be another heir to the Hearst millions,— and all we will need then will be the millions," 1908, PAH Papers.

56. "Lose a Million Dollar Mine Suit," *San Francisco Chronicle*, 29 July 1904. The suit was against Putnam Mining Company.

57. "Mrs. Hearst Withdraws Aid," *New York Times*, 28 May 1904; "Mrs. Hearst's Poverty," *Wilkes-Barre* (Penn.) *Record*, 27 May 1904.

58. "Withdraws Her Hand," unidentified newspaper article, [1904], PAH Papers.

59. PAH to Mrs. Grace Gallaudent Kendall, 3 April 1905, PAH Papers.

60. PAH to San Francisco Settlement Association directors, 15 May 1904, PAH Papers.

61. "Gives Property to College Settlement," *San Francisco Chronicle*, 4 June 1904; "Mrs. Hearst Makes an Explanation," *San Francisco Bulletin*, 4 June 1904.

62. William E. Curtis, "Curtis Describes Mrs. Hearst's Work," *Philadelphia Press* and *Washington Evening Star*, 6 November 1904.

63. B. I. Wheeler to PAH, 20 April 1904, PAH Papers.

64. PAH to J. Peck, 8 March 1904, Peck Family Letters, 1891–1947, Bancroft Library, Berkeley; PAH to O. Peck, from Butte, Montana, 22 June 1896, Orrin Peck Papers; PAH to J. Peck, 28 February 1904 and 1 August 1904, Peck Papers.

14. War and Suffrage

1. PAH to Janet Peck, 7 February 1905 and 19 April 1905, Peck Papers; floor plan of apartment, PAH Papers; PAH to O. Peck, Cairo, 28 February 1905, Orrin Peck Papers.

2. PAH to J. Peck, 7 December 1905, Peck Papers.

3. Ibid., 8–12 March 1904, Peck Family Letters.

4. Ibid., [16–18] April 1905, Peck Papers.

5. "London Newspaper in Hearst Family," *New York Times*, 30 April 1911; Ethel Whitmire to PAH, undated [c. 1914], PAH Papers.

6. WRH to PAH, undated [1910?]; idem, Paris, undated [1907?]; and idem, London, undated [1912 or 1913?], WRH Papers.

7. Ibid., undated [1910?], "On Board . . . Mauretania."

8. Benjamin Ide Wheeler to PAH, 23 April 1906, PAH Papers.

9. WRH to PAH, after the fire and summer 1906, WRH Papers.

10. Matilde L. Barreda to PAH, 17 October 1906, PAH Papers.

11. Susan J. Braly to PAH, 17 June 1907, PAH Papers.

12. Lillian (Mrs. Charles S.) Wheeler to PAH, 24 May 1906, PAH Papers.

13. J. B. Reinstein to PAH, 4 May 1906, PAH Papers.

14. Susan J. Braly to PAH, 8 December 1906, PAH Papers.

15. Unsigned telegram, 12 April 1906, WRH Papers.

16. PAH to Alice (Mrs. Jasper) MacDonald, 1 June 1906, PAH Papers.

17. Ibid.

18. WRH to PAH, undated [1907?], WRH Papers.

19. Ibid., undated [1908].

20. WRH to PAH, undated, [1908]; and idem, undated[1907?], WRH Papers. The baby had pyloric stenosis, an obstruction or constriction of the opening (pylorus) that leads from the stomach to the intestine, a condition sometimes occurring in newborns.

21. Ethel Whitmire to PAH, 2 October [1914?], PAH Papers.

22. Ibid., 5 September 1914.

23. WRH to PAH, "on the train," undated [1913?], WRH Papers. Will owned a German newspaper in New York.

24. E. Whitmire to PAH, undated [c. 1914], PAH Papers.

25. WRH to PAH, telegram, 30 April 1908, WRH Papers.

26. Ibid., WRH to PAH, on board the *Lusitania*, and from Queenstown, 1908.

27. Ibid., from *New York American*, 10 November 1908.

28. Ibid., 16 November 1908.

29. Ibid., undated [1908], and telegram, New York, 16 September 1909.

30. Ibid., 11 November 1912.

31. Swanberg, *Citizen Hearst*, 280.

32. "Unveil Memorial to Maine Heroes," *New York Times*, 31 May 1913.

33. WRH to PAH, telegram, 14 May [1914?], WRH Papers.

34. Ibid., telegram, 28 April 1915.

35. Ibid., telegram, 9 June 1915; "on the train," undated [1913?]; and telegrams from New York, undated and 30 April 1908.

36. Ibid., WRH to PAH, telegram, 3 July [1916?].

37. Ibid., telegram, San Simeon, 1 August 1915.

38. Ibid., 10 October 1915.

39. Ibid., the St. Charles, New Orleans, [1915]; and 22 October 1915.

40. Ibid., 2 December 1915; William Randolph Hearst, Jr., to author, 22 December 22, 1981; Swanberg, *Citizen Hearst*, 356.

41. One great-granddaughter, Randolph's daughter, Patty, would become famous in the early 1970s in a bizarre kidnapping in which she was held hostage by militant social revolutionaries, was caught with her captors in a bank robbery, and sentenced to prison in Pleasanton in the valley below the site of her great-grandmother's hacienda.

42. William Randolph Hearst, Jr., to author, 22 December 1981.

43. WRH to PAH, telegram, 2 December 1915, WRH Papers.

44. Ibid., 26 September 1916.

45. Ibid., telegram, Montello, Nev., 30 November 1916.

46. Ibid., WRH to PAH, 16 September 1918.

47. Ibid., telegram, 17 January 1916.

48. "Andy Lawrence is Feted by Exposition Directors," undated newspaper article, PAH Papers, referring to Lawrence's speech at honorary banquet in San Francisco, 20 August (1915?). In June 1915 Will had ordered that Lawrence, whom he called "a vindictive little person" who "has threatened to make trouble," be removed from the Chicago paper, after consulting with Edward Clark and Solomon Carvalho, his business advisers, who believed that Lawrence's "removal was necessary to the successful development of the property."

49. Robert C. Pavlik, "Something a Little Different: The Architectural Precedents and Cultural Context for La Cuesta Encantada," unpublished article by historian for Hearst San Simeon State Historical Monument, San Simeon, California, 1988, citing Longstreth, *On the Edge of the World*, 223, 225; Frank Morton Todd, *The Story of the Exposition* (New York: G. P. Putnam's Sons, 1921), 1:57–58, 63, 67; Robert A. Reid, *The Blue Book: A Comprehensive Official Souvenir View Book on the Panama-Pacific International Exposition at San Francisco 1915* (San Francisco: R. A. Reid, 1915), 80, 151; and James A. Barr et al., *The Legacy of the Exposition: Interpretation of the Intellectual and Moral Heritage Left to Mankind by the World Celebration at San Francisco in 1915* (San Francisco: J. H. Nash, 1916), 76.

50. PAH to Adolph C. Miller, chairman of the U.S. Commission to the Panama Pacific Exposition, Department of Interior, Washington, D.C., undated night-letter [1915?], PAH papers.

51. "Women of the Hour," [*Oakland Tribune?*], undated, PAH Papers.

52. "The Exposition Ladies Again," undated and unidentified editorial, [1915], PAH Papers.

53. Interim Certificate No. 65 of 500, shares of capital stock in "The Woman's Board of the Panama-Pacific International Exposition & World's Fair, a corporation," 7 February 1912, PAH Papers; Richard A. Harrison to stockholders and directors of Woman's Board, 12 March, PAH Papers.

54. *Bulletin of the Woman's Board*, 14 January 1916, 2–6; "Women of the Hour," PAH.

55. Stella G. S. Perry, "Shall I Go to the Panama-Pacific Fair? What It Offers of Special Interest to Women," *Ladies Home Journal*, 19 June 1915.

56. Mrs. Frederick G. Sanborn, "Work and Purposes of the Woman's Board of the Panama-Pacific International Exposition," *California's Magazine* 1 (July 1915): 372–76.

57. PAH to Charles Grafley, [December] 1914, PAH Papers.

58. Swanberg, *Citizen Hearst*, 346–47.

59. Anna Pratt Simpson, *Problems Women Solved* (San Francisco: The Woman's Board, 1915), 114–25.

60. "Signal Honor is Conferred on Mrs. Hearst," undated and unidentified newspaper article, [1915], PAH Papers.

61. WRH Papers.

62. P. Simpson, diary, 7 December 1915 to 20 January 1916, PAH Papers.

63. "Mrs. Hearst Makes Protest," *New York Times*, 14 July 1916, Will in 1910 had sent two reporters to Mexico and published articles in his *Cosmopolitan Magazine* favorable to President Diaz. See John Kenneth Turner, *Barbarous Mexico*, (Austin: University of Texas, 1969), 207, 216–17. He joined other U.S. citizens with extensive holdings and investments in Mexico who favored annexation of northern Mexico in 1914 to protect American interests.

64. Simpson diary, 7 December 1915 to 20 January 1916. In 1895 Murray Taylor, who oversaw management of the Mexican and San Simeon ranches, wrote WRH that the 22,000 head of Mexican cattle were worth $14 a head. See Murray F. Taylor to WRH, 19 July 1895, PAH Papers.

65. Bonfils, *Life and Personality of Phoebe Apperson Hearst*, 128–29; Frona Eunice Wait Colburn, "Phoebe Apperson Hearst, as I Knew Her," *Overland Monthly and Out West Magazine*, September 1923, 23–24; Bill Boldenweck, "A Second Look / July 22, 1916, S.F. Explosion that Rocked the West," *San Francisco Examiner*, 26 July 1982.

66. "An Uncrowned Queen," *New American Woman*, August 1916, 17.

67. Arthur Brisbane to PAH, 30 December 1916, PAH Papers.

68. Daniel O'Connell, San Francisco attorney writing for Anti-War Society of California, to PAH, 28 March 28, 1917, PAH Papers.

69. PAH to an unidentified French woman, 1918, PAH Papers.

70. PAH to Mr. Gale, [c. 23 September 1918], PAH Papers.

71. Philip King Brown to PAH, 22 April 1917, PAH Papers.

72. Randolph Apperson, to PAH, 2 June 1918, PAH Papers.

73. Bonfils, *Life and Personality of Phoebe Apperson Hearst*, 121. Bonfils, a "sob-sister" columnist for the Hearst papers, used the pen name Annie Laurie. WRH asked her to write a biography of PAH after her death and had one thousand copies printed, to be given to immediate family and public libraries.

74. Brooks biography and card drawn by Louisa Cutts Powell, University of California student, 25 May 1912, PAH Papers.

75. Depositions to Alameda County Justice of the Peace and Notary Public, Pleasanton, Calif., 5–19 June 1912.

76. PAH to WRH, telegram, 11–12 June [1912], WRH Papers.

77. PAH Papers.

78. "Asilomar, the First Fifty Years, 1913–1963," Asilomar Conference Grounds, Pacific Grove, California.

79. Susan Lincoln Tolman Mills to PAH, 27 April 1908, PAH Papers.

80. Ibid., 24 February 1911.

81. Ibid., 13 March 1912.

82. Annie W. Maybeck to PAH, 19 December 1917, PAH Papers.

83. Ibid.

84. Bernard Maybeck to PAH, 22 October 1917, PAH Papers.

85. Ibid., 15 December 1918, PAH Papers. Maybeck then was leaving service as District Housing Commissioner with the U.S. Shipping Board Emergency Fleet Corporation in San Francisco.

86. Georgia S. Wright, "Maybeck's Plan for Mills College," *The Californians* 2 (July/August 1984); and Maybeck, "Phoebe A. Hearst Architectural Plan for Mills College," PAH Papers.

87. Mrs. Wallen Maybeck to author, Berkeley, Calif., 12 March 1985.

88. Bernard Maybeck to PAH, Christmas 1902, PAH Papers.

89. Annie Maybeck to PAH, 3 September 1912, PAH Papers.

90. Bernard Maybeck to PAH, 17 July 1901, PAH Papers.

91. Annie Maybeck to PAH, 27 July 1899, PAH Papers.

92. Ibid.

93. Ibid., 2 November 1910.

94. Ibid., undated.

95. Gunther W. Nagel, *Iron Will: The Life and Letters of Jane Stanford*, rev. ed. (Stanford: Stanford Alumni Association, 1985), 8–9.

96. PAH to Susan B. Anthony, 7 April 1898, Hearst Papers, San Simeon.

97. PAH to a Mrs. Wattles, 28 August 1911, PAH Papers.

98. Selina Solomons, *How We Won the Vote in California, A True Story of the Campaign of 1911* (San Francisco: The New Woman Publishing Co., n.d.); copy with California Historical Society, San Francisco.

99. PAH to Mrs. Caroline Severance, undated [1911?], Severance collection.

100. "English Women's Fiery Campaign is Approved by Calgary Suffragette," *Calgary News-Telegram*, 25 February 1913, 1.

101. "Mrs. Hearst is for Suffrage," undated and unidentified newspaper article, PAH Papers.

102. PAH to Daniel G. O'Connell, 16 and 22 October 1916, PAH Papers, and Inez Haynes Irwin, *The Story of Alice Paul and the National Women's Party* (Fairfax, Va.: Delinger's Publishers, 1964), 160.

103. Hon. Phoebe A. Hearst, Honorary President of Woman's Board of Panama-Pacific International Exposition and Regent, University of California, "California as a Field for Women's Activities," *California's Magazine*, 1 (July 1915): 371–73.

15. Mortality and Immortality

1. Swanberg, *Citizen Hearst*, 364–67, 374, citing *New York American*, 24 April, 17 May, 27 July, 1917; and *New York Times*, 5 March, 22 and 30 June, 4, 5, and 30 October, 2 and 3 November 1917.

2. Susan J. Braly to PAH, 20 January 1919, PAH Papers.

3. E. Whitmire to PAH, undated [1918?], PAH Papers.

4. Swanberg, *Citizen Hearst*, 362–63.

5. WRH to PAH, telegram, 15 March 1912, *WRH Papers*. Will and Millicent Hearst never divorced, despite his long relationship with Marion Davies, which lasted until his death in 1951. Millicent reportedly refused to give him a divorce and remained Mrs. William Randolph Hearst until her death in 1974.

6. Adela Rogers St. John, interview with Gerald G. Reynolds and W. J. Truft, 17 May 1971, San Luis Obispo, transcript in Hearst San Simeon State Historical Monument archives.

7. PAH Papers.

8. 10 June 1915, PAH Papers.

9. WRH to PAH, telegram, 3 December 1918, and idem, undated telegram, 29 November 1918, Phoebe Hearst Cooke Papers.

10. Charles S. Wheeler, "Brief in Support of the Showing that Certain Transfers to William Randolph Hearst were not made in Contemplation of Death," before the U.S. Internal Revenue Bureau, First District of California, in the Matter of the Estate of Phoebe A. Hearst, Deceased, 21 May 1921, 63–64, copy in Charles S. Wheeler Papers, Bancroft Library, Berkeley.

11. Ibid., throughout and 49, 52.

12. Ibid., 64–65.

13. Randolph Apperson to PAH, 11 December 1918, PAH Papers.

14. Wheeler, "Brief," 84.

15. Ibid., 16, 47.

16. Ibid., 69–70.

17. Ibid.

18. Flint interview, 20 February 1960.

19. *San Francisco Examiner*, 14 April 1919.

20. "Public Drinking Fountain Will Mark Philanthropies to Mrs. Hearst," *San Francisco Journal*, 2 April 1923.

21. Flint interview, 20 February 1960.

22. Sara Holmes Boutelle, *Julia Morgan, Architect*, (New York: Abbeville Press, 1988), 176; Pavlik, "Something a Little Different," citing Conversations with Walter Steilberg in The Julia Morgan Architectural History Project, ed. Suzanne B. Reiss, (1976), Bancroft Library, 53–58.

23. WRH to PAH, 1906; idem, from Piedra Blanca Ranch, San Simeon, San Luis Obispo County, 30 August 1917; idem, from San Simeon, undated [1917?], *WRH Papers*.

24. Wheeler, "Brief"; Swanberg, *Citizen Hearst*, 431.

25. WRH, Jr., to author, 22 December 1981.

26. PAH's astrological chart in PAH Papers, as interpreted by John Sandbach, Kansas City, Mo., January 1986.

27. Annie Laurie, "Friend of All, Noblest of Women Rests," *San Francisco Examiner*, 14 April 1919, 1.

Bibliography

A. Unpublished Sources and Manuscript Collections

Archives, University of California, Berkeley
"Centennial Records of the University of California," 1868–1968
"Gifts for Lands and Buildings."
"The International Competition for the Phoebe Hearst Architectural Plan for the University of California," 1900.

The Bancroft Library, University of California, Berkeley
Hubert Howe Bancroft Biography of George Hearst, unpublished page proofs prepared for "Chronicles of the Kings, 1887–1890." C-D 361.
Thomas F. Barry Diary. May–August 1879. Photocopy. 79/88z.
Adele S. Brooks. "Report on Letters, Records, Certificates, Documents, and Papers of All Descriptions Belonging to Mrs. Phoebe Apperson Hearst."
Edward Hardy Clark. "Reminiscences of the Hearst Family." 1979 transcript of taped interview by Wesley Cook, 1967. 80/73c.
George Hearst Letters and Autobiography, 1877–1890. 73/38c.
Phoebe Apperson Hearst. Papers, c. 1864–1918. 72/204c.
William Randolph Hearst. Letters, 1892, 1903–18. 87/232c.
William Randolph Hearst. Papers, 1863–1951. 77/121c. Papers, 1873–1902. 82/68c.
Donald H. McLaughlin. Transcript of taped interviews by Harriet Nathan, Regional Oral History Office, 1970–71. 76/63c.
Peck Family Letters, 1891–1947. 74/196c.
Charles S. Wheeler. Papers.

California Historical Society, San Francisco
Almarin Brooks Paul. "Reminiscences, 1878–83." MS 3010.
Evan Dollarhide Biography. MS 2170/2.
Janet M. Peck. Papers, 1860–1956. MS 1672.
Orrin Peck. Papers: Correspondence with the Hearsts, 1882–1921. MS 1673.

California State Library, California Section, Sacramento, catalogue files for Hearsts.

Hearst San Simeon State Historical Monument, San Simeon, California
Hearst Papers (uncatalogued).

The Huntington Library, San Marino, California
George Hearst. Papers.
Peck Papers. Correspondence between P. A. and W. R. Hearst and Orrin and Janet Peck.
Severance Collection. Letters from P. A. Hearst to Caroline Maria (Seymour) Severance, 1907 and 1911.

Mount Vernon Historical Society, Mount Vernon, Virginia
Minutes of the Mount Vernon Ladies Association of the Union, 1890–1919.

Ph.D. Dissertations
Carol Roland, "The California Kindergarten Movement: A Study in Class and Social Feminism." University of California, Riverside, 1980.

Phoebe Apperson Hearst Memorial Historical Society, St. Clair, Missouri
Hearst Papers (uncatalogued).

Miscellaneous
Phoebe Hearst Cooke Papers, private collection.
"Phoebe Apperson Hearst." Program script. Radio Station KMBC, San Francisco, June 1961.

McCollum, A. James. "William Randolph Hearst." Lecture to Family Club, San Francisco, 30 August 1973.

Transcripts of interviews with Anne Drusilla Apperson Flint by W. A. Swanberg, 18 January 1960 and 20 February 1960. Collection of W. A. Swanberg.

R. H. Lowie Museum of Anthropology, University of California, Berkeley
"Report of Dr. G. A. Reisner on Work in Egypt, 1899 to 1905." ·

San Francisco Public Library
Golden Gate Kindergarten Association. Annual reports, 1889–1906.

Society of California Pioneers Library, San Francisco
Catalogue files for George, Phoebe Apperson, and William Randolph Hearst.

Van Pelt Library, University of Pennsylvania, Philadelphia
William Pepper Papers.

B. Published Sources

Allen, W. W., and Avery, R. B. *California Gold Book.* San Francisco, 1893.

Altrocchi, Julia. *Spectacular San Franciscans.* New York: E. P. Dutton, 1949.

Bonfils, Winifred Black. *The Life and Personality of Phoebe Apperson Hearst.* San Francisco: J. H. Nash, 1928.

Boltzmann, Ludwig. "Summer in Berkeley—1904." *Westways,* September 1976, 45–49.

Boutelle, Sara Holmes. *Julia Morgan, Architect.* New York: Abbeville Press, 1988.

Butler, Nicholas Murray. "The Washington Memorial Institution." *American Monthly Review of Reviews,* July 1901, 56–59.

Cardwell, Kenneth H. *Bernard Maybeck.* Salt Lake City, Utah: Peregrine Smith Books, 1983.

Clark, Eva Turner. *Jacob Clark of Abbeville, South Carolina, and Some of His Descendants.* New York: Downs Printing Co., 1926.

Coblentz, Edmond D. *William Randolph Hearst: A Portrait in His Own Words.* New York: Simon and Schuster, 1952.

Cohen, Daniel. "Charles Tiffany's 'Fancy Goods' Shop and How It Grew." *Smithsonian,* December 1987, 58.

Colburn, Frona Eunice Wait. "Phoebe Apperson Hearst, as I Knew Her." *Overland Monthly and Out West Magazine*, September 1923, 23–24.

Cook, H. T. *The Hard Labor Section*. 1923. Reprint. Greenwood, S.C.: Attic Press, 1979.

Duffield, Isabel McKenna. "Washington in the '90s." *Overland Monthly*, October 1929, 318.

Eastham, Voncille McCord. "PAH and the PTA." *Missouri Parent-Teacher*, February 1973.

Elasser, A. B. "Treasures of the Lowie Museum: An Exhibition at the Robert H. Lowie Museum of Anthropology, University of California, Berkeley, January 2–October 27, 1968." Exhibition catalogue. Berkeley: University of California, 1968.

Farish, Thomas Edwin. *The Gold Hunters of California*. Chicago: M. A. Donohue, 1904.

Ferlinghetti, Lawrence, and Nancy J. Peters. *Literary San Francisco*. San Francisco: City Lights Books and Harper & Row, 1980.

Ferrier, William Warren. *Ninety Years of Education in California, 1846–1936*. Berkeley: Sather Gate Book Shop, 1937.

Fielder, Mildred. *The Treasure of Homestake Gold*. Aberdeen, S.D.: North Plains Press, 1970.

Forte, H. S. *Pen Pictures from the Garden World: Santa Clara County*. Chicago, 1888.

Frederikson, V. M., and A. B. Elasser, eds. "Ancient Egypt: An Exhibition at the Robert H. Lowie Museum of Anthropology of the University of California, Berkeley, March 25–October 23, 1966." Exhibition catalogue. Berkeley: University of California, 1966.

"George Hearst." In *The Resources of California*. San Francisco, 1885.

Goode, James M. *Capitol Losses*. Washington, D.C.: Smithsonian Institution Press, 1979.

Garnett, Porter. "Stately Homes of California." *Sunset Magazine*, April 1914, 843–47.

Gregory, Ralph. "George Hearst in Missouri." *Bulletin of the Missouri Historical Society* (January 1965): 76–77.

Hargrave, Arthur. *The Family Story*. San Francisco: The Family, 1978.

Harpending, Asbury. *The Great Diamond Hoax and Other Stirring Incidents in the Life of Asbury Harpending*. Norman: University of Oklahoma Press, 1958.

Hart, Jerome A. *In Our Second Century*. San Francisco: Pioneer Press, 1931.

Hearst, Phoebe A. "California as a Field for Women's Activities." *California Magazine* 1 (July 1915): 371–3.

Henderson, Sam. "The First Citizen Hearst." *Golden West*, July 1974, 18–24.

Hittell, John S. *The Commerce and Industries of the Pacific Coast*. San Francisco, 1882.

"Honest George Hearst." *American Magazine*, 21 March 1981.

Hunt, Rockwell D. *California and Californians*. Vol. 4. Berkeley: Type-Ink, 1926.

Irwin, Inez Haynes. *The Story of Alice Paul and the National Women's Party*. Fairfax, Va.: Denlinger's Publishers, 1964.

Kantor, J. R. K. "The Best Friend the University Ever Had." *California Monthly Journal*, November 1969.

Lewis, Mary Kay, ed. *Polished Corners: A History of the National Cathedral School for Girls*. Washington, D.C.: Mount Saint Alban, 1971.

Lewis, Oscar. *Here Lived the Californians*. New York: Rinehart & Co., 1957.

Lockwood, Charles. "The Transcontinental Connection." *San Francisco Examiner and Chronicle*, 22 April 1979.

Longstreth, Richard. *On the Edge of the World*. Cambridge: MIT Press, 1983.

Lyman, George D. *The Saga of the Comstock Lode: Boom Days in Virginia City*. New York: Charles Scribner's Sons, 1934.

Maybeck, Bernard. "House of Mrs. Phoebe A. Hearst in Siskiyou Co., Cal." *Architectural Review*, January 1904, 65–66.

McCoy, Esther. *Five California Architects.* New York: Praeger Publishers, 1975.

Murray, Ken. *The Golden Days of San Simeon.* Garden City, N.Y.: Doubleday, 1971.

Murray, W. W. "Wyntoon." *Siskiyou Pioneer* 3, no. 1 (1958): 13–20.

Myrick, David F. *San Francisco's Telegraph Hill.* Berkeley: Howell-North Books, 1972.

Nagel, Gunther W. *Iron Will: The Life and Letters of Jane Stanford.* Rev. ed. Stanford: Stanford Alumni Association, 1985.

National Addresses on the Life and Character of George Hearst. U.S. Congress. Washington, D.C.: Government Printing Office, 1894.

Older, Fremont, and Cora Older. *George Hearst, California Pioneer.* 1933. Reprint. Los Angeles: Westernlore, 1966.

Owens, Billie Louise, and Robert James. *Sons of Frontiersmen: History & Genealogy of Rowland, Whitmire & Associated Families.* Canon City, Colo.: Master Printers, 1976.

Pavlik, Robert C. "Something a Little Different: The Architectural Precedents and Cultural Context for La Cuesta Encantada." Unpublished article, San Simeon, Calif.: Hearst San Simeon State Historical Monument, 1988.

Phelps, Alonzo. "George Hearst." *Contemporary Biography of California's Representative Men.* Vol. 2. San Francisco, 1882.

Preston, Douglas J. "A Daring Gamble in the Gobi Desert Took the Jackpot." *Smithsonian,* December 1987, 102.

Rickard, T. A. *A History of American Mining.* New York: McGraw-Hill, 1932.

Sanborn, Mrs. Frederick G., "Work and Purposes of the Woman's Board of the Panama-Pacific International Exposition." *California's Magazine* 1 (July 1915).

Shuck, Oscar T. *Bench and Bar in California.* San Francisco: Occident Printing House, 1888.

Simpson, Anna Pratt. *Problems Women Solved.* San Francisco: The Woman's Board, Panama-Pacific International Exposition, 1915.

Solomons, Selina. "How We Won the Vote in California: A True Story of the Campaign of 1911." San Francisco: New Woman Publishing Co., n.d.

Steffans, Lincoln. "Hearst, the Man of Mystery." *American Magazine* 63 (November 1906): 1–22.

Sumner, George Leland. "Historical and Genealogical Newberry County, South Carolina," 1950, private publication.

Swanberg, W. A. *Citizen Hearst.* New York: Charles Scribner's Sons, Paperback, 1961.

Tebbel, John. *The Life and Good Times of W. R. Hearst.* New York: E. P. Dutton, 1952.

Thane, Elswyth. *Mount Vernon: The Legacy.* Philadelphia: J. P. Lippincott, 1967.

Turner, John Kenneth. *Barbarous Mexico.* Austin: University of Texas Press, 1969.

Twain, Mark [Samuel Clemens]. *Mark Twain's Autobiography.* 2 vols. New York: Harper & Brothers, 1924.

Watkins, T. H., and Roger Olmsted. *The Mirror of the Dream.* San Francisco: Scrimshaw Press, 1976.

Webb, Catherine J. *History Reconstructed: Stories of Tallman, Ianthus, Horace, and Samuel Rolfe.* Berkeley: Type-Ink, 1978 (privately printed).

Wilkins, Thurman. *Clarence King: A Biography.* New York: Macmillan Co., 1958.

Wright, Georgia S. "Maybeck's Plan for Mills College." *The Californians* 2 (July/August 1984).

Index